The global onal agreement n of financial r not well understood. Because ir ough informal, non-binding accords, so eak treaty substitutes or by-products of nationa y cast as independent variables that can inform the behavior of regulators and market participants alike.

This book explains how international financial law "works" – and presents an alternative theory for understanding its purpose, operation, and limitations. Drawing on a close institutional analysis of the post-crisis financial architecture, it argues that international financial law is often bolstered by a range of reputational, market, and institutional mechanisms that make it more coercive than classical theories of international law predict. As such, it is a powerful, though at times imperfect, tool of financial diplomacy and poses novel opportunities and challenges for the evolving global economic order.

Chris Brummer is a Professor of Law at Georgetown University. He has also taught, or is slated to teach, at several leading universities as a visiting professor, including the universities of Basel and Heidelberg and the London School of Economics. Before becoming a professor, he practiced law in the New York and London offices of Cravath, Swaine & Moore LLP.

Soft Law and the Global Financial System

RULE MAKING IN THE 21ST CENTURY

CHRIS BRUMMER

Georgetown University Law Center

CAMBRIDGE
UNIVERSITY PRESS

CAMBRIDGE UNIVERSITY PRESS
Cambridge, New York, Melbourne, Madrid, Cape Town,
Singapore, São Paulo, Delhi, Mexico City

Cambridge University Press
32 Avenue of the Americas, New York, NY 10013-2473, USA

www.cambridge.org
Information on this title: www.cambridge.org/9780521181679

First published 2012
Reprinted 2012
1006626460
A catalog record for this publication is available from the British Library.

Library of Congress Cataloging in Publication Data

Brummer, Chris, 1975–
Soft law and the global financial system : rule making in the 21st century / Chris Brummer.
    p.   cm.
Includes bibliographical references and index.
ISBN 978-1-107-00484-9 (hardback) – ISBN 978-0-521-18167-9 (paperback)
1. International finance – Law and legislation. I. Title.
K4444.B78   2012
343 .03–dc23   2011033660

ISBN 978-1-107-00484-9 Hardback
ISBN 978-0-521-18167-9 Paperback

Contents

Acknowledgments

The prospect of writing a book on any subject can be daunting for just about anyone, law professors included. Indeed, unlike the eighty-page law review articles that dominate our field and are structured along consistent (and at times repetitive) patterns, books place unfamiliar demands on the academic lawyer. Not only are we tasked with pushing the boundary of knowledge, as we do in our more traditional scholarly journals, but we are also charged with doing so while writing for a broader, generalist audience. It thus opens new opportunities to have an impact on, and potentially even help to shape, policy debates, though it also places new demands on those of us more comfortable with shorter and more technical exercises.

Fortunately, I have benefited enormously from a wide range of support that has made the leap a little less forbidding. I owe an enormous debt of gratitude to my former colleagues at Vanderbilt University, where I started my career, who provided the perfect intellectual climate for learning how to execute large-scale projects, affect the course of scholarly debates, and nurture hazy hunches into full-blown academic theories and policy prescriptions. Subsequently, my new colleagues at Georgetown have provided invaluable input during the writing process and have both cheered and challenged my thinking and assumptions about markets, regulation and global governance. Finally, my research has benefited from my association with the Milken Institute's ever-expanding community of economic and financial policy thought leaders who have consistently helped me to maintain the energy and sense of purpose required to complete a project of this scope.

The book builds on earlier scholarship, including articles first published in the California (Berkeley), Chicago, Georgetown, Southern California (USC) and Vanderbilt law reviews, as well as Oxford's Journal of International

Economic Law.[1] As such, it benefits from the comments provided by many different scholars over time: Robert Ahdieh, Douglas Baird, Margaret Blair, William Bratton, Lisa Bressman, William Burke-White, Steven Davidoff, Anna Gelpern, Andrew Guzman, Paul Heald, Larry Helfer, Eva Huepkes, John Jackson, Don Langevoort, Adam Levitin, Kathleen Mc-Namara, David Millon, Erin O'Hara, Christoph Ohler, Saule Omarova, Katharina Pistor, Bob Rasmussen, Alvaro Santos, Heidi Schooner, Dan Sokol, Hans Stoll, Randall Thomas, Bob Thompson, Joel Trachtman, Pierre Verdier, Rolf Weber, and Todd Zywicki. I have also periodically enjoyed a unique glimpse into the thinking of regulators both in the United States and abroad. Above all else, my work would not have been possible without the opportunity to learn from and observe some of the most able "technocrats" in the business – Sherman Boone, Robert Fisher, Elizabeth Jacobs, Peter Kerstens, Robert Peterson, Paul Saulski, and Ethiopis Tafara.

Additionally, the book has benefited from a team of exceptionally strong editors who have worked tirelessly to keep it accessible (and in English). Many, many thanks to Mary Arutyunyan, Stephen Bowne, Alicja Kozlowska, Stephen Scher, and Professor Yesha Yadav – five people who have diligently and patiently waded through every word of this manuscript and offered consistently keen and thoughtful advice on to how to improve the book in both form and substance. John Berger has had the patience and good humor to shepherd me through the process at Cambridge University Press and has given consistently good advice about the publishing process.

Finally, this book would have never taken its present shape without the patience of family – Chauncey, Isabelle, Savoy, and Dena. And a special note of thanks to my wife, Rachel. From Ghana and Benin, to London and Paris, on absurdly too many "vacations" it's been you, me, and the laptop. It takes a special person to have condoned with your grace such obsessive behavior – especially from a guy who so obviously never deserved you in the first place.

---

[1] See Chris Brummer, *Stock Exchanges and the New Markets for Securities Laws*, 75 U. Chi. L. Rev. 1435–1491 (2008); *Corporate Law Preemption in an Age of Global Capital Markets*, 81 S. Cal. L. Rev. 1067–1114 (2008); *Post-American Securities Regulation*, 98 Cal. L. Rev. 327–383 (2010); *How International Financial Law Works (And How It Doesn't)*, 99 Geo. L.J. 257–327 (2011); *Why Soft Law Dominates International Finance – And Not Trade*, 13 J. Int'l Econ. L. 623–643 (2010); *Territoriality as a Regulatory Technique: Notes from the Financial Crisis*, 79 Cin. L. Rev. 499–526 (2010).

Key Abbreviations

BIS   Bank for International Settlements
CPSS   Committee on Payment and Settlement Systems
EU   European Union
FATF   Financial Action Task Force
FSAP   Financial Sector Assessment Program
FSB   Financial Stability Board
FSF   Financial Stability Forum
G-20   Group of Twenty Finance Ministers and Central Bank Governors
GAAP   Generally Accepted Accounting Principles
IADI   International Association of Deposit Insurers
IAIS   International Association of Insurance Supervisors
IASB   International Accounting Standards Board
IASC   International Accounting Standards Committee
IFAC   International Federation of Accountants
IFRS   International Financial Reporting Standards
IMF   International Monetary Fund
IOSCO   International Organization of Securities Commissions
ISDA   International Swaps and Derivatives Association
OECD   Organisation for Economic Co-operation and Development
WTO   World Trade Organization

Introduction

The Perils of Global Finance

Although financial crises have never been pleasant for people who have to live through them, they now seem to be more common and devastating than at any time in living memory. Large-scale financial crises sparked by loose lending and asset bubbles have occurred on average nearly once every three years since the 1990s – and in countries as diverse as Mexico, Thailand, and, of course most recently, the United States. Moreover, their impact has grown as ever more financial institutions from all over the world have become more central and indispensible to international capital markets. These developments have helped ensure that when financial crises occur, the global economy shrinks, companies go out of business, and countless jobs are lost, often in different countries and continents.

Perhaps, then, it is not surprising that people are now more interested than ever before in the issue of international financial market regulation. Whether it be on the pages of the *New York Times*, the *Frankfurter Allgemeine*, or *Le Monde*, scarcely a week has gone by since 2007 without a front page story on the machinations of the "G-20," "IOSCO," the "Basel Committee," or other seemingly arcane international institutions that are crafting key regulatory policies for the world's financial markets.

In some part, popular interest is due to the now widespread acknowledgment of financial regulation as a basic matter of economic prudence – and survival. Financial markets, when left to their own devices, have proven fertile grounds for disastrously bad behavior and poor decision making.[1] Banks take on extreme leverage to fuel speculative and often foolhardy bets involving poorly understood investments; conflicts of interests can skew incentives such that analysts insufficiently assess and report risk; con men can develop

---

[1] Robert Kuttner, *Financial Regulation After the Fall* 3 (Demos Effective Regulation for the 21st Century Report Series, 2009), *available at* http://www.demos.org/pubs/reg_fall.pdf.

fraudulent schemes to cheat investors out of their savings; and executives are empowered to act in their own short-term interest instead of the interests of the firms for which they work and shareholders. Ultimately, when gambles go awry, and animal spirits wane, financial institutions can fail – from commercial banks and investment banks to insurance conglomerates and money market funds – and in the process stifle lending and other financial activities necessary for running a modern economy. Indeed, the bankruptcy of just one institution can create panic in the marketplace, strangle the provision of credit in an entire financial system, and cause investors to pull hundreds of billions of dollars from an economy overnight. When severe enough, crises of confidence can even require national governments to intervene and participate in the markets that they would otherwise oversee, and in the process transform financial market crises into sovereign debt fiascos where the very creditworthiness of even the largest leading economies is questioned, a fact illustrated by both the ongoing Eurozone crisis and Standard & Poor's historic downgrade of the US credit rating.

Concerns about financial market regulation have also intensified as the world has become increasingly aware of the transmission belt of risk that can effectively export financial risks across borders. Over the last twenty years, failures in even marginal or peripheral economies have upended major financial institutions halfway around the globe that had large exposures to failing foreign companies and financial conglomerates and markets. And the locales generating risk have seemingly multiplied. No longer do commentators argue or assume that financial shenanigans and crises were primarily a problem of developing countries. Instead, the last financial crisis has showed with painful clarity that even the United States – from its unregulated credit default swaps to toxic subprime securities to the Bernie Madoff scandal – can suffer momentous lapses in regulatory oversight, and accordingly generate consequences for the global economy far greater than those once imagined with emerging markets.

Nevertheless, even the most fastidious observers of financial markets tend to have little familiarity with the specifics of international financial regulation. They may have heard of the Basel Committee or the G-20, especially in the wake of the financial crisis, but little else. And even the media may have only a limited understanding of how standards are set within the international system and, more generally, of how and under what circumstances international financial law – the diverse set of regulatory rules, standards, and best practices governing capital markets – actually "works." Instead, players in the international regulatory system are routinely referred to in shorthand as "a global body" or "group of regulators" without much attention paid to the means by which rules are propagated, or for that matter, what it even means to have "rules."

The contributions of academic writers to the study of international financial law have been similarly mixed. Understanding the supervision and oversight of the international financial system involves many disciplines, including international law, political science, and "corporate law" (which depending on one's views can itself entail a variety of fields like finance, securities, insurance, and banking). This complexity makes international financial law tough both to teach and to write about and often leads to a variety of disciplinary biases. Academic contributions have, as a result, ranged from the parochial to the profound.

Legal scholars, perhaps surprisingly, have been least likely to tackle the emerging field head-on. Business law scholars have tended to focus on domestic corporate, banking, and securities regulations since most international accords are dependent on national governments for their implementation. Similarly, legal philosophers, especially of the positivist bent, have argued that international financial law does not qualify as "law," given the absence of a centralized, coercive authority – a world government in effect – to implement its dictates. Even international lawyers have had little enthusiasm for international financial law, due in no small measure to its lack of traditional signposts of legitimacy and solemnity. In contrast to most other areas of international economic law (like trade, tax and, to a lesser extent, monetary law), international financial agreements do not take the form of legally binding treaties. Instead, global rules and standards are promulgated as informal, non-binding "soft law" agreements, often between regulatory agencies – and by international institutions with amorphous legal identities. International financial law has, as a result, occupied a backseat when compared to other areas of international law with more obvious features cognizable under traditional international legal theory.

By comparison, international relations scholars have arguably presented more compelling studies of international financial law. More sensitive to the competitive pressures unleashed by global financial markets, scholars in the field have, with increasing sophistication, examined the rise (and in some cases, fall) of many international economic institutions and their increasing prominence as standard setters in the area of international financial rule making. International relations scholars have also emphasized the distributional consequences inherent in international financial rule making. In the process, they have identified various means by which states pursue their national interests while also illuminating both the coordination challenges preventing cross-border regulation and the tactics needed to secure cooperation.

Yet even international relations theorists rarely examine international law as a category distinct from international politics. Political scientists tend not to talk about the prospect of international financial regulation *as law*.[2] Instead, they view law as the product of power relations between countries. Consequently, international financial law is almost always cast as a dependent variable or a signpost of power positions, as opposed to an independent variable informing the behavior of a host of regulatory and financial actors. Realist narratives of sovereign power fail to explain, however, why international financial law should exist at all in a world of deep distributional challenges. Assuming that countries indeed follow their own national interest, international codes, best practices and standards – especially the nonbinding ones like the ones shaping the global financial system – should provide minimal credibility or comfort to those relying on them. Compliance with particular standards often begins to resemble a zero-sum game. Once a regulatory choice is no longer beneficial to a party, there are, at least according to standard understandings of soft law, few (if any) incentives for that party to act on its commitments. Backtracking on promises should be costless. Existing models are, as a result, ill equipped to explain the puzzle of why soft law is so heavily negotiated and bargained over, much less *ever* relied on to communicate commitments in international financial regulation.

The tendency to overlook international financial law reflects an incomplete understanding of soft law – both of its impact on financial markets and of the unique institutional ecosystem in which it operates. As to the first point, existing theories of international financial regulation routinely underemphasize the role of market participants and international organizations in promulgating and backing global financial standards. Theorists, instead, routinely view markets and firms as a means by which state policy is exerted and rarely study them as independent variables that can affect the strength and pull of international financial standards. And though some scholars have identified a few of the key institutions governing international finance, few have comprehensively inspected how disparate organizations interact with one another as part of an international regulatory architecture. Consequently, theorists have failed to pinpoint the design features that can bolster, as well as reduce, the effectiveness of the global regulatory system. Instead, scholars generally rely on the theoretical models developed in other areas of international law, like the burgeoning "network" literature of global governance, that speak to the institutional specificities of international financial regulation. In doing so, they

---

[2] Jack L. Goldsmith & Eric A. Posner, The Limits of International Law 83 (2005).

fail to explain the existing soft law system and often overlook alternative routes to regulatory reform.

This book engages these and other issues in an effort to stake out a more nuanced understanding of international financial law. It argues that in order to understand how soft law works in the global financial system, we need to examine the broader institutional environment in which it operates. To do so, the book builds, on the one hand, on long-standing insights from international law that soft law can have important advantages as a coordinating mechanism. But it breaks, on the other hand, with pervasive views that assume soft law to be necessarily "nonbinding." Instead, it argues that the degree to which an instrument is coercive or "binding" is less a matter of obligation than enforcement. Where standards and best practices – even if informal – are backed by mechanisms that enforce compliance, they can be viewed from a functional standpoint as species of international law, albeit promulgated by means other than traditional treaty-making processes. And here, the book argues, international financial regulation, though not emanating from traditional authoritative sources, is indeed bolstered by a range of often complex enforcement technologies that render it more coercive than traditional theories of international law predict.

At the same time, the book notes that key features of the international regulatory system – including its considerable substantive and qualitative blind spots – help to explain general questions that have long interested students of international relations, such as when or why states fail to comply with or to implement international rules. The book predicts that the effectiveness of international financial law will depend, in part, on the benefits (or costs) of conforming to a standard as measured against the benefits (or costs) generated by reputational, institutional, and market disciplines. This analytical framing yields, in turn, important insights into reform. Efforts at reform have typically focused on whether the existing soft law architecture should be replaced with more "hard law" commitments and formal international organizations. This book shows, however, that the toolbox of options available to regulators is both broader and deeper than is commonly assumed, and that many of the most important choices are not necessarily between hard and soft law as such, but between different institutional arrangements.

To the extent to which international financial law intrudes more deeply into the fabric of domestic regulatory supervision, and as more national regulatory agencies are either tasked with or commit to implementing international standards and best practices, it makes sense to ask whether global mechanisms and forums properly represent and reflect the interests of both national and international stakeholders and constituents. Though operating at an "international" level, "international" financial law is not always "global" to the extent that some countries participate more than others and play more important roles in the promulgation of international standards. It also evades key domestic processes like treaty ratification and adopts more administrative modes of rule making. In light thereof, this book provides the conceptual tools with which we can begin to systematically think through the implications of such structural and procedural features embedded in the global financial system, and proposes a framework for addressing potential democratic deficits, legitimacy and accountability.

In doing so, this book provides the theoretical building blocks for studying international financial law as a coherent discipline. Because international financial codes, best practices and standards do not resemble other more traditional areas of public international law, international financial law is not generally understood as comprising a body or pattern of common principles, strategies, or instruments. This book challenges this tendency, and sets forth a holistic framework for understanding the qualitative features of the global financial system. At the same time, the book shows that any broad attempt to posit international financial law as "law" outright, or to deny it altogether, would be far too sweeping.[3] To be sure, many areas of international financial law exhibit key attributes of efficacy, legitimacy, and obligation – perhaps the three most common signposts of legality – whereas in other situations it does not. Context is thus very important. That said, there are important general principles that illuminate the operation and implications of international standard setting and the kinds of institutional features that can affect any of the common attributes of legality.

WHAT IS FINANCIAL REGULATION?

Although international financial law is still an emerging field when compared to international human rights or more traditional economic areas like trade, the demand for financial market regulation is not in itself new. The roots of its modern incarnation can be traced to the regulatory responses to the excesses of the 1920s, an otherwise golden era for the US economy, though one plagued by unbridled and often highly leveraged capital markets speculation. Investors – ranging from individuals to leading investment banks, commercial banks, and insurance companies – jockeyed to make quick winnings in companies

---

[3] Joshua Kleinfeld, *Skeptical Internationalism: A Study of Whether International Law Is Law*, 78 FORDHAM L. REV. 2451 (2010).

connected with the new technologies of radio, air flight, utilities, and automobiles. Many of these investments were made with borrowed money and with little understanding of the companies concerned. Financial services professionals often misrepresented the economic prospects of the investments that they sold, and thousands of fraudulent companies were formed for the purpose of duping investors into parting with their savings. The value vested in the exchanges soared as money poured into stocks and bonds.

On October 24, 1929, as it is famously recounted, the market ultimately "crashed" from the weight of bets gone bad, losing 9 percent of its value. In the month following the crash, one of the most dramatic in history, the capitalization of companies trading on the exchange fell from $80 billion to $50 billion, wreaking havoc on the US economy. By 1932, stocks had lost nearly 90 percent of their value. Millions of retail investors lost their life savings, leading to deep declines in consumer confidence and spending. Highly leveraged financial institutions had insufficient cash on their books to cover the bets that they had made. In the banking crisis that followed, nearly four thousand banks could not even honor withdrawal demands by customers, just as insurance companies scattered around the country could not honor claims by policyholders. These difficulties sparked bank runs across the country as depositors panicked over the security of their savings, setting off a worldwide run on gold deposits and causing other banks to fail through the mass withdrawals. With distrust of financial institutions rampant, lending between financial institutions halted, choking off credit and liquidity to the broader economy, ushering in a deflationary cycle marked by a decade of still-record 25 percent unemployment in the United States.

In response to these failings and the events leading up them, the federal and state governments in the United States, as well as various capitalist governments observing from afar, undertook regulatory reforms to help prevent financial crises from arising again and sapping the health of national economies. Key to these efforts was the regulation of capital – with a sectoral focus on banks, via banking regulation; on securities transactions, via securities regulation; and on insurance companies, via insurance regulation. This focus was due, in part, to the role of so many institutions as "culprits" in the financial crisis leading up to the Great Depression. After all, these institutions lay at the heart of a modern financial system – that is, the myriad economic and financial institutions and mechanisms whereby funds are channeled from savers to borrowers, enabling those with productive investment opportunities to avail themselves of much-needed capital.

Each regulatory sector had its own areas of emphasis. Bank regulation largely concerned commercial banks – the institutions that receive deposits of money from the general public and that lend out those deposits to other banks, institutions, and individuals. Historically, commercial banks have been regarded as the most critical pillar of a nation's economy. They act as the generative and backup source of liquidity for all other financial institutions and are the means by which monetary policy, usually through interest rates, is exercised. Consequently, banks are important channels for moving and directing capital in the national and international economy. Their failure, especially in large numbers, can rapidly deprive society of liquidity and increase the costs of credit. The focus of bank regulation is not to protect bank customers – though national banking authorities or governments generally guarantee deposits. Instead, the purpose of banking laws is to ensure that banks are prudently run, with adequate capital and liquidity, and are involved in safe, delimited commercial activities that do not unduly jeopardize the bank's health.

Similarly, insurance laws focus on the permissible investments of insurance companies to ensure their financial solvency and soundness, thereby enabling them to honor their long-term obligations to policyholders. Given that insurance companies market their services, insurance regulation aims to guarantee the fair treatment of current and prospective policyholders and beneficiaries by both insurers and the people who sell their policies. Like banks, insurance companies are required to meet and maintain certain financial requirements in order to conduct business and must abide by fair trade practices with regard to their terms of business with consumers.

Securities regulation governs the issuance, sale, and subsequent trading of securities instruments like stocks and bonds as well as, potentially, more exotic instruments like derivatives. Securities regulations involve three basic subfields. First, securities laws try to make available for investors useful, high-quality information regarding firms and potential investments. They prescribe the kind of disclosure that companies are required to make to the public when selling securities – a process that, among other things, involves the drafting of a prospectus containing financial statements detailing the economic condition of the firm. Second, securities regulation dictates how securities are traded and touches upon the procedures and constraints imposed during the trading process. Third, securities regulation governs stock exchanges and other venues for the sale of securities, as well as brokers and dealers – that is, those financial players (often housed as subsidiaries of investment banks) that either trade securities on their own behalf or for others (together, "broker-dealers").

Despite the seemingly disparate concerns, all sectors of financial regulation share two important points of focus. They all seek to reduce information asymmetries that increase the risks to which the institutions are exposed. Banking, by its nature, involves the credit risk that borrowers may fail to repay their loans to banks. One significant element of this risk is that banks are less knowledgeable about a borrower's revenue streams, market conditions, and organizational integrity than the borrower itself. Similarly, a significant element of an insurance company's risk (over and above spates of insurance claims) involves potential customers of insurance claims being more knowledgeable about their propensities to generate insurance claims than their issuers. Even securities transactions involve considerable risk insofar as investors and traders of securities are likely to have significantly less information about a firm's prospects for future success than the issuers of the securities. As a result, despite the myriad supervisory and prudential regulations in place, virtually all financial institutions are subject to various disclosure and capital reserve requirements in case investments go bad.

Financial regulations are also largely focused on the systemic risk generated by financial institutions. When a firm can no longer internalize the risks associated with its financial activity, it may collapse. With most firms, such collapses create losses for the firm's shareholders and creditors. However, with financial institutions, a collapse can have serious repercussions on other market participants and also the wider economy. Depositors may withdraw their money from a failing bank, precipitating a general perception that other banks are equally troubled and generating a run on banks by depositors en masse. In a rush to secure their asset bases and reduce the risks among themselves, banks may call in loans previously made to one another, compounding the systemic distress. Suspensions of both interbank lending and lending to corporate clients can slow economic growth and exacerbate wide-scale financial distress.

The failure of an insurance company can result in financial losses for clients with outstanding claims – which, depending on the severity of loss and their dependence on insurance coverage, may affect their ability to continue operations. Likewise, the collapse of a securities firm can severely disrupt international capital markets. When a major financial conglomerate files bankruptcy, some of the outstanding obligations to other firms go unmet, potentially imperiling the financial stability of borrowers and counterparties that depend on the firm's performance. Additionally, because a large securities firm can hold vast quantities of securities both to serve as collateral for loans and to maintain orderly markets, any major financial stress that it experiences could force it to sell off large swaths of its inventory to meet collateral calls – which can cause the stock market to decline as securities flood the market. The capital bases of other firms can then plummet in concert with the stock market's decline, forcing them to sell off their inventory and exacerbating the extent of decline. Interfirm lending can dry up altogether, creating a credit crunch for financial institutions. In light of these risks, international financial regulation has worked increasingly to establish best practices and oversight for these activities to ensure the stability of the global financial system.

THE RISE OF CROSS-BORDER CAPITAL

For much of the postwar period and up through the late 1980s, the objects of financial regulation – banks, the buyers and sellers of securities, and insurance companies – were primarily domestic actors. Banks tended to take deposits from local actors and lend to nearby businesses. Investors would invest in businesses that they knew, usually on nearby exchanges. And local insurance companies would provide products and services to their respective local constituencies. But as international trade linkages have deepened with globalization, so has finance, to the point that it now flows even more freely than the trade of goods.

Three dynamics have helped the rise in cross-border capital flows: deregulation, technology, and financial innovation. The first development, deregulation, involves the easing of governmental regulations over both capital and financial products. Throughout the 1990s, most countries sought to increase inward foreign investment. To do so, many countries introduced a range of measures that allowed "sophisticated" investors, among them foreign financial institutions, to raise capital or engage in complex financial transactions with light governmental supervision. More permissive institutional rules were also introduced, especially in the United States, which allowed greater affiliation between commercial banks and securities firms, and in the process generated greater incentives for traditional depositary institutions to seek higher-yielding returns in overseas ventures. Meanwhile, rules on currency convertibility were eased, facilitating the ability of foreign investors to repatriate capital and thus reduce the risk of investment. And thousands of investment treaties were entered into between countries in which governments, hungry for foreign capital, promised to compensate firms should their investments be seized or expropriated. Advances in information technology have also spurred cross-border, outward investment. Innovations in information technology have enabled the transmission of virtually real-time information over the Internet concerning securities traded on foreign capital markets. Earnings reports, government filings, and market developments can be disseminated via the Web pages of issuers, financial advisers, the government, and online news services – along with near-instantaneous quotations on most publicly traded securities. Equally important, "the digitalization of information has brought instantaneous transmission, interconnectivity, and speed to the financial markets."[4] Banks can provide billion dollar loans to clients at the push of a button, and issuers now readily raise capital in multiple countries and jurisdictions. Likewise, investors can purchase stocks and bonds in foreign markets in a matter of milliseconds through electronic trading. Because of these developments, investors, companies, and financial services professionals enjoy more choices than ever as to where to set up their operations, and can participate in far-flung markets virtually anywhere, instantly, regardless of national origin and boundaries.[5]

Financial innovation has, as a final important development, only accelerated the trend. New instruments make it possible to transfer various permutations of risk on a far larger scale and to every part of the globe.[6] Rather than lending money to one institution and keeping the loan on its books, banks can sell the loans to others, who then pool the loans and segment and synthesize them to create new asset classes. With techniques like securitization, otherwise illiquid loans and local assets like real estate mortgages can be pooled and then sliced into new securities to be sold to investors anywhere in the world. For example, a bank loan (or a piece of it) made in Boise can end up on the balance sheet of a bank in Berlin. Innovations in derivatives instruments, which themselves often evade easy categorization (and thus regulatory oversight), have also spurred greater volumes of cross-border finance by allowing institutions to contract with one another through swap and option agreements that are commonly traded on electronic derivatives exchanges all over the world. Consider, for example, the now notorious credit default swap. With these instruments, a lender that has lent money to a borrower can seek assurance from a third party that, if the borrower defaults, the third party will cover the lender's losses.[7] Such arrangements may appear pedestrian. Yet they have helped spur cross-border financial transactions. For one, they have helped internationalize the provision of risk insurance. Bank X (located in Country Y) can enter into a credit default swap agreement with Insurer Z (from Country W) to hedge against a loan to a local company, often without the insurer having to comply with the same regulations that would apply with standard insurance products. Additionally, credit default swaps have allowed investors to speculate on debt issues and the creditworthiness of entities referenced in

---

[4] Saskia Sassen, Losing Control?: Sovereignty in an Age of Globalization 43 (1996).

[5] *Id.* at 40.

[6] Howard Davies & David Green, International Financial Regulation: The Essential Guide 8 (2008).

[7] Dick K. Nanto, Cong. Research Serv., RL 34742, The U.S. Financial Crisis: The Global Dimension with Implications for U.S. Policy 10 (2009), *available at* http://graphics8.nytimes.com/packages/pdf/globalconcrs.pdf.

credit default swap contracts. They can be thus be used to create synthetic long and short positions in issuers of the debt. In short, investors can purchase protection on domestic and foreign companies betting that they are about to default on loan obligations, and alternatively sell protection where they believe default is less likely than the overall market presumes.

GLOBALIZATION AND FINANCIAL RISK

For the last two decades, economic theory has not been shy about the perceived benefits of this free-flowing "democratization" of capital. For nearly a generation, economists have trumpeted the changes in financial markets, largely on the basis that they allow the world's savings to be directed toward their most productive uses, regardless of location. This development, many economists argue, allows businesses and companies that would otherwise not have access to funding (given the limited resources of their home countries) to secure financing for growth. Furthermore, financial globalization has allowed for the diversification of risk. No longer are investors from one country precluded from investing in another, with the consequence that country-specific risk is diminished.

Yet during this same period, globalization has demonstrated – with ever more apparent consequences – that international investment is not without its own significant drawbacks. The highest profile challenges have been those relating to financial crime. The same instruments that make possible international investment facilitate international fraud, a point emphasized by Ethiopis Tafara and Robert Peterson. Fraudsters from one country, for example, can solicit unwitting investors in another through telephone calls, email, and the Internet to market Ponzi schemes fake investment opportunities and services. And as a distribution system for the sale of financial systems and products has gone global, fraudulent activities at any point in the sale of securities can affect a wide range of stakeholders. Fraudulent disclosures in accounting statements, bankbooks and offering memoranda for new securities regularly have a worldwide (and instantaneous) distribution and can effect the investment decisions of hundreds of thousands if not millions of investors. Thus, fraud perpetuated by multinationals like Enron, Parmalat, WorldCom, Vivendi, and Adelphia all involved deceptive financial statements that were relied on by investors throughout the world. The recent Madoff scandal cost Normura Holdings, a Japanese company, $300 million of exposure; Union Bancair Privee, a Swiss private bank, $850 million; Banco Santander, a Spanish bank, $3.1 billion; and Benbassat & CIE, a Swiss private bank, $935 million. The Allen Stanford Ponzi scheme was perhaps the most international of all with nearly 75 percent of all of his (worthless) securities sold to Latin American investors through offices in Venezuela, Colombia, Mexico, and Ecuador. The announcement of this fraud caused a bank run that Hugo Chávez was compelled to counteract by announcing that his government would back all losses.

Still, in many ways, these risks pale in comparison to other more damaging implications that globalization of the financial markets holds for financial stability. Increasingly frequent financial crises over the last two decades have shown that globalization can exacerbate asset bubbles throughout the world and also even encourage poor investment decisions. One institution in Germany can, in principle, make a loan to a bank in Namibia, which can then increase the number of loans it makes in the country. This process sometimes produces good results, as demonstrated in China and India, where capital-hungry firms used foreign resources to modernize and become more competitive. But sometimes this process does not. As capital becomes more readily available, competition among banks and other financial institutions to provide loans increases and incentivizes firms to enter into riskier lending transactions in search for higher yields. In cases where investments are poorly regulated, financial institutions may be tempted to enter sectors with which they are unfamiliar or to make loans to less creditworthy individuals in order to achieve higher profits. When loans and investments do not pan out, an institution may find its very existence imperiled, and if too large, its demise can threaten the economy of the country in which it is based and others as well.

The most obvious materializations of such risk arose during the Mexican and Asian financial crises of the mid and late 1990s, where the liberalization efforts of developing countries were not supported by sound regulatory oversight. After nearly a decade of stagnant economic activity and high inflation in Mexico, the government liberalized the trade sector in 1985, adopted an economic stabilization plan in 1987, and gradually introduced market-oriented institutions. As part of these reform efforts, banks were privatized, lending and borrowing rates were freed, and reserve requirements, as well as rules regarding the qualifications for bank officers, were eliminated.[8] Consumers took advantage of the generous credit terms by reducing savings and increasing borrowing, just as banks ratcheted up their extension of credit 277 percent from 1988 to 1994, or 25 percent per year. Ultimately, the credit bubble popped, and the government was forced to float the peso, which within a week of its

[8] Francisco Gil-Diaz & Agustin Carstens, *Pride and Prejudice: The Economics Profession and Mexico's Financial Crisis*, in MEXICO 1994: ANATOMY OF AN EMERGING MARKET CRASH 165, 165 (Sebastian Edwards & Moises Naim eds., 1998).

flotation crashed from a 4:1 ratio against the dollar to more than 7:1. Moreover, the country was faced with imminent default on its short-term, dollar-indexed government bonds, Tesobonos. With Mexico teetering on the brink, the International Monetary Fund (IMF) and the United States intervened to rescue the country, first by buying pesos in the open market and later by extending emergency loans of over $40 billion.

Similar problems arose with Thailand's liberalization in the 1990s. In an effort to encourage greater foreign investment, domestic banking rules were liberalized, and local banks were permitted to accept foreign deposits and thereby expand their lending capacities.[9] However, the increased lending resulted in lower interest rates, which increased competition among Thai banks and squeezed their profit margins, forcing them to enter into riskier activities. Such liberalization efforts in Indonesia allowed the number of banks to increase from 64 in 1987 to almost 239 in 1997, leading to similar competitive effects.[10] Korean policy changes allowed finance companies to engage in private equity transactions as well as lending and borrowing in foreign currencies, activities with which they had little experience. Throughout the region, increased lending brought lower credit standards as banks failed to undertake thorough evaluation and monitoring of borrowers. Thus, although capital inflows allowed annual bank lending to grow by 18 percent in Indonesia and Thailand and by 12 percent in South Korea, the lending entailed high levels of risk. This risk was reflected in the default rates on loans leading up to the crisis: in Indonesia the default rate was 17 percent; in Korea and Malaysia, 16 percent; and in Thailand, 19 percent. The stability of US banks, which were heavily invested, was threatened.[11]

As in the Mexican crisis, Asia's reliance on short-term and electronically mediated financing made it vulnerable to a sudden reversal in capital flow. Thailand was the first domino to fall. Whatever the reasons for the reversal in Thailand's capital flow, the result was a speculative run on the country's currency that it could not defend: up to 40 percent of foreign investment capital fled the country in 1997 and 1998,[12] and on July 2, 1997, when the government was forced to float the baht, it collapsed. The baht reached its lowest point of 56 units to the US dollar in January 1998. The Thai stock market dropped

[9] MALCOLM COOK, BANKING REFORM IN SOUTHEAST ASIA: THE REGION'S DECISIVE DECADE 56 (2008).

[10] KERN ALEXANDER ET AL., GLOBAL GOVERNANCE OF FINANCIAL SYSTEMS: THE INTERNATIONAL REGULATION OF SYSTEMIC RISK 204 (2006).

[11] Craig Burnside et al., *Prospective Deficits and the Asian Currency Crisis* (Fed. Reserve Bank of Chicago Working Papers Series Research Dep't, No. WP-98-5, 1998), *available at* http://www.chicagofed.org/digital_assets/publications/working_papers/1998/wp98_5.pdf.

[12] Tran Van Hoa, *Causes of and Prescriptions for the Asian Financial Crisis, in* THE CAUSES AND IMPACT OF THE ASIAN FINANCIAL CRISIS 11, 14 (Tran Van Hoa & Charles Harvie eds., 2000).

75 percent as investor confidence plummeted. The IMF stepped in on August 11, 1997, with a rescue package totaling more than $17 billion and on August 20, 1997, with another $3.9 billion. Nevertheless, the repercussions of Thailand's crisis were felt across the region. The effects spread to Malaysia, for example, where just days after the baht devaluation, stock exchanges experienced mass sell-offs and lending rates skyrocketed. The two economies fell into deep recession. Similarly, Indonesia's currency, the rupiah, came under attack by speculators, along with the South Korean won and the Filipino peso. In all, the entire region lost billions in capitalization and spiraled economically.

This dynamic was present, but to a lesser extent, in the recent 2008 financial crisis. European banks, among others, served as key purchasers of US securitized mortgages, and as the housing bubble began to implode, the value of these mortgages declined precipitously. Europe's biggest bank, UBS, had some of the largest losses and, in early 2007, was forced to write off $3.4 billion. The German bank IKB announced in July 2007 that "Rhinebridge," a structured vehicle operated by IKB, had invested heavily in the US subprime market; a consortium of German banks, including Deutsche Bank and Commerzbank, had to create a €3.5 billion bailout fund to rescue it. These kinds of banking failures ultimately caused credit markets around the world to freeze, prompting another round of failure in 2008 as banks highly dependent on capital could no longer secure short and medium term financing for their operations.

The domino effect illustrated above pinpoints a third and perhaps more worrisome drawback of financial globalization – the delocalization of risk and the morphing of national or local systemic risks into crises with global reach. For the first two decades of the post-war period, financial crises were largely national phenomena. To be sure, banks could fail and firms could fall – but their financial repercussions remained largely local. Firms had little contact and dealings with one another across national boundaries, so institutions were rarely dependent on the stability of a foreign counterpart. As a result, only the macroeconomic effects of failure had spillovers, especially when failures weakened the overall economy. Now, however, financial dealings are often deeply international. In the simplest case, when one institution loans to institutions or invests in products sold in another country, and those transactions turn sour, the investor, regardless of location, will suffer a loss. The Mexican crisis, for example, resulted in near historic losses by US banks, which as David Singer notes, had invested and reinvested more than $23 billion, an amount equal to approximately 465 percent of the total capital bases of the top seventeen US banks.[13]

---

[13] David Andrew Singer, Regulating Capital: Setting Standards for the International Financial System 43 (2007).

Since the early 1990s, financial innovation has multiplied the ways in which risk has become delocalized. Bank loans are now just one slice of cross-border financial activity, as other financial activities have become more central to financial intermediation and payment systems. Institutional funds and investors provide short-term financing that complements and supports the traditional long-term financing provided by commercial banks; investment banks and firms often act as insurance providers for domestic companies (and vice versa) by agreeing to cover parties for losses that they incur in transactions through exotic instruments like credit default swaps; and sophisticated individuals and investors routinely make cross-border bets as to the direction of prices concerning key commodities, interest rates, and virtually any other object bought and sold in the global economy, usually with minimal regulatory oversight. With the growth of this "shadow" banking system, the failure of not only banks, but even securities firms and other financial institutions, can imperil the financial system. Many of the players in such a system are interlinked by cross-affiliated credit relations, as well as other business and functional relationships, that render nationally based resolution difficult, if not impossible.[14] AIG's performance on its credit default swaps originated in the UK but was guaranteed by its US parent. The US Lehman Brothers' holding company guaranteed the liabilities of eighteen affiliates located in countries as diverse as England, Luxembourg, Japan, and Germany, creating cross-border disputes as to the holder of claims against the now defunct company.

SOFT LAW AND THE GLOBAL FINANCIAL SYSTEM

Against this backdrop, cross-border regulatory cooperation has been increasingly viewed as a necessary tool for providing financial market stability and consumer protection. Global problems, it is argued, require, at least in part, global responses, of which there have been many – with more to come. This book grapples with how the international financial system engages with these challenges. How rules are made and how they are enforced is the subject of this book. And further, who makes the rules? Why and under what circumstances do actors comply with these rules? And what do these processes tell us about possible improvements to the regulatory architecture?

Perhaps surprisingly, even in the large volumes published on global governance, these questions tend to escape close analysis, often as a result of overestimating the relative power of competitive markets and governmental agencies.

---

[14] Eva Hupkes, *Rivalry in Resolution: How to Reconcile Local Responsibilities and Global Interests*, 7 EUR. COMPANY & FIN. L. REV. 216, 220 (2010).

Some scholars portray regulatory coordination as the mere by-product of competitive processes unleashed by financial globalization. As technology has made banks, companies, and even investors ever more mobile financial actors, pressure has built on regulators to retain market participants and their business, and to draw new business to their shores, with the consequence that countries effectively bid down the price of doing business by watering down regulations geared to enhance transparency or financial stability. International rules as such represent the outcome of a self-determined "race to the bottom" driven by market preferences. Meanwhile, other commentators tend to view international financial law as the product of global regulatory cartels, immune in many regards to market preferences, and which, if unchecked, could produce new forms of global governmental dominance. Thus from this perspective, rules are in some regards overdetermined by oligopolistic behavior of governmental authorities.

This book takes a more modest tack and acknowledges that regulators are both competitors and essential partners in the international financial system, with varying and, at times, changing incentives with regard to whether and how to cooperate. In chapter 1 ("Territoriality and Financial Statecraft") the book provides a backdrop to international financial cooperation by first evaluating in close detail the tools with which national financial authorities act, or are empowered to act, as independent sources of cross-border rules and regulations. The chapter enables us to see that regulatory power, even at the international level, is above all else tied to the relative size, or rate of growth, of a regulator's local capital market. Where regulators enjoy large or quickly growing capital markets, especially in comparison to others, they not only wield territorial power over their local markets but can also more easily, project their policy preferences beyond their borders through both traditional domestic regulation and extraterritorial tactics. When, however, global allocations of capital are more diffuse – and thus spread among more countries – so is regulatory power.

From this perspective, financial globalization has had inevitably enormous consequences for dispensations of global financial governance. The emergence of a unified European capital market and the spectacular rise of the BRIC countries – Brazil, Russia, India, and China – have eroded the traditional economic hegemony of the United States and, with it, the country's means of unilaterally shaping international financial law through domestic rule making and market oversight. Increasing numbers of countries are, in the wake of these developments, better situated to retaliate against the interposition of any extraterritorial rules, and mobile market participants are better positioned to evade them. Consequently, even as financial centers seek to attract market participants and transactions to their borders, incentives for cross-border coordination of some sort have risen, not only for foreign financial centers seeking to promote their own burgeoning policy preferences, but also for the United States, the traditional regulatory hegemon.

How coordination takes place at the global level between regulators is the focus of chapter 2 ("The Architecture of International Financial Law"). Besides providing a blueprint for the global regulatory architecture, which involves a range of increasingly vertically integrated institutions including international agenda setters, standard setters, and monitors of compliance, the chapter inspects the organizational features of the law making process. The chapter shows that four sets of institutional design options pervade the rule making bodies. At the most basic level, international standard-setting bodies may be exclusive or universal in their membership. Additionally, some institutions may permit leadership and decision making by a select group of elite members, whereas others may require full group participation. Third, organizations can have various degrees of involvement by national authorities, with some animated by "private legislatures" consisting of market participants where regulators wield only indirect control over the standard-setting process. Finally, some international standard-setting bodies may serve as forums for coordination between regulators with similar sectoral mandates, whereas others host regulators with different mandates and administrative portfolios. The chapter shows that although these key institutional design features are for the most part grounded in soft law, they nonetheless hold important consequences for allocations of regulatory power and effectiveness at the global level. Thus even in an increasingly hierarchical system, international financial law is comprised of highly variable processes of organizational governance, each with their own comparative advantages.

Chapter 3 ("A Compliance-Based Theory of International Financial Law") explores why and under what conditions states comply with international financial rules. To do so, the chapter draws on (and sometimes critiques) classical international law and the law and finance literatures to develop a theory of international financial law based on various compliance technologies. The chapter shows that international financial law, in contrast to most other areas of soft law, enjoys a variety of not only reputational, but also market and institutional disciplines. And when these disciplines are activated, international financial law is often more coercive than traditional international legal theory predicts. Nevertheless, the chapter does not adopt a full-throttled endorsement of the existing international financial architecture. Instead, the book shows that disciplinary constraints are often hampered by a range of institutional flaws that limit the "compliance pull" of global financial standards. Monitoring is far from a comprehensive exercise. Participation in some of the most important surveillance programs is voluntary, and the process depends on self-reporting by national regulators and the firms. Furthermore, the information generated through monitoring is often not shared with the broader international regulatory community or market participants. The compliance pull of international financial law will thus be highly dependent on the particular array of institutional technologies supporting its prescriptions.

Next, in chapter 4 ("How Legitimate Is International Financial Law?") the book examines the more conventional concerns of legitimacy and accountability in international financial regulation, and poses broader theoretical questions concerning their relation to systemic risk. Scholars have frequently been skeptical of the significance of regulatory authorities, and specifically "independent" agencies, in financial market governance – partly because many of these authorities and agencies are subject to only modest legislative and executive oversight. International standard setting can be viewed as further exacerbating democratic deficits, given the exclusivity of international organizations and their at times limited engagement with the broader public. There has thus been concern about the degree of obligation and legitimacy implied by international financial standards, accords and obligations. The chapter shows, however, that overlooked administrative features and innovations relied on in contemporary international standard setting provide legitimacy enhancing benefits that require rethinking long-standing models of democratic governance. Indeed, the international regulatory architecture reveals an increasingly democratic and pragmatic character that, though far from perfect, allows for more input from the standpoints of legitimacy and accountability than most commentators assume.

Chapter 5 ("Soft Law and the Global Financial Crisis") turns to explore the limits of international financial law, while additionally providing deeper substantive content to the structures sketched out in earlier sections of the book. As a contemporary case study, it points out the range of gaps and regulatory black holes persisting at the international level prior to the 2008 crisis and then traces international responses from 2008 to 2011. Based on an analysis of the substantive content of international financial law at the time and the reform efforts immediately undertaken thereafter, the chapter theorizes broad political dynamics that have stymied full consensus on key issues and from them teases out what can be viewed as some key limitations of international financial law. The chapter shows that, though not without considerable successes, neither the soft law quality of international financial law nor the institutional apparatus backing it guarantees coordination, full implementation of standards, or error-free regulation.

Finally, chapter 6 ("The Future of International Financial Law") considers how international financial law is likely to develop in the post-crisis world. It argues that increasingly common calls for a "World Financial Organization" modeled after the World Trade Organization (WTO), where one treaty-based organization would act as the primary international standard setter for financial regulation, are highly impractical and unlikely. Instead, international finance is likely to continue to develop in fits and starts, with national regulators acting as backstops when there are gaps in the international regulatory system. Nevertheless, the same dynamics that drive cooperation are likely only to intensify as financial globalization continues, incentivizing even the regulators of the largest and most powerful financial centers to coordinate their activities. Chapter 6 thus concludes by identifying best practices in financial diplomacy that will prove most effective for regulators in both promoting their policy preferences and stabilizing the global financial system.

This book, like any book of this scope, has its share of limitations. Despite the wide array of financial market initiatives that are brought together and theorized, the book still hews to "financial market" regulation in its more narrow sense. I do not focus extensively on monetary law or trade law (or other important areas of international economic law), though I make occasional references to both as a means of comparison and as a way of teasing out the often special policy considerations involved in supervising financial markets. There are several reasons for this narrow scope. First, as I discuss later in the book, other areas of international economic law, like trade, rely heavily on hard law, and the purpose of this book is to better understand the predominance of soft law in international financial regulation. I thus found it conceptually easier to keep to one field in which to observe the processes by which soft law is generated and deployed, while referring, when helpful, to other related areas of international economic governance in order to draw contrasts and highlight especially salient points.

I also focus on financial regulation because doing otherwise would add extra layers of complexity to what is already a complex subject. Good scholarship, especially in new areas of research, is incremental. To my knowledge, no book has provided either a theoretical overview of the operation of international financial regulation as a species of "law" or, for that matter, an in-depth analysis of the international regulatory architecture since the 2008 crisis. This book attempts both in one concise volume. I have thus chosen to focus on financial market regulation without adding to the burden by tracing in detail the institutional and economic dynamics of international trade and monetary policies, which have only indirect importance for the descriptive interventions that are made in the following chapters.

There are consequences to narrowing the scope of the book. Monetary law can have important implications for financial regulation. Interest rates can affect the incentives of banks to engage in risk taking (just as currency fluctuations can affect the quality of bank assets) and, in the process, drive institutions into insolvency. Capital requirements for banks can affect lending by financial institutions and with it, the growth of the economy and inflation. And key institutions in international monetary and economic affairs, like the IMF and World Bank, may also coordinate activities that indirectly impact financial market regulation and financial sector development through jawboning, conferences and research. I have chosen, however, to focus on the more critical and primary role played by these institutions with regards to enhancing compliance with international financial rules, which is where the book places its emphasis.

Few statistical studies of regulatory standard setting exist, so this book largely relies on qualitative empiricism. Specifically, I use close institutional analysis and a range of case studies to tease out the possibilities and limitations of international financial law as a tool for cross-border rule making. Insofar as the international regulatory system is made up primarily of soft law organizations and institutions, and since soft law itself is continually evolving, the book's specific observations concerning the relationships between institutional actors are and will remain subject to change. That said, I believe the roles played by international financial law – as a focal point for discipline and as a means of coordination and persuasion – will continue to be relevant and, indeed, become more essential as globalization continues to spur the growth and development of new international financial centers. Wherever possible, I not only identify institutional particularities but also categorize those particularities as elements germane to international financial standard setting. As the international system evolves, and as patterns of governance emerge, the basic regulatory strategies and techniques identified in the following pages will, I believe, proliferate, even if under different institutional guises. Thus, the theory developed in this book as to how international financial law now "works" can provide a useful analytical framework for understanding and reforming the global regulatory system as it adapts and responds to new challenges.

1

Territoriality and Financial Statecraft

International (global) financial law cannot be fully understood without first examining how financial regulation is administered at the domestic (national) level. This is not only because national governments and regulatory agencies are ultimately responsible for coordinating international policy and implementing it, a point that we explore in the following chapters. It is also because national regulatory authorities can, under the right circumstances, leverage their own capital markets and formal legal dictates in ways that export their own regulatory preferences, allowing them to become unilateral sources of international financial law. Their ability to do so informs as a result both how and when regulators coordinate policies with foreign counterparts.

In light thereof, this chapter identifies and catalogues some of the regulatory strategies employed by national financial authorities to oversee not only local markets and market participants, but also foreign actors, and examines how these tools affect incentives to cooperate across borders. The chapter begins by showing that the primary tools for regulatory oversight are grounded in notions of "territoriality," with jurisdiction over markets and market participants being tied to events occurring in, or associated with, certain geographic markers. It then argues that, contrary to traditional theories of globalization that view territoriality as a limitation of regulatory authority, territoriality in practice constitutes a diverse array of tactics that, especially for regulators of large capital markets, can be leveraged to exert authority unilaterally over both mobile market participants and other foreign regulators. Territoriality can, as such, be understood as a means of not only controlling local geographic spaces and markets, but also of projecting economic regulatory power abroad. Nevertheless, the chapter shows how financial globalization has complicated both territorial and extraterritorial applications of national law by both increasing the evasive power of regulated market participants and by reallocating financial and regulatory power around the world. This "democratization" of capital has, on the one hand, resulted in new expenditures and made the task of regulation more demanding, even among traditional economic superpowers, but it has also, on the other, increased incentives for better-coordinated intergovernmental cooperation.

ADMINISTRATIVE DELEGATION AND NATIONAL REGULATORY AUTHORITY

A plethora of actors – among them heads of state, legislatures, and courts – are inevitably active in any country's financial affairs. Yet no actors are more important than the national "regulatory agencies" – specialized government bureaucracies charged with crafting rules for the participants in their local markets. Regulatory agencies are largely responsible for establishing the day-to-day rules that govern market participants' activities, for policing the market for violations of these laws, and, in some cases, for adjudicating conflicts.

The pole position of regulatory agencies is usually authorized by domestic legislators who "delegate" authority to agencies to oversee either specific sectors of domestic financial markets or broader fiscal or economic activities. Once power has been bequeathed to an agency or department, regulators generally take the lead in interpreting general legislative guidelines that the legislatures have provided, a process that usually requires much granular rule writing and policymaking.[1] Courts rarely play a defining role in standard setting and are instead charged with helping to define the reach and powers of regulatory authorities. The importance of heads of state has traditionally resided in their naming leaders of agencies and departments that undertake the task of financial and economic oversight[2] (though recently heads of state have exerted more influence in helping to set general agendas for financial rule making).

Political scientists and administrative law scholars have frequently drawn attention to the centrality of regulatory bureaucracies in financial affairs – largely due to the power that they wield over activities with considerable economic consequences. Several explanations have been advanced to support the broad delegation of authority to specialized regulatory agencies.

Expertise

Perhaps the most cited explanation for the centrality of administrative agencies in financial regulation is the expertise that they enjoy. Significant expertise is

---

[1] David Andrew Singer, Regulating Capital: Setting Standards for the International Financial System 20 (2007).

[2] Lisa S. Bressman & Robert B. Thompson, *The Future of Agency Independence*, 63 Vand. L. Rev. 599, 632 (2010).

required to oversee financial markets: supervisors are required to understand how market participants operate, what they do, and what kinds of risks they pose. By contrast, elected officials usually come from all walks of life, and as generalists they rarely possess the training or experience, or even the time, necessary for micro-managing financial affairs like capital-adequacy standards for financial institutions or disclosure regimes for securities offerings. On account of this complexity, scholars and policymakers have seen the growth of specialized regulatory agencies as a natural consequence of the increasingly complex nature of financial markets.

Efficient Rulemaking Processes

Delegation can also enhance efficiency. Traditional legislative processes are subject to a range of potential holdups by entrenched and politically connected constituencies. As a result, in many democracies the legislative process can be onerous and tedious, often requiring numerous attempts by legislators, in multiple parliamentary or congressional sessions, to achieve even basic regulatory objectives and reforms. Coordination is required among different legislators, who often have disparate interests and perspectives, and who can at times single-handedly stymie or prevent laws from being passed or even considered. By comparison, regulatory agencies are not subject to the same procedural roadblocks – allowing them to respond more swiftly to changing market or economic conditions than would otherwise be possible in many legislative forums.

Political Insularity

Given their circumvention of traditional legislative processes, regulatory agencies are assumed by many commentators to be insulated from the politics that can distort and undermine sound decision making and public policy. The argument goes that legislators may have short-term interests, like reelection or stifling a competitor party's legislative successes, which lead to suboptimal policy making. Politics may, for example, lead legislators to vote against or block initiatives that would otherwise be good for the national economy. Or alternatively, they may be inclined to push for a certain course of interest not out of interest for the national economy or even their local constituents, but instead to protect well-organized special interests. Thus where decision making resides in the hands of the legislative branch, decisions can be stunted or flawed, or greatly delayed, all as such pose enormous problems where financial market developments require quick, dispassionate responses.

Regulators, in contrast, are generally not under the same pressures. Although the heads of supervisory agencies may face confirmation hearings by legislators, they are not usually elected officials and thus do not face the same political pressures that legislators do. And their decisions as such are not generally exposed to the same spotlight and publicity. As a result, it is assumed that officials will be less partisan, as well as more willing to make the tough, necessary decisions that politicians would not, if so required."[3] Independence, made possible through legislative grants of administrative authority, thus facilitates more technocratic and unbiased exercises of oversight and supervision.

Legislative Shirking

A less charitable interpretation of the ostensible political insularity argues that delegation allows political actors, especially legislatures, to shirk responsibility. Instead of taking responsibility for unpopular, though perhaps necessary, actions, politicians can delegate rule making authority and the attendant political backlash to third parties. When agencies are forced to take unpopular decisions, politicians can avoid taking any blame. Meanwhile, when an agency takes actions that are successful or popular, politicians can applaud the agency for its work and take credit for their own involvement in any relevant consultations or administrative or rulemaking processes. Delegation thus provides a kind of political option that can be exercised by political actors whenever circumstances suit them.

Private Sector Contacts

Finally, some scholars note that regulatory agencies, especially those overseeing financial markets, tend to be best able to constructively incorporate the participation of the private sector in the decision making process. Contact with the private sector is vital for regulatory agencies to be effective, especially as finance has become more complex and some public officials have found it difficult to keep track of capital market developments. To this end, regulatory agencies have developed a number of ways to tap the finance industry's expertise. Private sector involvement is perhaps most obvious in jurisdictions where national authorities rely on a variety of "self-regulatory organizations" (SROs) – private sector authorities that police their own members – for both technical advice and the execution of policies. For example, both the UK Financial Services Authority (FSA) and the US Securities and Exchange

---

[3] *Id.*

Commission (SEC) regularly incorporate the monitoring and policing capabilities of stock exchanges, broker-dealers, and accountants to forward their objectives. Meanwhile, as John Braithwaite notes, virtually every major regulator additionally receives advice from consumer panels, organized interest and stakeholder groups, and other "epistemic communities" of private actors that counsel officials as to preferred or optimal regulatory strategies.[4]

HETEROGENEITY IN REGULATORY DESIGN

Although various common explanations are available to explain the pervasiveness and centrality of regulatory authorities in financial affairs, regulatory agencies are far from homogeneous – a point many commentators often overlook. Indeed, the literature tends to gloss over the significant heterogeneity of institutional forms characterizing administrative agencies as they conduct international affairs and to speak as if "the performance of regulation was a lodestone – as if all regulatory agencies were of the same makeup character."[5] However, regulatory agencies differ significantly from one another in their institutional and qualitative features. These differences inform, at least in part, how regulators interact with one another, both at home and abroad.

Scope and Content of Delegated Authority

Regulatory agencies differ dramatically from one another with regard to their formal mandate. Regulators can act as supervisors and rule makers for very different segments of the market – securities, banking, and insurance, for example – and concomitantly have delimited spheres of general market authority relating to prudential regulation or consumer protection. Thus, objectives and priorities can be quite distinct. Additionally, regulatory authority can emanate from finance ministries that act as governors of fiscal and even tax policy, and that coordinate regulatory initiatives in their respective countries.

Even when regulators are assigned the same firms or sectors of the economy, mandates can vary significantly, as is evident in the formal policy objectives of regulatory agencies. For example, some central bankers have as their mandate bank supervision and financial stability per se. Other central bankers may have mandates that include the promotion of national bank competitiveness (a feature perhaps most notably associated with Chinese oversight); yet

---

[4] JOHN BRAITHWAITE & PETER DRAHOS, GLOBAL BUSINESS REGULATION 161 (2000).
[5] Peter L. Strauss, *The Place of Agencies in Government: Separation of Powers and the Fourth Branch*, 84 COLUM. L. REV. 573 (1984).

others, like the German Bundesbank, will have a historic or legal obligation to guard against inflationary spirals that can derail the local economy. Depending on the circumstances, mandates can determine agencies' priorities and policy preferences when bargaining with other regulators domestically or across borders.

A frequently cited example of differences in delegated authority can be seen in the securities regulation of the United Kingdom and the United States. Securities regulators in the United Kingdom are tasked with the promotion of confidence in markets and the maintenance of a competitive capital market. By contrast, the US SEC has no such mandate; instead, it is tasked with advancing investor protection and maintaining market integrity. As a result, the two countries have traditionally had different approaches to regulating markets. The US SEC has been more aggressive and rules oriented with regards to its enforcement. The United Kingdom's securities regulator has (until the onset of the 2008 financial crisis) promoted what are considered to be more gentle "principle-based" regulatory approaches that are somewhat less stringent, and largely friendlier to firms issuing securities.

Regulatory agencies also differ with regard to the scope of their authority. Some regulators enjoy a mandate to regulate broad swaths of the financial economy, such as where central banks are responsible for not only monetary policy, but also bank supervision, or where financial supervision over insurance, securities and banking is consolidated in a single authority. Meanwhile, other agencies have a more limited or focused mandate. Authority may additionally be demarcated between the national and local (or regional) levels of governance, or national regulators may share power with local states and political organizations. In the United States, for example, banking regulators share chartering authority over depositary institutions with the local states; and securities authorities, while having direct authority over disclosure and trading, share authority over corporate governance with the states. In the European Union, a system of "cooperative federalism" reigns, as regulations are mainly promulgated via EU directives at the federal level and are implemented and supervised by member states.[6]

Mandates can vary according to the regulatory strategy authorized in each jurisdiction. In the United States, for example, regulation is largely product based, with securities regulators regulating "securities" – but not commercial banks and only indirectly financial products like derivatives that are commonly associated with securities regulation in other countries. Under "twin

---

[6] Howell E. Jackson, *Learning From Eddy: A Meditation upon Organizational Reform of Financial Supervision in Europe*, in PERSPECTIVES IN COMPANY LAW AND FINANCIAL REGULATION 523 (Michel Tison et al. eds., 2009).

peak" models of regulation, such as in Australia, agencies are organized into administrative units designed to advance specific regulatory objectives – for instance, the soundness of banks and systemically important financial institutions (SIFIs). Both approaches differ considerably from the ultra-consolidated forms of supervisory regulation traditionally practiced in the United Kingdom prior to the 2008 crisis, where the financial services authority regulated securities firms, insurance providers, and depositary institutions as well as a range of financial products.

Such divisions have important implications for managing coordination. When, for example, the United States and the United Kingdom sought during the crisis to regulate derivatives, the British financial authority, the Financial Services Authority, had to meet not only with the SEC, the agency responsible for disclosure tied to many derivative products, but also with the Commodities Futures Trading Commission, the US agency primarily responsible for derivatives trading, and even the Financial Industry Regulatory Authority, an SRO for US securities dealers. The cross-border negotiation dynamic can change significantly when two players increase to three and the interests at stake multiply. At the same time, where a regulatory agency is consolidated to the extent to which it internalizes the costs of any bad decision making, such as where deposit insurers and some central banks are directly responsible for saving failed institutions, it may be less likely to take on even efficient policies where they potentially undermine market confidence in domestic financial institutions. Or consolidation may create bureaucracies with insufficient close contact with financial actors and as a result possess an inadequate understanding of their specific needs.[7]

Resources

Regulators can also vary dramatically with regard to the resources at their disposal. Whether measured in terms of regulatory budgets or enforcement efforts, regulatory intensity varies widely across jurisdictions. The United States, for example, spent nearly $6 billion on financial regulation in 2004 alone[8] and employs more than forty-three thousand people in the financial regulatory industry. France and Germany have budgets that are less than a quarter of that enjoyed by US regulators (once one adjusts for economy and population

---

[7] Christian Tietje & Matthias Lehmann, *The Role and Prospects of International Law in Financial Regulation and Supervision*, 13 J. INT'L ECON. L. 663, 667 (2010).

[8] Howell E. Jackson, *Variation in the Intensity of Financial Regulation: Preliminary Evidence and Potential Implications*, 24 YALE J. REG. 253, 255 (2007).

size).[9] Few developing countries have the resources to muster even a fraction of European levels of funding for surveillance and monitoring activities. These disparities can affect both the interest and the capability of regulatory agencies in high-intensity enforcement.

Political "Independence"

The degree of structural and formal independence among regulatory agencies can be pronounced as well. Often, regulatory agencies are structured in ways that may render them insulated from the pressures of national politics as well as the direct influence from both the executive and legislature. Though tasked with implementing legislative mandates, independent agencies generally operate beyond the authority and direct control of executive departments and legislators, and the leaders of such agencies often cannot be fired at will. In some countries, independent agencies may additionally be required to have a minimum degree of representation by the primary political parties on key decision making bodies and commissions. The idea behind such institutional features is that by insulating agencies from the day-to-day politics of decision making, their policies will more likely have a technical, as opposed to purely ideological or political basis As a result, the agency's initiatives and rules will be more effective and enjoy more acceptance by market participants (if not actual political accountability).

Structural independence is a common feature among central banking authorities. Most economists believe independence better ensures the long-term performance of national economies. Because central banks are pivotal players in determining money supply and operate as lenders of last resort for domestic banks, most experts believe that judgments made by such key actors need to remain insulated from political influence. Independence is also a defining feature among a variety of securities regulators. Like the US Securities and Exchange Commission, agencies in many leading jurisdictions, including the Netherlands and Australia, are administratively separated from both the executive and legislative and thus enjoy what is more structural independence and leeway.

Not all agencies follow the model of agency independence, however. Most, if not all, finance ministries, including the US Department of the Treasury, are executive agencies (and part of the executive branch). In such instances, power is more clearly centralized and associated with the head of state, insofar as agency leaders generally serve at the pleasure of the president or prime

---

[9] Id.

minister. Additionally, in many countries, finance ministers are themselves elected officials and as such are more sensitive to the immediate political pressures facing the governing party and head of state. Securities commissions, too, need not be structured as independent agencies. China's securities commission, for example, is commonly described as an independent agency and as one whose developmental path was influenced by its US counterpart. But it is, like all administrative bodies in the country, subject to the State Council, an administrative authority (cabinet) of the People's Republic of China, chaired by the premier. As a result, the State Council enjoys veto power over the initiatives taken by the regulatory agency and can, at least potentially, dictate regulatory policy.

Finally, even when regulators enjoy formal structural independence, their practical authority may be quite limited. The extent to which regulatory agencies control their budgets and fund their operations differs dramatically. In some instances, regulatory agencies may be self-funding and, as such, derive their revenue from fines or fees imposed on regulated actors. By contrast, other agencies, even when ostensibly independent (like the SEC in the United States), may receive funding from annual appropriations processes that take place in the legislative branch. In such circumstances, agencies are incentivized to be more sensitive to the political ramifications of their decisions and, in order to ensure adequate funding for their activities, may attempt to placate legislative appropriators or at least to avoid aggravating them.

Internal Decision Making

How regulatory agencies are governed internally can vary along many dimensions. Regulatory agencies may be run by one person or by groups of assorted membership size and with distinct rules with regard to who or how many people must agree on a particular policy path for it to be implemented. In the United States, independent agencies are generally run by multimember commissions or boards whose members serve fixed and staggered terms.[10] Diversity can also be an important feature of regulatory bodies, especially with regard to leadership positions. For example, each Federal Reserve district can have no more than one Federal Reserve Board member representing it, and the president should ensure in his selection deliberations adequate representation of financial, agricultural, industrial, and commercial interests, as well as geographical diversity. Similarly, regulatory agencies may be subject to bipartisan membership requirements. For example, of the five SEC commissioners, no

---

[10] Bressman & Thompson, *supra* note 2, at 610.

more than three may belong to the same political party. Such constraints are not always the norm. In some regulatory agencies all may hail from the same region of the country or political party. Indeed, domestic administrative rules may require that all members be of the same party.

Given this variation, decision rules are important, as is the authority accorded to presiding members or agency heads. When regulatory agencies work on a consensus or supermajority basis, it can be difficult for those agencies to advance any radical reforms, such as a significant tightening or loosening of existing regulatory standards. By contrast, simple majority rules or the vesting of decision-making authority in one person enable more flexibility and, from a practical perspective, more regulatory decision-making power.

Private Sector Participation in Regulation

As discussed above, virtually all regulatory agencies consult with domestic firms and market participants. Yet the degree of formal decision making and involvement of the private sector differs significantly. For example, in the United States, self regulatory organizations ("SROs") often take the lead in regulating key financial market participants, like stock exchanges, and are embedded in the regulatory process. Indeed, involvement can go beyond even the SRO model of self-regulation to actually involve private participants in the decision-making process alongside regulators. This is seen with the open markets committee, an organization that helps determine monetary policy in the United States – but in doing so enjoys participation from five regional Reserve Banks that are themselves corporations with stock held by domestic commercial banks. By contrast, in other countries private institutions may be cut off from direct participation in devising monetary and banking policy even though, as in China and Russia, the state may act as a participant in national and international capital markets with its own profit-seeking objectives, or may play key roles in the internal affairs and activities of private financial institutions.

Similar variations in approaches are evident in agency leadership. In some countries, like China and Japan, agency directors are often career civil servants and work their way up through bureaucracies to assume leadership of an agency. In other countries – the United States and United Kingdom being perhaps the most salient examples – leaders hail from the private sector. The logic is that private sector leaders will, like SROs, have technical expertise superior to civil servants and thus be better positioned to understand and oversee markets. Private sector leaders will, however, likely make different regulatory decisions than those hailing from government. For example, they are more likely than career civil servants to be unaware of the social or political implications of their regulations and are also more likely to empathize with business and market interests. As a result, leaders from different regulatory traditions may have very different starting positions from which they reach policy decisions.

Private parties can also play different roles in expanding or curtailing official supervisory power. In some jurisdictions, for example, regulatory agencies may have the right to meet with private external auditors of financial institutions to discuss their reports. Or local statutes may require auditors to communicate directly with national regulatory authorities.[11] Private actors may similarly amplify supervisory authority through litigation. In a growing number of jurisdictions, for example, especially when securities transactions are involved, private rights of action supplement the enforcement of laws on the books. Howell Jackson reports that in the United States nearly three thousand actions per year are generated in the form of both proceedings from securities arbitration panels and class actions.[12] If there were no access to private action, it is probable that more regulators would be needed to secure compliance with domestic laws (notwithstanding the sizable US regulatory workforce). Considering the potentially higher legal risks and compliance costs that firms face owing to law suits by investors, regulators in jurisdictions with private remedies may favor regulatory reforms that impose stricter standards. Additionally, they may reject close supervision from international authorities in the belief that compliance with their laws is already high given the active participation of "private" attorneys general.

Finally, the degree of influence wielded by private firms and individuals can vary across regulatory boundaries owing to differences in local market organization and coordinated action. In some countries, regulated industries have close personal or, as noted above, professional ties to regulators or may be embedded in national regulatory systems. Meanwhile, in other countries, relevant market actors have weaker histories of collusiveness and thus less-effective lobbying tools and contacts with which to lever their policy preferences. These domestic structural differences can contribute to the degree of pressure and influence that parties have in their home jurisdictions – and by extension, affect the ultimate policy objectives of regulators.

TERRITORIALITY AS A REGULATORY TECHNIQUE

Financial regulators and administrative officials do, of course, share one immutable characteristic – they *regulate*, which is to say that they govern private conduct in their markets in an attempt to prevent fraud and other

---

[11] James R. Barth et al., Rethinking Bank Regulation 122 (2011).
[12] Jackson, *supra* note 8, at 256.

forms of misconduct and to promote market stability. Conceptually, regulation can take various forms, though practically, at the domestic level in the United States, regulation is almost inevitably tied to the administration of hard law as spelled out under a national statute passed by Congress. In some cases, regulators may prescribe a process that must be followed in order to engage in particular activities: for example, a regulator may require notification of certain types of transactions or that particular public statements and disclosures be made; or a regulator may demand that individuals or institutions put up a certain amount of cash reserves to cover any activities or bets they make; or perhaps a regulator may require that a license be obtained in order to do business. Regulators may choose to prescribe or altogether ban certain practices; for example, insider trading or risky "short selling" activities, where securities are borrowed from a third party and then sold to the market with the intention of buying back identical assets later to return to the lender. In any case, when the regulated entities or individuals do not abide by their commitments, they can be subject to penalties if caught by the regulator, usually in the form of civil fines, or they can be sued by interested parties, such as investors that have received fraudulent or materially incorrect information from them.

Regulatory governance need not assume the form of pronouncements given the force of law. In some countries, including the United States, agencies publish a variety of documents: staff legal bulletins, policy and interpretive releases concerning statutes, and interpretive and no-action letters responding to written requests from private parties to clarify the legality of certain activities. Many agencies have enforcement and supervisory authority (albeit with different degrees of resources), which permits them to investigate and prosecute violations of their statutes or to resolve disputes and issue orders through a hearing or trial-type process. All of these activities demonstrate how regulators go about their delegated responsibilities concerning the interpretation, application, and implementation of financial statutes and agency policies. Nonetheless, formal rule making is the dominant mode of governance by agencies and remains at the center of domestic regulatory activities.[13]

Key to domestic regulation is the common technique that regulatory agencies use to wield their authority – the "territorial" approach to regulation. See Figure 1.1. Under this approach, entities operating in a designated geographic space (usually coterminous with national borders) and seeking to access that area's investors, capital, or market intermediaries are deemed subjects of regulation.

---

[13] Bressman & Thompson, *supra* note 2, at 609.

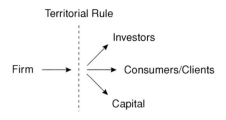

FIGURE 1.1. The Dynamics of Territorial Regulation

How geographic borders are defined for regulatory purposes is not always a straightforward matter.[14] Instead, jurisdiction is often defined by what can be described as territorial proxies. In countries with national banking regulators, jurisdiction generally arises and territorial contact is made when an institution takes deposits from persons in that jurisdiction.[15] In the case of securities law, territoriality is largely conceived through sale of securities to the "public" in a particular jurisdiction or the use of an instrumentality associated with securities transactions that physically exists in a particular jurisdiction (like stock exchanges or other centralized trading venues).[16] Once jurisdiction applies, certain regulatory requirements take effect. In the case of banks and insurance regulation, the consequence is that foreign banks must comply with capital reserve requirements and periodic examinations. And securities firms, along with issuers, must register with the host country's national securities regulator or, in the absence of a national regulator, with the relevant stock exchange authorities, meaning that periodic disclosures must be made.

In many respects, the territorial approach proves a simple and altogether powerful mode of domestic governance. When geared toward domestic activities, it inherently recognizes and embraces the principle that countries have authority over actions that take place within their borders. By attaching onto

[14] This observation holds true not only to the regulation of financial transactions, but also (and even especially) to corporate governance more generally. Under, for example, the real seat doctrine the authority over a company's internal affairs belongs to the state in which the company's central management decisions are being implemented on a day-to-day basis. *See* Werner F. Ebke, *The 'Real Seat' Doctrine in the Conflict of Corporate Laws*, 36 INT'L LAW. 1015, 1015 (2002). Meanwhile, under the incorporation theory, the state in which companies are incorporated trigger jurisdiction, thereby granting promoters choice of law as to what principles should govern the internal affairs of the firm. *Id.*

[15] Here the United States serves as a partial exception to this rule. To be sure, where a bank takes deposits in the United States, it will become subject to regulation by a government entity. Precisely which entity will, however, turn in part on the form of charter that a bank selects (e.g., state or national), though in either case federal regulation applies at least indirectly under FDIC deposit insurance supervision.

[16] Christopher J. Brummer, *Stock Exchanges and the New Markets for Securities Laws*, 75 U. CHI. L. REV. 1435, 1441 (2008) (describing jurisdiction of US securities regulation).

geographic proxies, like deposit taking, stock exchanges, and the investing public, financial regulations can have deep geographic coverage, touching virtually all "transactions that occur within [a country's] borders, or that have substantial effects within its territory."[17]

In this way, domestic authorities – whether in the form of a legislature, regulatory agency, or independent commission – enjoy what commentators have described as a "regulatory monopoly" over the conduct of financial activities in their relevant jurisdictions.[18] By law, domestic companies have to comply with domestic regulations. Similarly, foreign firms become subject to local laws and, in doing so, are generally afforded national treatment: they are treated no differently from local firms and must comply with the same rules as their local counterparts.

Territorial regulation need not, however, be entirely domestic in its reach. By operating as a gateway to investors, consumers, and capital, territoriality can be leveraged in a way that can affect foreign firms (at a minimum, those operating in the country) and, potentially, the conduct or approach by foreign regulators, as some affiliates, and even some parent firms, adopt the rules or standards of the state exercising territorial jurisdiction. At the most basic level, as already mentioned, foreign firms operating in a country will often have to comply with that country's domestic rules and thus internalize the costs and benefits of the relevant regulatory regime. In such cases, firms may have to make disclosures that are not usually required under their home regulatory regimes, as well as comply with various capital, corporate governance, and procedural requirements.

Territorial rules can move up the corporate ladder to parent companies. The US Financial Services Modernization Act of 1999, for example, has for over a decade required that all foreign bank seeking to be licensed as financial holding companies satisfy risk-based capital standards on a global basis and also satisfy the Federal Reserve that its global operations are well capitalized.[19] This consolidated form of supervision confers to the federal government the power to evaluate the operations of international regulators and

---

[17] Frederick Tung, *From Monopolists to Markets?: A Political Economy of Issuer Choices in International Securities Regulation*, 2002 WIS. L. REV. 1363, 1395 (2002).

[18] *See, e.g.*, Roberta Romano, *The Need for Competition in International Securities Regulation*, 2 THEORETICAL INQUIRIES L. 387, 390–96 (2001) (asserting that a market for regulatory regimes is superior to a monopolist regulator or "regulatory cartel" of internationally harmonized regimes); Tung, *supra* note 17, at 1379 (noting that many scholars view the territorially-based approach to securities regulation as allowing "each national regulatory agency to enjoy something of a 'monopoly' in terms of the regulation it chooses to supply within its jurisdiction").

[19] KERN ALEXANDER ET AL., GLOBAL GOVERNANCE OF FINANCIAL SYSTEMS: THE INTERNATIONAL REGULATION OF SYSTEMIC RISK 27 (2006).

to conduct inspections of foreign affiliates and foreign regulatory agencies.[20] Similarly, the EU's Financial Conglomerate Directive and draft Alternative Fund Investment Directive permit operations and access to customers only when companies, as well as their parent companies, either comport with EU rules or are subject to regulation deemed to be equivalent to that exercised in Europe.[21]

Extraterritoriality does not always come in the form of de jure rules that are pushed "upstream" to parent companies and affiliates. If compliance is required by a subsidiary entity, the relevant behavior may voluntarily be adopted by the parent entity or other affiliates in the corporate group in order to streamline operations. Managers of firms may prefer to transact under one set of rules in order to minimize the transaction costs of operating in multiple jurisdictions and to create a more harmonized compliance culture organizationally. For example, rather than adhering to Standard X (a strict set of disclosures) in one country and then hiring different lawyers to facilitate compliance with Standard Y (a more permissive set of disclosures) in another country, a firm will merely abide by Standard X in order to minimize compliance costs.

This particular kind of de facto internationalization of national standards is also possible when one country imposes certain kinds of national corporate governance requirements. Take, for example, the Sarbanes-Oxley Act of 2002[22] concerning issuers of securities and the EU's rules on credit-rating agencies as originally proposed in 2008.[23] The aim of both initiatives was to have firms monitor their internal controls and potentially institute new governance structures and committees. Although both initiatives were directed at local market participants, potentially their effects could have been international in

[20] Other countries are empowered to impose similar restrictions. *Id.* at 47.
[21] Michael Gruson, *Supervision of Financial Conglomerates in the European Union*, 4 CURRENT DEV. IN MONETARY & FIN. L. 425 (2008), *available at* http://www.imf.org/external/np/leg/sem/2004/cdmfl/eng/gruson.pdf (describing consolidated supervision under the EU Financial Conglomerate Directive); *see also* FRESHFIELDS BRUCKHAUS DERINGER LLP, EU DRAFT DIRECTIVE ON ALTERNATIVE INVESTMENT FUND MANAGERS: IMPLICATIONS FOR THE REAL ESTATE INDUSTRY (2009), *available at* http://www.freshfields.com/publications/pdfs/2009/jul09/26360.pdf (describing draft EU Directive for hedge funds and private equity firms).
[22] Sarbanes-Oxley Act of 2002, Pub. L. No. 107-204, 116 Stat. 745 (2002) (codified in scattered sections of U.S.C.).
[23] *Commission Proposal for a Regulation of the European Parliament and of the Council on Credit Rating Agencies*, at 8, COM (2008) 704 final (Nov. 12, 2008), *available at* http://ec.europa.eu/internal_market/securities/docs/agencies/proposal_en.pdf (describing proposed transparency and independence requirements for credit-rating agencies operating in Europe); *see also* Press Release, Brussels Council of the European Union, Financial Services: New Rules on Credit Rating Agencies, Bank Capital Requirements, Cross-border Payments and E-money, and a Programme to Support the Effectiveness of EU Policies (July 27, 2009), *available at* http://register.consilium.europa.eu/pdf/en/09/st12/st12380.en09.pdf.

scope since some regulated entities may have found it rational to change all of their operations to reflect these requirements. Common legal processes and administrative structures can be developed to harmonize functions across firms. Companies may thus be able to minimize the transaction costs associated with undertaking new compliance procedures in each jurisdiction. Furthermore, by operating with the highest common denominator (the most stringent requirements), legal risk can be minimized where operations are deeply international and where multiple subsidiaries work across borders.

Similar forms of de facto internationalization of national standards occur when a national authority applies rules to its own firms that are then "passed on" indirectly to foreign clients. For example, the EU has long considered, as part of its regulations for credit-rating agencies, a range of reforms that would impose elevated capital requirements on banks, insurance firms, and other financial institutions that enter into financial transactions whose risk assessments rely, in part, on credit-rating agencies that have not been registered by EU authorities.[24] In the wake of the credit crisis and the resultant regulatory concerns, authorities have been seeking means to ensure that credit-rating agencies are properly supervised and regulated. And the potential impact is considerable. In practice, a change would help export European rules by forcing credit-rating agencies to register – a move that would allow them to be competitive with other (registered) European institutions and to effectively court European banks as clients.

These examples illustrate that, as a regulatory concept, "territoriality" best describes not so much the effect or scope of law, but the means by which it is generated. Even more importantly from the regulator's standpoint, territoriality can afford potentially extraterritorial prudential and supervisory power. In an age of globalized financial transactions, the appeal of extraterritorial regulation is obvious. As business activity has become increasingly cross-border, strong extraterritorial regulation has permitted regulators to reach beyond their territories to affect the activities and conduct of not only foreign market participants, but in some cases foreign regulators as well.

"DIRECT" EXTRATERRITORIAL LEGISLATION

National regulators need not rely exclusively on territorial legislation in order to export their rules unilaterally. In theory, regulators can adopt purer forms of extraterritorial regulation that apply more directly to international actors and activities. This section addresses three possibilities. First, regulators can apply

---

[24] *Commission Proposal for a Regulation of the European Parliament and of the Council on Credit Rating Agencies, supra* note 23, at 9 (requiring registration as a requirement where firms intend to use the ratings for regulatory purposes).

laws directly and exclusively addressed to foreign firms. Second, jurisdiction can be structured in such a way that even the most inconsequential or tangential contact with the state triggers its authority, and jurisdiction might even extend to events that take place overseas but have a domestic effect. Third, jurisdiction can arise whenever foreign acts have an "effect" on the regulating country. Each will be discussed in turn.

In the first case, a country simply passes laws that apply directly to foreign firms. For example, a country could pass a law that outlaws any bank in the world from engaging in fraudulent conduct with any of that country's nationals – even when the depositors are themselves overseas when transacting with the firm. Such instances of extraterritoriality are virtually nonexistent in the financial world, in part because the courts are reluctant to take on cases so lacking in national interests. But extraterritorial laws are theoretically possible, as demonstrated by the United States' Alien Tort Claims and its international progeny, which permit foreigners to sue for human rights violations that occur abroad.[25]

As a second course of action, regulators can assert jurisdiction extraterritorially whenever foreign companies engage in conduct that has effects in the country asserting jurisdiction. In practice, this kind of extraterritorial strategy has been used to most spectacular effect in antitrust actions. For example, in 2001 the European Commission blocked a merger between General Electric and Honeywell – even after the US Department of Justice had sanctioned it – largely on the basis of the deal's anticompetitive implications for European markets.[26] Effects-driven jurisdiction has at times been applied by courts, thus amplifying the reach of US securities laws. In *Des Brisay v. Goldfield Corp.*, for example, a US federal court ruled for the plaintiff when the plaintiff alleged that an issue of stock in Canada to insiders of a Canadian company at an unfairly low price had adversely affected the value and price of the company's shares listed on the American Stock Exchange.[27] Although fraud had been perpetrated on a Canadian company, and the foreign defendant never entered the United States in connection with the fraud, the court found that "the adverse effect on the equity of US shareholders was sufficient to support jurisdiction."[28]

A final subspecies of direct extraterritoriality, similar to effects-based jurisdiction (and indeed often employed in conjunction with it), arises through the

---

[25] For a description of the Alien Tort Claims Act, *see generally* Harold J. Berman, Commentary, *The Alien Tort Claims Act and the Law of Nations*, 19 EMORY INT'L L. REV. 69 (2005).

[26] *See* Michael Elliott, *The Anatomy of the GE-Honeywell Disaster*, TIME, July 8, 2001, http://www.time.com/time/business/article/0,8599,166732,00.html.

[27] Des Brisay v. Goldfield Corp., 549 F.2d 133, 135 (9th Cir. 1981).

[28] Id.

implementation of what can be considered tenuous contacts with territorial proxies. It is best illustrated using the United States as an example; it remains the country most likely to exert extraterritorial financial law. The Securities Act of 1933 provides that it is unlawful to offer or sell any security without register-ing it when the offering or sale used any "means or instrumentality of interstate commerce."[29] "Interstate commerce" is defined in the statute to include "trade or commerce in securities or any transportation or communication relating thereto ... between any foreign country and any State, Territory, or the District of Columbia."[30] The statute is silent as to the scope of registration require-ments. It can be construed to encompass virtually any offering of securities made by a United States corporation to foreign investors; a telephone call to the United States in connection with the sale of a security abroad exclusively to foreign investors[31] is arguably enough to trigger the statute. Consequently, the rulemaking authority of the Securities Exchange Commission has at least historically had potentially international implications, though the Supreme Court has recently sought to curtail the scope of antifraud provisions.[32] Direct extraterritorial jurisdiction has, as one might expect, several clear advantages over domestic and extraterritorial territoriality. Territorialism's inherent limi-tation – that authority is tied to certain geographic markers – is at least theo-retically overcome. A regulator can directly address foreign activities without having to substantiate significant contacts within its domestic territorial bor-ders. In this way, activities that might be consummated entirely overseas but that have repercussions for local financial markets or the national economy can be addressed through domestic prudential and supervisory regulation. Direct extraterritorial regulation may be able to significantly affect the behavior of foreign firms. Additionally, the very promulgation of international standards or rules may have a deterrence effect on the possible conduct of overseas actors. And like classic territorial regulation, it can be wielded unilaterally with no cooperation required from a foreign counterpart to promulgate the rules, though it must, of course, be verified or upheld by domestic judicial authorities.[33]

---

[29] Securities Act of 1933 § 5(a), 15 U.S.C. § 77e(a) (2010).

[30] *Id.* § 2(7), 15 U.S.C. § 77b(a)(7) (2010).

[31] *See* Schoenbaum v. Fistbrook, 405 F.2d 200, 206 (2d Cir. 1968) (explaining the extraterritorial application of federal securities laws). For a detailed discussion of the effects test in securities regulation, *see generally* Michael D. Mann et al., *Oversight by the U.S. Securities and Exchange Commission of U.S. Securities Markets and Issues of Internalization and Extraterritorial Juris-diction*, 29 INT'L LAW. 731 (1995).

[32] *See*, e.g., Morrison v. National Australian Bank, 130 S. Ct. 2869 (2010) (curbing the extraterri-torial application of the Securities and Exchange Act of 1934).

[33] Courts may, of course, themselves impose strict limitations on the power of regulators, the subject of the conflicts of law literature. *See generally* Hannah L. Buxbaum, *Conflict of*

THE POLITICAL ECONOMY PROBLEM

Despite the advantages catalogued above, the unilateral "exportation" of regulation by national authorities to other jurisdictions – both in its indirect territorial guise and in its more explicit form – is difficult. Ultimately, two obstacles stymie such actions. First, there is what can be considered a "political economy problem": regulators do not act in a vacuum, and when their actions have negative consequences for foreign regulators, they may be punished. Second, the increasingly diverse sources of finance, a product of financial globalization, not only exacerbate the political and possibly economic costs of unilateralism, but also make extraterritoriality less practical and weaken the incentives for tough domestic territorial rules.

The political economy problem of extraterritorial regulation arises when a country's attempts at extraterritorial export sparks reactions, some retaliatory, from other regulators that can imperil an agency's ability to achieve its long-term strategic objectives. A most basic consequence of extraterritorial regulation is the potential erosion of image and respect in the international community of regulators. The international system generally frowns upon unilateral extraterritorial conduct, in part because it often implies the violation of long-standing principles of international law. The very notion of sovereignty, for example, demands that states have full authority over their respective territories, and principles of comity have long required that governments give effect to the executive, legislative, and judicial acts (and authority) of other countries. As a result, extraterritorial legislation (directly or indirectly) is generally found to be an acceptable practice only when it can be justified by significant interests of the intervening regulator.

Yet, as seen above, states may often have only tenuous interests in the foreign actor or conduct, or the interests of other states may be superior with regard to the regulated activity or individual. Moreover, even where a regulator has a legitimate policy or national interest, other authorities may perceive the regulation as too broad and intrusive and as not sufficiently tailored to that interest. As former Chief Justice Rehnquist noted such conflicts of law under such circumstances can generate "international discord."[34] Ensuing disagreements can then undermine the international reputation of an agency

---

Economic Laws: From Sovereignty to Substance, 42 VA. J. INT'L L. 941 (2002). Indeed, often considerations will involve a balancing of interests between countries. Yet even here, there is a focus on territorial power that at least historically has often upheld the exercise of extraterritorial authority.

[34] Equal Emp't Opportunity Comm'n v. Arabian American Oil Co., 499 U.S. 244, 248 (1991).

and its ability to promote policies, and also tarnish the personal or professional reputations of its civil servants.

Discord can be particularly high where extraterritorial regulation generates costs that are born primarily by foreign regulators and market participants. Extraterritorial regulation could require a foreign firm to comply with new (or different) standards, or force it to move to another jurisdiction altogether in order to avoid the reach of the foreign regulator. At the same time, the assertion of regulatory authority by a foreign agency potentially infringes on the ability of local regulators to oversee and supervise firms as they see fit. Firms in an affected jurisdiction may have to change their corporate governance structure or disclosure requirements in ways that conflict with local law, and thus in the process undermine the authority of the national regulator. In addition, the exertion of extraterritorial regulation can imply that a foreign agency finds the local laws in a relevant jurisdiction to be less sound than those practiced domestically, and erode market confidence in the target country's regulatory regime and supervisors.

By engaging in extraterritorial regulation, a regulator may thus appear thus self-interested and insensitive to the costs and consequences that its laws may have for other regulators and firms. The regulator can develop a reputation for being unwilling to abide by expectations of comity and international laws of sovereignty. Appearing to have an inclination to engage in unilateralism can, as a result, have a variety of adverse consequences for a regulator. Once a regulator is judged to be self-interested and uncooperative, other regulators may decide to refrain from cooperating with it or helping it achieve its strategic objectives.[35] A regulator can always go down the path of least resistance and decide not to help its foreign counterpart enforce its extraterritorial rules when it seeks assistance when prosecuting a violation (where witnesses or the proceeds of misconduct are located abroad). In more dramatic circumstances, a regulator could pull back from cooperation altogether. It could, for example, refuse to engage in joint regulatory projects and refrain from robust information sharing and enforcement cooperation.

How does this passive retaliatory conduct look in practice? Consider Germany's response to the economic instability caused by the global economic crisis and, more specifically, the speculative "attacks" against Eurozone currencies in 2010. In May of that year, just after the euro lost nearly 20 percent of its value vis-à-vis the dollar, Germany's market regulator announced a ban

---

[35] This idea has been articulated by a variety of theorists, but for a comprehensive assessment, *see* Andrew T. Guzman, How International Law Works: A Rational Choice Theory 71–111 (2008).

on so-called naked short selling of Eurozone government debt and shares of major financial companies – a ban applying, among other things, to naked credit default swaps involving Eurozone debt. The ban was intended to prevent the kind of financial-market speculation that was then exacerbating Greece's financial woes, but the decision was made without consultation with, or even advance warning to, the other EU member states. Therefore, Germany's unexpected and unilateral decision raised concerns in the EU about regulatory arbitrage and fragmentation within the EU. In response, a range of regulators, including the British Financial Services Authority, announced that they would not apply or help enforce the rule with regard to German institutions operating in their jurisdictions – voiding, in effect, any practical impact of the rule.

A regulator can respond to extraterritorial rule making by another regulator with extraterritorial rule making of its own.[36] In some (rare) situations, a response might take on an explicitly retaliatory character aimed at disciplining the extraterritorial regulator. In others, it may merely take place as a reciprocal breach of established principles of comity in a related area. Consider, for example, the long-standing differences between the United States and Europe with regard to the treatment of financial statements by foreign issuers. Since the 1990s, European regulators had requested their US counterparts that they permit foreign issuers to make disclosures according to the International Financial Reporting Standards (IFRS), a common set of accounting rules in Europe, as an alternative to US Generally Accepted Accounting Principles (GAAP). After years of debate and prodding, the SEC relented, albeit only partially, by permitting disclosure under IFRS but requiring reconciliation with US GAAP. Frustrated with the sluggish pace toward acceptance of IFRS – especially in light of widespread European acceptance of US GAAP and changes made to IFRS to appease US regulators – the EU threatened that, if the SEC did not accept IFRS financial statements without a reconciliation, it would act to require a reconciliation to IFRS of US GAAP financial statements filed in Europe.[37] Ultimately, in response to this pressure, in April 2005, the SEC backtracked. It devised a roadmap that culminated in permitting foreign issuers to report in IFRS without reconciling to US GAAP.

More frequently, however, extraterritorial conduct may also serve as a kind of "precedent" justifying extraterritorial regulation in unrelated financial matters.

---

[36] *Id.* at 42–49 (discussing retaliation and reciprocity as disciplinary responses in international relations).

[37] Stephen A. Zeff, *IFRS Developments in the USA and EU, and Some Implications for Australia,* 18 AUSTL. ACCT. REV. 275 (2008), *available at* http://www.ruf.rice.edu/~sazeff/PDF/AAR%20Dec%202008%20article.pdf.

Consider, for example, the promulgation of the Sarbanes-Oxley Act, a law that, though applied territorially, forced foreign companies with US listings to restructure their corporate governance in ways that at times conflicted with the corporate governance requirements in Europe. Foreign regulators and politicians protested the extraterritorial reach of the legislation, though their protests were (mostly) ignored, and few reforms to the legislation were made.[38] This event created a precedent, however, for the European Commission when it enacted stiff corporate governance requirements for (primarily US) credit-rating agencies as a reaction to the 2008 financial crisis. After EU authorities had promulgated some initial proposals, the US SEC, like European officials earlier, protested the unilateral exertion of regulatory power. The SEC did so, however, from a weakened position, having earlier employed similar regulatory tactics itself.

The mode of jurisdictional authority that regulators employ can be important. For example, all else being equal, traditional territorial regulation generates fewer political costs than direct extraterritorial legislation. The latter challenges international law more obviously than even aggressive territoriality insofar as it either is addressed directly to actions that take place overseas or at least implicitly does not limit the rules to domestic application. There are fewer obvious justifications for direct extraterritorial legislation. Territorial regulation can be justified on the basis that it is applied domestically and addresses either actors or transactions that are local. Moreover, when territorial regulation is promulgated, regulators can argue fairness and impartiality: foreign companies voluntarily subject themselves to host country regulation by coming to the country to do business – in other words, firms "opt in" to the regulatory regime of the host state. Usually, no such justifications are available when extraterritorial laws are explicitly addressed to foreign companies and actions taking place abroad.

TRANSACTIONAL DECOUPLING

Regulatory export is becoming increasingly difficult as international sources of both capital and financial investment diversify. As a tool for international regulatory export, territoriality relies on a regulator's authority over strategically important financial markets. Simply put, the more important a country's financial markets, the greater the influence of its local regulators. This raises the question: what makes a market important?

---

[38] For an analysis of the difficulties for European companies, especially in Europe, *see* Lawrence A. Cunningham, *From Convergence to Comity in Corporate Law: Lessons from the Inauspicious Case of SOX*, 1 INT'L J. DISCLOSURE & GOVERNANCE 269, 272 (2004).

The size of a country's financial markets is one obvious consideration. Where a market hosts a large share of the world's investors, financial institutions, or financial transactions, its domestic regulators wield considerable power since more investors, issuers, and counterparties transact there. Moreover, economies of scale can heighten positive feedback dynamics, or "network effects," that reinforce the desirability of the standards and rules governing the market. For example, as US stock exchanges were required by regulators to ensure that listed firms comply with US GAAP in their financial disclosures, even firms not directly subject to US regulatory requirements came to adopt the standards, in part because they came to be used, required, and understood by so many investors and firms.

Some markets may be strategically important owing to their high growth rate – either with regard to participation by investors and firms or the rate of return available from the markets' underlying investments. When a particular market is able to offer outsized gains due to the rapid underlying economic growth of the country in which it is located, it will attract investors and financial services companies like investment banks, brokerages, and private equity firms. Similarly, high growth in consumer markets or particular segments of the services market – for instance, the growth of a country's high net worth individuals – can attract large numbers of firms, from commercial banks to hedge funds, to service them.

Finally, some markets are unique in providing investments that are unavailable or rare elsewhere. Frequently, markets try to create certain kinds of niches, often tied with financial innovation. This strategy is usually associated with derivatives – complex instruments like swaps and options whose value depends on other underlying events, benchmarks, or asset classes. However, niches can be created by markets specializing in certain kinds of instruments – like the infamous "credit default swaps" tied to the US housing market that were securitized in the United States or the Islamic bonds designed to comply with Sharia law throughout the Middle East. When markets provide unique instruments, they may succeed in attracting investors seeking to diversify their portfolios.

If a capital market is large or significant enough to the global economy, its rules can at least conceivably become *lex financiaria* – not necessarily the international law of finance per se, but the rules and practices followed by firms in their financial activities nonetheless. Likewise, its regulatory authority can come to exert what international relations theory views as "hegemonic" authority – the financial and regulatory power over other groups, regardless of the explicit consent of the latter. In such circumstances, the hegemon's rules and standards can become (quite literally) the gold standard, the ones against which other jurisdictional rules are judged and compared.

In practice, only one country, the United States, has consistently wielded such authority over the last sixty years. Its capital markets, led by New York City, have largely dwarfed those in other cities – with the exception of its long-standing rival, London – and thus most multinational companies seeking financing beyond their own shores came to the United States to raise capital on its world-class exchanges. This migration gave the national securities authority, the SEC, indirect influence over the provision of both domestic and global securities rules. Similarly, the United States has been well positioned to inform, and in some instances even design, global banking regulations. Not only have foreign companies and financial institutions come to the United States in order to secure dollar-based financing (given the currency's traditional reserve status), but those seeking to transact with US clients and customers have often established US branches to do business – activities that often brought them under the supervision of state or federal authorities in the United States.[39]

Yet as economists and political scientists now regularly attest, this dominance has waned considerably over the last two decades, if not in absolute terms, then at least relatively. The reasons for this decline are myriad. Perhaps the most important political factor is the centralization of rulemaking authority in Europe. Once a common currency, the euro, was established under the Treaty of Maastricht in 1992, two important projects accelerated the process of European regulatory centralization. First, the Financial Services Action Plan of March 2000 provided a framework policy deemed necessary to integrate European national and financial services industries. Much more so than in the past, the "new laws centralized regulatory authority by harmonizing national rules in ways that often required a single set of EU standards and regulations."[40]

The second important development was the inauguration of the Lamfalussy Process, which provides for a four-stage process of rule making over the financial services industry.[41] The process is in many ways an unwieldy exercise involving the elaboration of legislation by the EU Commission and three sectoral-based regulators (themselves the product of collaboration by the EU Commission, EU Council, and EU Parliament), but it made possible a shift in the transatlantic balance of regulatory power. Prior to centralization efforts, there was no distinctive approach to capital market regulation, and nations

---

[39] William F. Kroener, III, Comment, *Towards Interdependence: A Decline in U.S. Dominance?*, 24 Law & Pol'y Int'l Bus. 1135, 1136 (1992–1993).

[40] Elliot Posner, *Making Rules for Global Finance: Transatlantic Regulatory Cooperation at the Turn of the Millennium*, 63 Int'l Org. 665, 681 (2009), *available at* http://politicalscience .case.edu/faculty/posner/IO.pdf.

[41] *Id.*

largely remained passive; at the most, US regulatory leadership was challenged "along the edges."[42] National differences among EU states undermined potential efforts to show a unified front and maintain a common position (and, indeed, at times still do).

However, as Brussels began to take charge of financial services oversight, the EU increasingly began to resemble a second regulatory "superpower," whatever its ultimate structural flaws and internal divisions. Its jurisdiction extended to the important financial centers of Amsterdam, Berlin, London and Paris. By adopting common policies on the freedom of movement of capital, labor, and enterprise, EU member states have helped create the largest and deepest pools of capital and customers in the world. Now, EU institutions bargain externally with other states on financial matters, and the federal government monitors the harmonization of national laws to comply with EU law, with the consequence that the collective power of EU member states has expanded dramatically.[43] This process is expected to accelerate, as a new systemic risk board has been established to warn about dangers building up in the financial system. The Lamfalussy committees have also been replaced by three new EU supervisory authorities in the areas of securities, banking, and insurance and pensions, which wield greater powers, including the ability to draft technical standards with legal force when endorsed by the Commission.

Another critical development since the early 1990s has been the rising importance of emerging countries as centers of financial market activity. By far the most important countries in this regard are Brazil, Russia, India, and China. In virtually every sector, a wave of market participants – such as brokerages, stock exchanges, investment banks, and even investors – have migrated from home markets to foreign shores to transact alongside domestic actors. The key driver behind this development has been the consistently rapid economic growth in these regions. Successful, export-driven economies have ushered in soaring trade and capital account surpluses and, in the process, boosted tremendous wealth creation in these countries, with hundreds of millions

---

[42] *Id.* at 677.

[43] Daniel W. Drezner, All Politics is Global: Explaining International Regulatory Regimes 37 (2007) (arguing that a strong case can be made for viewing the EU as a single actor in the wake of the Maastricht treaty). *See* Gregory C. Shaffer & Mark A. Pollack, *Hard vs. Soft Law: Alternatives, Complements and Antagonists in International Governance*, 94 Minn. L. Rev. 706 (2010) (noting that "[b]ecause of the size of the EU's internal market, once the EU member states harmonize regulatory policies at eh EU level and develop corresponding EU-level regulatory institutions, the EU is well positioned to exercise economic clout as a global actor"); *see also* Roberta S. Karmel, *The EU Challenge to the SEC*, 31 Fordham Int'l L.J. 1711 (2008) (noting how European integration has given the EU more power in influencing the SEC decision making).

TABLE 1.1. *Projected GDP growth between 2007 and 2050*

Country	GDP at market exchange rates in $US (indices, with US = 100)	
	2007	2050
United States	100	100
Japan	32	19
China	23	129
Germany	22	14
UK	18	14
France	17	14
Italy	14	10
Canada	10	9
Spain	9	9
Brazil	8	26
Russia	8	17
India	7	88
Korea	7	8
Mexico	7	17
Australia	6	6
Turkey	3	10
Indonesia	3	17

more people now enjoying incomes between $6,000 and $30,000.[44] Moreover, emerging markets exhibit far better economic fundamentals and better growth prospects than their developed counterparts. Not only do they enjoy much larger foreign reserves and less sovereign indebtedness, but their domestic household finances and savings rates are considerably greater than those in the United States and Europe.[45] Global investors are, as a result, more confident in the ability of emerging markets to grow over the next several decades, an optimism grounded in both real and expected growth in the gross domestic product (GDP) of emerging economies. See Table 1.1.

Additionally, the degree and quality of oversight in emerging markets can increasingly be compared to that practiced in traditionally dominant financial centers. A decade ago, US and UK markets were viewed as premier financial systems enjoying unrivaled quality of regulatory oversight. This reputation

[44] Dominic Wilson et al., *Is this the 'BRICs Decade'?*, Brics' Monthly, May 2010, http://www2 .goldmansachs.com/ideas/brics/brics-decade-doc.pdf.

[45] *See* John Stepek, *Emerging Markets Will Be the Winners from this Crisis*, MoneyWeek June 15, 2009, http://www.moneyweek.com/news-and-charts/economics/emerging-markets-will-be-the-winners-from-this-crisis-15672.aspx.

was, in part, a response both to the roaring economies in the region and to the regulatory failures in developing countries that upended the global financial system throughout the 1990s. Since then the regulatory reputations of developed financial centers have suffered, especially in the wake of the 2008 crisis. By comparison, some analysts and investors are exploring the value and benefits of alternative regulatory methods and approaches embraced by countries that have best weathered the crisis – many of which are members of the BRIC club. Most commentators agree that Asian securities markets, though far from perfect, have come a long way with regard to disclosure and regulatory supervision. In 1998, China created a central securities regulator, promulgated its first securities law, reduced the number of nontradable, state-owned shares in its equity markets, and relaxed restrictions on foreign institutional investors seeking to invest in its markets. Brazil has also taken steps to strengthen the reputation of its financial markets. In 2001, the World Bank announced a $14.46 million loan to Brazil to help it strengthen its Central Bank and Securities Commission, and the country has also been working to improve corporate governance and investor voting rights in connection with a set of priority initiatives by the Organisation for Economic Co-operation and Development (OECD).

These developments have helped support a "decoupling" of transactions from traditional money centers as capital and market participants migrate to ever more diverse parts of the world. Although the trend is still nascent, evidence already shows that multinational banks have expanded aggressively beyond their home jurisdictions in order to offer depository, advisory, and wealth management services in countries with rapidly growing middle-class and upper-income residents – services that are often available only when banks submit formally to full prudential oversight by national authorities. Similarly, insurance companies have merged with counterparts overseas to break into new markets and to offer expanded risk-management services, including derivatives underwriting. Reinsurance companies, too, have been driven to combine and expand beyond national borders to achieve sufficient size to underwrite the, at times, billions of dollars of risk generated by traditional insurance companies, their clients.

Yet no industry has been more affected by financial globalization and the BRIC emergence than securities issuance and trading. In the wake of financial globalization, the United States has experienced a dramatic decline in its market share in securities transactions; in particular, the global IPO market – those initial public offerings done outside of a company's home country. As late as 1996, nearly 44.5 percent of all IPOs took place in the United States. By 2007, none of the year's twenty largest global IPOs took place in the United States, and just 10 percent overall. Instead, numerically, most IPOs were in London, a financial center long sporting nonintrusive ("light touch") regulatory oversight; and in value terms, the lion's share was raised in BRIC countries – $106.5 billion of the total $255 billion raised in IPOs worldwide. In part because of these trends, exemplified by Hong Kong's $52 billion of public offerings in 2010, as compared to the New York Stock Exchange's $35 billion, BRIC stock exchanges significantly outperformed those in Europe, Japan, and the United States over the last decade, providing returns on equity of 200–900 percent.[46] This success helped drive the migration and expansion of banks, brokerages, and financial services professionals beyond the financial centers of London and New York to Hong Kong, Mumbai, and São Paulo.

IMPLICATIONS FOR REGULATORY POWER

The rise of transactional decoupling has a range of important strategic implications for territorially based regulation worldwide.[47] Financial globalization exacerbates the stakes of extraterritorial regulation, whatever its guise. Countries that were once only remote destinations for capital now wield more regulatory clout and significance, and are better positioned to check traditional leaders' efforts to exert extraterritorial influence. As competitive, world class financial centers have arisen in Europe and emerging markets so, too has the ability of their local regulators to project their national prerogatives abroad as an increasing number of foreign institutions now participate in their capital and consumer markets.[48] In a multipolar world of financial power, greater reflection is required by regulators of the traditionally dominant financial

---

[46] Wilson et al., *supra* note 43, at 3.
[47] It is, after all, notable that China in particular may face significant write-offs with regard to its own imprudent domestic lending in real estate, much like the United States. *See* Vishesh Kumar, *China Curbs Bank Loans as Asset Bubble Worries Grow*, DAILY FIN., Jan. 20, 2010, http://www.dailyfinance.com/story/china-curbs-bank-loans-amid-bubble-worries/19324151/. Some experts contend, however, that even in the event of such bubbles "bursting," the domestic fallout would be considerably less than that in the 2008 crisis in the United States. Katie Benner, *What happens if China's 'Bubble' Pops?*, CNN, Feb. 5, 2010, http://money.cnn.com/2010/02/05/news/international/china_bubbles.fortune/index.htm.
[48] As in other forms of extraterritoriality, the policy consequences have been most obvious in the antitrust space, where China is increasingly blocking international deals with only secondary implications for its markets. *See Antitrust in China: Beijing is Asserting its Authority in Extraterritorial Deals*, FIN. TIMES (Asia Edition), May 5, 2009, at 8. (Noting how China's Ministry of Commerce imposed restrictions on the $1.6bn takeover by Japan's Mitsubishi Rayon of the UK's Lucite international, forcing the latter to sell half of its production of one polymer at cost, as well as restrictions on InBev's $52 billion acquisition of Anheuser-Busch).

centers as they attempt to unilaterally solve global capital market challenges – and, indeed, even domestic capital market challenges.

The accelerated development of foreign capital markets also makes it easier for firms to evade any one country's rules. Instead of acting as an outright determinant for firms and investors, prohibitions and rules often can be evaded by moving cross-border. Mobility can be physical, such as where a bank relocates from one country to another, or it can be along transactional lines, where, for a example, a bank reroutes trading revenues from London to Singapore in order to avoid limitations on bonuses on bank trading activities. In either event, mobility can create a de facto "choice of law" for market participants. Territoriality as a technique consequently has more limited repercussions than ever before. Indeed, not only is there greater technical ability for capital and market participants to transact in foreign locales, but there is more reason to do so. More financial centers offer greater liquidity, reliable expertise, and speed, plus a global array of market participants. And customers and clients can move and transact in foreign markets.[49]

Perhaps as challenging as mobility are the increasing practical difficulties of, and resources required for, monitoring and enforcing territorial rules. Globalization implies that more transactions are undertaken in more places by more individuals and firms. Enforcement in such a world becomes increasingly demanding. In the future, resources will have to be devoted to the adjudication of claims and to the potential explosion of cases to be settled in domestic courts. Furthermore, in order to prosecute (or sue) violators of extraterritorial laws, the assistance of foreign regulators will be sought when violators or witnesses are located abroad. That assistance may not eventuate since foreign counterparts may reject the merits of the substantive rules that are being enforced. Thus, mobility can give some markets (that chose not to follow the lead of other regulators) a virtual "veto power" over key areas of regulation. And when one country decides to raise its standards, and another does not, firms

---

[49] *See generally* ERIN A. O'HARA & LARRY E. RIBSTEIN, THE LAW MARKET (2009) (As a contemporary example of how such mobility operates in practice, consider the draft Alternative Investment Funds Managers Directive, a legislative initiative announced in April 2009 requiring stricter oversight of private equity and hedge funds operating in the EU. Even before its ratification by the EU, over twenty hedge funds started leaving the EU, and specifically London, the capital of EU activity, for less stringent jurisdictions such as Switzerland. Moreover, twenty percent of fund managers are expected to leave the city by 2011 to escape the reach of the regulation and prospects of bonus taxes by the UK government. This kind of mobility, of course, bears on regulatory competition, touched on in the previous chapter. As market participants have more choice as to where to list or trade their securities, or deposit their savings, or transact with others, they can wield influence over the decisions of national regulators by threatening to leave and operate elsewhere).

may merely move to the weaker or less costly jurisdiction, making regulators hesitant to raise standards.[50]

REGULATORY SUASION AND SPECIAL-TREATMENT STRATEGIES

Even before the onset of the global financial crisis, changes in national regulatory tactics among national financial authorities were well underway. Since the early 1990s, administrative agencies in the United States and Europe, once content with largely domestic regulatory strategies, have hired personnel with both market know-how and foreign policy expertise: foreign policy analysts, experts, and area specialists often work alongside traditional regulators and enjoy civil service tenure. Moreover, the general trend of technocratic control has accelerated via further specialization by regulatory agencies. Virtually every regulatory agency charged with domestic supervisory responsibilities – whether it be financial ministries, securities regulators, or banking authorities – has instituted an "office of international affairs" to spearhead cooperation efforts with their foreign equivalents. We will get to know just how they do this in group settings in the following chapter, but for the moment let's consider the basic toolset available to regulators on a unilateral basis.

Technical Assistance

For well-resourced agencies like those in Australia, the United Kingdom, and the United States, technical assistance programs have been especially helpful tools of financial diplomacy that allow regulators to influence the policy direction of other countries. Through such programs, well-resourced regulators provide management-level training to regulators in other jurisdictions. In more elaborate programs – such as the SEC's two-week-long International Institute for Securities Market Development or the International Regulators' Seminar sponsored by the United Kingdom's Financial Services Authority – a national regulator may invite counterparts from other countries to its headquarters and conduct training exercises and lectures. Additionally, regulators may make their staffs available as consultants or have them conduct training programs abroad and in developing countries to provide country-specific advice and capacity building. Much, if not most, of such work is provided for free and funded by national development agencies and the World Bank.

The benefits of technical assistance are not simply one-sided. At a most fundamental level, technical assistance helps governments develop both policy

---

[50] Shaffer & Pollack, *supra* note 42, at 736–37.

and supervisory mechanisms to prevent financial crises that can undermine national and international markets; since the interests between the assisting and assisted countries are frequently "situationally interdependent," improvement in another's welfare improves one's own. Additionally, because technical assistance provides grounding in the basic principles and approaches employed by the assisting agency, it helps to reduce gaps in regulatory philosophy, understanding, and possibly adjustment costs. For example, if country A sponsors a technical assistance program to help country B develop better surveillance programs, the costs of enforcement cooperation are reduced, and the likelihood of the two countries working well together increases.

The efficacy of technical assistance is not always certain, however. By its nature, technical assistance is voluntary – the recipient country is not obligated to undertake any specific regulatory reform. When technical assistance programs propose policies that could undermine a country's local market participants, the country is free to ignore them. Furthermore, the scope of technical assistance is inherently limited. Few developed countries are in need of technical assistance (or at least would admit it), and even emerging markets are quickly developing their own sophisticated supervisory expertise. Moreover, the 2008 financial crisis, which started in the United States, undermined the credibility of developed countries as "experts" in financial market regulation. As a result, the proselytizing impact of technical assistance is limited to the most needy recipients of assistance. Participation in technical assistance programs allows, above all, for networking and better familiarization with the shape and function of foreign regulatory regimes. These are opportunities, beneficial to coordination, but the actual impact on foreign regulators is less than one might predict.

Mutual Recognition Strategies

Mutual recognition is another means of regulatory persuasion, with the often more tangible or immediate rewards of regulatory adjustment. In its simplest form, mutual recognition means that one country recognizes the other's regulatory oversight as equivalent and thus allows the market participants of the partner country to conduct business with no additional regulatory hurdles beyond compliance with the partner's regulatory regime.

Though formally a means of liberalization, in practice mutual recognition is often used to enhance or project certain regulatory preferences. Mutual recognition is perhaps most commonly associated with the legislative practice of the EU. If one EU nation judges a market participant to be compliant with EU standards, then that approval is valid for the entire region. Thus, under the

EU's Prospectus Directive, for example, any prospectus prepared for equity and low-denomination debt securities will need approval only from a relevant regulator of a single designated member state. Once approved, issuers can use the same prospectus in any member state, subject only to the issuance of a certificate of approval by the competent authority (which initially approved the prospectus) – the so-called passport effect.[51] Similarly, under the second Banking Coordination Directive, adopted in 1989 and implemented in 1993, EU authorities created a single license for banking, which permits a bank established in one member country to open branches in any other.

These instances of EU practice are not, however, typical of all instances of mutual recognition – or of its implications for convergence. In the examples cited above, mutual recognition has a supervisory focus. That is, the EU adopts certain core rules and principles that must then be implemented and enforced by member states. Only implementation and enforcement are left to the members. The prior, independent existence of an EU baseline serves as a policy bulwark against the bidding down of regulatory standards that might well occur if mutual recognition programs functioned as backdoor policies for registrants.

The absence of some kind of regulatory backstop or supervisory oversight as seen in the EU mutual recognition schemes can undermine mutual recognition as an instrument of regulatory suasion. Consider, for example, the Multijurisdictional Disclosure System (MJDS) program, a mutual recognition scheme adopted by the United States and Canada. Under the MJDS, Canadian foreign private issuers that meet eligibility criteria qualifying them as large, established companies are viewed as meeting certain of the SEC's securities registration and reporting requirements if they provide disclosure documents prepared according to the requirements of the relevant Canadian securities authorities.[52] By using a Canadian prospectus, issuers can avoid a range of administrative costs associated with US documents. Furthermore, the SEC does not review prospectuses prepared under the MJDS, which saves much time. Because the arrangement is "mutual," US issuers also enjoy expedited access to Canadian markets, though only a fraction have chosen to do so, given the immediate advantages of US markets. The program is thus largely

---

[51] FRIED FRANK LLP, MEMORANDUM: THE EU PROSPECTUS DIRECTIVE (2005), *available at* http://www.ffhsj.com/siteFiles/Publications/80000148E4AAC4F3C1A706258BB7CA66.pdf.

[52] Once the Canadian securities regulator grants approval, a wrap-around document is attached to the prospectus. This document provides certain information required by the United States securities regulators such as taxes, civil liability, and GAAP reconciliation in certain circumstances. Ruth O. Kuras, *Harmonization of Securities Regulation Standards Between Canada and the United States*, 81 U. DET. MERCY L. REV. 465, 469 (2004).

viewed as a boon to Canadian issuers seeking to raise capital in the United States.

Mutual recognition programs are viewed as largely deregulatory programs because they entail reciprocal (and simultaneous) changes in national-level hard law governance structures. This means a loss of national regulatory control and authority for participating regulatory agencies. However, mutual recognition programs can and do periodically constitute means of regulatory export. In the case of the MJDS, Canadian regulators were required to institute a range of changes associated with both issuance rules and supervisory activities as a condition for participating in the program. The SEC eked out additional concessions from Canadian regulators over time. In 2000, for example, the SEC publicly considered abandoning the program outright. The agency considered two matters inadequate – the reconciliations between Canadian companies' financial statements and generally accepted US accounting principles, and the oversight that Canadian regulators, particularly the Ontario Securities Commission, had exercised over prospectuses filed under the MJDS. The deliberations prompted several important reforms in the supervision of issuances, including the allocation of increased resources for that purpose. When Sarbanes-Oxley was passed by the US Congress, questions arose as to whether Canadian firms would be required to abide by the new US legislation, which imposed a range of additional (and costly) requirements on issuers. Canadian firms and regulators felt that compliance was not warranted and resisted prospective application of such rules to Canadian firms making offerings in the United States. Partly in response to this resistance, the SEC formally considered various policy changes that would, among other things, dismantle the MJDS. After further negotiations with the United States, Canadian regulators eventually conceded to the SEC and implemented key Sarbanes-Oxley provisions at home, which ultimately bolstered the cross-border arrangement.

Sarbanes-Oxley's repercussions on the MJDS illustrate an important limitation of regulatory export through mutual recognition. Because mutual recognition is not legal convergence, it does not create a level playing field across borders. If the legal regimes are sufficiently similar when entering into an agreement, this lack of convergence may not be a problem. National regulatory frameworks are never static, however; they change continually with regard to their substantive intensity and breadth. This dynamism can challenge the robustness of mutual recognition when one party makes a significant change to its national regulatory regime.

Such change need not take the shape of enhanced regulatory stringency. Having entered into a substantive mutual recognition arrangement, one of the parties may decide to dramatically lower its domestic standards. By lowering its standards, it acquires a "twofer" – it can become a more attractive jurisdiction for issuers seeking low-cost regulation, and it can act as a backdoor to the partner jurisdiction when foreign issuers from a third country decide to submit to its local (weaker) regulatory jurisdiction. This type of conduct not only deflates the trust and understanding on which mutual recognition arrangements are based, but also clashes with the partner jurisdiction's regulatory philosophy and undermines the supervision of its markets and protection of investors.

Seeking to avoid the earlier shortcomings of the MJDS, modified mutual recognition strategies have been employed by the SEC – in particular, to incentivize change and liberalize markets. The most high-profile strategy has been the "substituted compliance" program (later renamed "mutual recognition") introduced by SEC officials in 2008, just before the financial crisis. Under this initiative, foreign exchanges and foreign broker-dealers from select countries are eligible to enjoy preferential access to US investors if they comply with foreign regulations that are comparable to those of the United States. The SEC must therefore seek partners who, as in typical mutual recognition arrangements, recognize one another's institutions and procedures governing market regulation as "comparable," thereby allowing market participants or products in the market segment covered by the recognition regime to operate freely in the host market. Substituted compliance departed from the earlier MJDS insofar as it required an actual application for exemptive relief from national regulatory authorities for the mutual recognition scheme to become effective, thereby creating a multi-tiered process of granting market access.[53] Among other things, "eligible market participants would need to apply for, be vetted and finally granted an exemption on a case by case basis. Thus while the home country supervisors retain ultimate authority over foreign players active in their jurisdiction, the host country, the SEC, would grant individual exemptions to market participants."[54]

To establish a framework for such exemptions, substituted compliance entails that the SEC and its chosen foreign counterpart sign a nonbinding mutual recognition "arrangement" laying out their intent to liberalize market integration. At the same time, bilateral memoranda of understanding would be signed allowing for enhanced enforcement cooperation and information sharing. This arrangement would also contain an undertaking by the foreign regulators to describe "in detail how certain regulatory preconditions required

---

[53] Steffen Kern, Deutsche Bank, EU-US Financial Market Integration: A Work in Progress 12 (2008), *available at* https://www.dbresearch.de/PROD/DBR_INTERNET_EN-PROD/PROD0000000000225963.pdf.

[54] *Id.*

by the SEC are met, and a similar undertaking by the SEC providing for reciprocity." US regulators would then evaluate the country's regulations, determining whether they were comparable to those in the United States. Once the SEC had blessed the laws of their home jurisdictions, stock exchanges and broker-dealers in those countries would be able to apply for exemption from SEC registration based on compliance with their home countries' laws. Consequently, shares traded on or through those countries could be marketed and sold to US investors without compliance with US disclosure and corporate governance rules.

The first mutual recognition agreement was signed on August 25, 2008, between the United States and the Australian financial authorities. The program has yet to be implemented in the wake of the financial crisis, and most commentators are unsure whether US regulators will proceed with the initiative. Indeed, there is widespread concern that a consequence of the initiative could be regulatory arbitrage: companies could list on Australian exchanges to access US investors. This concern is exacerbated by the ostensible failings of earlier deregulatory initiatives that contributed to the crisis. The program's regulatory architects nevertheless believe that it provides key incentives for foreign counterparts to adopt more US-styled regulatory features: although convergence might be costly or involve the adoption of rules contrary to a regulator's traditions or philosophy; the regulator's domestic market participants could benefit from a range of competitive advantages, especially over other market players in nonparticipating jurisdictions; under the initiative, securities do not have to be registered in the United States in order to access capital markets there (since compliance only with the home state regulator is required); exchanges in the complying jurisdiction could potentially enjoy greater liquidity; and foreign regulators that secure agreements could receive political payoffs (for example, raises or promotions from agency executives and political elites, or jobs in the private sector). Regulators that support the initiative hope that advantages such as these might increase regulators' net payoffs. Of course, the optimal outcome would be the importation of US law, and as common or more closely related standards are adopted, positive network effects may stimulate better consensus between market participants and their regulators.

Are hopes in this regulatory strategy justified? Hardly any empirical information is available. The comparability assessment with Australia has not been made public, so we do not know what concessions were made between the two jurisdictions when negotiating their agreement. Substituted compliance – like mutual recognition more generally – is most likely to be effective as a means of raising regulatory standards in two circumstances. First, preferential market access may provide sufficient incentive for adjustment when a regulator of a big, capital-rich market enters into a mutual recognition policy with the regulator of a significantly smaller capital market. In this situation, all else being equal, the big market regulator would be reluctant to coordinate at the smaller regulator's standards since adjustment would entail high costs (more of its firms would have to make compliance changes). By contrast, the regulator of the smaller market would have greater incentive to make concessions in order to enable its firms to access clients, customers, and investors on terms that are more competitive than those available to firms in other countries.

Second, substituted compliance and mutual recognition programs are most feasible when adjustment costs in the target jurisdiction are low. That may happen, for example, when few conditions are placed on a prospective counterparty to a mutual recognition agreement (such an agreement almost entirely facilitates market access or a deregulatory program). Another example involves countries that share similar regulatory approaches, philosophies, administrative techniques, or enforcement intensity – such as the substituted compliance initiative between the United States and Australia. In these instances, regimes are comparable or even equivalent, and few adjustments are needed unless one regulator seeks convergence at a higher, more intense level than is currently the case in either jurisdiction.

My principal point is that the potential for mutual recognition as a change agent is likely circumscribed. A regulator must wield a considerable amount of market power to be able to single-handedly achieve significant regulatory change in another jurisdiction through a mutual recognition agreement. This power differential will become less and less common, especially since many emerging economies now not only enjoy sophisticated domestic markets, with local firms having access to increasingly diverse sources of capital. If a regulator's local markets are so small that regulatory adjustment is worth the benefits of preferred market access, it is probably only a minor regulatory player, and the strategic significance of its regulatory conversion will be limited. Finally, if only few conditions are placed on partners to attain liberalized market access, then mutual recognition holds little power as a change agent unless regulators in both jurisdictions aspire to a higher regulatory standard. Mutual recognition may serve as a useful means of reducing inefficient duplication of compliance processes, but that is not reason enough to consider it a powerful or significant instrument of regulatory statecraft.

CONCLUSIONS

Financial globalization has had a considerable impact on financial regulation, in terms both of <u>cost</u> and <u>practicality</u>. As economic and financial activity becomes more widely dispersed, so does regulatory influence – making the imposition of local rules and regulations, even on a territorial basis, more complicated than ever before.

Territorial control nevertheless continues to be significant. Financial global-ization generates new challenges for unilateral action, and national regulatory power remains an important aspect of financial statecraft, even at the interna-tional level. Nation-states – and by extension, regulatory agencies – still wield formal authority over resources and capabilities in their territories. As such, they possess significant regulatory influence. But as the allocation of financial capital and resources evolves, different countries come to wield influence in their own right. Though the United States and the EU may have diminished powers of extraterritorial export, new regulatory capabilities are becoming available to other countries and regions. These regions are increasingly wield-ing their hard law capabilities to exercise both domestic and international influence. The evolving, multipolar world of financial regulation operates along the lines of a "conservation theory" of international financial law: in an age of increasing financial globalization, regulatory power is not so much destroyed as transferred.

Changes in the global financial economy shift the burden of noncoopera-tion, whatever form it takes. In the past, in a world of regulatory hegemony, going it alone was potentially an option for a great financial power like the United States. Peripheral powers had no choice but to make do with the deci-sion making of large market actors. Countries were forced to accommodate or work within the international system as determined by the gravity of de jure or de facto regulatory preferences. Today, these tools are no longer as effective and carry costs that must often be internalized by regulatory authorities of both small and large financial markets.

As a result, multipolarity, especially in a world of cross-border financial transactions and regulations, generates imperatives to cooperate, and national regulators must expand their traditional policy toolset in order to put that cooperation in motion.

- The growing complexity of financial markets means that national finan-cial authorities must increasingly gather and share *information* about national regulatory strategies in order to meet rising policy challenges. Specifically, regulators must understand the interests and actions of for-eign financial authorities and market participants, as well as the impact of prospective national rules on foreign national strategies, and vice versa.
- National regulators are additionally incentivized to *engage* their for-eign counterparts, preferably at a global level. By engagement, I do not

necessarily mean the espousal outright of foreign rules or adopting an inflexible global standard (as we shall see later in greater detail). For reasons of both cost and competitive advantage, significant incentives can restrain regulators from adopting the practices of others or working together on common ground. But along with acting locally and seeking to strengthen their own markets, even the most self-centered regulators will have to more proactively coordinate with foreign homologues. That is to say, to be most effective, formal and informal administrative rulemaking processes will increasingly have to incorporate the participation of not only domestic, but also foreign, market participants and regulators.

- In a world of dispersed financial and economic power, it is essential to maintain policy flexibility and the capacity to *compromise*. Big powers can no longer push through their preferences at the local level and expect the world to always fall in line. Instead, uncompromising, unilateral action to promulgate one's regulatory standards risks new forms of policy retaliation by counterparts that can undermine local firms' dealings abroad. Rule making consequently requires more creativity and flexibility than in the past, elevating the importance of bargaining and negotiation.

Importantly, multipolarity in the international system does not necessarily mean that interests between different national regulatory authorities are themselves becoming "polarized." In some instances, the development of domestic markets and stakeholders may drive countries toward a convergence of interests, especially with regard to the regulation of practices that hold broadly negative economic or financial consequences. Furthermore, as financial centers develop and gain breadth, the interests of regulators and market participants may change; countries may transition to more generally accepted standards in order to enhance their legitimacy or to improve the reputation of domestic financial services. Regulators may resist new standards, however, when their divergent local practices are viewed as competitive advantages critical to the success of domestic financial centers.

Financial globalization does, however, highlight in stark terms that a single national regulator cannot single-handedly impose its will globally on all actors, all the time, and on its own, through local hard laws and regulations. Territoriality can help project power, but ultimately (like extraterritoriality) its effectiveness is not assured. Instead, territorial power both defines and is defined by financial might. And in a world of steep macroeconomic imbalances and skewed economic growth and financial market activity, the result has been a shift not only in the allocation of territorial regulatory power, but also, as we will explore in the two following chapters, in *how* it is wielded.

2

The Architecture of International Financial Law

Financial globalization makes international engagement necessary as mobile market participants and capital more easily escape unilateral national regulatory supervision. Regulatory authorities have responded to the challenge by seeking to promulgate global standards, best practices, and prudential guidelines through a range of international forums and organizations. That international institutions should constitute focal points for such interactions is not surprising. Because of the constantly evolving nature of the global capital markets, many problems require continuous attention and new policy solutions rather than one-shot solutions. In such a world, corralling purely ad hoc alliances to deal with regulatory problems as they arise is a highly inefficient approach.[1] Institutions help actors develop habits of cooperation and allow sustained attention to be brought to bear on common problems.

That said, the forums in which regulators participate are qualitatively different from those that have traditionally preoccupied theorists and practitioners of international law. Since the mid twentieth century, global rule making has been increasingly the province of "international organizations" – institutions defined by academics as grounded in a formal ratified treaty and enjoying "state membership, tangible manifestations of organizational bureaucracy, and an adequate legal pedigree."[2] Academics have extolled these features because they evince consent-based legitimacy: they require states to formally commit to participation along clearly demarcated terms specifying the powers and obligations of the body concerned. The powers accorded to such institutions have also often been considerable and include

[1] Stephen G. Brooks & William C. Wohlforth, *Reshaping the World Order: How Washington Should Reform International Institutions*, FOREIGN AFF., Mar.-Apr. 2009, at 51.
[2] David T. Zaring, *International Law by Other Means: The Twilight Existence of International Financial Regulatory Organizations*, 33 TEX. INT'L L.J. 281, 305 (1998).

the ability to interpret the treaties on which they are based, adjudicate disputes, and supervise members' conduct.

By contrast, in the international financial system, the production of international standards and rules arises through largely informal institutional arrangements grounded in nonbinding bylaws, charters, and accords – which, as such, are not recognized under international law. Nevertheless, these organizations are highly sophisticated institutional players in terms of both their internal design and their external orientation as pieces of a larger regulatory system. Individually, each employs varied strategies of rule production and monitoring. At the same time, organizations operate – despite their ostensibly "peer-to-peer" modes of technocratic cooperation – in hierarchical systems of regulatory influence and power. As a result, the operation of international financial law departs in significant ways from increasingly influential "transgovernmental" models of international governance that presume essentially egalitarian relationships and networks among regulators.

TRADITIONAL "INTERNATIONAL ORGANIZATIONS"

Describing the international financial architecture is no easy task, in part because the development of the relevant financial institutions has not followed any neat or obvious historical narrative. To name just a few odd features of the evolution of international financial regulation, the institutions that are now responsible for monitoring standards are older than the standard setters themselves. And many of the most important standard setters are among the youngest, born of the 1997 Asian financial crisis and the 2008 global financial crisis, and have usurped roles of other older bodies. There are also challenging methodological obstacles. The details of the international architecture are constantly evolving – a point recently highlighted by the 2009 G-20 London Summit, which not only created a new agenda-setting body with a range of surveillance powers but also relaunched existing institutions with more aggressive mandates (both of which are discussed below). And as has been recounted extensively, in many of these organizations, particularly the G-20 and the Basel Committee, deliberations among officials are nonpublic, making them difficult to assess from the outside.

Yet perhaps the most difficult challenge derives from the fact that the production of international financial law departs from the classical model of public diplomacy embodied by formal "international organizations." As Jose Alvarez has noted in his authoritative work on the matter, international organizations are generally recognized as having several core attributes,[3] two of which are especially important for our present purposes. First, international organizations have long been considered to be those established by international agreements between states. That is, not only are they the product of interstate relations, but they are also grounded in instruments recognized as comprising international legal obligations. Second, international organizations are viewed as possessing independent legal personalities that are distinct from their individual members. In that way, "treaty parties have entrusted somebody other than themselves with developing and maintaining their common will."[4]

It is not surprising that official international agreements are commonly viewed as a defining feature of international organizations. International treaties and articles of agreement establish a legal personality that approximates those of modern corporations and business entities in many domestic legal systems. As such, they facilitate independent action at the international level. Formality serves an expressive function articulating to the international community sustained activity in a given issue area by the organization. It also enables international organizations to create subsidiary or supplemental organs that likewise possess robust legal authority and legitimacy to carry out institutional mandates.

Official founding charters and agreements can additionally help organizations promote deep forms of discipline. A robust international charter enables organizations to make rules that are not only hortatory in character, but also binding on members and legally recognized as such. Legal charters can facilitate the settlement of disputes among members by establishing official tribunals, panels, and courts. Indeed, a range of institutional attributes often accompany international organizations, including secretariats whose workforce can carry out or support the mission of the organization. Consequently, academics, like the popular media, have long favored international coordination arising through universally recognized, and usually high-profile, international institutions and organizations – like the UN and more recently the WTO–that have headquarters, experienced civil servants, and sizable budgets.[5]

---

[3] Jose E. Alvarez, International Organizations as Law-Makers 6 (2006).
[4] Id.
[5] Janet Levit, A Bottom-Up Approach to International Lawmaking: The Tale of Three Trade Finance Instruments, 30 Yale J. Int'l L. 125, 126 (2005)

Given the range of issues they address, international organizations can vary with regard to how they are run. That said, an internal, tripartite structure is common to many of them.[6] This structure consists of

> a plenary body consisting of the full membership, charged with broad powers to discuss policy, and meeting infrequently; an organ of more reduced membership capable of exercising some select powers, particularly implementation, and capable of meeting on a more regulator basis; and a staff or secretariat of ostensibly "independent" international civil servants drawn and broadly representative of, member state and headed by a "Secretary" or Director" general.[7]

Voting procedures in international organizations can, meanwhile, vary considerably. Some have majority voting whereas others adopt supermajority or even unanimity requirements, frequently in response to members concerns regarding sovereignty. Consensus-based decision making, where formal votes are not taken, has at least traditionally been less common since it has been considered "less protective of sovereign consent than the more traditional procedures providing for 'one state, one vote' common to 19th-century treaty-making conferences."[8]

THE KEY QUALITATIVE FEATURES OF THE INTERNATIONAL REGULATORY SYSTEM

International financial regulation often departs from traditional modes of international organization. Indeed, many of the features common to formal international organizations are rare in the international financial system. In this section we explore some of the salient features and key differences.

Informal Institutions

Unlike traditional international organizations, most international regulatory organizations rely on "soft" administrative structures. International regulatory organizations are generally not set up by traditional international law instruments. Instead, they are usually founded under informal bylaws, agreements, and declarations with no formal sense of international obligation or existence. In limited circumstances, international regulatory organizations

---

[6] Alvarez, *supra* note 3, at 9.
[7] *Id.* at 9.
[8] *Id.* at 10.

may be incorporated domestically in order to contract and carry on local activities in the country in which their headquarters are based. In virtually all circumstances, these soft international institutions lack dispute settlement organs. They can, however, take on a variety of other roles, including the disciplining of members when they fail to live up to their obligations as members of the organization – a point that we elaborate in the following chapter.

Informal mandates, like formal articles of agreement for international organizations, permit countries to develop institutional focal points around which coordination can arise. This process does not, however, require full-scale delegations of authority from countries to supranational entities. Furthermore, the substantive content of foundational charters can vary across organizations. Some are brief outlines of the organization that are posted on websites and that summarize basic duties of parties and committees. Others take the form of elaborate founding documents that detail the roles and responsibilities of different institutional organs. Traditional explanations for informal legal mandates focus on their procedural efficiency. By adopting informal rules of organization, participants retain the flexibility to convene quickly in order to create and reform institutions to meet new and unexpected challenges. Such flexibility is often unavailable to formal international organizations where the dismantling, enlargement, or reform of membership standards often require renegotiation of treaties and ratification procedures involving legislatures of member countries. As a result, soft institutions are subject to much more institutional change and adaptation.

Meanwhile, formal international organizations generally play supporting roles in the international regulatory system.[9] As will be seen below, formal organizations help monitor countries' compliance with rules promulgated by informal standard setters, and one, in particular, provides administrative support and analysis for regulatory organizations lacking their own secretariats. Rarely, however, are formal organizations a direct source of international financial law.

Agency Domination

The second feature of the international regulatory architecture is an extension of a pattern we explored in the previous chapter: international financial

---

[9] These supporting roles can be important in determining how institutions execute their mandates, however, a point we will explore in greater detail.

regulation is, like its domestic counterpart, dominated by regulatory agencies and officials. This is not to say that heads of state and even market participants play no important role (I address this point below in the discussion of agenda setting and private legislatures, as well as in chapter 4's discussion on legitimacy). Nevertheless, from a practical standpoint, regulatory agencies are *the* central players in crafting cross-border rules and regulations. Indeed, there are virtually no venues of international standard setting from which financial authorities are absent.

Participation by regulatory authorities can arise at various points and in different capacities. A regulator may meet with its counterparts to hammer out international standards in their particular financial sector, whereas at another stage the regulator may interact with dissimilar agencies or even heads of state. And in contrast to many foreign ministries, which are run and dominated by a few senior officials, financial diplomacy can be devised and conducted by both heads of agencies and mid- and lower-level civil servants, depending, in part, on their expertise. When agreements are finally secured, cross-border accords are implemented by national regulatory agencies, giving the accords an international, and potentially globally reach.

Fragmentation

Far from being dominated by one centralized, supranational authority, international financial law is a fragmented regulatory domain. No one preeminent institution promulgates all financial standards, adjudicates disputes, or facilitates compliance. This situation contrasts considerably with that of such international organizations like the WTO, under whose legal umbrella virtually all multilateral ("global") trade negotiations are now conducted, and disputes resolved. Instead, institutions of various sizes, shapes, and objectives participate in the regulatory process – and no one institution has a monopoly (or even explicit authority) over the day-to-day activities of all others. As such, new forums can be created, launched, and reformed, just as responsibilities can be shared or moved from one institution to another in the face of novel regulatory challenges.

NETWORK THEORY AS A DESCRIPTIVE FRAMEWORK

Because these features depart so significantly from classical conceptions of diplomacy, many scholars resort to describing the international financial system by way of metaphor or conceptual abstraction. By far the most dominant refrain is that the international financial system (and indeed most modern coordination efforts among regulators) comprises governmental "networks," an idea popularized by Anne Marie Slaughter's *New World Order*.[10] Through networks, or informal government-to-government contacts between administrative agencies, decision making is not so much vested in the hands of uninformed political elites but is, instead, guided by a stable of skilled technocrats, mainly midlevel bureaucrats, who develop shared expectations and trust, allowing them to dispense with time-consuming treaties and formal international organizations.[11] Regulators execute and rely on less formal instruments that permit rapid responses to keep pace with quickly evolving financial markets.[12] In this way, "standards are primarily a function of science and technical considerations rather than a function of the distribution of power between national, regional, or non-state actors."[13]

In this fragmented world of administrative policymaking, network theorists argue that policies are not advanced by military force or coercion, but by the power of persuasion and attraction.[14] In addition to attempting to shape how their own domestic markets are regulated, these domestic regulators promote their own regulatory approaches as the ones that other countries should follow. The international financial system is thus animated by collegial, relatively unstructured interagency interactions between governmental administrative bodies that foster collective problem solving and policy innovation. Regulators, many of whom share the same academic and professional experiences, develop deep relationships and a sense of community that help guide the coordination process. Competitive advantages among countries in furthering their policy preferences are directly tied to economic factors, though not according to the traditional rules of market power: regulators of larger, richer markets have more resources and are often better positioned to promote their agendas – by hosting conferences, scholars, and regulators. They also have the personnel available to draft position papers, assess reform programs, and shape disputes. Regulators of small markets, by contrast, have fewer resources and are at

---

[10] *See generally* ANNE-MARIE SLAUGHTER, A NEW WORLD ORDER (2004).

[11] *See generally* Pierre-Hugues Verdier, *Transnational Regulatory Networks and Their Limits*, 34 YALE J. INT'L L. 113, 148 (2009); *see also* Charles K. Whitehead, *What's Your Sign?: International Norms, Signals and Compliance*, 27 MICH. J. INT'L L. 695, 704 (2006).

[12] Kal Raustiala, *The Architecture of International Cooperation: Transgovernmental Networks and the Future of International Law*, 43 VA. J. INT'L L. 1, 1, 30 (2002-03).

[13] Walter Mattli & Tim Buthe, Setting International Standards: Technological Rationality or Primacy of Power?, 56 WORLD POL. 1, 12–13 (2003).

[14] *Id.*

least likely to try to emulate powerful ones by aspiring to similar levels of success.[15]

Using network theory, scholars have come to better grasp the diversity of forms through which international coordination is mediated. Network theory has the virtue of underscoring the multilayered and ultimately multinodal contacts that exist between regulators and international bodies. International relations theory has long anticipated a "two-level" game of cooperation based on the work of domestic politicians, who must manage both domestic special interests and their strategic objectives abroad.[16] Network theory complicates this model by emphasizing another important feature of some international coordination – the informal, peer-to-peer bargaining between domestic regulators in their promotion of new regulatory standards. In this community, regulators must not only keep abreast of domestic special interests and the expectations of their home governments but also cultivate allegiances and respond to the concerns of their international homologues.

Nonetheless, network theory is an intrinsically limited conceptual tool. Beyond highlighting the increasing "connectivity," or personal and professional contacts, between regulators, the term does little to explain just *how* regulators and institutions are connected. Regulators are merely assumed to be bound and related to everyone, a notion that, though in some ways true, does not provide insight into the workings and implications of the international regulatory architecture. Network theory also tends to downplay the institutional design of network actors and international organizations. Because the latter are grounded in nonbinding agreements and limited secretarial support, they are deemed to be amorphous and disorganized forums with few cognizable institutional structures. Network theory identifies and describes some broad and abstract qualities of regulators but does not integrate them into an analytical framework for conceptualizing the regulatory "order" and how institutional designs affect international financial law. In the following section, I provide a more concrete blueprint of the international regulatory architecture.

A SNAPSHOT OF THE GLOBAL FINANCIAL ARCHITECTURE

For the uninitiated, understanding the complexities of the global regulatory system can be a daunting task. Thus in order to get a sense of how the system works, it is better to look at the forest before inspecting the trees. Just like many

---

[15] JOSEPH S. NYE, JR., SOFT POWER: THE MEANS TO SUCCESS IN WORLD POLITICS 5 (2004).

[16] Robert D. Putnam, *Diplomacy and Domestic Politics: The Logic of Two Level Games*, 42 INT'L ORG. 427 (1988).

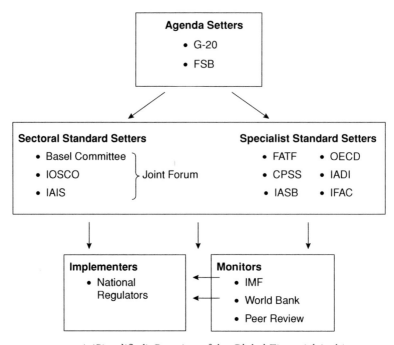

FIGURE 2.1. A (Simplified) Overview of the Global Financial Architecture

national regulatory systems, the international regulatory system consists of entities that specialize in setting agendas for the international regulatory system, bodies that focus on standard setting itself, and institutions that then monitor the system and check for compliance with the regulatory stipulations. See Figure 2.1.

The first activity, agenda setting, is most associated with the G-20 and the Financial Stability Board (FSB), both of which operate at the core of the international system. These bodies represent the largest and most influential economic powers and their leaders, and by extension 90 percent of the world's financial markets. They determine the areas that need to be addressed through regulation across financial sectors and what, broadly speaking, needs to be done for achieving agreed-upon objectives.

The work of actually devising prescriptive guidance for market participants is largely undertaken by institutions that set standards relating to specific financial sectors or issue areas. Standards can differ considerably with regard to their specificity and flexibility. In most cases, they are more targeted than the policy objectives and directions articulated at the agenda-setting level and are intended to be incorporated by a variety of legal systems and cultures. These standards are then made available for consumption by national regulators, who implement standards through their domestic lawmaking or supervisory authority.

Monitoring can take place in a variety of ways, including peer reviews conducted by members of the standard-setting bodies themselves (a topic we will explore in greater detail in the following chapter). At this point, however, it is important to highlight the dominant monitoring role played by the World Bank and IMF. Besides being among the most high-profile actors in the international financial system – owing to their hard law status and important role in international economic development – they are charged with evaluating compliance with rules that are considered to be the most critical for the functioning of sound financial systems. As such, they routinely carry out examinations of national regimes to evaluate the extent to which international best practices have been adopted by regulatory authorities.

From a bird's-eye view, international regulatory processes demonstrate a clear inter-institutional logic. National regulators wield their local expertise at the national level and then set global standards by participating at the international level through agenda- and standard-setting bodies. Meanwhile, the IMF and World Bank leverage their experience in economic development and stabilty to exercise oversight in financial regulation – not as primary originators of financial market policy, but as observers of policy compliance.

The chart above has its limitations, which deserve brief mention. Like a map of the world, the chart has a two-dimensional quality and fails to reflect the different national regulators and international institutions that participate at different and multiple points along the organizational chart. Some, though not all, national regulators participate in agenda- and standard-setting bodies, just as some, though not all, standard-setting bodies can be members in some, but not all, agenda-setting bodies – a point that we will return to shortly. The chart and the following chapter also do not account for the work of either the World Bank or IMF on issues like transparency and creditor rights (I have intentionally made this choice since their work in these areas only indirectly addresses financial market regulation as commonly understood).[17] The key point to understand at this juncture is that the global financial system is characterized by a functional division of labor informing the regulatory activities and responsibilities of each actor.

---

[17] The IMF, for example, is responsible only for standards aimed at helping ensure that governments are providing a clear picture of the structure and finances of government, as well as transparency regarding central bank activities in monetary affairs and as lender of last resort. Meanwhile, the World Bank, promulgates important principles on insolvency and creditor rights, though focuses on corporate creditors, and not bank insolvency and financial stability. Instead, these matters are the province of the Basel Committee.

Now, let's inspect the trees more closely. Among the highest-profile actors are the international agenda setters – organizations with broad and diverse memberships, including both regulatory and, to a lesser extent, political actors that are tasked with defining broad, strategic objectives for the international system. Two agenda setters are especially central to international financial regulation: the G-20 and the newly constituted FSB.

The Group of 20

The present Group of 20 finance ministers and central bank governors, perhaps today's most visible body for international economic coordination, has its origin in a series of meetings convened among the finance ministers of France, Japan, the United Kingdom, the United States, and West Germany in the early 1970s. The meetings were initiated in response to a series of economic challenges caused by that decade's oil crisis, including the collapse of the Bretton Woods monetary system and the growing problem of inflation in many developed economies. In 1975, the group was expanded to include Italy, and a year later Canada was invited to attend. This group of what were the seven largest industrialized countries, termed the G-7, has met each year ever since, often with head-of-state participation. In a setting that is more informal than IMF meetings, leaders are able to discuss problems affecting the global financial system. It is hoped that such informality will foster more candid discussion and cooperation among the participants on global economic matters.[18]

The G-7 eventually helped establish additional "G" groups to accommodate new political and strategic objectives. In 1962, for example, the G-7 countries joined Belgium, Netherlands, Sweden (and eventually Switzerland) to participate as the G-10 in the General Arrangements to Borrow, which provides financing for the IMF beyond the standard quota subscriptions of its member countries. In 1994, after the fall of the Soviet Union, Russia began to participate in meetings (owing to its status as one of only two nuclear superpowers) and, in 1997, became a full-fledged member of an expanded G-8.

The biggest organizational development came in 1999, in the wake of the Asian financial crisis, when the G-7 finance ministers recommended the establishment of, among other things, a "Group of 20" to promote "open and constructive discussion between industrial and emerging-market countries on key

[18] Putnam, *supra* note 17.

issues related to global economic stability."[19] No formal criteria were used for membership in the new organization, but the G-20 has publicly explained that "systemic significance for the international financial system" was a major factor, especially as it became obvious that even jurisdictions in emerging markets could endanger the global economy.[20] In addition to the G-8 members, the G-20 includes Argentina, Australia, Brazil, China, India, Indonesia, Mexico, Saudi Arabia, South Africa, South Korea, Turkey, and the EU.

Until the financial crisis of 2008, the G-20 was largely a dormant player in international economic affairs. The G-7 operated as the primary G-Group and agenda setter, though its role as such was limited. With the 2008 financial crisis, however, the G-20 was revived. The growing consensus was that global economic governance required the participation of key emerging countries – many of whom were effectively underwriting the economic growth of developed countries. In response to this consensus, the G-20 was officially dubbed the primary forum for international economic coordination. Thus, although the G-8 and G-20 continue to meet independently, the bulk of international coordination now arises under the G-20's larger policy umbrella. As with earlier G-groups, finance ministries, as both technocratic and political entities, have tended to dominate financial diplomacy. Since the 2008 crisis, however, heads of state routinely participate in "Leadership Summits" can set the pace for regulatory coordination as well as provide a forum for discussing and even "ratifying" standard-setting initiatives.

Despite its importance in global economic affairs, the G-20 has no permanent staff. Instead, a chair is selected annually from among the group's twenty members and is responsible for creating a temporary secretariat to handle the group's work for the duration of its term. In addition, the chair combines with the chair from the previous year and the chair slated for the following year to form the management "Troika," which is responsible for ensuring continuity in the group's work across the years. Additionally, the G-20 does not use any formal voting system. Rather, the G-20 is focused on achieving consensus. According to its Web site, every "G-20 member has one 'voice' with which it can take an active part in G-20 activity. To this extent the influence a country can exert is shaped decisively by its commitment."[21]

---

[19] *About G-20*, G-20, http://www.g20.org/about_what_is_g20.aspx (last visited March 10, 2011).

[20] *Frequently Asked Questions*, G-20, http://www.g20.org/about_faq.aspx (last visited March 10, 2011).

[21] *Id.*

As both a regulatory and political medium, the G-20 has a range of legislative products, including communiqués and declarations, usually published at the end of summits that inform the public about agreements reached by G-20 members. In these public declarations, the G-20 leaders collectively articulate shared viewpoints on the economic policies and on the causes of, and solutions to, microeconomic and macroeconomic challenges. To date, they have touched on a diverse array of topics, such as raising the quality of capital held by banks, restructuring the IMF's early warning system, and coordinating with standard setters for better financial regulation, especially with regard to derivatives and credit-rating agencies. Communiqués also inform the public as to future initiatives and frequently task other international bodies to implement agreed-upon priorities. The heft and credibility of these communications can be reinforced with other instruments. Working groups comprising representatives from G-20 countries have, especially in the wake of the 2008 crisis, been tasked by countries to develop reports and recommendations to strengthen international standards in areas like accounting, risk management, disclosure, and prudential oversight.[22] Similarly, on at least one occasion, the group has published a progress report – as a kind of self-assessment evaluating what has been done with regard to previous commitments.

Financial Stability Board

The second important agenda setter is the FSB, which in many ways operates as a technocratic extension of the more political G-20. Like the G-20, the FSB evolved from a predecessor, in this instance the Financial Stability Forum (FSF). Like the G-20, it was launched by the G-7 in the wake of the Asian financial crisis as increased evidence emerged that one cause of the crisis was an absence of prudently managed financial institutions throughout the region.[23] No organization up to that point had focused much attention on the weaknesses in national regulatory supervision. This absence of oversight created systemic risks to the global economy. Countries could have a reasonably stable fiscal position – and thus satisfy existing monetary and economic authorities like the World Bank and IMF – but still create enormous risks to the financial system.

[22] The working groups produced a range of key reports including G-20 Working Group 1, Enhancing Sound Regulation and Strengthening Transparency, and the G-20 Working Group 2 report, Reinforcing International Cooperation and Promoting Integrity in Financial Markets. For an analysis, *see* Mario Giovanoli, *The Reform of the International Financial Architecture After the Global Crisis*, 42 N.Y.U. J. INT'L L. & POL. 81 (2009).

[23] HOWARD DAVIES & DAVID GREEN, GLOBAL FINANCIAL REGULATION: THE ESSENTIAL GUIDE 111 (2008).

In 1999, the FSF was given the task of analyzing specific vulnerabilities in financial systems – though not necessarily through macroeconomic policy assessments, which at the time were the province of the IMF. To carry out this task, the FSF drew on senior representatives of national financial authorities (central banks, regulatory and supervisory authorities, and ministries of finance), international financial institutions, standard-setting bodies, and committees of central bank experts from the G-7. Working groups were created "to study potential systemic risks related to a variety of challenges including highly leveraged institutions, offshore financial centers, and short term capital flows."[24] The forum also published a compendium of best practices devised by other international organizations. However, the FSF's powers were limited, and it exercised no mandate to generate standards, even voluntary ones.[25]

In the wake of the 2008 Financial Crisis, the FSF was superseded by the FSB and given a broader mandate to more vigorously assess and improve the financial system. Perhaps most significantly, its regulatory focus has shifted from micro-prudential regulation to macro-prudential regulation.[26] The organization is no longer exclusively focused on particular firms or sectors, but is tasked with examining leverage levels in the financial system as a whole.[27] The FSB was additionally charged with conducting reviews of firms to spot potential trouble and with reporting situations that potentially threaten the stability of the global financial system. The organization increasingly operates as a clearing house for information sharing and contingency planning. Recently, it embarked upon the creation of a supervisory college to monitor the largest international financial services firms.

Key organizational features were transformed in the creation of the FSB. Membership was increased from roughly a dozen to thirty-six actors and institutions (including all members of the G-20). The institutional architecture also changed. The organization's permanent secretariat was enlarged to include approximately twenty people, and a full-time secretary general was tasked with providing administrative support with the help of the Bank for International Settlements (BIS; described below). The FSB also now includes a Plenary of the full membership, which is itself assisted by three standing committees to

---

[24] KERN ALEXANDER ET AL., GLOBAL GOVERNANCE OF FINANCIAL SYSTEMS: THE INTERNATIONAL REGULATION OF SYSTEMIC RISK 75 (2006).

[25] *Id.*

[26] As Ellis Ferran & Kern Alexander noted, "[m]embership carries with it obligations to pursue the maintenance of financial stability, to maintain the openness and transparency of the financial sector, to implement international financial standards, and to submit to periodic peer reviews." Ellis Ferran & Kern Alexander, Soft Institutions and Hard-Edged Power: What Role for the European Systemic Risk Board? 162 (2010) (unpublished manuscript) (on file with author).

[27] *Id.* at 13.

help coordinate policymaking – one geared toward supervisory and regulatory initiatives, another focusing on cooperation, and a third on implementation of FSB agendas. Other committees can be established when necessary. Finally, alongside the plenary is the Standing Committee – whose members are determined by an FSB chairperson – which provides operational guidance between plenaries. Besides the G-20, the FSB is the only major forum where finance ministries, arguably the most political of all regulators, participate (heads of state have no active role in the organization).

Importantly, although the FSB has limited formal rulemaking authority, it has become an increasingly important de facto source of broad standards, especially in the wake of the financial crisis. During its transition to the FSB, the FSF issued a series of reports and principles to strengthen the global financial system, including its 2008 *Report on Enhancing Market and Institutional Resilience*, which offered broad guidance for improving banking capital-adequacy requirements, accounting standards, and margin requirements for certain trading activities. Similarly, in its *Report of the Financial Stability Forum on Addressing Procyclicality in the Financial System*, the FSF proposed a range of measures to mitigate regulatory and market mechanisms that help drive bubble-economies.[28] As the FSB, the institution has additionally promulgated *Principles for Sound Compensation Practices* and elaborated them with implementation standards to strengthen adherence.[29] It has also been involved in developing a global regime for regulating hedge funds[30] and credit-rating agencies.[31] Along with other groups, it also guidelines for use by national authorities to assess whether a financial institution, market, or instrument is systemically important.[32]

SECTORAL STANDARD SETTERS

Agenda setters are not generally involved in the day-to-day standard-setting process. Instead, the actual task of devising standards for the ultimate adoption or implementation by national regulators and authorities is done by standard-setting bodies that comprise less political actors (for example, no heads of state or finance ministries). The standards determined by standard-setting bodies

---

[28] Fin. Stability Forum, Report of the Financial Stability Forum on Addressing Procyclicality in the Financial System (Apr. 2, 2009).

[29] Ferran & Alexander, *supra* note 27, at 14; *see also* Fin. Stability Bd. [FSB], FSB Principles for Sound Compensation Practices: Implementation Standards (2009).

[30] FSB, Progress Since the Pittsburgh Summit in Implementing the G20 Recommendations for Strengthening Financial Stability 11–12 (2009).

[31] *Id.* at 12–13.

[32] Ferran & Alexander, *supra* note 27, at 15.

are, in many ways, more familiar to market participants than the proclamations of agenda setters. The most dominant category of standard setters can be thought of as "sectoral" in nature since their mandates focus on entire financial market sectors.

Basel Committee on Banking Supervision

The best-known and oldest of the sectoral standard setters is the Basel Committee on Banking Supervision, a group charged with the oversight of banks and other large financial institutions. Like the G-7, the Basel Committee was created in the 1970s in response to the new risks and turmoil wrought by a rapidly changing banking industry. With rapid increases in oil prices, as well as increased exchange rate volatility, banks of all sizes began to seek more investment opportunities abroad, such as lending to foreign governments and companies. And to hedge their risk and earn higher yields from speculation, they engaged in a wide range of currency-related transactions. Many of the banks wading into these new transactions were not especially sophisticated from a transactional standpoint; they were old-line, deposit-taking institutions with little expertise in activities as exotic as foreign exchange trading. They neither fully appreciated their competitive disadvantage nor saved sufficient reserves to cover their losses in the event of bets gone bad.

These structural issues came to a head with the failure of the famed Herstatt Bank in Cologne, Germany. Like many banks of the time, Herstatt was a universal commercial bank and engaged in not only deposit taking, but also a range of complex foreign exchange–related financial transactions with a diverse range of institutions throughout the world. When its investments went bad, the company filed for bankruptcy, shocking the global financial markets. Foreign exchange trading ground to a halt as traders grew concerned that their foreign counterparts would not follow through on their obligations.[33] Moreover, many counterparties to foreign exchange transactions with Herstatt failed to receive the currency they had bought because of the six-hour time difference between the close of business in Germany and the close of business in New York. When German regulators closed Herstatt at 6:00 p.m. local time, the counterparties in New York were left exposed for the full value of the deutsche mark payments that they had made earlier in the day.

Even before Herstatt, many regulators had expressed frustration at their inability to monitor and supervise foreign banks with local branches, given

---

[33] DAVID ANDREW SINGER, REGULATING CAPITAL: SETTING STANDARDS FOR THE INTERNATIONAL FINANCIAL SYSTEM 38 (2007).

that the failure of a foreign bank could adversely affect the domestic market. The collapse of Herstatt underscored an additional twist to such risk – that of settlement risk, which could potentially leave any financial institution exposed to failures abroad. The fiasco spurred what had historically been domestic and inwardly looking banking authorities to establish an institutional mechanism to both supervise cross-border activities of banks and strengthen the resilience of the international banking system as a whole. Within a year of the crisis, a committee of central bank governors and banking regulators of the then G-10 countries was established in Basel, Switzerland, and based at the Bank for International Settlements, to work toward shoring up and strengthening international bank regulation. Since then, membership of the Basel Committee on Banking Supervision has been expanded to include members of the G-20, and the committee's work has been supported by various subcommittees chaired by alternating countries that focus on policy development, the implementation of standards, and international regulatory coordination among members and non-members alike.

The committee's initial legislative achievements were modest. In 1975, the committee's first legislative act, the Basel "Concordat," articulated broad principles that central banks should follow in bailing out banks facing imminent failure. Specifically, the Concordat holds that parent banks should be held liable for the financial difficulties of their foreign branches, a position that moves the burden of failure away from the states hosting banking activities to the home country (and its regulator). A later amendment in 1983 additionally contained the principle of "dual key supervision," which provides that regulatory authorities shall be permitted to assess the ability of other national authorities to supervise and carry out their respective responsibilities and, where such oversight is not available, to potentially deny entry to an organization.[34] The committee has also been active in improving the exchange of information on national supervisory arrangements, in promoting the effectiveness of techniques for supervising international banking business, and in setting minimum supervisory standards in areas of interest. In 1997, the Basel Committee released its *Core Principles for Effective Banking Supervision*, which – along with the more granular *Core Principles Methodology* for operationalizing the core principles – has been used by countries as a benchmark for assessing the quality of their supervisory systems and for identifying future work to be done to achieve a baseline level of sound supervisory practices.[35]

---

[34] ALEXANDER ET AL., *supra* note 25, at 48.

[35] *See* BASEL COMM. ON BANKING SUPERVISION [BASEL COMM.], CORE PRINCIPLES FOR EFFECTIVE BANKING SUPERVISION (2006), *available at* http://www.bis.org/publ/bcbs129.pdf; BASEL COMM., CORE PRINCIPLES METHODOLOGY (2006), *available at* http://www.bis.org/publ/bcbs130.pdf.

The Basel Committee is perhaps best known for its 1988 accord on capital adequacy (referred to interchangeably as the Basel I Accord or Basel I), which famously required banks of member countries to maintain an 8 percent ratio of their "capital" to "risk weighted assets."[36] The agreement was ultimately adopted by each member and nearly one hundred nonmembers. Under the agreement, different kinds of financial activities are assigned different risks. The riskier the activities and the higher the risk weighting, the more capital that banks are required to hold on their books to maintain the 8 percent threshold (capital includes a variety of instruments, including governmental securities). These rules were refined in a new round of negotiations in 2004 (Basel II), which were designed to give the world's largest banks substantial discretion in the methodologies and systems used to generate their own internal risk ratings and which are expected to be fully implemented in the next several years by each Basel Committee regulator.[37] Since the 2008 financial crisis, however, the emphasis on such discretion has waned, and efforts have been focused on creating a new generation of capital requirements (under a "Basel III" regime), on identifying systemically important financial institutions (within a global context), and on determining what bank-compensation and corporate-governance practices would strengthen financial stability.

International Organization for Securities Commissions

The key standard setter for securities regulation is the International Organization of Securities Commissions (IOSCO). Its history, like that of the Basel Committee, is tied to the rapid internationalization of securities markets. The impetus for its development was not, however, tied to market failure generally. Instead, as financial globalization enabled greater mobility of fraudsters, authorities wanted to ensure both robust (and common) approaches to securities regulation and sufficient cooperation to enforce national rules when criminals, evidence, and witnesses were in other countries. Only as securities firms began to reveal themselves as potential sources of systemic risk did financial stability come to the fore as a regulatory objective of the organization.

Just as IOSCO's scope has expanded in fits and spurts, so has its membership. In 1974, regulators from North and South America established the then Inter-American Association of Securities Commissions to tackle common securities-related challenges. As its title suggests, it was a geographically

---

[36] BASEL COMM., INTERNATIONAL CONVERGENCE OF CAPITAL MEASUREMENT AND CAPITAL STANDARDS 13 (1998), *available at* http://www.bis.org/publ/bcbsc111.pdf.

[37] BASEL COMM., INTERNATIONAL CONVERGENCE OF CAPITAL MEASUREMENT AND CAPITAL STANDARDS: A REVISED FRAMEWORK (2004), *available at* http://www.bis.org/publ/bcbs107.pdf.

limited organization geared largely toward coordinating interactions in the Western hemisphere. As cross-border trade increased, however – and with it, the need to coordinate with regulators in Europe and other parts of the world – the association was reorganized as the International Organization of Securities Commissions. Its membership expanded to include not only the United States and other regulators from the Americas, but also nearly fifty other countries. By the late 1990s, virtually every national regulator had sought and gained membership in the organization. Today there are nearly 150 members, and the secretariat (unaffiliated with the BIS) is in Madrid. In addition to these securities regulators, which are ordinary members and have the right to vote, secondary financial market regulators can also participate as nonvoting members when a country has more than one financial market regulator. IOSCO also hosts affiliate members – including self-regulatory agencies that participate in the Self-Regulatory Organizations Consultative Committee and provide direct market input from the perspective of exchanges.

Compared to the Basel Committee, IOSCO's legislative achievements have been modest. Until relatively recently, IOSCO has boasted as its most significant piece of legislation the *Objectives and Principles of Securities Organization*, a set of 30 principles outlining the organization's view as to what makes for high-quality securities regulation. It has also promulgated *International Disclosure Standards for Cross-border Offerings and Initial Listings by Foreign Issuers*, which spells out the nonfinancial disclosures that a foreign company should make to authorities and investors when selling securities abroad.[38] In 2008, IOSCO adopted more aggressive means of facilitating enforcement cooperation through its Multilateral Memorandum of Understanding (MMOU), an agreement that memorializes a process whereby regulators can seek assistance from their foreign counterparts to help prosecute cases in which witnesses or the proceeds of fraud are located in other jurisdictions. And in the wake of the financial crisis, the organization has developed reports advocating better regulation of securitization markets and exotic financial instruments, and has promulgated a high-profile code of conduct for credit-rating agencies.

International Association of Insurance Supervisors

The sectoral standard setter for insurance is the International Association of Insurance Supervisors (IAIS), established in 1994. Unlike IOSCO and the

---

[38] INT'L ORG. OF SECURITIES COMM'NS [IOSCO], INTERNATIONAL DISCLOSURE STANDARDS FOR CROSS-BORDER OFFERINGS AND INITIAL LISTINGS BY FOREIGN ISSUERS (1998), *available at* http://www.iosco.org/library/pubdocs/pdf/IOSCOPD81.pdf.

Basel Committee, which developed somewhat organically among like-minded regulators, the IAIS is the direct consequence of lobbying by banking and securities regulators – through IOSCO and the Basel Committee – to form an international counterpart to their groups. Up to that point, attempts at international coordination had been limited. The United States' occasional efforts in this context, though real, were somewhat half-hearted – partly because few regulators believed that insurance companies posed a systemic threat to economies, and partly because US regulation was itself a matter of regional (state-level), not national, prerogative.

By the early 1990s insurance companies had begun to ramp up their international activities, both as insurance providers and participants in insurance-related markets and investments in complex financial transactions. There were growing concerns among regulators as to the safety and soundness of reinsurance providers – companies that provide insurance for insurance companies. Although these providers enjoyed diversified exposure to risk through their international activities, they were often based offshore or subject to little regulation. Regulators began to worry about the industry as a potential source of systemic risk to the financial system as a whole.[39] As in the banking sector, regulators in the United States and elsewhere began to recognize that the failure of a reinsurer could lead to the failure of a client, which in practice can be located in another country or jurisdiction.

The IAIS, like IOSCO, enjoys an extremely broad membership – nearly 180 members – which includes not only national and local authorities, but also international organizations and nearly 120 (nonvoting) insurance professionals who act as observers. Its legislative track record, however, has long been regarded as meager. One reason for its performance is that, being a new standard-setting body, it is still catching up with standard setting and cross-border coordination. For example, it was only in 2003 that the IAIS developed a set of core principles for effective insurance supervision that articulated best practices for insurance companies and the conduct of cross-border insurance activities. And it was not until 2002, and again in 2007, that the IAIS forwarded its *Principles on Capital Adequacy and Solvency.*[40] Intended as an initial step toward more detailed capital-adequacy standards like those available under the Basel Capital Accord, the principles articulate standards for evaluating the solvency of life- and non-life-insurance undertakings. In 2007, following the lead of other supervisors, the IAIS drew up an MMOU on cooperation and information exchange. Virtually all of these initiatives were reinvigorated in

---

[39] Davies & Green, *supra* note 24, at 73; Singer, *supra* note 34.
[40] Int'l Ass'n of Ins. Supervisors, Principles on Capital Adequacy and Solvency (2007).

2008 with the failure of the international insurance giant, AIG, whose collapse in the midst of the crisis upended global financial markets and required an eventual takeover by the United States. In the response to the debacle, the organization is contemplating "comprehensive" approaches to the regulation of insurance companies that would encourage more consolidated regulation of insurance firms and their global affiliates.

The Joint Forum: Coordination Among the Sectoral Giants

Efforts to coordinate between the IAIS, IOSCO, and Basel Committee are routinely undertaken by the Joint Forum on Financial Conglomerates (Joint Forum). Consisting of an equal number of senior bank, insurance, and securities supervisors, the Joint Forum enjoys the participation of thirteen countries: Australia, Belgium, Canada, France, Germany, Italy, Japan, the Netherlands, Spain, Sweden, Switzerland, the United Kingdom, and the United States. The EU Commission attends as an observer. The Joint Forum's original mandate focused primarily on diversified financial firms with complex organizational and management structures whose large-scale activities cross national borders and sectoral boundaries. The Joint Forum has accordingly explored a range of challenges common to the banking, securities, and insurance sectors, including the regulation of financial conglomerates, and has focused on how information can be better exchanged between supervisors both in and among different areas of sectoral expertise. Additionally, the Joint Forum has examined ways to enhance supervisory coordination and has performed cross-sectoral comparisons of core principles issued by the sectoral standard setters.

SPECIALIST STANDARD SETTERS

International Accounting Standards Board

Alongside the primary sectoral standard-setting bodies outlined above are other important standard-setting bodies that enjoy much more limited mandates concerning very specific, often complex problems. The first is the International Accounting Standards Board (IASB), an organization led by accountants and auditors whose objective is to develop a single set of global accounting standards for investors, creditors, and regulatory authorities. In contrast to the organizations discussed above, it is grounded – at least from the standpoint of its internal affairs – by hard law and is incorporated as a nonprofit in the US state of Delaware.

The IASB began life in 1972 as the International Accounting Standards Committee (IASC), which was itself the product of the Tenth International Congress of Accountants, a body tasked in 1966 to examine methods of harmonizing accounting standards across jurisdictions. The impulse for the IASC's formation was that, in the face of rapid growth in international trade and investment, financial reporting practices differed considerably among countries.[41] Removing such differences through harmonization of accounting would, at least in theory, facilitate international trade and investment. To do so, the IASC promulgated a range of important legislative products. The most important was the International Accounting Standards (IAS), a set of guidelines laying out how particular types of transactions and other activities should be reflected in financial statements like cash flow and balance sheets.

For the first two decades of its existence, the IASC languished as an international standard-setting body, even as its membership grew exponentially. The IAS assumed only a minor place in international accounting. This lackluster debut owed in some measure to the dominance of the US Generally Accepted Accounting Principles; firms were required to comply with these principles in order to be listed on (the then dominant) US exchanges. But the slow start was also because of the low quality of the IAS. Initially, the standards merely represented the lowest (acceptable) common denominator as the IASC was initially geared toward eliminating practices that were already by and large viewed as unacceptable.[42] As a result, unlike the US GAAP, the IAS frequently permitted alternative treatments of basic balance sheet line items.

By 1987, the IASC began to develop a more ambitious agenda, motivated by a closer cooperation with the International Organization of Securities Commissions and the prospect of that organization endorsing its standards and promoting them among its members. The IASC undertook the high-profile Comparability and Improvements Project, aimed at developing one harmonized approach under the IAS. The project revised ten important international accounting standards. In 1995, the IASC entered into an agreement with IOSCO to produce a comprehensive, core set of high-quality standards for cross-border listings on securities exchanges. Ultimately, IOSCO provided only partial support for the initiative. In 2000, it recommended that its members allow companies to use the IAS but also permitted members to require supplementary information and reconciliation for certain items and to eliminate some of the options.

---

[41] Kees Camfferman & Stephen A. Zeff, Financial Reporting and Global Capital Markets: A History of the International Accounting Standards Committee, 1973–2000 22 (2007).

[42] *Id.* at 253.

Additionally, the IASC has undergone a series of changes designed to make it more independent of special interests. As opposed to earlier organizational structures, where professional associations had representatives that participated in the standard-setting process, members are now independent experts from the industry selected by a board of trustees (whose members are themselves chosen by national and international regulatory officials) based on their professional competence and practical experience.[43] To achieve geographical diversity, membership is divided among the regions as follows: four members from the Asia/Oceania region, four from Europe, four from North America, one from Africa, one from South America, and two appointed from any area, subject to maintaining overall geographical balance.

These changes ushered in a variety of legislative successes. In 2000, the European Commission announced plans to require all companies listed throughout Europe to use international financial reporting standards issued by IASB by 2005 (as well as some existing IAS standards). The move ultimately affected nearly seven thousand companies in the EU and lifted IFRS to the dominant standard in the Eurozone area. Australia, Hong Kong, and South Africa then followed the EU's lead in requiring the use of IFRS. By 2010, nearly one hundred countries had either required or accepted IFRS as an accounting standard. In acknowledgment of this move toward harmonization, and concerned that US companies might have to reconcile their financial statements with IFRS or adopt it outright when transacting abroad, the SEC, the primary holdout on IFRS, decided in 2007 to accept IFRS rather than require US GAAP in SEC filings by foreign issuers. It also, to the surprise of many, blessed efforts by Financial Accounting Standards Board (or "FASB," the private sector organization in the United States that establishes financial accounting and reporting standards) to update and reaffirm a Memorandum of Understanding to harmonize all major accounting standards – a process that was given new life in 2009 when the G-20 called on regulators to achieve a single set of global accounting standards by June 2011.

IASB has focused much of its attention on the accounting issues emerging from the global financial crisis, including those identified by the G-20 and the FSB as having caused and exacerbated the financial market turmoil in 2008 and 2009. As the IASB has increasingly taken direction from these agenda setters as well as from traditional securities regulators, its own mandate has at least implicitly been broadened from merely devising a harmonized set of rules for enhanced cross-border trade to helping address systemic risk problems.

---

[43] The members are selected to establish an appropriate mix of recent practical experience of standard setting, or of the user, accounting, academic or preparer communities *See* INT'L ACCOUNTING STANDARDS BD., DUE PROCESS HANDBOOK FOR THE IASB (2008). At present there are 15 members. By July 1, 2012, the number of members has to be 16.

Most notably, the question of how to value assets in times of financial stress has received careful attention: under such conditions should assets (especially derivatives) be marked to current market conditions (causing problems for balance sheets), or should banks be given greater leeway to reclassify portfolios and value them more favorably based on their expected market factors.

The International Federation of Accountants

The International Federation of Accountants (IFAC) was started in 1977 at the eleventh annual World Congress of Accountants in Munich, Germany, where sixty-three national professional accountancy bodies signed the (non-binding) constitution establishing the organization. At the first meeting of the new organization, a twelve-point work plan was developed that contains many of the objectives held by the organization today, including developing international standards, establishing a code of ethics for accountants, developing report-management processes and techniques, and fostering closer relationships with users of financial statements.[44] Since then, it has been at times closely affiliated with the IASB; in 1981, all members became members of the IASC, though twenty years later the two organizations once again separated as each underwent changes in their membership policies.

In the early days of the IFAC, various institutional organs developed and promoted international standards in the areas of auditing and assurance, ethics, and education. One of those organs, the International Auditing and Assurance Standards Board, has been responsible for the International Standards on Auditing (ISA), which have been adopted or are used as a basis for national auditing standards in more than one hundred countries.[45] Another organ has promulgated international public sector accounting standards for national and local governments, which have been adopted or are currently under consideration by more than fifty countries.[46] The organization regularly publishes reports and conducts surveys of members. It publishes an influential code of ethics for professional accountants, which is intended to serve as a model for national ethical guidance for accountants and is periodically updated, featuring new rules on independence.

In comparison to the IASB, the IFAC is a rather low-key organization, though it has at various times attracted considerable attention, most notably in 2001. Following the collapse of Enron, where the firm's auditors helped

---

[44] INT'L FED'N OF ACCOUNTANTS, IFAC: 30 YEARS OF PROGRESS ENCOURAGING QUALITY AND BUILDING TRUST 1 (2007), *available at* web.ifac.org/download/IFAC_History_-_Nov_2007.pdf.
[45] *Id.* at 3.
[46] *Id.*

enable fraud, regulators around the world focused considerable attention on the regulation and effectiveness of auditors and the accountancy profession. In the United States, for example, the Sarbanes-Oxley Act established "new corporate governance requirements for public companies and created a new entity, the Public Company Accounting Oversight Board, to develop standards for listed entities and to conduct inspections of the work of audit firms."[47] The IFAC, spurred by the United States and coordinating with a range of other standard setters like IOSCO, the Basel Committee, and the FSF, established similar internal institutional reforms. Perhaps most notable was the formation of the Public Interest Oversight Board in 2005 to oversee the organization's activities and to ensure that they are adequately responsive to the public.[48]

Committee on Payment and Settlement Systems

Clearing and settlement systems – that is, agreed-upon technologies, procedures, and rules for the transfer of funds among a group of participating firms – have also become subject to more international oversight. Payment systems can become a source of systemic risk when large transactions are processed, and often have international consequences to the extent that participants in such systems are foreign firms. Thus the Committee on Payment and Settlement Systems (CPSS), established in 1990, was launched by the then G-10 to provide internationally valid guidance for key back-office activities concerning both the verification of information in financial transactions in which securities are sold (clearing) and the subsequent delivery of securities certificates after trades are made (settlement). The CPSS has worked with IOSCO to publish its *Recommendations for Central Counterparties* establishing comprehensive standards for risk management by central counterparties and also including recommendations for securities settlement systems to improve the infrastructure for financial activities.[49] Additionally, the CPSS publishes its *Core Principles for Systemically Important Payment Systems*.[50] The document, first published in 2001, establishes standards and guidelines for processing interbank payments and spells out in broad terms how payment systems may best be legally and operationally established to limit the risks arising in the processing of large-value payments between financial institutions.

---

[47] Id.
[48] Public Interest Oversight Bd., http://www.ipiob.org/ (last visited Nov. 29, 2010).
[49] Comm. on Payment & Settlement Sys. [CPSS] & Technical Comm. of IOSCO, Recommendations for Central Counterparties (2004), *available at* http://www.bis.org/publ/cpss64.pdf.
[50] CPSS, Core Principles for Systemically Important Payment Systems (2001), *available at* http://www.bis.org/publ/cpss43.pdf.

To carry out its work, the CPSS undertakes studies of payment and settlement system, either on its own initiative or at the request of the G-20 (formerly the G-10). It regularly publishes reports on topics such as securities settlement systems, large-value funds transfer systems, specialized foreign exchange transactions, clearing arrangements for exchange-traded and over-the-counter derivatives and retail payment instruments, including electronic money.[51] The CPSS also publishes the "Red Book" on payment systems, which provides extensive studies of member countries' payments and settlement systems. It is revised periodically and updated annually.[52]

Financial Action Task Force

The Financial Action Task Force (FATF) was created in 1990, largely as a response to what had been only moderately effective efforts at curbing money laundering – a series of financial transactions that generate an asset or value from the result of an illegal act. In 1988, the United States spearheaded efforts to draft the Basel Committee's *Statement of Principles on Money Laundering*, and in the same year the UN Vienna Convention Against Illicit Traffic in Narcotic Drugs and Psychotropic Substances was drafted and signed; after going into force (which occurred in 1990), it would legally obligate parties to criminalize and extradite money laundering and to cooperate on international enforcement.[53] By 1990, only six countries had adopted strict money-laundering statutes that would require banks to improve information gathering associated with organized crime and to share that information with authorities. In order to speed up progress, the G-7 finance ministers convened a summit with the president of the Commission for the European Communities and invited eight nonsummit participants to join what would become the FATF. Today, the organization's members number thirty-five countries, and it has a secretariat in Paris at the Organisation for Economic Co-operation and Development, though is independent of it. The FATF has also created eight affiliated regional bodies, whose purpose is to ensure the implementation of FATF standards beyond the core FATF membership.

The FATF's key legislative achievements include the *40 Recommendations*, a set of comprehensive principles for action against money laundering.[54] They cover the criminal justice system and law enforcement, the financial system

---

[51] COMM. ON PAYMENT AND SETTLEMENT SYS., http://www.bis.org/cpss/index.htm (last visited Nov. 29, 2010).

[52] *CPSS – Red Book: CPSS Countries*, BANK FOR INT'L SETTLEMENTS, http://www.bis.org/list/cpss/tid_57/index.htm (last visited Apr. 25, 2011).

[53] JOHN BRAITHWAITE & PETER DRAHOS, GLOBAL BUSINESS REGULATION 106 (2000).

[54] FIN. ACTION TASK FORCE, FATF 40 RECOMMENDATIONS (2004), *available at* http://www.fatf-gafi.org/dataoecd/7/40/34849567.pdf.

and its regulation, and international cooperation. As with other standard-setting bodies, the FATF consistently reviews the principles and has introduced a methodology (its "Interpretative Notes") to clarify the application of specific recommendations. Its mandate has grown to combat terrorist financing in addition to money laundering. Specifically, in October 2001, FATF members agreed to and issued nine new international standards, known as the *Special Recommendations* (and collectively with the original set the "*40 + 9 Recommendations*"), which sets out common approaches and standards for financial institutions to detect, prevent, and suppress the financing of terrorism and terrorist acts.

Unlike some standard-setting bodies, the FATF not only prepares and consistently updates its recommendations to accommodate developments in the international financial system, but also monitors the implementation of its principles. Specifically, states that join the FATF are subject to reviews from one another to track their compliance, and reports discuss members' regulatory actions. Moreover, the organization has created a list of codes and criteria to identify countries that refuse to abide by its standards, as well as a schedule of disciplining countermeasures, including prohibitions on financial institutions in member countries from transacting with scofflaw states. For these and other reasons I elaborate in the following chapter, the FATF's recommendations have been extraordinarily successful and widely implemented among FATF members and around the world. The FATF is thus commonly considered one of the most successful and ambitious international standard setters.

Organisation for Economic Co-operation and Development

Ironically, although the OECD is a hard law organization with a broad mandate, its role in financial regulation is limited. Established in 1961 under an international convention, it has three main aims: to promote policies designed to achieve sustainable economic growth in member countries while maintaining financial stability; to contribute to sound economic expansion in member, as well as nonmember, countries in the process of economic development; and to contribute to the expansion of world trade.[55]

With regard to international financial regulation, the OECD's most important standards are its *Principles of Corporate Governance*,[56] which was first

---

[55] Convention on the Organisation for Economic Co-operation and Development, Dec. 14, 1960, 12 U.S.T. 1728, 888 U.N.T.S. 179, *available at* http://www.oecd.org/document/7/0,3343, en_2649_201185_1915847_1_1_1_1,00.html [hereinafter OECD Convention].

[56] *OECD Principles of Corporate Governance*, OECD (Apr. 22, 2004), http://webnet.oecd.org/oecdacts/Instruments/ListBySubjectView.aspx (follow "Corporate Governance" hyperlink; then "Recommendation" hyperlink).

promulgated in 1999 and revised in 2004. This work sets forth standards and guidelines for countries to devise or retain effective corporate governance frameworks, including the rights, roles, and responsibilities of stakeholders, shareholders, and company executives and management.[57] The principles have been adopted as one of the key standards for sound financial systems by the FSF and have formed the basis of the corporate governance component of the World Bank and IMF monitoring.[58] The OECD works closely with the FATF; in addition to generally supporting the FATF's recommendations, OECD members discipline institutions that do not comply with them. The organization has also taken the lead in examining, through a series of reports and initiatives, how weaknesses in corporate governance contributed to the financial crisis.

The OECD describes itself as a forum where governments can compare policy experiences, seek answers to common problems, identify good practice, and coordinate domestic and international policies.[59] Its membership has grown from twenty at the time of its establishment to thirty-one in 2010.[60] The OECD requires that a prospective member have a market economy, and admission is subject to the unanimous consent of the existing members.[61] Although OECD membership is limited, OECD maintains cooperative relations with more than seventy nonmembers.[62] Under the cooperative arrangement, non-members not only participate in the activities of the OECD, but also adopt published standards. The OECD has a permanent secretariat that helps carry out the work mandated by the OECD Council. The secretary-general, as the chair of the council and head of the secretariat, connects national delegations with the secretariat's activities. The OECD's technical work, however, is performed by specialized committees, working groups, and expert groups

---

[57] RICHARD WOODWARD, THE ORGANISATION FOR ECONOMIC CO-OPERATION AND DEVELOP-
MENT 72 (2009).

[58] Id.

[59] About the Organisation for Economic Co-operation and Development, OECD, http://www
.oecd.org/pages/0,3417,en_36734052_36734103_1_1_1_1,00.html (last visited Nov. 29, 2010).

[60] The members and accession dates are as follows: Australia (1971), Austria (1961), Belgium
(1961), Canada (1961), Chile: (2010), Czech Republic (1995), Denmark (1961), Finland (1969),
France (1961), Germany (1961), Greece 1961, Hungary (1996), Iceland (1961), Ireland (1961),
Italy (1962), Japan (1964), Korea (1996), Luxembourg (1961), Mexico (1994), Netherlands (1961),
New Zealand (1973), Norway (1961), Poland (1996), Portugal (1961), Slovak Republic (2000),
Spain (1961), Sweden (1961), Switzerland (1961), Turkey (1961), United Kingdom (1961), United
States (1961). See List of OECD Member Countries, OECD, http://www.oecd.org/document/
58/0,3343,en_2649_201185_1889402_1_1_1_1,00.html (last visited Nov. 29, 2010).

[61] OECD Convention, supra note 56, 12 U.S.T. at 1738, 888 U.N.T.S. at 187–89.

[62] Members and Partners, OECD, http://www.oecd.org/pages/0,3417,en_36734052_36761800_1_1_
1_1_1,00.html (last visited March 11, 2011).

mandated by the council. Committees comprise representatives from OECD members and usually work on a one-country, one-vote basis.[63] Currently, there are approximately 250 committees and groups working under the OECD.

International Association of Deposit Insurers

Founded in 2002, the International Association of Deposit Insurers is the most recently established standard setter. The IADI has sixty-two member organizations, six associates, and twelve partners. The six associates are representatives of other agencies that have developed or are considering developing a deposit insurance system. Thus far, the IADI's primary legislative product has been the *Core Principles for Effective Deposit Insurance Systems*, issued in 2009 as a joint project with the Basel Committee.[64]

According to the organization's by-laws, the supreme authority for all matters concerning the organization lies in the General Meeting of the members, which elects an executive council consisting largely, though not exclusively, of developed countries and which has itself established six standing committees to assist the performance of its activities. Much of the IADI's work is initially addressed through the Executive Council. All members of the Executive Council serve on at least one of the association's seven standing committees, which other members and associates may join. In addition to the Executive Council, the IADI has created a range of regional committees for Africa, Asia-Pacific, the Caribbean, Eurasia, Europe, Latin America, and the Middle East and North Africa. These committees are intended to encourage information sharing and the exchange of approaches and views among agencies hailing from diverse parts of the world. Finally, a range of parties, including international organizations, financial institutions, and professional firms, have entered into a cooperative arrangement with IADI to serve as observers in order to help promote the organization's work.

International Swaps and Derivatives Association

The final organization requiring mention is the International Swaps and Derivatives Association (ISDA), a trade association of firms and professional service providers in the over-the-counter derivatives industry. The ISDA is known for its role in developing the ISDA Master Agreement, the authoritative contractual framework document used in derivatives transactions to

---

[63] WOODWARD, *supra* note 58, at 48.
[64] BASEL COMM. & INT'L ASS'N OF DEPOSIT INSURERS, CORE PRINCIPLES FOR EFFECTIVE DEPOSIT INSURANCE SYSTEMS (2009), *available at* http://www.bis.org/publ/bcbs156.pdf.

memorialize contractual obligations between parties. The Master Agreement's popularity stems in large part from its standardization of certain terms that are used as defaults in derivatives transactions, as well as from its definition of key terms, allowing parties to save time and money in crafting agreements. Because a wide range of industrial and financial institutions participate to some extent in the derivatives market, the ISDA plays an important standard-setting role in the industrial and financial sectors. Tasks in the ISDA's mission statement include "promoting practices conducive to the efficient conduct of the business," "promoting the development of sound risk management practices," and "fostering high standards of commercial conduct." However, the terms and principles that the ISDA promotes are not sanctioned by any government-run international standard setter, and the organization has no official enforcement capacity. Instead, because the ISDA promulgates a default contract, on the basis of which parties craft customized agreements, private litigation or arbitration is the primary means of discipline among parties. For this reason, it is not commonly recognized as a "regulatory" body in the same sense as the other standard setters discussed above. That said, ISDA has created in-house "determination committees" consisting of dealers and buy-side investors that have authority in private disputes involving ISDA contracts to determine whether a credit event has occurred and to make determinations on any substitute reference obligations.

INTERLUDE: THE BANK FOR INTERNATIONAL SETTLEMENTS

Before we proceed to monitoring in the international regulatory system, it is appropriate to identify an important actor that, though not formally an agenda or standard setter, provides critical assistance for both activities – the BIS. Established under a charter approved at the Hague Convention in 1930, the BIS was originally geared toward ensuring the transfer of German reparations payments after World War I. Its responsibilities grew as the international economy matured; the bank eventually held some deposits of central banks and came to operate as "a central bank for central banks." It also plays a key role in helping central banks keep abreast of global economic and market developments, as well as issues relating to monetary and financial stability. See text box 2.1.

The BIS is a unique organization. It is both a formal international organization and a private market participant whose shares are publicly traded. In the latter capacity as a private market entity, the BIS offers a broad array of for-profit services designed to assist central banks and other monetary authorities in the management of their reserves. In its more regulatory capacity, the BIS provides economic, monetary, financial, and legal research and supports

---

Text box 2.1. Key Activities of the Bank for International Settlements

- Conducts economic, monetary, financial, and legal research to support the activities of the Basel-based committees
- Serves as a hub for sharing statistical information among central banks, and for publishing statistics on global banking, securities, foreign exchange, and derivatives markets
- Provides financial services to assist central banks and other official monetary institutions in the management of their foreign reserves

Source: BIS website

---

the meetings of but the FSB and all Basel-based standard-setting authorities, including the Basel Committee, the CPSS, and IAIS. The BIS is also a self-described "hub for sharing statistical information among central banks and for publishing a wide range of analytical products concerning global banking, securities, foreign exchange, and derivatives markets."

THE INTERNATIONAL "MONITORS"

The last important group of actors concerns institutions that collectively can be described as the international "monitors." Though they may act as sounding boards for policy development, these organizations are not the main drivers of regulatory standard setting, and they do not generally originate best practices for capital market participants. Instead, they are primarily responsible for identifying whether (and the degree to which) regulators comply with international financial law. Like the standard-setting process, monitoring can be decentralized. Usually, it takes place under the auspices of the IMF and World Bank. That said, standard setters, too, can undertake monitoring of their members' compliance with their collective legislative products.

Delegated Monitoring Under Bretton Woods

The two most prominent monitors of financial regulatory policy are the IMF and the World Bank. Both were created in the 1940s to avoid the economic protectionism and monetary instability that characterized global finance in the years following the great depression. The World Bank works with other institutions to provide loans, advice, and an array of customized resources to more than one hundred developing countries. The IMF was originally created to provide financial and technical assistance to countries experiencing balance of payments problems. As such, its traditional expertise lies not in financial regulation, but in fiscal and monetary affairs.

With the 1978 amendment to the IMF's Articles of Agreement and the abandonment in the early 1970s of the par-value system, decisions on a member country's exchange rate moved into the domain of domestic policy.[65] IMF surveillance was introduced as a means providing discipline for freed currencies and exchange rates. Specifically, under the amended Article IV, members were required to "collaborate with the IMF to assure orderly exchange arrangements and to promote a stable system of exchange rates" – an obligation that has at least been interpreted to include surveillance of member countries' policies with regard to exchange rate management.[66] Such surveillance activity was envisioned to provide a means of dialogue, persuasion, and peer pressure to spur domestic policies that both served members' self-interest and contributed to international stability and prosperity.[67]

In the wake of the Asian financial crisis in the late 1990s, the scope of surveillance expanded well beyond monetary affairs. National and international regulatory authorities agreed that capital market crises could have severe implications for the stability of the global financial system and exchange rates. G-7 leaders, in particular, pressed for increased surveillance activities directed toward capital market management and activity to gain better understanding of how financial globalization affected international economic stability.

Thus in 1998, the FSF was tasked with identifying internationally accepted prudential standards that could help brace against and prevent global financial crises – and, in doing so, relied on the standard setters (and specialists) outlined above. The purpose behind this activity was clear: "if countries were to reap the benefits of access to international capital without 'excessive risk' of contagious international financial stability, they would have to strengthen their financial systems."[68] The IMF and World Bank were then asked to coordinate the surveillance of compliance with these standards. Both institutions already had considerable expertise in one key area, transparency, especially in

---

[65] Biagio Bossone, Int'l Monetary Fund, IMF Surveillance: A Case Study on IMF Governance 9 (2008), *available at* www.ieo-imf.org/eval/complete/pdf/05212008/BP08_10 .pdf.

[66] Articles of Agreement of the International Monetary Fund art. IV, July 22, 1944, 60 Stat. 1401, 2 U.N.T.S. 39, *available at* http://www.imf.org/external/pubs/ft/aa/.

[67] Bossone, *supra* note 66.

[68] Jacob Vestergaard, Discipline in the Global Economy?: International Finance and the End of Liberalism 91 (2008).

light of their place in the global financial system as lenders of last resort and bridge-loan providers. Because both the IMF and World Bank mandated that their members commit to pursuing policies conducive to orderly economic growth, they seemed the natural institutions to take on surveillance in a broader scope of regulatory affairs.

Central to the global surveillance system administered by the IMF and World Bank is the Financial Sector Assessment Program (FSAP). The program is intended to toughen the assessment and monitoring of member countries' financial systems so as to develop, as needed, strategies and policies for strengthening those systems. FSAP reports are prepared by the staffs of the IMF and the World Bank with the participation of experts from national or international agencies. FSAP reports consist of three volumes. The third volume (the "Assessment of Observance of International Standards and Codes") contains a detailed appraisal of selected financial sector standards, codes, and good practices. This appraisal is divided into modules, whose focus and content may vary from country to country.

Usually included in financial sector assessments by the World Bank and IMF are Reports on Observance of Standards and Codes (ROSCs). See Table 2.1. Like FSAP reports, they focus on countries' adherence to targeted international codes and principles, but unlike those reports, ROSCs can be prepared separately by IMF and World Bank staff and are not strictly limited to prudential financial sector issues. The ROSCs address standards in areas as diverse as accounting, auditing, anti–money laundering and countering the financing of terrorism, banking supervision, corporate governance, insolvency and creditor rights, insurance supervision, monetary and financial policy transparency, payments systems, and securities regulation. (Other standards are also produced by the IMF for areas like fiscal transparency, corporate insolvency and creditor rights, and government transparency for monetary affairs – but as mentioned above, they are outside the scope of our analysis on financial market regulation).

FSAP results are shared with member countries to help them identify the "strengths, vulnerabilities, and risks" of national financial systems and design appropriate policy responses.[69] In addition to the findings of the FSAP team, the staff of the IMF and World Bank prepare separate reports to their respective Executive Boards to help them carry out annual (usually less intrusive) surveillance as dictated under Article IV of the IMF Articles of Agreement. Article IV *requires* that each member collaborate with the fund and other members via

---

[69] *Id.* at 90.

TABLE 2.1. *Key financial market standards, codes, and principles for which reports on observance of standards and codes (ROSCs) are produced*

Issue Area	Relevant Standard Setter	Form of Publication
Banking supervision	Basel Committee	*Core Principles for Effective Banking Supervision*
Securities	IOSCO	*Objectives and Principles for Securities Regulation*
Insurance	IAIS	*Insurance Core Principles*
Market integrity	FATF	*40 + 9 Recommendations*
Corporate governance	OECD	*Principles of Corporate Governance*
Accounting	IASB	*International Accounting Standards; International Financial Reporting Standards*
Auditing	IFAC	*International Standards on Auditing*
Deposit insurance	IADI	*Core Principles for Effective Deposit Insurance Systems (co-authored with the Basel Committee)*
Payment and settlement	CPSS	*Core Principles for Systemically Important Payment Systems; Recommendations for Central Counterparties (co-authored with IOSCO)*

Source: Daniel W. Drezner, All Politics Is Global: Explaining International Regulatory Regimes 137 (2007).

surveillance to assure financial stability (or more precisely, "orderly exchange arrangements and to promote a stable system of exchange rates").[70]

Non-delegated Monitoring

Monitoring need not be outsourced to the IMF and World Bank. International standard setters can independently undertake surveillance of compliance with their best practices, rules, and standards through both formal and informal peer review processes. Members of the FATF, for example, participate in a mutual or peer-evaluation process whereby they monitor one another's implementation of the FATF recommendations through on-site reviews. And with

---

[70] The report to the IMF's Board is a Financial System Stability Assessment (FSSA). The report to the World Bank's Board is a Financial Sector Assessment (FSA).

regard to nonmembers, the FATF's International Co-operation Review Group analyzes the legislative and regulatory frameworks of high-risk and noncooperative jurisdictions and reserves the right to recommend specific actions to induce compliance.

A similar example of in-house monitoring can be found in IOSCO's Multilateral Memorandum of Understanding, an agreement that lays out procedures and commitments for enforcement cooperation and information sharing among securities regulators. As a precondition to joining IOSCO, prospective members must first become signatories of the MMOU. Regulators must formally indicate their commitment to mutual cooperation and assistance with regard to IOSCO members and also demonstrate that they have the rights and powers under their own national laws to comply with the terms and conditions of the agreement.[71] This process requires the applicant regulator to fill out a questionnaire on the its home state laws that.[72] Based on a review of the questionnaire responses, IOSCO verification teams make specific recommendations to a screening body regarding the applicant's ability to comply with each MMOU provision cited in the questionnaire.[73] IOSCO officials then decide whether to accept the application.

Again, most formal forms of monitoring are carried out through the IMF and World Bank, either in the course of their economic surveillance activities or in connection with their lending activities for client states. Monitoring by international standard-setting bodies themselves is, however, on the rise – a point we pick up in the following chapter. To the extent that an organization both sets rules and evaluates members with regard to their compliance with those rules, it takes on roles as both lawmaker and judiciary. As such, the organization begins to take on in striking fashion some of the features associated with traditional international organizations.

That said, organizations operating at the international level may be wary of concentrating both activities in the same institution. Monitoring is often a source of friction and generates an environment of tension. It inherently involves some sort of verification process, which – when exercised by foreign governments in particular – can be construed as infringing economic sovereignty or as politically motivated. Moreover, the conclusions from

---

[71] IOSCO, Multilateral Memorandum of Understanding Concerning Consultation and Cooperation and the Exchange of Information 12 (2002), *available at* http://www.iosco.org/library/pubdocs/pdf/IOSCOPD126.pdf.

[72] *Id.* at 16–19.

[73] *Id.* at 12.

monitoring can be debatable and, as such, cause disagreements among member countries. Frictions can spill over to the standard-setting process and erode rule making at the very outset. When monitoring and standard setting are independent of each other, the likelihood of such risks materializing is reduced, even where (as is often the case) international monitors themselves rely on national regulators and standard-setting bodies for guidance and assistance in carrying out their assessments.

Finally, national regulators can and do themselves engage in various forms of monitoring via national (and international) technical assistance programs, which allow them to probe the regulatory architecture of other countries. National regulators can also evaluate one another in the course of conducting financial diplomacy. As Dan Tarullo has noted, because regulators frequently interact in promoting rules, they are able to monitor in broad terms the seriousness with which counterparts are committed to certain principles, albeit imperfectly. Some institutions like the G-20 and the FSB additionally publish follow-up declarations that assess progress made with regard to previous agenda items, which as we will see can enhance greater compliance discipline.

THE PREDOMINANCE OF CONSENSUS

The architecture of international financial law is striking for not only the increasingly intricate relations among institutions, but also the internal design of international policymaking bodies themselves. As we saw earlier in this chapter, network theory generally assumes that international regulatory forums are somewhat amorphous bodies. No doubt this view arises because those forums are grounded in soft law, and because the overall regulatory architecture is highly fragmented and unsettled. As a matter of descriptive theory, however, international standard setters are far from simple organizations and often exert their own sophisticated institutional and political economies.

One source of complexity relates to the rules according to which decision making takes place. See text box 2.2. A range of such decision-making rules is available to an organization. Some organizations, for example, may make decisions according to majority vote – a democratic process that respects the general will of participants. It allows for relatively swift decision making since not all voting members need agree with a particular course of action. The notion of majority rules implicitly acknowledges the inevitability of disparate opinion. Simultaneously, it allows organizations to address the current challenge and to be in a position to respond flexibly to new ones.

Text box 2.2. Decision Rules for Key Standard-Setting Bodies

Institution	Voting rule
G-20	Consensus
FSB	Consensus
Basel Committee	Consensus
IOSCO	Majority vote of Presidents' Committee or Executive Committee, except resolutions to amend the by-laws, which require 2/3 vote of Presidents' Committee Consensus is emphasized, and most day-to-day operational decisions by committees and working groups require consensus
IAIS	2/3 vote of General Meeting to adopt principles, standards, or guidance, or to amend bylaws Majority vote of General Meeting or Executive Committee for residual matters
FATF	Consensus
IASB	Publication of standards requires 10 of 16 votes (9 if fewer than 16 members are sitting) A majority vote is generally required for other decisions The constitution requires members to "work with one another in reaching consensus views," which are required in interpreting standards

---

Yet most organizations, with the important exception of the private standard-setting bodies, do not operate by majority rule. Instead, they adopt some form of supermajority governance – usually in the form of consensus-based decision making adopted in an institution's underlying organizational document or expressed or declared by members and their leadership in a communiqué of some sort. What consensus means in practice is, however, not always obvious. Usually, it indicates that no formal tallies of voting are made. It also generally suggests unanimity as a voting requirement – or at least a requirement that no standard adopted is vociferously opposed by any member. As such, it represents a normative expectation that displaces more flexible, supermajority rules.

Consensus can be a costly organizational feature. Internal disagreements can be sharp and deep due to the potential impact of particular rules on members' divergent national interests. Consensus can exacerbate the problem by enabling different members and, by extension different jurisdictions to wield veto power over the promulgation of potentially sound regulatory policies. It can give rise to a range of strategic dynamics that can stymie coordination.

Perhaps most important, consensus can incentivize actors to potentially with-draw or withhold their support for any particular regulatory reform in order to extract concessions of their own.

There are, nonetheless, certain strategic advantages that can arise through consensus-based decision rules. First, by raising the bar for the adoption of a legal standard, it potentially minimizes the likelihood of regulatory error. All parties must agree (or at least concede) to a particular piece of legislation. Moreover, the chance that one global standard will create disproportionately negative burdens for a minority of members, without their consent, is signifi-cantly reduced. Simply put, by having a consensus-based requirement, states must allow all parties to have a voice in decision making. Small or finan-cially less significant countries cannot be overlooked or ignored. Instead, the sponsors of any particular piece of legislation are required to coordinate with all parties and to take into consideration the potentially negative implica-tions of their particular approach or standard for the broadest constituency of actors.

Higher legislative hurdles can also confer a solid veneer of legitimacy on the organizational rules promulgated. Rules cannot be adopted without over-whelming support. And when all (or almost all) members of an organization agree to a certain standard or rule, it is likely that the rule will be regarded as well considered and as the most appropriate course of action. Such legitimacy may help facilitate the propagation of a rule, especially where it generates considerable compliance costs for a diverse set of market actors.

PRIMARY INSTITUTIONAL DESIGN CHOICES

International regulatory bodies are structured and organized differently, even where they are tasked with similar duties or objectives. Specifically, inter-national standard setters can be thought of as diverging along four sets of institutional design options. At the most basic level, international standard-setting bodies may be exclusive or universal in their membership. Second, some institutions may permit leadership and decision making by a select group of elite members, whereas others may require full group participation. Third, organizations can have various degrees of involvement by national authorities, with some animated by "private legislatures" consisting of market participants where regulators wield largely indirect control over the standard-setting process. Finally, some international standard-setting bodies may serve as forums for coordination between regulators with similar sectoral mandates, whereas others host regulators with different mandates and administrative portfolios.

Exclusive Versus Universal Membership

Membership is an important issue in international standard setting. To the extent to which an agency is permitted to participate in an international regulatory body, it can directly promote, and potentially export, its regulatory preferences. On the other hand, where it is excluded, rules can be made and propagated without its consent, and contrary to its interests or those of domestic stakeholders.

The international architecture is animated by two basic approaches toward membership. Some standard setters have adopted a "universal" model of membership, whereas others are more "exclusive" in their outreach and membership. In the former case, organizations are largely global in scope and have few membership requirements. Two organizations that exemplify this approach are IOSCO and the IAIS. Since its inception, IOSCO has been largely identified as (and identifies itself as) a universal standard setter for securities regulation (though recently it has required modest levels of enforcement cooperation and information sharing from new members). Similarly, the IAIS has had a global, multilateralist orientation and has either invited or permitted scores of regulators – from the most highly developed to newly emerging markets – to join in its regulatory efforts.

Other international organizations are much more selective and are largely confined to a finite number of elite actors. They can thus be considered "exclusive" in their membership. Members are typically regulators of large capital markets or strategically important ones – including regulators that represent key countries in particular geographic areas or oversee markets that are quickly expanding. The most obvious example of an exclusive organization is the G-20, where well over 150 countries are not members. Because of its exclusivity, countries that attain membership in it usually have strong claims to participating in other exclusive bodies, some of which are increasingly based on G-20 membership.

Centralized Versus Decentralized Organizational Leadership

Membership does not by itself guarantee rule making authority. In some instances, all members in an organization will have equal input and opportunity to address a particular topic. In others, tasks may be centralized or delegated to an internal group of actors. In the Basel Committee, for example, decisions have traditionally been highly decentralized in the sense that all members participate in the standard-setting process. The group relies, as do most international organizations, on working committees in which not all members participate. The suggestions and proposals made by the group, however, must eventually be vetted by the rest of the membership body in order for policy to be formally promulgated. Without a consensus among the members, the proposed policy will not become law.

Other institutions, by comparison, are more flexible. IOSCO is, as noted above, an open membership organization, and virtually every regulatory agency has a representative on the President's Committee, the one organ that possesses all powers necessary or convenient to achieve the purpose of the organization. It is also consensus driven, meaning all members must in theory agree to legislation for it to be sanctioned as an official product of the agency. IOSCO also has four regional standing committees, as well as an Executive Committee and an Emerging Markets Committee to take actions in support of IOSCO's objectives. Yet none of these organizations constitute IOSCO's policymaking core. Instead, most legislation originates in the Technical Committee, a working group comprising eighteen agencies that oversee the world's largest and most developed securities markets. In principle, the members of the Technical Committee, after reaching agreement among themselves about standards, can pass on their proposals to the rest of the organizational body for approval. But additionally, and indeed often more important, the Technical Committee can promulgate its own standards. That is, members can take a policy stance on a particular issue and then issue guidance independently as a product of the Technical Committee – and thus without the explicit approval of all other IOSCO members. As a result, even with a large membership and a high consensus threshold, expedited and, indeed, voluminous policymaking is still possible, though potentially at the expense of universal membership participation.

Private Legislatures Versus Public Legislatures

Closely related to considerations of both membership and centralization is the question of whether and to what extent private parties should be involved in the standard-setting process. Until now, we have focused on the role of regulators in the standard-setting process. There is, however, one notable exception to this phenomenon. In a practice best described as "private legislatures," practitioners themselves can create, interpret, and enforce their own rules on the basis of their professional experience.[74]

---

[74] Alan Schwartz & Robert E. Scott, *The Political Economy of Private Legislatures*, 143 U. PENN. L. REV. 595 (1995); Levit, *supra* note 6, at 127.

The concept of private legislatures – as well as private rule making more generally – is one that is historically associated with coordination among and between domestic parties. International legal scholarship has generally shied away from nonstate actors in order to emphasize the legitimacy and authority of traditional international law, which requires the formal participation or practice of sovereign states. Nonetheless, private actors consistently assume an important role in fixing international standards, even in the financial context. As we have seen above, in the IASB and IFAC, for example, private bodies – accountants and auditors – have traditionally been the shapers and crafters of international legislation and have spearheaded coordination efforts in their fields. Elsewhere, many private organizations and professional organizations play an important role, independent of governmental agencies and bodies, in helping to shape the cross-border conduct of particular market participants and industry players. For example, under the Institute of International Finance and the International Banking Federation, major banks and securities firms have organized to consult with international standard-setting bodies, for which they research issues and put forward draft regulations. Although these industry groups are not standard-setting organizations with governmental backing, they do issue recommendations for global policy directly to governmental officials and, in the process, shape the terms of debate and the way in which regulators perceive risks and regulatory challenges.

Like financial regulators, private legislatures are technocratic actors that craft specific, often complex rules for homogenous groups of market participants. They arguably carry more expertise, however, than even the financial regulators, which may have only a vague understanding of specific market transactions and deal structures. By contrast, private actors have on-the-ground experience in the issues for which they craft rules. This superior knowledge of market practice often enables them to engage in more informed decision making than their governmental counterparts.

Private legislatures are not, however, without their drawbacks. As Bill Bratton and Lawrence Cunningham have often noted in their work on the IASB, members may promote rules that benefit their members and not the public.[75] Although they ostensibly place market concerns (as opposed to political or regulatory turf battles) in the forefront, participants in private legislatures may nonetheless act as a cabal and promulgate rules that enrich themselves at the

---

[75] *See, e.g.*, William W. Bratton & Lawrence A. Cunningham, *Treatment Differences and Political Realities in the GAAP-IFRS Debate*, 95 VA. L. REV. 989, 1000 (discussing the how private standard setters can be asked to resolve political issues, generating questions for legitimacy).

price of others and the public or that create costs that are borne by outside organizations and persons. This membership in a private legislature is homogeneous and open only to either the providers or users of particular services.

Although private legislatures may have a keen sense of the issues concerning market participants in discrete transactions, they are often ill informed as to the social costs of the transactions (and of their proposed rules). It is here that regulators – working in the service of the state, operating in larger institutional structures, and coordinating with counterparts across agencies – often have strategic informational advantages over private legislatures. In short, because private legislatures have but one constituency (themselves), they can suffer from a kind of institutional bias or hubris and provide rules and standards with only limited welfare-enhancing benefits.

Meeting these challenges has often required both significant, frequent organizational change in the structure of private legislatures and indirect or direct participation by regulatory agencies. The IASB and IFAC were both originally private sector initiatives. They comprised professional organizations almost exclusively and, as such, sought to create norms across borders with which members would comply. Over time, however, their character evolved to take on much more public characteristics. As noted above, the IASB, in particular, has changed dramatically, growing in independence and geographic diversity over the last three decades. As early as 1981, it created a Consultative Group comprising representatives of various organizations with an interest in financial reporting, including the World Bank, International Chamber of Commerce, IOSCO, and the International Bar Association. And since 2009, the IASB operates under a Monitoring Board – largely comprising key governmental and standard-setting bodies like IOSCO's Technical and Emerging Markets Committees – which approves of the trustees of the IASB's governing body and ensures that they execute their duties in light of the organization's governing constitution. The trustees, in turn, appoint the members of the IASB and other important administrators, and also annually approve the budget and strategy of the organization. Similarly, IFAC has become subject to a Public Interest Oversight Board, which itself operates under the leadership of members nominated by a variety of actors including sectoral standard setters, the World Bank, and the European Community.

Many of these structural changes were institutional responses to pressure exerted from governmental authorities that were concerned with the potential undue influence that private special interests could wield in setting standards that benefited them at the expense of the public. Governmental authorities consequently demanded more involvement in the standard-setting process and more organizational independence from professional associations before they would seriously consider moving from their own national standards. Such reforms, though widely regarded as reasonable, nonetheless illustrate the limitations of private legislatures – namely, that those seeking global prominence are still ultimately dependent on national regulatory authorities and, by extension, on national governments. Private legislatures must, in short, "sell" legislative products to national regulators. Otherwise, their "rules" will receive no domestic enforcement and likely remain unimplemented. National regulators can simply choose to adopt or promulgate their own national or international standards that depart from those pursued by private associations.[76]

Owing to their strategic need to sell their legislative products, private legislatures rarely, if ever, wield the same standard-setting power that institutional actors like IOSCO or the Basel Committee possess. To be sure, IOSCO and the Basel Committee face challenges of implementation, though when they seek to convince public regulators and policy officials to adopt best standards, their sell-side efforts are facilitated by the fact that their members are themselves regulators and, as such, have already bought into a reform program through their embrace of a standard in the organization's legislative process. And when the organizations seek to promulgate standards beyond their membership, they can do so from the position of a peer regulatory authority, or more. By contrast, not only do private legislatures lack the same veneer of authority and credibility, but their nongovernmental nature also requires more aggressive selling of their legislative products, and exposes them up to the very real risk – and frequent criticism – of catering to, and currying favor with, strategically important members of other standard setters in order to gain recognition of their rules.

Sectoral Versus Cross-functional Membership

Finally, organizations can assume a functional or cross-functional institutional structure. In the former case, members all come from the same general sector. Certainly, they may have relationships with other regulatory entities and bodies and even have regularized interactions with them; for instance, another standard-setting body or national regulator may participate as an observer. But membership and formal decision making is reserved for members with particular, typically sectoral experience. Thus, securities regulators interact with securities regulators, banking regulators with banking regulators, and so on. The Basel Committee, IAIS, and IOSCO stand as exemplars of functional entities.

---

[76] The latter was the case in the G4's role in international accounting standards. *See* Donna L. Street, *The G4's Role in the Evolution of the International Accounting Standard Setting Process and Partnership with the IASB*, 15 J. Int'l Acct. Auditing & Taxation 1, 109–26 (2006).

Text box 2.3.   Three Cross-functional Organizations: the G-20, FSB, and Joint Forum

Organization	Membership
G-20	Finance ministers; banking regulators; periodic participation by heads of state; IMF/World Bank
Financial Stability Board	Finance ministers; banking regulators; supervisory authorities; international standard setters (sectoral and specialist); IMF/World Bank
Joint Forum	International standard setters (sectoral); banking regulators; supervisory authorities

---

The members of cross-functional organizations represent diverse groups of regulatory authorities whose experience and responsibilities reflect that very diversity. Cross-functionality can be seen in FATF, where financial authorities and law enforcement officials cooperate to prevent terrorist financing and money laundering, as well as in IASB, insofar as its members are selected on the basis of diverse experience in accounting, auditing, investment, and industry. But it is perhaps most recognizable in the Joint Forum, FSB, and G-20. See text box 2.3. The Joint Forum brings together the IAIS, IOSCO, and Basel Committee, along with other regulators in the sector, to discuss issues common to the banking, securities, and insurance sectors, including the regulation of financial conglomerates. The FSB provides a forum for national and regional regulatory prudential regulators and supervisors to interact with one another and with international organizations. Finally, the G-20 enables banking regulators to interact with finance ministers and, in some cases, with political leaders and heads of state.

In the existing regulatory arrangement, cross-functional organization is generally reserved for those institutions that operate as broad regulatory agenda setters. By meeting across disciplines, cross-functional networks allow regulators to identify gaps in the international architecture as well as inconsistencies in approaches or points of emphasis. Different levels of experience are culled, from the macro-perspective of international organizations and institutions to the more granular perspective of individual national regulatory authorities. Fuller information can, as a result, be gathered, and a range of technical expertise is provided with regard to helping establish the direction of international regulatory policy. It also allows for a broader policy buy-in since a diverse array of actors participate in the agenda-setting process.

It is worth noting, however, that cross-functionality is often a matter of degree, and the amount of interaction across sectors can often be obfuscated

TABLE 2.2. *A comparison of institutional design features of key agenda setters and standard setters*

	Exclusive	Centralized	Public	Cross-functional
G-20	Y	N	Y	Y
FSB	Y	N	Y	Y
Basel Committee	Y	N	Y	N
IOSCO	N	Y	Y	N
IAIS	N	Y	Y	N
IASB	Y	N	N	Y
FATF	Y	N	Y	Y

by focusing exclusively on membership per se. Participation can be practiced in a variety of ways and does not always fit along neat lines of "membership." Many bodies, for example, have other organizations as associate members or observers, or have working groups or task forces where other standard setters participate. Furthermore, cross-functionality does not necessarily imply that all sectoral representatives will have equal input into decision making or even that all sectoral actors will have similar prominence in the international regulatory system. For example, national securities regulators like the US Securities and Exchange Commission do not participate in the G-20 unless, as in some countries, securities regulators are part of a larger, consolidated regulatory body that also serves as a country's primary banking regulator. The FSB, by contrast, has a less exclusive form of cross-functionality in that national securities and insurance regulators participate alongside finance ministers and banking regulators. Such differences can have important implications for how the agenda-setting process unfolds and how the relationship between national regulators domestically plays itself out.

EXPLAINING INSTITUTIONAL HETEROGENEITY

The governing international architecture can thus be described as one of considerable heterogeneity. As visually summarized in Table 2.2, standard-setting bodies differ along basic institutional design choices.

In virtually all cases (the important exception being the Basel Committee), these diverse design features are spelled out in advance by an institution's founding documents. As described above, bylaws and charters describe the objectives and procedural workings of various international institutions. These instruments are not, however, typical hard law international agreements but, instead, informal arrangements with no formal legal status. Their specificity can vary greatly, from elaborate bylaws spelling out membership in committees and working groups to sparse organizational charts. Nevertheless, the basic design choices memorialized in the agreements have important consequences for the amount and substance of the legislation that emerges from international standard- and agenda-setting bodies.

Why does such diversity characterize the international regulatory community? To be sure, no one book can explain all of the reasons why each of the institutions described above has evolved the way that it has. However, there are a broad set of rationales that provide some explanation for the institutional heterogeneity that one sees in the global financial system.

Path Dependency

One important factor is the institutional path dependency of organizational evolution and development seen in international financial regulation. In short, institutions tend to share some of the organizational characteristics of their predecessor, sponsoring, or founding organizations.

IOSCO, as we have already seen, began as the Inter-American Association of Securities Commissions and comprised a disparate array of regulators from North, Central, and South American countries regularly participated in its coordination and information-sharing activities. The decision to expand its membership arose in 1983, in Quito, Ecuador, as members sought to transform the organization into a global regulatory player. In light of its origins, it is not surprising that its transformation was inclined toward universal membership, at least at some level. Had it been otherwise, with membership based on strategic size and importance, some of the members of the antecedent Inter-American group would have effectively legislated themselves out of a position on the world stage. It is also not surprising that some members became key members on both the organization's regional associations and its Emerging Markets Committee.

By contrast, some institutions evolved from and borrowed formats that were highly limited in nature. Membership in the Basel Committee and FSB has been based on variations of various "G" groups that either brought them to life or tasked them with carrying out specific responsibilities. The Basel Committee, for example, contains the original G-10 members, who originally formed the group, plus members in the expanded G-20. The FSB was created by the then G-7 as the FSF and originally included (with a handful of exceptions) that group's membership along with existing international institutions involved in international financial oversight. But in 2008, when the FSB was tasked with responding to the financial crisis, it expanded to include the G-7's membership in addition to its own. The G-7 itself was the legacy of an earlier "Library Group" from the 1970s, consisting of the finance ministers of France, Germany, the United Kingdom, and the United States – and which provided a means for the then major industrialized democracies to informally launch new ideas, resolve disputes, and coordinate policies.

Intuitively, these patterns make a lot of sense. Given that countries seek to protect their interests, an organization's membership should be expected to reflect its promoters. Yet institutional origins do not fully explain design features like membership. Perhaps most obviously, such accounts do not explain first-order design choices, such as why particular countries are chosen to participate in any one body. And origins do not fully explain why many organizations have grown only incrementally beyond the original group of members, whereas others have undergone dramatic changes in the number and types of agencies participating in them.

Coordination Logics

Institutional design theory helps fill in the gaps by highlighting the important coordination considerations that can inform organizational structure and membership, especially by rational, self-interested parties.

Long-standing coordination theory presents several lessons, one of the most important being that, as a general matter, problem-solving organizations frequently seek to establish the smallest membership possible for addressing any common challenge. Smaller forums make problem solving both faster and less costly, especially in organizations that have supermajority or consensus-based decision rules. As membership increases in size, however, more players must be satisfied with legislation (or appeased), and opportunities increase for players who are seeking to exploit unanimity and to delay the legislative process in order to secure their policy preferences.

Coordination logics thus help explain not only exclusive organizations like the G-20 and the Basel Committee, but also centralized management structures in universal organizations like IOSCO and the IAIS. All else being equal, where fewer individuals negotiate, fewer preferences must be identified and fewer players appeased. Smaller negotiation sets – memorialized by exclusive membership organizations or in structural innovations within multilateral institutions like working groups and technical committees – are generally viewed as more efficient coordination opportunities. Not only are there fewer members and thus likely fewer preferences to be negotiated (and lower bargaining costs), but institutional rules are likely to mobilize actors that share several core characteristics – like wealth, geographic location, domestic financial market size, private market status, or regulatory philosophies. Owing to their similarities, participants in exclusive arrangements may have a clearer understanding of one another's expectations and objectives or may enjoy greater trust and familiarity through their shared background and earlier interactions. Although collective problems may not be eliminated, they can be significantly reduced, even minimized.

That said, membership size does not by itself determine the costs and benefits of any particular institutional arrangement. The nature of the issue area to be addressed by parties is also important. Some problems, in short, are inherently difficult to resolve among many parties, especially when some jurisdictions have higher switching or compliance costs than others, or when a standard may generate skewed advantages for one jurisdiction's market participants. Regulators' solutions to challenges may thus leave one or more parties dissatisfied or even worse off than they were before the cross-border negotiations were launched. Meanwhile, other regulatory standards – like those involving procedural matters like enforcement cooperation, information sharing, and technical assistance – constitute what are relatively pure coordination problems. Participants share common preferences and the benefits of cooperation are generally reciprocal, making coordination easy. In such instances, the deployment of a multilateral organization can help facilitate cooperation by serving as a forum for expansive regulatory interaction and the broad participation of members in those forums that decide policy should not necessarily generate high coordination costs.

Just as some problems can potentially be addressed through coalitions, others may require engagement by all regulators, big and small, in order to be effective. This kind of policy approach has been historically tied to issues like fraud and consumer protection. Criminals can locate themselves virtually anywhere and can be increasingly associated with issues relating to systemic risk, where the failure of any institution – whether banks in New York, Italy, or Thailand – can set off a range of consequences that can undermine the global economy. Large and diverse negotiation sets can generate new opportunities for resolving conflicts and reaching mutually beneficial arrangements. When the parties have different priorities, for example, and thus price the costs or benefits differently, albeit not antagonistically, joint gains from cooperation are possible. This situation may arise especially in cross-functional networks like the G-20 or the FSB, where political elites with broad mandates periodically participate in organizational proceedings. In such settings, cooperation might be achieved through simple horse trading along different sectors. Alternatively, actors may be able to incentivize agreement by linking compliance with a particular standard with market access in other related or unrelated financial sectors.

Power

The institutional designs embodied in soft law instruments can entrench power relationships that can, in turn, influence the kind of policy that emerges from these organizations. Even a cursory review of various institutional designs shows that certain institutional formats can provide privileged points of input for some regulators and also keep others out. Exclusive institutional designs permit a narrow band of decision makers to participate in groups as members. Innovations within a structure can change the amount of input any one regulator has in the legislative process. Likewise, institutional design and procedural rules can have an enormous impact on the form and substance of an organization's legislative products. Privileged players are able to construct rules that allow them to forward their policy preferences.

At the initial design stage, whether or not a potential party is able to have its preferred institutional design realized depends on that regulator's negotiating leverage. A regulator may, for example, threaten to withhold participation unless its organizational preferences are accepted. This kind of strategy certainly arises at the bilateral level with regard to substantive issues, as we saw in Canada's relations with the United States, and has been an important means by which regulators – including the EU, the United States, and Japan – have influenced the policy of accounting, securities, and banking organizations. National regulators can also threaten to create alternative competing forums for coordination. Between 1992 and 2001, for example, a group of national accounting standard setters representing Australia, Canada, New Zealand, the United Kingdom, and the United States formed a working group (known as G4 + 1) and threatened to create an alternative standard setter of accounting if key structural and substantive changes were not made in the IASC.

Some regulators can decide to withhold funding if their priorities are not addressed – a frequent concern for international organizations due to their relatively small secretariats and dependence on the full participation of key constituent regulators. Such concerns have been most notably tied to high-profile organizations like the United Nations, where the United States, in particular, has periodically withheld 20 percent of its contributions to the United Nations' regular budget in an attempt to compel the organization to reform its voting rules on budgetary matters. Withholding funding commonly arises in international standard setting. As recently as 2007, the European

Commission ordered the IASB to improve its governance or risk forfeiting its annual funding of what was then £4.3 million.

As with regulatory export more generally, those regulators that oversee the largest capital markets will usually dictate terms with regard to institutional design and development. The prospect of their nonparticipation tends to have the greatest implications for an organization's success. If major financial powers do not participate in an organization, not only will it potentially be perceived as weak, but it may also, in practice, fail to obtain the degree of coverage of major capital markets needed for its rules to inform or affect the behavior or firms in nonparticipating jurisdictions. That said, even regulators of large markets run risks where they refrain from participating in international regulatory forums. Among other things, organizations may simply proceed without their input and still cobble together sufficient buy-in to create pressures on firms to switch to the organization's policy preferences. And even if powerful regulators of major markets are able to sway the policy of international standard setters from the outside, they may do so in ways that undermine their credibility as neutral technocrats.

Once regulators opt into an institution and participate as members, they help create a positive-feedback dynamic by which they increase the attractiveness of the organization to those outside the network. International organizations are, in other words, much like a foreign language. As the number of people who participate in the language community increases, the attractiveness of learning the language increases for those outside the system. As the number of members of grows, and as more members acknowledge the organization as a source of international financial law and its pronouncements, nonmembers become more incentivized to accept existing governance structures and standards.

Initial decisions among members concerning an organization's institutional design can also have lasting repercussions. Generally, as organizations mature, new members will be poorly positioned to negotiate new policies or institutional structures in the absence of buy-in from incumbents since consensus-based or supermajoritarian decision rules give incumbents leverage to block reforms. To be sure, regulatory changes are possible and – as we see in shifts in the G-20, FSB, and other organizations – do occur, especially if outsiders come with new clout that buffers the network effects generated by international organizations. But early membership in international organizations can hold important advantages that help explain the durability of institutional designs and the relative stability of membership rosters in most organizations.

Not surprisingly, regulators enjoying privileged membership or organizational status have been reluctant to share their authority with others. Throughout the 1990s, for example, members of groups like the G-7 and

IASB consistently evinced a deep reluctance to transition to other broader platforms, even as emerging economies grew – in part because members did not want to cede their influence by operating in larger groups. Similarly, the Basel Committee refrained from expanding for many years, leading to charges of its being an oligopolistic regulatory forum of developed countries. Even ostensibly universal organizations are reluctant to expand policy cores. IOSCO's Technical Committee, for example, has expanded its membership only once since its creation (in 2009), when it invited Brazil, China, and India to join in response to the economic crisis.[77]

Power politics are pervasive but are rarely asserted outright. Instead, other motives are usually offered for actions by regulators that support or promote their influence in the regulatory system. International accounting again serves as a good example. International regulators had, as mentioned above, long voiced criticism of the IASB due to its ostensible lack of "independence," and various regulators – most vociferously the SEC – urged structural reforms. Importantly, however, the reforms that took place involved not only broad moves away from the professional associations, but also changes that highlighted the power of several key members. A monitoring board was created and made responsible for appointing the agency's board of trustees (and by extension the personnel). The Monitoring Board was itself staffed by six key members: a representative from the European Commission, the chair of the IOSCO Emerging Market Committee, the chair of the IOSCO Technical Committee, the commissioner of Japan Financial Services Agency, the chairman of the US SEC, and as an observer, the chairman of the Basel Committee on Banking Supervision. As a result, the regulators of the largest financial centers had special input and powers regarding the direction of the body. Additionally, constitutional changes were made that explicitly allowed the IASB to rely on members for research on policymaking activities – benefiting, of course, those regulators with superior budgets and resources.

Legitimacy

Finally, design features can reflect various social logics and pressures that may have practical repercussions. This topic will be addressed extensively in chapter 4, but for now suffice it to say that organizations are driven to incorporate the institutional practices considered by constituents and stakeholders to be appropriate. To the extent that they succeed in doing so, organizations can

---

[77] Douglas W. Arner & Ross P. Buckley, *Redesigning the Architecture of the Global Financial System*, 11 MELB. J. INT'L L. 185, 210 n.114 (2010).

increase their legitimacy and their survival prospects, and can strengthen their position relation to other, similar organizations that may not have fully incorporated such practices.[78] Standard-setting bodies thus adopt whatever practices they believe that their institutional environment deems suitable or proper, at times irrespective of whether such practices reduce costs relative to benefits.[79]

Legitimacy is understood by different persons, countries, and cultures in different ways, though it is almost always associated to some extent with democratic governance and participation. When participation in decision making is broadly based and diverse sets of persons and countries are able to participate in international forums, more perspectives are brought to bear on any regulatory approach or problem. Additionally, when membership is universal, there are fewer opportunities for participant countries to create rules that are self-serving or that may harm or disadvantage any nonparticipating jurisdiction's market participants unfairly. By contrast, when organizations are more exclusive in their membership, or are more centralized in their decision-making processes, they can be deemed less legitimate. Institutions become more open to charges of ideological and capture by constituent members, and nonparticipants can become skeptical of standards emerging from them. Rules may consequently be less persuasive for financial authorities as governing standards and thus have a diminished impact on the governance of cross-border market participants.

Legitimacy has, as a consequence, been a rising concern in the international regulatory community, especially as financial globalization has moved apace and as developing countries have sought to participate in international standard setting more fully. Indeed, recent changes in the makeup of various agenda- and standard-setting organizations – such as the G-20's displacement of the G-7, and the expansion of membership in bodies like the Basel Committee, FSB, and IOSCO Technical Committee – were at least in part spurred by critical perceptions of earlier institutional arrangements as insufficiently representative of the global economy and the stakeholders in it. And as we explore later throughout chapter 4, demands for further reforms of both democratic governance and effective global standard setting persist.

CONCLUSIONS

International financial law is animated by various levels of governance. Domestically, financial regulatory authorities enjoy formal mandates, which are

---

[78] John L. Campbell, Institutional Change and Globalization 18 (2004).
[79] Id.

usually provided by legislatures. They then interpret and implement rules of parliamentary and congressional bodies in ways that give them a hard law effect. In carrying out their mandate, they also participate in international organizations that exhibit few of the institutional trappings associated with formal international organizations like secretariats, independent staffs, and large resources. Moreover, the primary products of these bodies are not hard law, but informal codes, standards reports, and best practices.

The allocation of various functional roles of international standard setters reveals an increasingly "vertically" integrated regulatory system. Broad-based and more-political institutions set agendas and assess gaps, whereas more-technocratic sectoral and specialist standard setters promulgate best practices and, in some instances, granularized rules. Monitoring has meanwhile been dominated by the IMF and World Bank. Regulatory agencies participate in multiple forums at different levels and generally have an important role moving the agenda and standard-setting processes forward.

Meanwhile, from a "horizontal" vantage point, we see a system consisting of highly variable processes of organizational governance. Despite their soft law foundations, the standard-setting bodies that drive standard setting and international agendas typically possess highly developed institutional structures, each with its own mix of membership rules, decision rules, and decision-making processes. Thus, even where institutions occupy roughly equivalent roles in the international regulatory system – as sectoral standard setters, for example, or as agenda setters – they can exhibit considerable heterogeneity in institutional design. Some, like the Basel Committee, are more exclusive than others; some are more technocratic and less political; and still others vary in the degree of market participation, with the ISDA, IASB, and IFAC providing the most obvious examples of market participants as legislating actors.

Returning, then, to our original discussion, several observations concerning the international regulatory structure compel a reassessment of traditional legal and international relations theory. Most notably, the international regulatory system reveals that formality is not necessarily required for sustained international governmental cooperation. Informal organizations can, even in the absence of hard law, organize highly complex patterns of institutional and regulatory interactions. Similarly, soft law, though legally nonbinding, is often relied on by parties to determine who participates (and how), committee structures, institutional agendas, strategies, and more. In such cases, which are common in international financial regulation, soft law serves as a building block and focal point for coordination, and creates patterns of relationships that link agencies, financial authorities, and heads of state.

The fragmented character of the international regulatory system, which itself is the product of at times ad hoc and informal cross-border relations, has its downsides. As intergovernmental forums with relatively meager staff resources, agenda- and standard-setting bodies tend to rely heavily on the resources of national regulators for their leadership, participation, resources, and expertise. Verticality also generates a kind of institutional interdependence – most importantly, a dependence upon the broad functional role played by agenda- and standard-setting organizations. The G-20, for example, for all of its power and prominence, relies on the Basel Committee to write banking standards and to provide input on the direction of banking regulation in the future. And as we will discuss in greater for the standards to be implemented, standard setters rely on monitors to comprehensively track compliance and to observe and investigate national regulatory policy.

That said, contrary to some of the more wistful network scholarship, there *is*, to be sure, a cognizable structure of relationships in the international system, albeit one that is dynamic, evolving, and highly malleable. The advantages of such dynamism are those tied to the soft law features undergirding the structure of the international system itself. International organizations – whether the FSF of the 1990s or the more recent incarnations of the IASB or the FSB – can be quickly created and, if necessary, relaunched in diverse institutional guises in order to respond to emerging crises. Thus, an institution like the G-20 can quickly usurp the traditional leadership and agenda setting of another institution, like the G-7, after only one summit meeting among heads of state and financial authorities. Likewise, the FSB can come to work in concert with institutions like the World Bank in assessing the stability of the financial system and in setting regulatory priorities and agendas. Such dynamism is a sharp deviation from traditional hard law institutions where, even if parties agree in principle to certain arrangements, new mandates often involve extended and drawn out legal renegotiations, (re)interpretations of founding documents, and treaty ratifications.

Each standard-setting body, even in its informality, is also a site of power and of power relationships that play themselves out continuously. Internally, each establishes a hierarchy of actors, hubs of (required and optional) interactions, and processes of decision making through informal charters, bylaws, and communiqués – all nonbinding but complied with by members for a variety of practical, political, and economic reasons. And externally, organizations generate rules, both for market participants and for regulators – some of whom have little direct participation in the standard-setting process. Soft administrative designs help establish and even entrench a hierarchy of relationships, actors, and points of view, even while leveraging consensus-based decision rules and embracing persuasion and information sharing as dominant coordination tools. This political economy of standard setting departs, of course, not only from traditional conceptions of international organizations, but also from the "peer-to-peer" nature of intergovernmental coordination long presumed by network theorists. In doing so, it does indeed reveal a new world order – though not entirely the one anticipated by Slaughter and her fellow network theorists.

Ultimately, the observations reveal that not all international organizations, or "nodes" in the "network" of regulators, are created equal. Different standard-setting bodies can involve and empower different regulatory and national authorities. In doing so, they mobilize different political resources, private actors, and market participants. Some organizations may deliver a narrow range of expertise and skills, while others will draw on broader sets of expertise, experience, and interests. A choice of various institutional designs can make some organizations appear more democratic and more accountable, and thus endow their rules and standards with greater intrinsic or social acceptability. We can perhaps best characterize the heterogeneity of international financial law as a set of institutional choices. This heterogeneity militates against the development of a "general" theory of the field, as is often possible in less organizationally diverse fields of law, even though a set of basic assumptions and considerations inform and help explain the institutional designs that we see animating the international financial system.

3

A Compliance-Based Theory of International Financial Law

In this chapter, we explore why – and to what extent – international financial law "matters." Whatever their organizational diversity, the international institutions discussed in the previous chapter are ultimately designed to generate standards to be *implemented* across legal systems of different cultures and legal traditions. When international financial rules and standards are adopted robustly across borders, regulators are better able to ensure adequate cross-border supervision of market participants, no matter where they operate. Opportunities for arbitrage and regulatory competition are dramatically reduced, and enforcement cooperation and information sharing among jurisdictions is enhanced.

Thus ultimately, the effectiveness of international financial organizations depends on regulators complying with the rules that have been agreed to. As we have already seen, however, financial regulatory standards often have disparate costs and benefits across jurisdictions and are thus rarely self-enforcing. If a regulator deems certain rules disadvantageous to its domestic markets, it may fail to honor its commitments. Likewise, if a regulator "lacks confidence that others will do what they say, it has no incentive to take action itself."[1]

From this perspective, international financial law is a curious species of cross-border coordination. Unlike many areas of international economic law – for example, trade, where countries make formal commitments to specific practices by signing treaties – the commitments made by international financial organizations have no legal effect and are unrecognized and nonbinding as a matter of international law. If noncompliance carries no negative consequences, a national regulator can ignore best practices and standards, or it can cherry pick certain aspects of international agreements. A regulator could

---

[1] *See* ANDREW T. GUZMAN, HOW INTERNATIONAL LAW WORKS: A RATIONAL CHOICE THEORY (2008).

officially adopt certain standards but then under-enforce them or ignore them altogether.

Why then are most agreements, rules and standards used for the promulgation of international financial law non-binding? In this chapter, we see that international financial regulation, though formally a species of "soft law," is bolstered by various disciplining mechanisms that render it, under certain circumstances, more coercive than traditional theories of international law predict. As a first-order principle, a regulator's record of compliance with international standards can affect its reputation, and with it, its ability to create coalitions and alliances in the future. Furthermore, international financial rules may, despite their informality, affect the cost of capital for firms operating in noncompliant jurisdictions. In doing so, international financial law can still influence the behavior of regulators and market participants alike. Finally, international standard setting bodies and organizations can act as sources of discipline by subjecting nonconforming regulators to institutional sanctions and shaming.

That said, the existing international financial architecture reveals its own institutional flaws that limit the "compliance pull" of global financial standards. As I show below, not only is monitoring far from comprehensive, but the information generated through monitoring is often not shared with the broader international regulatory community or market participants. And even when information is shared, it often goes unused due to the complex format through which it is disseminated. As a result, the risk-adjusted cost of defection can be low, increasing the likelihood of noncompliance when significant distributional tradeoffs arise. The ultimate strength of any given standard will thus depend on a variety of institutional factors that vary across sectors and organizational settings.

THE CENTRALITY OF SOFT LAW IN INTERNATIONAL FINANCIAL REGULATION

International financial law comprises what is in many ways a unique form of economic governance. As we have already discussed, unlike international trade and monetary affairs, when international laws are made by formal international organizations, regulatory coordination arises through interagency forums with, at best, ambiguous legal status. The initial commitments are not made by treaty but, instead, largely through "soft law" instruments that do not impose formal legal obligations. We saw several examples of these instruments in the previous chapter, as well as some of the legislative achievements of soft law institutions. To help our analysis, we can group the soft law instruments into three broad categories: best practices, regulatory reports and observations, and information sharing and enforcement cooperation agreements.

Best Practices

International financial law often takes the form of best practices, or rules of thumb, that promote sound regulatory supervision.[2] Best practices often concern discrete issue areas, like capital adequacy, optimal disclosure rules, or due diligence techniques for preventing money laundering and terrorist financing. These practices may be promulgated by coalitions of wealthy regional bodies or even by organizations of private actors blessed by national authorities. Best practices sometimes have a broader scope, however, and deal with the general features of sound oversight in a particular financial sector. Key regulatory "core principles" have been promulgated by each of the major international standard setting bodies – the International Organization of Securities Commissions (for securities regulation), the Basel Committee (for banking), and the International Association of Insurance Supervisors (for insurance), as well as other standard setters. As opposed to focusing on one discrete issue, they provide an overview of what broader qualities are necessary for sound supervisory and prudential oversight in a particular sector.

Best practices are also articulated through "codes of conduct" that offer normative pronouncements concerning the ideal conduct of private parties (rather than of regulatory officials). Codes promulgated by IOSCO, for example, prohibit certain forms of self-dealing among securities analysts and work to remove conflicts of interest that are often inherent in operations of investment banks and credit-rating agencies. Though codes of conduct are aimed at private actors and, even more importantly, are not legally mandatory, they are, like best practices, guidelines with which national regulators overseeing their own domestic firms and institutions are expected to comply. For this reason, they are of interest to both the private and public sector.

Countries differ radically from one another with regard to the character of their local market participants and the nature of regulatory challenges that they face as supervisors. Against the background of this diversity, best practices define the minimum shared standards necessary for a healthy or "good" financial regulatory system. They thus carry a significant normative valence. If a country deviates from them, the (rebuttable) presumption is that its approach will prove to be underdeveloped or insufficient. Additionally, best practices

---

[2] Best practices have not been very much analyzed from the standpoint of international law, though have been the subject of insightful scholarly examination in the domestic US context. *See* David Zaring, *Best Practices*, 81 N.Y.U. L. REV. 294–350 (2006).

often double as capacity-building modules: besides acting as normative instruments, they provide functional, off-the-rack rules of good governance that provide flexibility in implementation by allowing countries to take local needs and circumstances to be taken into account in tailoring their own rules. Countries need not start from scratch when creating regulatory approaches and strategies for new (or even old) problems – which would present a daunting and costly challenge, especially for developing countries. Instead, they can both learn from, and elaborate on, international best practices and guidelines that reflect broad, cross-border regulatory concerns and popular consensus.

Regulatory Reports and Observations

Though rarely acknowledged as such, the data that are collected, assessed, and utilized by national and international regulators to craft policy is another important source of international financial law. Reports create an official record of fact drawn on by financial authorities to regulate and supervise markets. At times, these records merely recount data; at others, they record official opinions and institutional perspectives as to financial data and their implications for the broader global economy. In either case, reports help establish a basis for policymaking and often generate normative undercurrents that help define the appropriateness of different regulatory responses. They also, by extension, generate a record of authoritative responses to particular policy challenges. As such, they play a distinctive role in the international financial system. In the wake of the 2008 financial crisis, for example, a range of reports from international organizations offered retrospective analyses identifying the causes of financial market disruptions or attempted to identify future challenges.[3] Other reports have centered on problems in existing regulatory approaches.[4]

Reports affect governance by helping establish tacit commitments by national authorities; for example, when reports identify problems in existing regulatory approaches, sponsors of the document are implicitly sanctioning future efforts to devise solutions to those problems. Reports also record expressions of limited consensus among regulators on the causes, if not the solutions,

---

[3] Monetary & Capital Markets Dep't, Int'l Monetary Fund, Lessons of the Financial Crisis for Future Regulation of Financial Institutions and Markets and for Liquidity Management (2009), *available at* http://www.imf.org/external/np/pp/eng/2009/020409.pdf.

[4] Group of Twenty Summit on Financial Markets and the World Economy, London, U.K., Apr. 2, 2009, *The Global Plan for Recovery and Reform* 47; Technical Comm., Int'l Org. of Securities Comm'ns [IOSCO], Report on the Subprime Crisis (2008), *available at* http://www.iosco.org/library/pubdocs/pdf/IOSCOPD273.pdf.

to emerging challenges, and in cases where they identify certain regulatory practices as "bad" or inefficient, sponsors of the report are tacitly rejecting such practices. In this way, reports take on covenant-like qualities and can serve as way stations to more elaborate regimes. Although signatories possess broad discretion as to future actions, they (and often outsiders) expect of each other that they will avoid any behavior that is contrary to the values or norms expressed in the reports. The reports are, for that reason, highly debated and negotiated instruments.

Information Sharing and Enforcement Cooperation

Finally, many international financial agreements spell out the procedural means by which greater information sharing and enforcement cooperation can be achieved. *Information-sharing* agreements, usually promulgated through memoranda of understanding, address the reality that many domestic financial institutions are globally active. As international actors, these institutions often find it difficult to gain adequate, relevant information for assessing the risk exposures of banks or the possibility of transnational fraud or money laundering. Consequently, national regulators of the banking and securities industries routinely enter into information-sharing agreements whereby the regulators commit to better coordination with one another in order to enhance their prudential oversight and monitoring at home.

Enforcement agreements, whether promulgated through MOUs or broader, information-sharing instruments, detail the terms by which different countries agree to provide one other with assistance when enforcing their domestic rules and obligations abroad. Securities regulators have been especially active in this area and have enacted scores of enforcement MOUs geared toward more effective cross-border cooperation. Through such agreements, gaps arising in transnational cases are narrowed; for example, if a con man in Germany perpetrates a securities fraud against a person in the United States, if the two countries have an enforcement agreement in place, US authorities would be able to use a formal process by which witnesses, evidence, or the proceeds of fraud are accessed with the help of officials in Germany.

COMPLIANCE UNDER "HARD" INTERNATIONAL LAW

As we discussed in the previous chapter, the predominance of soft law in international financial affairs diverges significantly from other fields of international law, especially international trade. Generally speaking, commitments between countries are memorialized as treaties, which often require approval by legislatures, and subsequently recognized internationally as binding on all parties.

One explanation for the popularity of hard law – and in particular, international treaties – is its potential for institution-building. As we have already discussed, international treaties enable the creation of formal institutions that help operationalize coordination and compliance with agreed-upon rules. In treaties, as in any contract, the limited information of the parties can make it difficult for them to anticipate and address all possible contingencies. Parties can anticipate this challenge by creating, or enabling the creation of, formal international organizations to supply missing terms and interpret unclear provisions. Grounded by and in hard law arrangements, such organizations can also monitor compliance by the parties, serve as forums for their disputes, and even exercise their legal authority to enforce parties' compliance with their treaty commitments.

The paradigmatic institutions cited as evidence for such evolutionary dynamics are the WTO and its predecessor, the General Agreement on Tariffs and Trade. In 1948, the United States and its principal economic partners initiated the GATT to promote freer and fairer trade, primarily through negotiated reductions of formal tariffs. Over time, the GATT evolved through successive rounds of treaty negotiations spurred by the United States. Parties took on deeper substantive commitments to reduce trade barriers, and the GATT came to include a secretariat and dispute resolution panels. In 1995, this evolutionary process culminated in the creation of the WTO – an international organization with a distinct legal personality and an almost universal, worldwide membership of more than 150 countries.[5] It has the authority to interpret laws and enjoys more efficient and formalized disciplinary mechanisms than the GATT, whose dispute resolution mechanisms were often delayed or altogether sidelined because disputants blocked proceedings or failed to implement decisions.[6]

Hard law, though not without its skeptics, is also seen as an important coordinating mechanism by public international law theorists. In particular, many theorists view it as a potential source of discipline in the international system. Andrew Guzman has identified several coercive effects of international law that incentivize countries to comply with its dictates. They can be summarized as follows.

---

[5] Joost H.B. Pauwelyn, *The Transformation of World Trade*, 104 MICH. L. REV. 1, 25 (2005).
[6] ROBERT GILPIN, GLOBAL POLITICAL ECONOMY: UNDERSTANDING THE INTERNATIONAL ECONOMIC ORDER 223 (2001).

Reputation and International Law

First, formal international obligations can create reputational pressures that incentivize compliance. When countries make official commitments and then renege on them, they send a signal to future potential treaty partners that they cannot be trusted, which can hamper future prospects for alliances and coordination with others. When a state enters into a treaty, it signals to the other party that it prefers mutual cooperation to noncooperation. Its hope is that this claim will be credible to the other state. If it is, the other state will enter into the agreement, assuming that the payoffs are sufficient. If one of the states then violates the agreement, its ability to make credible promises in the future will be reduced – a so-called loss of reputation.[7]

Those countries that honor their treaty commitments develop strong reputations that help them coordinate with others when they seek to advance their national interests.[8] Guzman notes that all else being equal, a

> state that is known to honor its commitments will find more partners when it seeks to enter into future cooperative arrangements, will be able to extract more generous concessions in exchange for its promises, and will be able to solve more problems of cooperation than will a state that has a less favorable reputation.[9]

A strong reputation can have tangible welfare-enhancing advantages for a country, just as a weak reputation can have real costs for a country. By way of illustrating the power of reputation, let us initially look at international environmental law – one area of regulation in which international treaties do exist. Suppose two countries, A and B, are seeking to lower their environmentally degrading carbon emissions. Suppose further that to do so is costly and requires changing over to different technologies. Given the costs, both countries could be hesitant about the change – one that could disadvantage local firms. To solve the problem, both commit to a treaty in which they agree to lower emissions at the same time. Assume, finally, that country A ultimately does not follow through on its commitment to reduce emissions.

What are the likely reputational costs for A? For starters, it will likely be hard for A to get B to cooperate again in the future, especially on environmental matters. As a result, if A tries to enter into another such treaty with B, it will need to make special efforts to demonstrate its seriousness. Such efforts

[7] GUZMAN, *supra* note 1, at 38.
[8] This idea has been articulated by a variety of theorists, but for a comprehensive assessment, *see id.* at 71–111.
[9] *Id.* at 34.

could mean switching first and adopting the new standard before others (in which case it is exposed to a possible defection by B), subsidizing some or all of the costs that B incurred in relation to the earlier treaty, or maybe even helping B in implementing the new agreement. And, of course, even given such concessions, B may avoid cooperation in view of A's tarnished reputation.

Reputation can thus either yield value in the form of higher payoffs or, instead, result in heavy costs. The shadow of the future, including future gains, acts as a kind of disciplining force against defections from international commitments. When a state enters into an international agreement, it is, in effect, pledging its reputation as a form of a bond. If it violate its agreements, it gives up some of this reputation collateral – which, in practice, means that its promises become less credible. When a state complies with an international rule, particularly one that is not immediately in the state's interest, it signals to the international community that it is willing to "sacrifice current gains in exchange for the ability to credibly enter into cooperative arrangements in the future."[10] The state's reputation improves, and it enjoys more support at a cheaper rate than it would otherwise.

Reciprocity and International Law

Reciprocity is another potential disciplinary strategy available under international legal commitments. A country returns like behavior with like – and thus responds to a defection from a commitment with a defection of its own. Some scholars consider this phenomenon the central component of the "meta theory" of all international law, even multilateral contexts, especially where commitments are official and clear. In practice, however, reciprocal behavior is usually most effective in bilateral contexts, where both parties prefer absolute gains represented by mutual cooperation over mutual defection. When a party decides to defect, and another party responds reciprocally, the defecting party will not secure the gains associated with cooperation. Additionally, it may incur reputational costs that can undermine its cooperative ventures in the future.

Consider a simple example in which two parties enter into an arms control treaty requiring that each maintain a reduced, equal number of nuclear weapons. Theoretically, the parties may be better off if both decide to dismantle their weapons, but each may also be strongly tempted to renege in order to achieve a strategic advantage over the other party. If defection is countered with a reciprocal abandonment of the treaty, both countries could find themselves worse off. In addition to potentially destabilizing the military situation,

[10] *Id.* at 35.

future cooperation efforts would be undermined because future promises to reduce weapons would be less credible. A one-time, opportunistic gain may result in less advantage than envisioned, along with future noncooperation costs.

Retaliation and International Law

Formal legal obligations also enable a range of retaliatory measures justified under international law. As Guzman again notes,

> [r]etaliatory sanctions can take on a variety of forms. They can include taking on some kind of economic action, such as levying duties or taxes on imports from the offending state or curtailing one's economic, financial or technical assistance to that state; reducing cooperation in some other area, and, where resources are available, potential military force.[11]

The WTO operationalizes what is likely the best-known form of retaliation in international economic relations. Through its dispute panels, it can authorize states that are harmed by rule violations by other states to retaliate by suspending equivalent concessions or other obligations under the covered agreements.[12] Consequently, the organization's enforcement strategy enjoys what Nzelibe rightly describes as a robust, tit-for-tat approach: "if state A is found to breach its obligations to state B and state A refuses to remedy the breach, state B can suspend an equivalent measure of its market access obligations to state A."[13] Though reciprocal in nature, it is retaliatory insofar as an aggrieved state need not target the sector in which a commitment violation has occurred. The WTO thus leverages institutions and actors in ways that permit strong monitoring and enforcement of commitments – which makes WTO rules directly applicable to member states.

Scholars have noted that retaliation (and for that matter, reciprocity) can have a deterrent function. "When a violation has taken place and is ongoing, sanctions can signal to the violating state that the sanctioning state will punish violations."[14] Retaliation helps establish the reputation of the retaliator as willing to punish certain violations – though it may be costly for retaliating states to administer, which undermines its optimality as a coercive mechanism.

---

[11] *Id.* at 47.

[12] Jide Nzelibe, *The Credibility Imperative: The Political Dynamics of Retaliation in the World Trade Organization's Dispute Resolution Mechanism*, 6 THEORETICAL INQUIRIES L. 215, 215 (2005).

[13] *Id.*

[14] GUZMAN, *supra* note 1, at 48.

As with other compliance theories, reputation, reciprocity, and retaliation are not consider to be sufficient in themselves to induce universal compliance. No particular sanction or set of sanctions – except, perhaps, the effective use of force, inherently prevents defection by a treaty counterparty. Some important countries may be "too big to ignore," with the consequence that the practical reputational consequences for them may well be negligible compared to other countries. When deciding how to act, a state will compare the relative payoffs associated with compliance and with noncompliance. As with a breach of any contractual obligation, noncompliance is tempting only if the payoff from a violation – from which any reputational, reciprocal, or retaliatory costs must be deducted – is larger than the payoff from compliance.[15]

EXPLANATIONS FOR SOFT LAW'S DOMINANCE IN INTERNATIONAL FINANCIAL LAW

Until recently, rational choice theories of public international law have seemed to have little relevance for international financial law since, by definition, international financial law lacks the legal obligation and formality of hard law instruments like treaties. Models rely on commitments that are "solemn" and, by extension, official in nature. By contrast, dominant explanations for soft law's prevalence as a coordinating mechanism for financial regulators have borrowed from two broader theories about the use of soft law: "contractarian" analyses, which characterize soft law as a risk-mitigation device, and "soft power" theories, which interpret soft law as an essential facilitator of ongoing, productive coordination and cooperation.

The Contractarian Analysis

Of the two, perhaps the most useful is the contractarian stream of international relations, articulated most prominently by Kenneth Abbott and Duncan Snidal and later by Charles Lipton. Drawing on law and economics frameworks, these scholars compare the costs and benefits of soft and hard law by analogizing the making of international agreements to that of contracts. By identifying the objectives that contracting parties have when drawing up a contract, they apply this information to the objectives that countries have when considering the appropriate form for memorializing international agreements.

One of the first and most important advantages of soft law, they argue, is that action can be undertaken quickly and efficiently, which is often an objective of bargaining parties. States, they note, not only seek to generate credible

---

[15] GUZMAN, *supra* note 1.

commitments and norms in following certain policies, but also seek to do so with speed and efficiency. In this regard, hard law is unattractive. Treaty making often entails months, if not years, of negotiation between heads-of-state or their representatives, and even after an agreement is reached, approval by domestic legislatures is typically required to ensure its maximum effectiveness. Soft law, by contrast, provides a decisively more efficient means of agreement making. Perhaps most importantly, it requires neither extensive participation by heads-of-state nor lengthy ratification procedures. Instead, agreements can be entered into at the highest levels of government – or even between administrative agencies and technocrats – with relatively little interference from outsiders. As a result, fewer interests need be accounted for, easing negotiation. Because of the flexibility afforded by soft law, parties can also amend accords relatively easily, so long as agreement among parties exists.[16]

Contractarians additionally argue that soft law involves far fewer "sovereignty costs," or constraints, that may limit a state's ability to follow its own national prerogatives. Sovereignty costs arise, at a most basic level, at any time that countries are no longer able to follow their national prerogatives. Hard law can often be quite restrictive: retaliation, reciprocal noncompliance, and damage to reputation act as important disciplines for most countries and are enabled and legitimized by the presence of formal international agreements.

Sovereignty costs are often especially steep under many hard law arrangements because countries must accept external authority over significant political or economic decisions. International agreements implicitly or explicitly empower international or supranational authorities – which are typically unelected and not subject to domestic forms of accountability – to act in ways that may limit states' ability to determine entire classes of issues.[17] Indeed, in some cases, such delegations of authority inform and determine the relations between a state and its citizens – and not just the relevant domestic market participants.

Scholars in both political science and law point frequently to the WTO and to the EU when highlighting the sovereignty costs implicit in treaties.[18] Other, lesser-known treaties, however, also provide illuminating examples.

---

[16] Charles Lipson, *Why Are Some International Agreements Informal?*, 45 INT'L ORG. 495, 500 (1991) (noting that although treaties often contain clauses permitting renegotiation, the process is slow and cumbersome).

[17] Kenneth W. Abbott & Duncan Snidal, *Hard and Soft Law in International Governance*, 54 INT'L ORG. 421, 437 (2000).

[18] *See* Douglas W. Arner & Michael Taylor, *The Global Financial Crisis and the Financial Stability Board: Hardening the Soft Law of International Financial Regulation?* (Asian Inst. of Int'l Fin. Law, Working Paper No. 6, 2009), *available at* http://papers.ssrn.com/sol3/papers. cfm?abstract_id=1427084 (noting that the starting point for international economic law is the WTO); *see also* Waltraud Schelkle, *EU Fiscal Governance: Hard Law in the Shadow of Soft*

Investment treaties allow investors to sue signatories in special international arbitral proceedings when a signatory interferes with the investors' rights to enjoy their foreign investments. Although investment treaties reduce risk for exporters of goods and capital, they also restrain the ability of states to undertake even beneficial regulation – a situation partly due to surprisingly expansive interpretations of "expropriation" by arbitral tribunals. For example, in the famous *Metalclad* case,[19] the prohibition against expropriation in the North American Free Trade Agreement enabled a US multinational to sue Mexico, the host government, when local authorities engaged in environmental regulation. Similarly, other companies, under the investor protection provisions of bilateral investment treaties, have sued Argentina for its attempts to regulate utility prices in the wake of the country's financial crisis.[20] Consequently, countries that have entered into such treaties have found themselves subject to severe constraints with regard to how they conduct essential state business.

The argument goes that soft law's informal status allows parties to avoid such unexpected sovereignty costs. Because such agreements are not legally binding, regulators can choose not to adopt certain of their elements. This flexibility applies both to actions prescribed in reports and to those detailed in instruments laying out best practices. Additionally, even when parties have signaled an intent to pursue a particular course of action, they may defect from such soft commitments if later circumstances suggest that compliance would not be in their best interests. International theorists predict that such defections from commitments carry no reputational consequences since no "legal" obligations have been violated. The typically open, prescriptive language of soft law agreements ("parties intend to" or "strive to achieve") creates no legal obligations under international law; there are no specific commitments that could, if not carried out, damage a state's reputation. Parties to soft law agreements have the opportunity to learn about the impact of certain policy choices over time, and they retain the flexibility to manage their own affairs.[21]

Law?, 13 COLUM. J. EUR. L. 705, 719 (2007) (describing interplay of soft and hard law in key EU financial domains).

[19] Metalclad Corp. v. United Mexican States, ICSID Case No. ARB(AF)/97/1, Final Award (Aug. 30, 2000).

[20] *See* Lucien J. Dhooge, *The North American Free Trade Agreement and the Environment: The Lessons of Metalclad Corporation v. United Mexican States*, 10 MINN. J. GLOBAL TRADE 209 (2001) (describing Metalclad case); William W. Burke-White, *The Argentine Financial Crisis: State Liability Under BITs and the Legitimacy of the ICSID System*, 3 ASIAN J. WTO & INT'L HEALTH L. & POL'Y 199 (2008) (assessing claims against Argentine for its regulatory responses to its financial crisis).

[21] Abbott & Snidal, *supra* note 17, at 423.

Finally, soft law helps facilitate agreement by lowering the risk of uncertainty that pervades policy issue areas. Potential parties to an agreement often are skeptical or anxious concerning the adoption of any particular approach. "The underlying problems may not be well understood, so states cannot anticipate all possible consequences of a legalized arrangement."[22] When entering into potentially long-term, durable agreements, such as those that address novel products or vehicles for investment or investment strategies, the uncertainty can be substantial because the full impact of the relevant rules is unknown. The wrong standard can, in theory, not only disadvantage domestic firms, but also prove to be inefficient by either overly burdening firms or providing inadequate oversight of financial activities.

Hard law deals with this situation in two ways. First, it can simply leave contentious terms imprecise or constricted (omissions that, in the eyes of some, render the agreement "soft").[23] Imprecision or absence of terms, however, weakens the usefulness of the agreement (perhaps even more so than by using soft law instruments) because uncertainty about the expectations of basic commitments can undermine the agreement's efficacy. International organizations may be empowered to fill in the interpretative gaps of treaties, but sovereignty costs can be significant. Second, as Larry Helfer notes, treaties may incorporate reservations or, more importantly, allow signatories to exit from commitments altogether.[24] Yet treaty exit is not always easy (or even permitted), and it can take decades for countries to provide proper notice to fellow signatories to extract themselves from their obligations.

By contrast, soft law provides a more attractive option by employing nonlegal obligations that allow participants to avoid unacceptable and unforeseen events.[25] Without formal legality, parties to agreements are able to see the impact of rules in practice in order to better assess their benefits, and the parties also retain the flexibility to bypass any unpleasant surprises that the rules may hold.[26] Thus, soft law affords strategies for both individual and collective learning whereby parties can work out problems over time.[27] Particularly in the financial regulatory context, soft law allows parties to experiment and, if necessary, to change direction when new information emerges or new costs arise. Soft law also serves as a communicative mechanism; as new challenges

[22] *Id.* at 441.

[23] *Id.* at 442.

[24] Metalclad Corp. v. United Mexican States, *supra* note 19.

[25] Abbott & Snidal, *supra* note 17, at 442.

[26] *Id.*

[27] *Id.*

arise, countries can signal to one another their intention to take a particular regulatory action or to adopt a particular regulatory approach.

Soft Power Theories

The value of soft law has been extolled by scholars of both international relations and international law, who have come to view soft law as a force in its own right. In this regard, network theorists have been the most vocal. Recall that network theory elevates inter–administrative agency processes to technocratic solutions that engender peer-to-peer collaboration and community. Key to the success of such collaboration, as framed by its leading exponents, is that these processes are distinctly noncoercive. Policies are neither advanced nor adopted by military force or economic coercion, but by the power of persuasion and attraction.[28] Smart regulators leverage their soft power to shape collective goals and policy agendas to respond to ever evolving and, at times, fast-paced challenges.

Soft law is an essential and, indeed, logical centerpiece of such a system. In contrast to hard law, which can lever sanctions or brute violence, soft law is not coercive; instead, it is an expression of cooperation. Soft law's primary objective is to produce dominant norms with which to coordinate behavior. Hard law is ill suited to this task: it commands in lieu of encouraging collaboration; it generates ossified, top-down rule making in lieu of the flexible, bottom-up governance required in a dynamic financial environment. Soft law is consequently cast by some scholars as an alternative model of international rule making, distinct from the traditional statecraft that operates among sovereigns.[29] In addition to facilitating low-cost collaboration, soft law serves as a driver for a collective approach to international engagement; countries can tackle complex, quickly evolving global problems that cannot be addressed unilaterally. Soft law is thus necessary as a means of building trust for sustained and effective collective action.

HOW THE DOMINANT EXPLANATIONS FALL SHORT

For all of their obvious differences, a common condition precedent undergirds both contractarian and soft power accounts of soft law effectiveness. Network theorists envisage soft law as a means of power in a world animated by similarly

---

[28] *Id.*

[29] Anne-Marie Slaughter & David T. Zaring, *Networking Goes International: An Update*, ANN. REV. L. SOC. SCI., Dec. 2006, at 211, 217.

situated, albeit decentralized, parties engaged in a cooperative joint venture. Likewise, contractarians – though acknowledging the potentially diverse range of viewpoints – often imply in their emphasis on efficiency that parties have relatively congruent interests that enable them to agree upon effective forms of cooperation.

This common presumption is not implausible. As we saw at the outset of this book, one of the key drivers behind international coordination is the desire to mitigate "systemic risk" – in particular, the economic spillovers generated by unsound regulatory practices in other countries. By acting together, it is hoped that the international community of financial authorities can impose minimal standards in every country to reduce the likelihood of institutional and legislative failings. For example, financial institutions can be assured that counterparties have met capital-adequacy requirements, and investors participating in foreign markets can be assured that foreign firms are making adequate disclosures.

The dominant perspective among legal scholars over the last decade is that international financial collaboration is a resolutely cooperative venture that cannot be reduced to the interests or relative power of regions or individual states.[30] The challenge of coordination lies in the information asymmetries between countries. Coordination involves two essential steps. First, a common standard must be identified (usually by experts) and agreed upon. This first step requires significant time and resources because the available data must be collected, assessed, and distilled in order to formulate an optimal rule. Second, each regulator must then choose to apply that regime, or arbitragers and fraudsters will target the weakest regime, in which case many of the efforts of those regulators that adopt the optimal rule will be effectively wasted. Thus – on this standard analysis – in order for soft law solutions to work, there must be both sufficient information sharing to find the optimal solution and sufficient trust between countries for leaders to feel confident that commitments will be honored and fulfilled.

Despite its plausibility, this common view of the international regulatory process is, as we have already seen, unrealistic. It fails to recognize that rules have distributive implications that can undermine existing agreements between parties and that can frustrate parties and prevent them from finding any common position. Four dynamics are of especially important in this context.

---

[30] *See id.* at 215–16 (describing the common interests regulators have to cooperate); Charles K. Whitehead, *What's Your Sign?: International Norms, Signals and Compliance*, 27 MICH. J. INT'L L. 695 (2006) (describing common interests and peer pressure of regulatory communities).

Divergent Regulatory Philosophies

Countries often have divergent regulatory philosophies, with the consequence that they disagree on the nature or extent of problems to be addressed. Even when countries agree on the nature of a problem, they will often disagree as to the appropriate policy solutions. For example, different regulators may have different views on the proper role of government in the marketplace, and these views, in turn, will inform their policy analyses and prescriptions. Leaders of some countries believe that government should take a prominent role in policing institutions. Others assert that the market should be subject to as little governmental intervention as possible and that a laissez-faire attitude best encourages a society's welfare.

Similarly, countries can have very different views on the relationship of the market and market participants to society. For example, some nations, such as the United States, believe that corporations exist for, and should be geared exclusively toward, maximizing profits for investors, whereas others may contend that corporations exist primarily to promote domestic industries, provide employment, or enhance a country's general welfare.[31] Similarly, the financial system may be viewed from the standpoint of promoting different policy goals. For example, some policymakers may view credit access as a means of providing "blind" liquidity such that capital can be directed to its most productive uses, whereas other policymakers may view credit access as a means of achieving certain policy ends, like expanded home ownership.[32] These different policy agendas can be problematic since they potentially lead to different regulatory decisions concerning the regulation of the relevant financial entities.[33]

Even more fundamentally, regulators often differ in what they view as acceptable risks. Financial regulation involves various trade-offs. As the economist Dani Rodrik has noted, "the more you value financial stability, the more you [may] have to sacrifice financial innovation" since financial regulation often limits the range of activities in which firms are permitted to engage.[34] Convergence is typically seen as a good thing, but convergence can actually occur in relation to what prove to be ineffective or inefficient standards, which are then internalized by firms and the greater economy.

---

[31] Lawrence A. Cunningham, *From Convergence to Comity in Corporate Law: Lessons from the Inauspicious Case of SOX*, 1 INT'L J. DISCLOSURE & GOVERNANCE 269, 272 (2004).

[32] GLOBAL FINANCE IN CRISIS: THE POLITICS OF INTERNATIONAL REGULATORY CHANGE 6 (Eric Helleiner et al. eds., 2010).

[33] *Id.* at 277 (describing French skepticism of the American model of profit maximization).

[34] Dani Rodrik, *A Plan B for Global Finance*, THE ECONOMIST, March 14, 2009, at 80.

Countries will weigh the trade-offs differently. Those that are more risk averse may be philosophically and economically more willing to sacrifice innovation and flexibility in order to avoid shocks to their financial systems; such countries would presumably be less averse to the costs of regulatory error and would seek to purchase greater financial stability than that to be achieved through other regulatory alternatives. Countries that are less risk averse would likely prefer greater flexibility to pursue financial innovation and to develop their domestic capital markets, despite potential systemic risks, in accordance with their own needs. Agreement can therefore be difficult to achieve: different nations will "want to sit on different points along the pareto frontier."[35]

Even when the benefits from cooperation are readily apparent, differences in regulatory philosophy may render it difficult for agencies to reach a consensus. Although some national regulators might be willing to enter into deeper cross-border dialogues and partnerships, others may well be disinclined to wander from their traditional regulatory missions and philosophies. In such circumstances, policy disagreements can lead to political or even diplomatic confrontations if countries seek to unilaterally export their national regulatory perspectives in order to gain influence and avoid the potential sovereignty costs of adopting regulatory models that run against their own preferences.[36]

Adjustment Costs

Significant adjustment costs further hamper the coordination process, a topic discussed in depth by Dan Drezner.[37] Because of history, culture, and custom, countries have vastly different starting points as to what kinds of regulations they have in place.[38] Effective compliance with a new international norm may require a country to revise its core regulatory framework and even its basic political structure in relation to the amount of power or discretion that administrative agencies can exercise.[39] These changes may be difficult to achieve in that regulatory agencies and lawmakers, accustomed

---

[35] *Id.*

[36] Daniel W. Drezner, All Politics is Global: Explaining International Regulatory Regimes 31 (2007).

[37] *See generally id.*

[38] *Id.* at 41. *See also* Mark J. Roe, *Legal Origins, Politics, and Modern Stock Markets*, 120 Harv. L. Rev. 460 (2006); Donald C. Langevoort, *The SEC, Retail Investors, and the Institutionalization of the Securities Markets*, 95 Va. L. Rev. (2009) (discussing different traditional market participation in the Europe and the United States and its implications for national regulatory approaches).

[39] Cunningham, *supra* note 31, at 278 (explaining the European public reactions to SOX).

to the status quo, may resist such reform.[40] Furthermore, adjustment almost inevitably requires the allocation of more resources to enforcement activities. For many states, especially in emerging markets, such resources are not available.

Regulators must also take into consideration the compliance costs borne by their domestic firms, as well as by foreign firms, when adjusting to new international standards. Changes in transparency requirements, though helping to inform investors and other market participants, often require firms to hire lawyers, accountants, and other financial services providers to ensure that their interactions with investors do not run afoul of new regulations. Similarly, reforms touching on corporate governance, like the Sarbanes-Oxley Act, may require some firms to jettison assets specific to previous domestic and regulatory regimes – changes that may substantially affect the organization of firms' internal affairs and management structures.[41]

Perhaps the most substantial adjustment costs are those involved in prudential measures aimed at improving the safety or soundness of a firm or financial institution. Rules that curb the scope of a bank's financial activities can force it to refrain from practices that are highly profitable. Similarly, higher capital standards require affected financial institutions to keep more capital on their books or more of their savings idle when lending in order to cover the possibility of loans not being repaid. As a result, banks make fewer loans, which decreases both their ultimate revenue and, more generally – since capital is taken out of the relevant economy – the growth of GDP.

In virtually all cases, new standards mean adjustment, which entails costs that may be unequally distributed. If a firm is operating in a jurisdiction already close to the international standard, or in one that becomes the international standard, it will internalize few costs. Firms in other jurisdictions, however, will spend more on compliance, for they need more counseling by auditors, lawyers, and other financial advisers.[42] Resources that could have been used

---

[40] DREZNER, *supra* note 36, at 46.

[41] *Id.* at 5. This was, for instance, the case with Sarbanes-Oxley, the US law which required of all firms, including foreign issuers, that their audit committees be independent. Though laudable in principle, this requirement conflicted with the statutorily required organization of German and Dutch firms, which required worker participation on supervisory board aimed (ironically) with disciplining CEO compensation. *See* Cunningham, *supra* note 31. Thus SOX's outlawing of non-independent audit committee members in some ways helped weaken German and Dutch controls on management. *Id.*

[42] *See, e.g.,* CRA INT'L, SARBANES-OXLEY SECTION 404 COSTS AND IMPLEMENTATION ISSUES: SURVEY UPDATE 3 (2005), *available at* http://www.crai.com/Publications/listingdetails .aspx?id=6928&pubtype (stating that the average Sarbanes-Oxley compliance cost per company for financial advisor services was $7.8 million).

elsewhere are allocated to compliance, putting these firms at a competitive disadvantage.

Competitive Market Pressures

Agreement can also be difficult because adopting particular rules may undermine a country's competitiveness in terms of attracting capital and financial transactions. In a world of globally mobile capital, countries compete with one another across borders for investment, investors, and financial institutions. To attract firms and transactions to their borders – thereby bring in resources and tax revenues – governments employ a variety of regulatory strategies to boost their countries' attractiveness as places in which to transact and invest. In some countries, stringent rules and regulations are applied to firms raising capital, as well as to banks and other depositary institutions.[43] In this way, firms operating in the country signal their commitment to transparency, strong corporate governance, and financial health. Other countries impose weaker regulatory standards. Many firms find that the costs of compliance generated by stringent regulation outweigh its benefits, so some countries adopt less stringent rules to minimize the cost of legal, accounting, and other advisory services tied to raising capital. Weaker standards may also make local institutions and market participants more competitive abroad. The adoption of a certain accounting rule, for example, can insulate banks from cyclical downturns in that fewer assets need to be written off in times of financial distress. Similarly, lower capital-reserve requirements allow banks to invest more of their money and thus to enjoy higher returns (though also exposed to greater risk).

Weak regulatory standards are most commonly associated with offshore financial centers. Smaller, capital-poor countries may have no other choice

---

[43] *See* John C. Coffee, Jr., *Racing Towards the Top?: The Impact of Cross-listings and Stock Market Competition on International Corporate Governance*, 102 COLUM. L. REV. 1757, 1780–82 (2002) (noting that the United States is one example of this regulatory competition technique). *See also* Rafael la Porta et al., *Legal Determinants of External Finance*, 52 J. FIN. 1131 (1997) (arguing that strong equity markets require strong minority rights). Indeed, securities markets may not be able to expand to their full potential in the absence of some mandatory legal regimes protecting minority shareholder rights. *See* John C. Coffee, Jr., *The Rise of Dispersed Ownership: The Roles of Law and the State in the Separation of Ownership and Control*, 111 YALE L.J. 1, 65 (2001). Nevertheless, even in the absence of highly developed law, equity markets can, and have, still developed. There are a variety of institutional accounts as to why this is the case. *See* Katharina Pistor & Chenggang Xu, *Governing Stock Markets in Transition Economies: Lessons from China*, 7 AM. L. & ECON. REV. 184 (2005) (arguing that administrative governance can substitute for formal legal governance). Usually, however, securities markets ultimately encounter shocks that result in a loss of investor confidence that legal institutions help buffer against.

than to offer weak regulations to market participants to attract capital. With no alternative, they maintain weaker standards as they have "nothing to lose" with regard to the rules they adopt. Cooperation may be difficult because the costs and benefits across jurisdictions differ so greatly – *even with regard to systemic risk*. Different countries have different degrees of exposure to the financial system. Some countries may, for example, be net exporters of "bad" financial products to foreign investors – whether stocks, bonds, or more recent exotic instruments such as mortgage-backed securities, covenant-lite loans, and credit default swaps. In such cases, countries have few incentives to cooperate and to adopt more stringent regulatory standards.

Even states that host large and potentially fragile financial institutions may have relatively few incentives to cooperate in adopting stricter standards. Consider the case of a Caribbean country that uses weak regulations to lure large banks to its shores. The light regulation of banks may cause banks to fail, and the fallout could endanger the country's economy. Nevertheless, as noted above, a small country may have no other means of luring financial institutions or transactions to its shores – or of keeping them there. Thus either the country adopts weaker regulations and hopes for the best, or it adopts stronger regulations and either fails to attract financial institutions or loses the ones that are there.

In all of these cases, global rules complicate strategic considerations. Perhaps most obviously, the adoption of strict global standards potentially nullifies a country's competitive position. The uniqueness of regulators with strong regulatory brands is reduced, while at the same the potential advantages of countries with weaker regulatory approaches are eliminated since the global playing field is leveled. Capital ends up being diverted to other jurisdictions, costing countries jobs and tax revenue – and also, in the process, potentially compromising the political support for ruling elites. Domestic actors may find themselves in the same situation – less competitive on an even playing field where firms operate under the same set of legal constraints. In such circumstances, institutions will lobby their political authorities and local regulators to shy away from the global standard at issue, and a state will be less likely to cooperate with others in crafting common rules.

IMPLICATIONS FOR COORDINATION (AND LEGAL THEORY)

Because of these asymmetric costs and benefits, international coordination can be much more complex and difficult than has been traditionally acknowledged in the literature. At a most basic level, the presence of heterogeneous preferences suggests that agreement may not be possible. Although parties recognize that they could be better off, they may disagree as to what action should be taken. One country may prefer an approach with lower adjustment costs, whereas a country with a different philosophy may choose another approach. Regulators may simply have fundamentally different, or even antagonistic, policy preferences. Persuasion will likely be insufficient for all countries potentially involved in a regulatory regime to reach agreement on issues with distributive implications. Similarly, although information sharing is useful to the extent that it can help create a bargaining space to avoid what come to be recognized as unfortunate outcomes, it is typically not sufficient, on its own, to generate consensus on any particular issue.

Instead, some form of strategic action will often accompany international negotiations where actors attempt to change the net payoffs of adopting a particular form of regulatory behavior. Such strategic action can include bargaining (where actors trade different kinds of concessions in order to create a mutually beneficial agreement), coercion (through political or economic means), or a combination of the two. In the absence of such strategic action, coordination will occur against the background of regulators' existing policy preferences. To consider a simple example, assume that a group of regulators all agree that they would like to strengthen capital-adequacy requirements for banks, but disagree as to how much. All the regulators could adjust their regulations to those of the minimum-standard regulator. Now assume that one regulator disagrees with the rest and believes that capital-adequacy standards should be weakened. In the absence of side payments or issue linkages, the likelihood of agreement is basically nil, particularly if the overarching organization is consensus based.

The contractarian framework speaks to this pitfall by highlighting the risk-mitigation features of informal rules. Yet herein lies a second, perhaps more important problem: enforcement. Asymmetric distributional effects undermine the durability of informal international agreements. Even when countries reach an agreement as to rules, new information (or opportunities) may arise that make noncompliance attractive. For example, a state may recognize an opportunity to attract new business or transactions to its borders by offering less onerous disclosure requirements. Or implementing a particular standard may be more costly (economically or politically) than authorities expected. Resources may have to be diverted to regulatory activities that are more valued by legislators or the general population, or the volume of financial transactions taking place in a country may unexpectedly suffer after entering into a particular international regime that imposes certain limitations on securities firms or banking institutions.

In such circumstances, soft law provides, at least as traditionally conceived, few disciplining mechanisms to prevent a country from backtracking on its commitments. Indeed, the availability of a cheap exit allows parties to take advantage of changing circumstances or more advantageous regulatory options. Regulators can avoid the adjustment costs of moving to a new standard, or choose another regulatory approach, even if it departs from international best practices or existing agreements.

In practice, defection can play itself out in several ways. Regulators will sometimes cherry-pick international agreements without embracing them comprehensively. If, for example, a global agreement on core standards contains fifteen best practices, a country may choose to comply with only those that promote its own competitive position or financial market strength. In such cases a country may ultimately adopt only a handful of the principles expressed in international agreements.

Alternatively, countries can adopt regulations but then under-enforce those rules at home – which amounts to a defection from its commitments. Problems of under-enforcement most frequently arise when countries have weak compliance cultures, as well as when institutions may themselves be owned by the government. But under-enforcement can also be due to supervisors having conflicting institutional mandates that lead to inconsistent enforcement – for example, when national authorities are tasked with both ensuring financial stability and fining (and by extension, weakening) banks that do not comply with its rules. Finally, some international commitments involve not only switching to or adopting new standards, but also creating new domestic regulatory structures that may prove costly to governments having other priorities. In such circumstances, signatories may agree in principle to certain kinds of conduct but may be incapable, either politically or institutionally, of implementing the agreement.

Existing explanations for soft law thus leave us with a puzzle. Why is soft law relied on so frequently to articulate global rules and standards? When compliance decisions begin to resemble zero-sum games, as opposed to win-win collaborations in which all countries and market participants benefit (or lose) equally, international legal theory predicts that a losing party will merely "defect" from any international commitments that are disadvantageous, especially since any obligations are informal. Soft law thus should be inadequate in facilitating deep and lasting convergence in situations where rules carry varying degrees of costs and benefits for different national market participants.

Broadening the theoretical optics traditionally used to examine soft law offers important clues that what is needed, among other things, is a radical rethinking not only international financial law, but also, more generally, of soft law and how it works. Ultimately, *legalization* is typically seen as the key dimension giving rise to law's coercive force. Even within contractarian and network frameworks, it is only hard law instruments that create binding obligations on states and that create pressure for states parties to comply with their commitments. By contrast, soft law, which is informal, does neither.

Emphasizing legal obligation as the primary feature distinguishing hard law from soft law is problematic. Even formal international obligations are often not honored, and defections from them do not necessarily carry high reputational consequences. Treaties are commonly ignored by states as they go about conducting international affairs. Indeed, many scholars disavow even international law as a legitimate category of "law," given the absence of a single entity to enforce rules and the frequent flouting of international rules. According to these scholars, international rules are inherently "nonbinding" in view of international system's limitations in constraining sovereign actors.

By privileging legalization, theorists imply (and at times state explicitly) that defections from soft law carry no reputational costs. Thus, by extension, soft law is unable to generate the necessary seriousness for commitment making. This view overlooks, however, the degree of commitment backing informal arrangements – and especially international financial agreements. Since regulatory actors have virtually no ability to promulgate legally binding international commitments, soft agreements are often imbued with significant solemnity. The theorists also miss the extent to which defection from soft law commitments has serious practical consequences for other parties and actors. Thus, this approach fails to articulate an accurate reputational theory for international financial affairs.

Reigning theories also fail to take into account the extralegal mechanisms that operate as sources of discipline. Two lacunas are especially apparent. For one, the realist impulse driving international relations theory generally passes over the important role played by nongovernmental actors, especially markets and firms that provide incentives for compliance. Instead, markets – like law – are generally viewed as instrumentalities of state power. They are rarely identified as independent factors that can inform the strength of international financial standards. This realist perspective departs dramatically from the longstanding insights of the law and finance literature that even where rules are not legally binding, they may influence the behavior of market participants who are seeking to signal efficiency, value, and strong corporate governance. Such insights have important potential implications for soft law and suggest that markets can have coercive effects when soft law is promulgated. A framework within which to comprehensively theorize and evaluate such dynamics, however, is missing entirely in these realist accounts.

The second lacuna is that descriptive theories of soft law ignore the role that international organizations and institutions play in securing compliance.

To a certain degree, this lapse is not surprising. Contractarians generally view international organizations as the by-product of hard law and the means by which treaties are operationalized and enforced. Meanwhile, network theorists recognize that institutions can be associated with and backed by soft law instruments, but diminish their importance precisely because these institutions are themselves not the product of treaties and thus enjoy only a "twilight" existence.[44] By contrast, political scientists and economists have long insisted in institutionalist accounts of global affairs that international organizations and institutions frequently shape the procedures by which norms and standards arise – and, in doing so, determine a wide variety of regulatory outcomes. Furthermore, in corralling different regimes and authorities, these organizations and institutions create new forms of legitimacy and compliance, even when undermining conventional (domestic) conceptions of accountability. These dynamics, which should not (and do not) turn on whether an instrument is soft or hard law, need to be integrated into existing legal theory.

A more comprehensive structural analysis is thus required that focuses not only on the degree of obligation both explicitly and implicitly expressed by an instrument – and by soft law, in particular – but also on the context and the political economy in which international financial law operates. What is needed is a closer examination of the players involved in coordination and of the processes by which financial laws gain global currency. From these observations, a framework can be established to better understand the international regulatory architecture and the degree to which international financial regulations exhibit their compliance pull on participating parties.

COMMITMENTS UNDER INTERNATIONAL FINANCIAL LAW

The observations made by rational choice theory, though helpful in highlighting the relevance of public international law more generally, have only limited import for international financial law. In traditional international legal scholarship, the advantages of reputation, retaliation, and retribution are largely reserved for "hard" international law, especially treaties. Not only do treaties represent the strongest form of international commitment – in which context they are characterized as "legally binding" – but they are also expressed in formal written documents and articulate relatively precise representations of parties' obligations. Violations thus naturally carry reputational effects that

---

[44] *See generally* David Zaring, *International Law by Other Means: The Twilight Existence of International Financial Regulatory Organizations*, 33 Tex. Int'l L.J. 281 (1998).

can undermine credibility. And as legally binding instruments, they regularly establish or recognize disciplinary processes that enable retaliation or reciprocity.

Soft law, by contrast, constitutes a seemingly less serious commitment. Because it is inherently nonbinding (and usually explicitly so), classical international legal theory assumes that there are costs on international actors when they choose to defect from agreements. Reputational effects are lacking, as are disciplinary measures to operationalize implementation.

Legal obligation as evidenced by an instrument's technical formality is a poor means, however, of identifying the true compliance pull of any international legal standard. Even informal agreements can express "commitments." Technically, a commitment is nothing more than a promise to do something, and promises can entail various degrees of obligation. In some cases, commitments may be relatively weak, as when observations made by members of an international forum (for example, in formal reports, as discussed earlier) are taken either as defining the preliminary outlines of a more elaborate regime to be developed or as expressing a limited consensus among regulators, typically as to the origins of, but not the solutions to, emerging challenges. In such cases, agreements take on the quality of broad, "negative covenants"; members continue to have wide discretion as to future actions but are at least expected not to engage in behavior contrary to, or conflicting, with the values or norms that have been expressed.

International financial law sometimes defines specific actions that the parties to an agreement intend to take: from a contractual standpoint, these actions are "affirmative" commitments between regulatory officials. The kind of regulatory action required can be diverse. Regulators may agree to assist one another, to apply certain regulatory standards in overseeing domestic market participants, or to submit to surveillance from the outside. In such diverse circumstances, international financial law is operationalized through myriad instruments, including bilateral or even multilateral MOUs or codes of conduct and best practices. And the breadth and nature of the obligations can be subject to various degrees of specificity, from broad principles of adherence to more granular responsibilities accompanied by explanatory methodologies or supporting documentation addressing the implementation of agreed-upon standards and principles.

Commitments can also be implied. As we have seen throughout the book, a vast body of international financial law is articulated through reports issued by international agenda-setting and standard-setting organizations. Some may include normative assessments in that they request or support specific policies or broad policy directions, while many others may be no more than fact-based assessments of recent events. Yet even here, in confirming a factual state of affairs in the world and the challenges or opportunities associated with it, reports can be important in indicating members' support for undertaking actions in line with, or responsive to, the reports' conclusions and recommendations.

That international financial law is not "legally" binding in the same sense as formal international treaties does not detract from the great solemnity that accompanies the making of these instruments, whatever specific form they take. Because international financial law is generally concluded between regulators, their obligations to one another are, for reasons discussed previously, necessarily informal. Perhaps most centrally, regulatory agencies do not have the power to unilaterally or independently enter into international treaties. Informality is thus a necessary element of most cross-border, interagency cooperation, but it does not detract from the seriousness of the commitments made. International financial agreements are often intrinsically important because they have critical consequences for counterparties. Among other things, regulators commonly rely on one another to execute their domestic mandates. A regulator, for example, may rely on another in order to gain access to witnesses or evidence concerning a domestic violation that may have geographically occurred in another jurisdiction. So it is no surprise that intergovernmental agreements are periodically concluded with great fanfare and at public, well-publicized events that include speeches, photo ops, regulatory officials from home and abroad, and even flags representing each agency's home country.

REPUTATION AS A REGULATORY TOOL

When international financial law articulates a regulator's commitment to abide by a certain policy, various disciplines, as in the general international law context, can enhance compliance. As with states, one important source of discipline is reputation, whereby regulators can use one another's past behavior with regard to compliance to predict future compliance with international obligations. Imagine, for example, a situation where two countries enter into a nonbinding, mutual recognition program, and one party's firms undertake changes in corporate governance in order for its market participants to gain special or preferential treatment by the other regulator. Imagine further that after changes are implemented, the would-be partner decides not to implement the program and thus not to ultimately provide such treatment. Although the agreement to establish the program may have been nonbinding, the aggrieved regulator will be less likely to enter into future cooperative agreements with the defecting regulator. Noncompliance causes, in other words, the counterparty (and perhaps other regulatory agencies, too) to reevaluate their expectations of a regulator's future behavior in relation to its international commitments. Once a party loses its reputational capital, others become less inclined to put their own resources at risk or to adjust their own standards with a view to cooperation.

A poor reputation for compliance can have additional costs for regulators, beyond the ability to credibly commit in the future (something even rational choice theorists fail to sufficiently emphasize). For example, a regulator can suffer diminished group influence – a real cost in a system designed to depend in many ways on the "soft power" of persuasion. Chronic noncompliance raises issues about the seriousness with which an agency is committed to pursuing the organization's goals and objectives. As a result, a poor reputation makes it harder for regulators to assume positions as opinion leaders, even if they occupy a privileged position in an organization's institutional structure. Finally, regulatory bodies with poor reputations will find it harder to convince other regulators to comply with their obligations when they themselves are unwilling to do so. If it has a poor reputation for compliance, or for implementing international standards, an agency will neither lead by example nor exert deep persuasive power by demonstrating the benefits of a policy. Nor will it reap the reputational payoff that comes with complying with international standards even under difficult circumstances.

Thus, as in the formal, public international law context, financial authorities compare the expected payoff from compliance to the expected payoff from violation. States will be tempted to violate a soft law agreement only if the nonreputational payoff from violation is larger than the nonreputational payoff from compliance.[45] In practice, the value of a strong reputation will not be the same for every regulator in all circumstances. Some states, especially poor developing countries with small financial sectors, may have limited interest in international financial affairs or may have an interest in having a strong reputation only with regard to particular sectors. Others, meanwhile, may already have, or may seek to build, broader, ongoing relationships in order to achieve more ambitious (global) policy objectives.[46] In such cases, reputations for cooperation can be valuable, and states will be more willing to bear the costs associated with enhancing or protecting them, including compliance with otherwise less than favorable commitments.[47]

---

[45] GUZMAN, *supra* note 1, at 74–77.
[46] *Id.* at 75–76.
[47] *Id.*

Violations of commitments will not always generate the same reputational costs. Financial centers seeking to gain size and global market share may find that the reputational payoffs for compliance with international standards are comparatively high, particularly when they are seeking to convince investors of the sophistication of their financial centers. They may thus be more willingly incur the costs of compliance – even though adjusting to an especially high international standard may be more burdensome for them than for their larger, more developed, or better-known counterparts. Violations may also have divergent reputational costs due to variations in the degree of obligation expressed by an instrument. Some obligations are more specific than others and, as such, give parties less flexibility both in how they define the commitment and in how they plan to comply with the obligations made. Other obligations are more ambiguous because of poor drafting, absent terms, or multiple paths to satisfy different commitments. To the degree that the fine details of an obligation are unclear, violation is more difficult to determine, and deviations from the standard may incur fewer reputational consequences.

Regulators may also have divergent reputations across issue areas, which depend in part on the structure and mandate of the domestic regulatory agencies. A financial authority in which securities, banking, and insurance supervisors are consolidated into one agency could conceivably have one reputation for how it complies with international securities standards and another for standards relating to payment systems. By contrast, when regulators wield more limited authority over narrow financial sectors, multiple reputations are harder to earn – though it is still possible. A securities regulator could develop one reputation for enforcement cooperation and an entirely different one for compliance with principles promulgated by IOSCO. Similarly, a banking regulator could have a glowing reputation for its compliance with the Basel *Core Principles* and a poor reputation for compliance with the more precise (and often more strenuous) dictates of the Basel rules on capital adequacy.

I do not wish to overstate the likelihood of such reputational compartmentalization. Most regulators will, after all, use any and all available information to generate realistic expectations of another regulator's conduct, with the consequence that poor conduct in one issue area could produce expectations of poor conduct others. That said, if "reputations are compartmentalized, it will be more difficult to generate compliance in areas where states have little interest in building a good reputation. It will conversely be easier to do so in areas where states have much to gain from a good reputation."[48]

---

[48] *Id.* at 105.

Although it is commonly – and correctly – noted within the field of traditional international law that reputational sanctions do not apply when no
commitments are made, the issue as to what constitutes a commitment can
be difficult to determine. As we have already seen, traditional international
law emphasizes the form in which a commitment has been made, taking as
its model the formal legal obligations created by instruments such as treaties.
And the standard position is that some such instrument is required in order to
create a commitment. The better approach, however, is to see whether or not
a governmental body actually espoused or made a commitment of any sort,
regardless of its formality. As we saw in the previous chapter, many standard-
setting bodies are far from representative, and their yet their members affirm
standards and make recommendations that they intend to be followed by
national regulators not themselves members of the standard-setting organization and not directly represented in the standard-setting process. In such cases,
the nonobservation of a standard should not affect a regulator's reputation for
compliance with its obligations. No commitment was made.

Of course, the nonreputational payoffs of noncompliance can swamp any
reputational benefits. Even a regulator eager to bolster its reputation will
violate commitments if the nonreputational payoffs are big enough,[49] as is
often the case when countries are desperate to attract capital and high-value
financial transactions and can be seen as competitive only through weak or lax
regulation. In circumstances where governmental agencies have fundamental
concerns of economic prosperity, reputation by itself will likely have only a
limited impact on a regulator's decision making. These observations suggest
that when the economic stakes of a policy are high, reputation on its own is
unlikely to decisively influence the behavior of regulatory agencies.

MARKET DISCIPLINES

Reputations for compliance or for credibility with regard to commitments are
not the only forms of reputation that are relevant in the international regulatory
arena. As we have seen, regulators can have reputations for unilateralism that
can similarly affect one's ability to cooperate. In this section we address a third
form of reputation – namely, the market reputation that a regime enjoys, along
with the costs and benefits that it implies for a regulator's market participants.

The relationship between a country's national regulations and costs of capital for local firms has been extensively explored in securities offerings and
disclosure. Various studies have shown that when a country mandates the

---

[49] *Id.* at 112.

disclosure of certain information and penalizes firms when they fail to comply
with national securities statutes, it provides a guarantee to investors that relevant, material information will be available to them on a timely basis. Firms, in
turn, can enjoy lower costs of capital since the listing on a market with strong
disclosure rules and practices has the effect of reducing the risk premium associated with potential fraud, bad corporate governance, and insider trading.
Law thus helps firms make a credible commit to disclosing bad information
just as promptly as good information.[50]

The impact of such disclosure laws on the cost of capital will generally
depend on their strictness and efficiency. Regimes that require more material
information will have a greater impact on the cost of capital than regimes that
require less information. When a country's commitment to transparency is
low, investors may have less, and less trustworthy, information on which to
base their investment decisions. In such circumstances, investors will charge
a premium for their capital.

Due to the impact that disclosure laws have on how potential investments
are perceived, many scholars surmise that foreign firms often intentionally
subject themselves to foreign disclosure and enforcement regimes, especially
that of the United States. By opting into a stricter foreign regime, firms are
often able to reduce perceived agency costs and thus offer increased returns
on investments. Drawing on the finance literature, John Coffee, for example,
has drawn attention to the fact that foreign corporations that list their securities both in their home markets and in the United States (and thus subject
themselves to US territorial laws) enjoy a valuation premium in comparison to
otherwise similar firms that do not cross-list. Specifically, foreign companies
that cross-listed shares in the United States had Tobin's q ratios that, in the late
1990s, were 16.5 percent higher than those of non-cross-listed firms from the
same countries. This figure rose to 37 percent for foreign firms that cross-listed
on a major US exchange.[51] Finance experts Hail and Leuz have additionally
found that when non-US companies cross-list in the US market, they incur
a cost of capital reduction that averages 13 percent and can be as high as 25
percent.[52]

Similar dynamics are at play with regard to capital reserve requirements in
banking and insurance. Although capital reserve requirements effectively act
as a charge on a bank's operations, they may nonetheless be the only means

[50] Stephen M. Bainbridge, *Mandatory Disclosure: A Behavioral Analysis*, 68 U. Cin. L. Rev 1023, 1033 (2000).
[51] John C. Coffee, Jr., Law and the Market: The Impact of Enforcement 8 (Columbia Law Sch. Law & Econ. Working Paper Grp., Paper No. 304, 2007).
[52] *See* Luzi Hail & Christian Leuz, *International Differences in the Cost of Equity Capital: Do Legal Institutions and Securities Regulation Matter?*, 44 J. Acct. Res. 485 (2006).

by which a bank's maximum return on capital can be achieved. Investors in debt instruments, as well as counterparties to derivatives transactions like swaps (transactions where two parties exchange promises to deliver certain securities or capital streams), may require strong credit. Part of the assessment of a potential party's creditworthiness may depend on an external evaluation, often by an auditor or credit-rating agency, of the participant's capital reserves. Thus, to the extent that capital reserves are low, banks may lose business or incur higher costs of participating in certain financial transactions.

High capital reserves may be important for those who invest in financial institutions and signal a reduced exposure to downside business cycles and damaging economic events. During an economic downturn, nonperforming loans and capital write-offs for defaulted loans may increase quickly and, in the process, destabilize financial institutions. Increases can undermine the institutions' perceived stability and can even spark solvency fears since the institutions are no longer able to attract counterparties or depositors. Investors in institutions with low capital reserves may thus require a bank to accept lower premiums and share prices for their securities to reflect the increased risk associated with investment, which then translates into higher costs of capital for banks and insurance companies.

Significant evidence is available that banks often keep higher amounts of capital on their books than is formally required under their national regulatory regimes in order to signal the stability and health of their financial institutions. Recently, Samu Peura and Esa Jokivuolle examined the capital levels of over one hundred large financial institutions among G-10 countries from 1997–2001. They found that the median risk-weighted capital ratio for all 128 banks was 11.2 percent during this five year period, with regional averages ranging from 11.9 percent for US banks to 10.8 percent for European banks.[53] Tarullo has additionally noted that over the last decade, the risk-based capital levels of the 10 largest US banks had nearly always been above Basel I's basic 8 percent threshold capital requirement, as well as above the US regulatory requirement of 10 percent required for banks to be recognized as 'well capitalized.' This level of capital worked to assure creditors, counterparties and investors of the banks' stability and helped to promote business dealings with nonbank financial institutions.[54]

Such preemptive, and in some ways defensive regulatory compliance, is in part due to the fact that compliance with international best practices and standards can help regulators and firms send important market signals to

[53] Daniel K. Tarullo, Banking on Basel: The Future of International Financial Regulation 142 (2008).
[54] Id.

investors and would be partners to financial transactions. To the extent to which international standards are considered welfare enhancing for investors, compliance by market participants and their regulators can decrease the cost of capital. And conversely, where a country deviates from international best practices, it can also be interpreted as having an *inferior* regulatory environment. In such circumstances, not only may firms be subject to higher costs of capital, but also investment dollars and lucrative transactions may concomitantly be diverted to other jurisdictions.

Notice that that these market disciplines can operate regardless of whether or not a regulator has committed to a particular regulatory standard. That is, a firm may subject itself to international standards, even where its home jurisdiction may not necessarily require it to do so. This dynamic differs from that associated with traditional public international law, where reputational pressures generally arise only when countries have made explicit commitments to abide by certain standards. In the international financial global marketplace, investors can in many instances evaluate national regulatory regimes and their relationship to established best practice in order to determine what kind of risk premium should attach to investments or counterparties should be attached.

More generally, international financial law can help shape the perceptions of investors, lenders, and other relevant market participants as to the value of any particular kind of conduct. Soft financial institutions may, for example, articulate norms that have not previously been systematized. What are, in fact, preferred practices have not been explicitly identified as such but are simply matters of habit or widely followed practice that are implicit and taken for granted. Once regulators identify and express best practices, international financial law, though nonbinding, those practices become explicit and prescriptive. International financial law can thus provide the publicity and prominence required to put those practices on a firmer basis and to make them more dominant.

Similarly, soft law can create practices or conventions where none exist by influencing market participants' expectations of how others will or should act. In the process it nudges along investor preferences. International financial law's influence is especially strong when investors are unsure of what to expect or demand from firms in light of new market or industry conditions. In those situations, soft law is a means of communicating the observations and preferences of a collective of diverse governmental actors – many of whom have supervisory responsibilities and thus access to insider or nonpublic information. As a consequence, investors "who perceive themselves as having limited information . . . can observe the actions of presumptively better-informed persons," and may therefore adopt the same expectations as regulators and impose risk premiums on firms that fall short.[55] Soft law can thus serve as an especially useful prescriptive instrument that helps guide investors in their investment strategy.

Firms thus frequently perceive adherence to major international standards as a means of enhancing their own reputations and facilitating lower-cost funding from banks and capital markets. The dominant corporate law scholarship has long demonstrated that some firms seek to become subject to the laws and supervision of major financial centers so that they can signal their strong corporate governance and disclosure to investors. Similarly, banks based outside of the Basel Committee member states' jurisdiction have similarly been known to adopt Basel capital guidelines and other international standards in order to show the world that they have moved to the latest, most sophisticated models and have received the approval of leading regulatory bodies.

INSTITUTIONAL DISCIPLINES

Finally, the institutions animating the international regulatory system can themselves exert discipline. Though not always retaliatory – some, for example, can be deployed against actors who never actually committed to any particular regulatory program or reforms – these disciplinary mechanisms are designed to supplement any reputational and market costs for noncompliance and are wielded through institutional processes. This section discusses four mechanisms (see Table 3.1) that are the most significant in the international regulatory system: financial assistance, shaming, capital market sanctions, and membership sanctions.

Financial Assistance (Conditionality)

Perhaps the bluntest potential institutional discipline for noncompliance with international regulatory standards arises when the IMF and World Bank make their financial and economic assistance conditional on the adoption of regulatory standards, as evidenced in the Financial Sector Assessment Program, which itself relies on and draws on a "Compendium of Standards" produced by standard setting bodies and recognized by the Financial Stability Board (and previously the Financial Stability Forum). The practice of "conditional" lending first started in 1952 and was associated with structural reforms that were necessary for countries to avoid balance-of-payment crises. After the Asian financial crisis, financial regulatory reforms were increasingly embedded in lending programs, and the IMF and World Bank were empowered to require client countries to make reforms relating to any of the core standards they monitored.

---

[55] Bainbridge, *supra* note 50, at 1038.

TABLE 3.1. *Key institutional disciplines*

Institutional discipline	Prominent institutional user	Relevant soft law instrument
Financial assistance (conditionality loans)	IMF/World Bank	FSB compendium of standards and FSAP program
Name and shame	FATF IOSCO FSB/IMF/World Bank	40 + 9 Recommendations Appendix B FSAP standards
Capital market sanctions	FATF	40 + 9 Recommendations
Membership sanctions	IMF FATF FSB IOSCO	Article IV 40 + 9 Recommendations Charter obligations MMOU

Despite its coercive element, financial assistance is largely designed to underscore the technically voluntary nature of country participation. The loan origination process consists of two documents. The first is a letter from a prospective borrower country to the World Bank (called the "Letter of Development Policy") or the IMF (called the "Letter of Intent") in which the government seeking financial assistance outlines specifically what it plans to finance with the proceeds from the loan that it is requesting. The letter also outlines steps that the government has taken in the past, as well as steps that it plans to take in the future, to improve its fiscal, regulatory, and market systems. This process establishes conditionality and guarantees country ownership of the reforms since the conditions of the loan are set by the government – thus individual state sovereignty is respected.[56]

The second important document is the credit agreement itself. Like all credit agreements, it includes the loan's terms, the borrower's and lender's representations, and the borrower's covenants and obligations. The agreement does not include a description of the project to be financed with the credit or loan, for that has already been outlined in the government's initial letter. In this manner, the borrowing government takes ownership of the loan, and it is the government, not the World Bank or the IMF, that sets the conditions of the loan in the initial letter (which is a government document). The Bank

---

[56] Gerhard Anders, *The Normativity of Numbers: World Bank and IMF Conditionality*, 31 PoLAR: Pol. & Legal Anthropology Rev. 187, 191–92 (2008).

or the IMF then declares its intention to disburse the money as long as the government honors its intention as declared in the letter.

In practice, this approach has clear limitations. Most important, it has been a useful lever only for countries that rely on World Bank and IMF assistance. Wealthy countries are more likely to host systemically important financial institutions because of the size of their local capital markets, but they are less likely to need IMF funding since they rarely experience currency crises of the sort that could cripple their economies, the 2010–11 Eurozone crisis notwithstanding. Furthermore, wealthy countries do not generally lack access to capital for their own developmental needs. They consequently do not need World Bank assistance and thus are not subject to World Bank loan agreements. As a result, the most critical financial centers are not governed by regulators subject to, or disciplined by, conditionality programs.

Second, even when countries do participate in IMF or World Bank lending programs, the degree of obligation implied by the loan is ambiguous. For its part, the World Bank views its loan agreement as legally binding under inter-national law since the agreements are signed by government ministries and explicitly contain representations on which the World Bank relies in order to extend the loan. Its credit agreements generally include a provision empow-ering it to suspend disbursement if the program described in the borrower's Letter of Policy is not carried out "with due diligence and efficiency."[57] By contrast, the IMF refers to "arrangements" rather than "agreements," thereby explicitly attempting to avoid any contractual implications. The IMF's former general counsel Joseph Gold has argued that the term "agreement" does not imply any contractual relationship – and by extension – hard or legal obliga-tion by the IMF, though the organization has not explicitly adopted the stance. But as with the World Bank, nonperformance empowers the IMF to suspend payments to a client country. Suspension can thus operate as a significant incentive for countries to adopt the two institutions' preferred policies.

Yet from a practical standpoint, even when these obligations are regarded as legally binding, their compliance pull can be weak. Enforcement can be diffi-cult, especially once the loans are disbursed; with the funds in hand, countries face fewer incentives to comply with obligations memorialized in loan agree-ments with international financial institutions. Moreover, even when loans are tranched and paid out on a staggered schedule, the IMF and World Bank are often disinclined to cut off disbursements of aid, even when not all loan condi-tions memorialized in loan documents have been realized. Historically, such inaction has been especially unlikely with regard to loan conditions relating

---

[57] *Id.* at 192.

to financial regulation – an area that has traditionally been deemphasized in comparison to obligations in other economic areas, such as a country's trade, monetary, and labor policies.

Name and Shame

An alternative approach to discipline is through a technique of disparagement commonly referred to as "name and shame." Through this approach, institutional actors do not rely on reputations to gradually coalesce or for market participants to make entirely uninformed, independent judgments regarding the value of particular regulations. Instead, they take the initiative themselves: not only is noncompliance disclosed to the public, but such disclosure is often supplemented with some form of official opprobrium by the institution.

Perhaps the most famous form of name and shame in finance is that practiced by the Financial Action Task Force. As discussed above, money laundering, a financial transaction that generates an asset or a value as the result of an illegal act, has long been an area of interest to police and banking authorities, largely because it is the modus operandi for financing prostitution and the drug trade. That said, not all countries have an interest in promoting tighter anti-money-laundering regulation – especially those that attract capital to their shores by offering secrecy and lax regulatory systems. Of particular concern to many regulators are so-called offshore financial centers, which are typically small, low-tax jurisdictions. Because these offshore centers hold few competitive advantages in their own right as financial centers other than their light regulatory governance, the adoption of stricter regulations could make them significantly less attractive destinations for foreign investment. These countries have historically been strongly inclined not to cooperate in anti-money-laundering efforts; in fact, they have typically resisted them.

To respond to this challenge, the FATF, with the encouragement of the G-7 finance ministers, adopted a more aggressive anti-money-laundering policy in 2000. The FATF devised standards to identify countries that were failing to adopt international standards and not cooperating with the international community in the fight against illegal financing. The resulting "blacklist" – a term that quickly gained currency to describe the FATF's list of identified countries – was eventually made public and was shared with domestic financial institutions. It was even used as the basis for capital market sanctions (discussed in the following section).

This strategy was developed, in part, from an approach taken with Turkey in 1996. There, the FATF saw one of its own members refuse to pass legislation criminalizing money laundering or to adhere to the group's primary legislation, the *40 Recommendations*. After nearly five years of relatively subtle negotiation aimed at getting the country to reverse course, the FATF opted for a more aggressive approach and issued a press release that, among other things, instructed banks and other financial institutions to scrutinize capital market transactions with Turkish businesses and individuals. In response to the public rebuke, the country instituted new money-laundering regulations just months later.

The idea behind name and shame is simple. By identifying noncompliance and also effectively superimposing and making public a country's *intent* not to cooperate, the technique heightens the potential reputational consequences of nonobservance of particular standards. Purposeful nonobservance, when it occurs, is a sign of the (implicitly nefarious) regulatory preferences of a particular country. Regulators in the identified jurisdiction are thus publicly ostracized and isolated from the members of the organization publishing the list. Additionally, by doing such shaming publicly, regulators are able to potentially sharpen the market consequences of noncompliance. Market actors, in short, can take cues from emphatic expressions of disapproval from regulators that a particular country presents special risks or dangers to the stability of the financial system.

Several name-and-shame lists have been published over the life of the program. The first and most extensive list came out in June 2000, when fifteen countries were identified as uncooperative in the fight against money laundering. A second high-profile list, with eight additional countries, was published the following year. In all, eight annual reviews of Non-cooperative Countries and Territories (NCCTs) have been conducted (not always resulting in a new list), and the exercise has largely been hailed as effective. Dan Drezner has reported that of the fifteen countries identified, four acquiesced completely to the FATF, passed all of the anti-money-laundering laws, and staffed the requisite agencies to implement them.[58] Another seven made significant concessions, and three passed laws that responded sufficiently to the FATF demands to avoid more significant sanctions.[59] Since then, the FATF's naming and shaming, as well as the prospect of reputational consequences, has been used to exert pressure on a wide array of countries – even the Vatican.

Capital Market Sanctions

Along with name and shame, organizations can also choose to adopt capital market sanctions – the imposition of special restrictions or outright

---

[58] DREZNER, *supra* note 36, at 143.
[59] *Id.*

prohibitions against market participants from countries that do not abide by certain regulatory standards. In a sense, capital market sanctions are present whenever members of international organizations impose in their home markets certain regulatory requirements that, when unmet, translate into costs for foreign market participants. What is meant here, however, are sanctions imposed by members of international standard-setting bodies against foreign market participants due to failures by their home governments to adopt the relevant international standards.

One of the earlier instances where capital market sanctions were used as instruments of financial regulation was in 1987. UK and US regulators entered into a bilateral agreement on banking standards in which they adopted more stringent, risk-based capital requirements for the two jurisdictions. After reaching an agreement, the two sought to have the same requirements adopted by the Basel Committee – partly in an effort to avoid putting their own banks at a competitive disadvantage other banks. Japan resisted, however, even after considerable negotiation. The United Kingdom and the United States ultimately won the day by signaling their willingness to exclude banks (and particularly Japanese banks) from their markets if they failed to abide by their regulatory standards. As David Singer and Ethan Kapstein note, the "tacit threat being made was that foreign bank activity could be reduced in the US and UK markets unless these banks adopted the new risk-based standard. Since Japanese banks were intent on expanding their activities in New York and London . . . this was a prospect that had to be taken seriously."[60]

After drawing up its NCCT blacklist in 2000 and promulgating a menu of possible countermeasures that could be imposed on countries that failed to adopt standards – including the "conditioning, restricting, targeting or even prohibiting [of] financial transactions" with noncooperative jurisdictions" – the FATF instituted a more targeted and muscular approach to money laundering. It directed sanctions against three countries: Nauru (identified in the first 2000 report), Myanmar, and the Ukraine (both identified in the second, 2001 report). In the case of the Ukraine, the sanctions involved the application of prospective information-gathering and record-keeping requirements on institutions that dealt directly or indirectly with Ukrainian institutions. In the case of Nauru, the sanctions involved outright prohibitions against financial activities with persons from Nauru. Under the weight of such sanctions and within five years of their application, both countries had reformed their domestic rules and oversight, and countermeasures were

---

[60] David Andrew Singer, Regulating Capital: Setting Standards for the International Financial System 60 (2007).

withdrawn. Since then, the FATF has called on its members and other jurisdictions to apply countermeasures only against Iran, given the perceived
significant gaps in Iran's financial system that enable the transfer of funds
terrorists.

Capital market sanctions are often difficult disciplinary mechanisms to
impose and retain. Though they are among the stiffest disciplinary measures
that organizations can impose, they usually involve some costs for not only
the country made subject to the sanctions, but also the country or countries
imposing the sanctions. Firms from countries subject to capital market sanctions may have to compete against firms that escape them, resulting in higher
costs of doing business or lost business altogether. But, domestic companies
may also lose opportunities to transact with foreign firms targeted by the sanctions. Thus, in practice, even domestic firms may face lower profits and higher
costs of doing business where sanctions are administered.

As a result, capital market sanctions require broad, robust participation
from major financial centers, as well as efforts to minimize the likelihood
of transactions merely moving offshore to regulatory safe havens. Attaining
such cooperation can be very difficult. Countries often have different perceptions of risk and good conduct, and the *intensity* of their preferences for
any one policy or regime. Thus, although countries may share basic views
with regard to the optimality of a particular approach, they may disagree as
to whether noncompliant countries should be punished – especially if there
is concern that they, too, could be punished in the future for their own regulatory lapses. Additionally, it can be challenging to convince a wide range
of (diverse) countries to impose sanctions that may, in fact, hurt and limit
the economic prospects of powerful special interests at home. Finally, capital
market sanctions potentially have consequences that extend beyond financial
policy, making it difficult for risk-averse countries to back sanctions. In short,
a country may choose to retaliate against sanctions in a way that is unrelated to
financial regulation but that undermines the welfare of the countries imposing
the sanctions in unexpected ways.

Capital market sanctions can nonetheless be a potent tool for regulators.
The mere prospect of capital market sanctions can decrease the value of firms
operating in the targeted jurisdiction. Not only may they incur higher costs of
capital – a prospect we see more generally with noncompliance and discuss
in the following section – but firms may experience lower rates of return due
to diminished demand for their services as prospective clients opt to avoid the
firms altogether or submit their potential transactions with those firms to more
stringent review. These pressures create considerable incentives for political
actors, governments, and regulators to comply with international standards

and to avoid the uncertainty that comes with the prospect of capital market sanctions.

Membership Sanctions

Finally, international organizations can impose sanctions on their members. This technique differs from name and shame and from capital market sanctions, both of which, though they may have indirect implications for a member's international standing, do not directly undermine or affect the advantages that members of international organizations derive from those organizations.

In theory, a variety of sanctions can be imposed on members that fail to live up to their institutional obligations. In theory, a member enjoying a key or privileged policy position – for example, through a seat on a technical committee – could potentially lose that seat, much as a country can lose its seat on a human rights panel in the United Nations, either temporarily or permanently. In practice, however, the most consequential sanction, and the only one identified in the international regulatory context, arises when a member of standard-setting body (and by extension, the home country represented by that member) is threatened with expulsion.

Though expulsion is rarely included as a remedy in the organizational documents of standard-setting bodies, hard law institutions like the IMF and World Bank do provide for the possibility of a member being "compelled to withdraw."[61] Most international institutions only list the requirements of membership. The FATF's mandate explicitly provides an agreement among members that "all countries should implement the FATF Recommendations effectively," just as the Financial Stability Board charter contains commitments by members to "implement international financial standards." Even IOSCO, a universal organization, now requires that new members sign the MMOU in order to join. Current members are also required to sign or, at the very least, to commit to seeking the legal authority that would permit the member to become a signatory. Otherwise, they risk a loss of membership.[62]

The prospect of revoked membership is (no pun intended) foreign to international standard-setting bodies, given their soft legal character and orientation toward persuasion and coordination. That said, the integration of membership standards into intergovernmental "networks" can, at least in theory, be an effective means of heightening compliance with international standards. First, it

---

[61] C.F. Amerasinghe, Principles of the Institutional Law of International Organizations 122 (2nd rev. ed. 2005).

[62] Id. at 12–13.

can have a dramatic impact on the standard's prominence and attractiveness. Often, the widespread adoption of standards among members generates what economists call "positive feedback dynamics," or networks effects, enhancing the attractiveness of those standards irrespective of the substantive nature of the obligations. By promoting widespread standards, firms no longer have to adopt multiple processes to accommodate multiple regimes; instead, one uniform regime is in place.[63]

Second, by conditioning access and excluding noncompliant regulators/countries, international organizations can recalibrate members' cost-benefit analyses concerning the adoption of a standard. Compliance generates the benefits associated directly with adopting the standards in question, but many other benefits are associated with membership in a standard-setting body: enhanced credibility and visibility as a member of a standard-setting organization; increased opportunities for information exchange; technical and enforcement assistance; and, most critically, a role in the standard-setting process and an opportunity to inform global standards. Loss of membership can thus present serious problems. And in the case of formal international financial institutions like the World Bank and IMF, the cost of lost membership can be exceedingly heavy, for it can translate into severely diminished recourse to loans and financial assistance in times of economic stress.

It is worth noting, however, that in practice, membership sanctions are, like capital market sanctions, rarely administered. Only hard law institutions have successfully employed membership sanctions, and even then only twice. The IMF and World Bank have expelled only one member: Czechoslovakia, in 1954, due to its failures to provide information as required by its Article IV commitments. Half a century later, in 2003 – after having suspended Zimbabwe's voting rights, borrowing rights, and technical assistance two years prior – the IMF initiated compulsory withdrawal procedures. But by 2009, after arrears were paid and Zimbabwe's cooperation on economic policies had improved, the proceedings were terminated.

By contrast, *no country* delegation has ever been expelled from an international standard-setting body, though Austria came close. Throughout the 1990s, international standard-setting organizations and international financial institutions complained about Austrian bank-secrecy laws, particularly the country's permissive stance regarding anonymous savings "passbook" accounts. In 2000, after exhausting what it felt to be more persuasive and softer avenues of coordination, the FATF threatened the ultimate sanction against Austria – expulsion from the organization (and the Organisation for Economic Co-operation and

---

[63] DREZNER, *supra* note 36, at 43.

Development) unless the country issued an unequivocal statement announcing that it would comply with the *40 Recommendations* and also prohibit and eliminate anonymous accounts.

Why is expulsion such a difficult remedy and so rarely administered? From a practical standpoint, exclusion not only runs against the objectives of members (to achieve broader participation and compliance), but can thwart problem solving to the extent that problems require full global responses. When a member is expelled from an organization or institution, the country is unlikely (unless it is seeking to have its membership restored) to be fully cooperative, or even helpful, in addressing particular policy problems.

Even when a standard-setting body's rules are clear that expulsion is justified and appropriate, the expulsion of members is a matter of discretion and thus requires the consensus of members. Such agreement may be difficult to reach in view of the diverse and sometimes antagonistic interests of members, not to mention the potentially wide differences of opinion as to what conduct merits expulsion. Membership sanctions, like capital market sanctions, can create considerable political blowback in other related (and even unrelated) areas of cooperation between countries, and countries may have economic and political relationships beyond the specific subject matter of finance that require certain degrees of allegiance. Against this background, generating a sufficient consensus to expel a particular member from an organization verges on the impossible. That said, the mere prospect or threat of expulsion can itself constitute a considerable sanction. Members will experience some isolation from other members and, in order to maintain their official status in the organization, will often have to rely on expending political capital to bolster support among colleagues. The member will also suffer diminished stature in the organization, which will weaken its capacity to direct or influence the organization and its policies.

MONITORING AND THE CONTINGENCY OF DISCIPLINE

Now that we have an overview of how discipline can operate in a world where information is readily accessible, we will shift gears and move to a closer inspection of how discipline operates in practice. All of the disciplinary effects outlined above depend on information dissemination of some sort: regulators need information in order to update their expectations regarding one another's credibility. Markets need information to price risk. Institutions rely on information to determine compliance with membership standards and act accordingly with regard to their financial support. Thus, to examine the international regulatory system's efficacy, it is necessary to understand not only how discipline is exercised, but also how the information needed for that purpose is obtained.

Like enforcement, how monitoring is carried out can vary across issue areas in terms of how it is performed. In some cases, it entails casual and distant, albeit sustained, observation of counterparts across the globe. For example, regulators may analyze the extent to which a country has formally incorporated international standards into its books; the adopted standards should be reflected in a country's domestic laws and organizational structure. In other cases, monitoring can include a deeper scrutiny of whether or not a country's regulatory system actually implements the objectives or principles espoused by international regulatory reforms. Such monitoring can include on-site verification activities, inspections of enforcement techniques, and analyses of regulatory capacity. Monitoring can also be done by regulators in their individual capacities or as members of relevant international bodies, and by third-party staff permanently employed by international organizations.

The particular means used in monitoring have a strong impact on compliance. Actors will discount the costs of defection relative to the likelihood of detection. When international accords are protected by robust surveillance mechanisms, and the likelihood of detection is high, actors will presume the full range of reputational, market, and institutional costs. Thus, when full information is available, a country that ignores its commitments or international best practices can expect reputational, market, and institutional sanctions – such as shaming or capital market sanctions. When the risk of detection is small, a country may decide that the benefits of defecting from a regulatory standard are worth the risk of detection. Monitoring thus serves as a condition precedent to discipline insofar as it is only through the detection and evaluation of regulatory conduct that reputational, market, and institutional disciplines can operate properly.[64]

THE PROBLEM OF FINANCIAL SECTOR ASSESSMENT PROGRAM MONITORING

Despite its importance, the architecture supporting monitoring has historically been quite weak, even with regard to the primary monitoring system – the FSAP. As you will recall, the FSAP constitutes the largest and broadest surveillance system in the international regulatory architecture. Along with

---

[64] Dave Grossman & Durwood Zaelke, An Introduction to Theories of Why States and Firms Do (and Do Not) Comply with Law, Presented at the Seventh International Conference on Environmental Compliance and Enforcement (Apr. 9–15, 2005), *available at* http://www.inece .org/conference/7/vol1/13_Grossman.pdf.

more specialized reports, such as the Reports on Observance of Standards and Codes (ROSCs) discussed in the previous chapter, it provides the means of assessing compliance with a fundamental set of core standards that most international standard-setting bodies promulgate. The following section demonstrates that the FSAP has historically suffered from three key weaknesses: participation has been voluntary; information regarding defection (which has often been difficult to interpret) has not always been made public; and actors have been able to subvert and undermine the negative image associated with defection through their own regulatory hype. The risk-adjusted cost of defection has as a result often been low, increasing the likelihood of noncompliance if significant distributional trade-offs arise.

Limited Scope

Although the FSAP provides the broadest tools for monitoring – and the only ones supported by a formal international organization – its scope is limited. IMF and World Bank officials do not provide surveillance assistance for all international financial standards. Instead, they focus on those key sets of core standards that have been identified by the FSB (and its predecessor, the Financial Stability Forum) as the most basic and fundamental to the international system. This narrowed focus excludes a variety of important standards, some of which are arguably of greater import than even the core standards incorporated into the FSAP process. The restricted ring of activity underscores, in part, the challenge associated with limited resources – a problem that often inhibits the monitoring process. Not only must monitors master the content and objectives of international regulatory standards, but they must also familiarize themselves with the regulatory context and particularities of the examinee. In its initial stages, this process includes interviewing national regulators and authorities, as well as examining the regulatory infrastructure of the client state. Monitoring can, in short, be costly, both for the examiners and the examinees, and the resources spent domestically for this purpose might well be seen as better spent elsewhere.[65] Consequently, when either the examiners or examinees lack the political will to sustain such programs, the intensity of surveillance will likely diminish.[66]

---

[65] Indeed, the observance report budget alone was approximately $3.8 million dollars without any verification capacity. *See* INT'L MONETARY FUND [IMF] & THE WORLD BANK, THE STANDARDS AND CODES INITIATIVE: IS IT EFFECTIVE? AND HOW CAN IT BE IMPROVED? 26 (2005), *available at* http://www.imf.org/external/np/pp/eng/2005/070105a.pdf [hereinafter Standards and Codes Initiative].

[66] ABRAM CHAYES & ANTONIA HANDLER CHAYES, THE NEW SOVEREIGNTY: COMPLIANCE WITH INTERNATIONAL REGULATORY AGREEMENTS 191 (2007).

Suboptimal Participation

The FSAP process is limited in scope and also has had low levels of participation. Until recently, participation in the FSAP process was largely voluntary. Only countries receiving aid from the IMF and World Bank could be required to adopt core standards under principles of conditionality established as the basis of loans. The lack of broad mandatory participation reflected, in part, domestic regulators' skepticism at being subjected to outside scrutiny by foreign regulators and international officials. Developing countries, in particular, were apprehensive about imposing on the entire world the standards developed by largely rich and developed countries. Voluntariness also reflected the assumption by powerful countries that it was in a country's self-interest to participate and to build its domestic regulatory capacity, and thus that surveillance was an inherently collaborative, noncoercive exercise. Seen in this light, surveillance provides an opportunity for domestic regulators to engage with other international experts, creating opportunities for dialogue and learning, and spurring the spread of international best practices.

Nonetheless, the flexibility of the FSAP has helped generate questionable dynamics. First, there is an adverse selection problem. In the absence of coercion through conditionality, the countries that are most likely to participate are those most in need of a signal of good governance *and* that do well in the assessment.[67] From this perspective, the FSAP comprises less a disciplinary mechanism than a means by which countries can bolster their own reputations through third-party assurances provided by the IMF and World Bank.

Second, many countries have opted out of the FSAP altogether. Regulators, institutions, and market participants are left to make inferences about what a country's nonparticipation means – an altogether difficult exercise. Nonparticipation may indicate a regulatory disagreement with particular standards and their appropriateness, or with the process by which standards are generated. Domestic regulators may have little trust in the capabilities of the monitors or may believe themselves to have few functional shortcomings. They may therefore have little interest in a participating in a time-consuming and officious inspection process. Finally, nonparticipation can also, of course, suggest noncompliance with international standards, but even so, the extent of noncompliance is difficult to assess without discussions with home-country officials.

---

[67] IMF, *Factsheet: The Financial Sector Assessment Program (FSAP)* (Mar. 23, 2011), http://www
.imf.org/external/np/exr/facts/pdf/fsap.pdf [hereinafter FSAP Factsheet].

Questionable Data Inputs

Data quality represents another important challenge to the FSAP process. Specifically, the data provided to international standard-setting bodies are self-reported by national authorities and are often sourced from information provided by regulated financial entities that are themselves subject to little supervisory oversight.[68] The logic behind this approach rests on two basic beliefs. First, self-reporting provides a focal-point analysis provided by the actor in the best position to provide the relevant information – the domestic regulator. Second, "national reporting can perform a policy function by encouraging self-examination. . . . [T]he process of preparing a national report may have a catalytic effect in promoting internal policy reform by mobilizing and empowering actors both within and outside government."[69]

The quality of the information provided in financial sector assessments and observance reports can potentially be compromised, even when independent data sources and country assessments are available. Perhaps most obvious, regulators undergoing surveillance – as well as the firms they oversee – will regularly interpret international benchmarks and standards in ways that make them appear compliant. Additionally, many countries, particularly developing countries, may have insufficient resources for accurate self-reporting, in which case the data supplied by regulatory authorities may not accurately depict the level or nature of compliance with international regulatory standards. Not only may regulators have insufficient human capital and compliance resources, but they may also, due to limited experience with financial supervision, under- or overemphasize both the steps that their regimes have taken to meet their commitments and, by extension, the extent to which their practices comply with international best practices.[70]

Stymied Information Sharing

The FSAP has failed to optimize information sharing regarding compliance with international standards. Historically, information gained from the key surveillance mechanisms – observance reports, financial sector assessments,

---

[68] *Financial Sector Assessment Program (FSAP)*, THE WORLD BANK, http://web.worldbank .org/WBSITE/EXTERNAL/TOPICS/EXTFINANCIALSECTOR/0,contentMDK: 22142161~menuPK:6459396~pagePK:210058~piPK:210062~theSitePK:282885,00.html (last visited Feb. 22, 2010).

[69] DANIEL BODANSKY, ART AND CRAFT OF INTERNATIONAL ENVIRONMENTAL LAW 239 (2009).

[70] CHAYES & CHAYES, *supra* note 66, at 14.

and the informal surveys on approaches and techniques conducted by national regulators – has been published only with the permission of the inspected country.[71] It has thus remained at that country's discretion whether information regarding its compliance is shared with other domestic regulators or market participants.[72]

Decisions to disclose have been case dependent. Market mechanisms can sometimes pressure countries to release surveillance reports (assuming that market participants are aware that monitoring was undertaken). If a country undertakes the FSAP, and then chooses not to disclose the results, a strong inference can be made that compliance with international standards may be weak.

A negative report could tarnish the market and regulatory reputation of a country. A country could suffer from both a loss in credibility and higher costs of capital. Consequently, if a regulator knows or expects that a report will draw negative conclusions as to its compliance, it may be inclined not to publish the results of the document. A disciplining mechanism working against this inclination is the desire to avoid the negative inference by other regulators and market intermediaries that, in choosing not to publish, the report's financial sector assessment is negative. Whether this incentive is sufficient remains unclear; at least one-quarter of countries undergoing observance reports – most of them developing nations – decide not to publish their financial sector assessments.[73] See Table 3.2.

Following the meltdown of global capital markets in 2008 and 2009, the relatively low participation rates have not gone without notice by commentators and international financial regulators, especially considering the virtual absence of participation by the one country largely thought to have caused the financial crisis, the United States. To address these challenges (see chapter 5), both the IMF and FSB are revamping their membership requirements. The IMF, for its part, has approved making financial stability assessments under the FSAP a regular and mandatory part of the fund's surveillance for members with systemically important financial sectors – a group that includes twenty-five jurisdictions. The FSB's members have meanwhile committed to undergo periodic "peer reviews," which will be published and which can use financial sector assessment reports "among other evidence."

---

[71] FSAP Factsheet, *supra* note 67 (noting that the voluntary nature of FSAPs is necessary for "buy-in" among participants).

[72] Alastair Clark & John Drage, *International Standards and Codes*, FIN. STABILITY REV., Dec. 2000, at 166, *available at* www.bankofengland.co.uk/publications/fsr/2000/fsr09art7.pdf.

[73] Standards and Codes Initiative, *supra* note 65, at 5.

TABLE 3.2. *G-20 ROSC/FSAP modules published*[74]

Country	FSAP/FSSA[a]	Banking supervision[a]	Insurance supervision[a]	Securities regulation[a]	Total ROSCs published
Argentina[75]	2001	04/15/1999			1
Australia[76]	10/23/2006	10/23/2006 4/15/1999	10/23/2006	10/23/2006	4
Brazil[77]	2003				0
Canada[78]	02/13/2008 2001	06/30/2000	06/30/2000	02/13/2008 06/30/2000	4
China[79]	Planned for 2010				0
France[80]	11/03/2004	06/08/2005 11/03/2004	06/08/2005 11/03/2004	06/08/2005 11/03/2004	6
Germany[81]	Planned for 2010 11/06/2003	11/06/2003	11/06/2003	11/06/2003	3
India[82]	2001				0

[74] The Ctr. for Int'l Governance Innovation, *The Financial Stability Board: An Effective Fourth Pillar of Global Economic Governance?*, (Stephany Griffith-Jones et al. eds., 2010), *available at*, http://www.cigionline.org/publications/2010/6/financial-stability-board-effective-fourth-pillar-global-economic-governance.

[75] Financial Sector Assessment Program, WorldBank.org, http://go.worldbank.org/ZRV7 QA8TS0 (last visited Jan. 6, 2011); Reports on the Observance of Standards and Codes, IMF.org, http://www.imf.org/external/np/rosc/rosc.asp (last visited Jan. 6, 2011).

[76] Reports on the Observance of Standards and Codes, *supra* note 212.

[77] Int'l Monetary Fund & World Bank, *The Financial Sector Assessment Program After Ten Years: Experience and Reforms for the Next Decade*, Aug. 28, 2009, *available at*, http://www.imf.org/external/np/pp/eng/2009/082809b.pdf.

[78] Reports on the Observance of Standards and Codes, *supra* note 212; Int'l Monetary Fund & World Bank, *supra* note 214; *Canada: Financial System Stability Assessment – Update*, IMF.org (Feb. 13, 2008), http://www.imf.org/external/pubs/cat/longres.cfm?sk=21710.0; *Canada: Financial Sector Assessment Program – Detailed Assessment of the Level of Implementation of the IOSCO Principles and Objectives of Securities Regulation*, IMF.org (Feb. 13, 2008), http://www.imf.org/external/pubs/cat/longres.cfm?sk=21713.0.

[79] Int'l Monetary Fund & World Bank, *supra* note 214.

[80] Reports on the Observance of Standards and Codes, *supra* note 212; *France: Financial Sector Assessment Program – Detailed Assessments of Observance of Standards and Codes including Banking Supervision, Insurance Regulation, Securities Legislation, Monetary and Financial Policy Transparency, Payments Systems, Securities Settlement, and Anti-Money Laundering and Combating the Financing of Terrorism*, IMF.org (June 8, 2005), http://www.imf.org/external/pubs/cat/longres.cfm?sk=18300.0.

[81] *Germany: Financial System Stability Assessment, including Reports on the Observance of Standards and Codes on the following topics: Banking Supervision, Securities Regulation, Insurance Regulation, Monetary and Financial Policy Transparency, Payment Systems, and Securities Settlement*, IMF.org (Nov. 6, 2003), http://www.imf.org/external/pubs/cat/longres.cfm?sk=16998 .0.

[82] Int'l Monetary Fund & World Bank, *supra* note 214.

Country	FSAP/FSSA[a]	Banking supervision[a]	Insurance supervision[a]	Securities regulation[a]	Total ROSCs published
Indonesia[83]	09/16/2010	09/16/2010		09/16/2010	2
Italy[84]	03/14/2006	03/14/2006	03/14/2006	03/14/2006	3
Japan[85]	09/05/2003	09/05/2003	09/05/2003	09/05/2003	3
Korea, Republic of[86]	03/19/2003	03/19/2003	03/19/2003	03/19/2003	3
Mexico[87]	10/11/2006 10/25/2001	10/11/2006 10/25/2001	10/25/2001	10/11/2006 10/25/2001	5
Russian Federation[88]	05/30/2003	05/30/2003	05/30/2003	05/30/2003	3
Saudi Arabia[89]	06/05/2006	06/05/2006			1
South Africa[90]	10/22/2008 2000			10/22/2008 2000	1
Turkey[91]	11/09/2007	11/09/2007			1

(continued)

[83] *Indonesia: Financial System Stability Assessment*, IMF.org (Sept. 16, 2010), http://www.imf .org/external/pubs/cat/longres.cfm?sk=24212.0.

[84] *Italy: Financial System Stability Assessment, including reports on the Observance of Standards and Codes on the following topics: Banking Supervision, Payment Systems, Insurance, Securities Regulation, Securities Settlement and Payment Systems, Monetary and Financial Policy Transparency, and Anti-Money Laundering and Combating the Financing of Terrorism*, IMF.org (Mar. 14, 2006), http://www.imf.org/external/pubs/cat/longres.cfm?sk=19033.0.

[85] *Japan: Financial System Stability Assessment and Supplementary Information*, IMF.org (Sept. 5, 2003), http://www.imf.org/external/pubs/cat/longres.cfm?sk=16865.0.

[86] *Republic of Korea: Financial System Stability Assessment, including Reports on the Observance of Standards and Codes on the following topics: Monetary and Financial Policy Transparency, Banking Supervision, Securities Regulation, Insurance Regulation, Corporate Governance, and Payment Systems*, IMF.org (Mar. 19, 2003), http://www.imf.org/external/pubs/cat/ longres.cfm?sk=16436.0.

[87] *Mexico: Financial System Stability Assessment, including Reports on the Observance of Standards and Codes on the following topics: Monetary and Financial Policy Transparency; Payment Systems; Banking Supervision; Securities Regulation; and Insurance Supervision*, IMF.org (Oct. 25, 2001), http://www.imf.org/external/pubs/cat/longres.cfm?sk=19978.0.

[88] *Russian Federation: Financial System Stability Assessment including reports on the Observance of Standards and Codes on the following topics: Banking Supervision, Insurance Supervision, Monetary and Financial Policy Transparency, Payments Systems, and Securities Regulation*, IMF.org (May 30, 2003), http://www.imf.org/external/pubs/cat/longres.cfm?sk=16578.0.

[89] *Saudi Arabia: Financial System Stability Assessment, including Reports on the Observance of Standards and Codes on the following topics, Monetary and Financial Policy Transparency, Banking Supervision, and Payment Systems*, IMF.org (June 5, 2006), http://www.imf.org/ external/pubs/cat/longres.cfm?sk=19307.0.

[90] Int'l Monetary Fund & World Bank, *supra* note 214; *South Africa: Financial System Stability Assessment, Including Report on the Observance of Standards and Codes on the following topic: Securities Regulation*, IMF.org (Oct. 22, 2008), http://www.imf.org/external/pubs/cat/longres. cfm?sk=22437.0.

[91] *Turkey: Financial System Stability Assessment*, IMF.org (Nov. 9, 2007), http://www.imf.org/ external/pubs/cat/longres.cfm?sk=21442.0.

TABLE 3.2 *(continued)*

Country	FSAP/FSSA[a]	Banking supervision[a]	Insurance supervision[a]	Securities regulation[a]	Total ROSCs published
United Kingdom[92]	03/03/2003	03/03/2003	03/03/2003	03/03/2003 03/15/1999	4
United States[93]	07/30/2010	07/30/2010	07/30/2010	07/30/2010	3

[a] Dates refer to conducted and published modules.

Poor Data Interpretation

A final possible impediment to market discipline is the inaccurate quantification of risk by reputational intermediaries. Even assuming that self-reporting and monitoring are effective, data have to be properly analyzed and assessed.

The quantification of regulatory risk and the advantages of any particular course of action are inherently difficult. No one wishes their home jurisdictions to be viewed as unsupervised or weak, so governments and market officials work hard to bolster their regulatory brands. Governments, for example, often proclaim their adherence to the highest regulatory standards in newspaper and magazine advertisements without specifying precisely what those rules are or how they may compare internationally. Similarly, stock exchanges, market intermediaries, and financial institutions hold themselves out in their promotional materials as secure and safe and as adhering to the highest ethical standards, even though they may be based in countries where they are subject to relatively weak supervision and where few metrics are available to gauge technological or regulatory expertise.

Hyperbole about regulatory excellence can often drown out pertinent information regarding the qualitative nature of a jurisdiction's oversight. This kind of cheap talk puts at risk unsophisticated market participants and less experienced investors who are unaccustomed to sorting through information at most

---

[92] Reports on the Observance of Standards and Codes, *supra* note 212; *United Kingdom: Financial System Stability Assessment including Reports on the Observance of Standards and Codes on the following topics: Banking Supervision, Insurance Supervision, Securities Regulation, Payment Systems, Monetary and Financial Transparency, Securities Settlement Systems, and Anti-Money Laundering and Countering Terrorist Financing,* IMF.org (Mar, 3, 2003), http://www.imf.org/external/pubs/cat/longres.cfm?sk=16364.0.

[93] *United States: Publication of Financial Sector Assessment Program Documentation - Financial System Stability Assessment,* IMF.org (July 30, 2010), http://www.imf.org/external/pubs/cat/longres.cfm?sk=24105.0; *United States: Publication of Financial Sector Assessment Program Documentation – Reports on Observance and Codes,* IMF.org (July 30, 2010), http://www.imf.org/external/pubs/cat/longres.cfm?sk=24108.0.

risk.[94] Cheap talk undermines risk assessments by providing irrelevant data to divert the attention of experienced actors, by potentially exacerbating peoples' misperceptions, and by overloading observers with short-term information that clouds judgments about long-term risks.[95] Consequently, managers of firms may be unaware of any signals regarding the advantages or disadvantages of raising capital in a particular jurisdiction, and analysts may inaccurately price the risk (or do so, albeit accurately, at higher cost) – which would not be the case in the absence of such statements.[96] As a result, "noise" can help deflect attention from, or diminish costs relating to, a domestic regulator's defections from, or noncompliance with, international standards.

FSAP reports and ROSCs are envisioned as addressing this challenge by identifying important standards that the international regulatory community recognizes and by then providing an in-depth analysis of compliance. Those reports, however, are not designed to interpret the data and do not provide ratings to market participants with regard to compliance. Instead, they usually (but not always) provide "a principle-by-principle assessment of observance of international standards."[97] It is therefore up to market participants to judge for themselves the significance of the information collected and compiled by international financial institutions.

This situation may present special challenges to private intermediaries, whose staffs, though generally trained in financial interpretation and analysis, may be poorly equipped to determine the pricing implications of regulatory decisions.[98] Even many attorneys may not appreciate the meaning of non-compliance in all cases. Market participants have consequently admitted to low ROSC utilization rates in their own work.[99] In a survey sponsored by the World Bank, 45 percent of market participants admitted to using ROSCs in their analysis either "not at all" or "to a very little extent"; 45 percent used them "to some extent"; 10 percent to "a large extent"; and *none* "to a very large

---

[94] *See* Donald C. Langevoort, *Taming the Animal Spirits of the Stock Markets: A Behavioral Approach to Securities Regulation*, 97 Nw. U.L. Rev. 135, 139–52 (2002) (surveying noise-trader research in economic literature).

[95] Erik F. Gerding, *Laws Against Bubbles: An Experimental-Asset-Market Approach to Analyzing Financial Regulation*, 2007 Wis. L. Rev. 977, 1002 (2007) (noting academic research demonstrating how even relatively financially sophisticated investors can behave like noise traders).

[96] This will especially be the case with thin markets, or for the purpose of this Article, where financial institutions raise money or transact with relatively little financial activity.

[97] Standards and Codes Initiative, *supra* note 65, at 44.

[98] Furthermore, even if lawyers are hired to assist analysts in their analysis, no lawyer will understand all of the diverse regulatory approaches adopted by countries, and thus general assessments of risk will be difficult and costly.

[99] Standards and Codes Initiative, *supra* note 65, at 24.

Text box 3.1. Modes of Monitoring and Their Characteristics

Monitoring source	Key characteristics
Informal peer review	Present in all standard-setting environments
	Most effective for pure coordination challenges
	Leverages easily observable data/highly transparent environments
Formal peer review	Practiced in FATF, IOSCO (for the MMOU), FSB
	Most effective in the context of distributive problems
	Leverages verification procedures to attain hidden information or data not easily observable
Nongovernmental stakeholders	Key agents include market participants and civil society (academics and commentators)
	Gathers information with regard to compliance in the course of professional duties or research

---

extent." The ultimate result of such structural flaws is that the risk-adjusted cost of defection is lowered. When information about compliance is not produced or shared, or is underutilized, noncompliance with international standards can be a relatively costless choice for national authorities. Consequently, the likelihood of noncompliance is increased when there are significant distributional tradeoffs.

MONITORING BEYOND THE FSAP PROCESS

Although FSAP reports are the broadest and, in many ways, the most high-profile type of regulatory monitoring undertaken by the World Bank and IMF, they are not the only sources of surveillance. Just as standard setting can take place beyond the auspices of the formal Bretton Woods processes, so can monitoring. When it is operationalized institutionally, it is usually done in-house by the standard-setting body that promulgates the standards, though such work can be supplemented by the work of third-party monitors. See text box 3.1.

Informal Peer Review

Virtually all international organizations depend to some degree on informal peer review processes, which have two important characteristics. First, as the term implies, "peer" review is generally performed by members of the organization themselves. Second, the "informality" of the process denotes that monitoring is not undertaken in connection with any formal membership obligation. It serves, instead, as a learning process that is intimately connected with the standard-setting process and through arm's-length observations of other members and their behavior.

Informal peer review can take place in several ways. In some instances, regulators are able to send employees overseas to work with foreign counterparts, enabling them to both learn about other regulatory practices and to observe how national and international standards are implemented. Most opportunities for review arise indirectly, however. One of the most important is when regulators discuss the interpretation or elaboration of new or existing international regulatory standards. As Dan Tarullo notes, such interactions provide participants with the opportunity to gauge the likely approach and commitment of their counterparts.[100] When regulators seek to promulgate methodologies or interpretations needed to implement broader standards or principles, they can gain important information regarding the seriousness of foreign financial authorities to particular standards and estimate the likely degree of present and future implementation in other jurisdictions.

Additionally, various other, observable data points are available for reviewing each other's conduct and making judgments about compliance. Perhaps most obvious, regulators can (and do) look to their own employees to see whether they have been effectively complying with international assistance and cooperation agreements. Thus, even in the absence of direct information about the conduct of other regulators, domestic regulators can see how they themselves are complying (or not) and use that as a basis for predicting the compliance behavior of other regulators. Regulators can also use economic reports and data to glean information about other jurisdictions' compliance. For example, a regulator may look to another jurisdiction's cost of capital or its lending activity to make judgments about the degree to which a foreign jurisdiction's banks are adhering to capital requirements, or it may examine a country's public records of administrative cases or lawsuits to glean information about enforcement intensity. By cross-checking reports with market data and information collected from local regulatory actors and market participants, inferential judgments can be made as to a foreign regulator's compliance with international standards.

Formal Peer Review

Informal peer review has its limits. Many forms of regulatory conduct are not easily observable from a distance, and producing data about compliance

---

[100] Tarullo, *supra* note 53, at 68.

in the absence of cooperation from a foreign jurisdiction may be both time and resource intensive. Some international standard-setting bodies therefore have more explicit, or "formal," peer review processes embedded in their organizational governance structures.

As monitoring mechanisms, formal peer reviews are functionally similar to the FSAP reports, though they do not rely, as FSAP reports often do, on what can be described as third-party surveillance. Under FSAP reviews concerned with payment systems, for example, the World Bank, not the Committee on Payment and Settlement Systems, takes the official lead in examining and publishing reports on countries' compliance with CPSS principles and best practices. Peer reviews, by contrast, are conducted in-house by the relevant agenda or standard setter. Thus, in the FSB, peer reviews are conducted through the body's Standing Committee on Standards Implementation, which, though itself may be comprised of individuals with a variety of institutional affiliations, is ultimately subject to the direction of the FSB's chairman and secretariat. A variety of standards are monitored, mostly related to information sharing and enforcement cooperation, and not to regulatory oversight. Peer review is also embedded in the FSB's Charter, though (as with many soft organizations) with no clear indication as to the consequences of noncompliance with the FSB peer review or FSAP process.

The most robust and famous form of formal peer review is associated with the FATF, which imposes serious penalties for noncompliance. States that join the FATF agree to undertake evaluations that monitor the implementation of the FATF recommendations and that assess the effectiveness of the anti-money-laundering and counterterrorist financing systems. The purpose of the activity is to determine whether "the necessary laws, regulations, or other measures required under the new standards are in force and effect, that there has been a full and proper implementation of all necessary measures and that the system in place is effective."[101] Evaluations are conducted by FATF experts or, when the evaluations address countries beyond the core FATF membership, by regional bodies in conjunction with the FATF. A key feature of the process is an on-site visit to the jurisdiction that includes comprehensive meetings with government officials and private sector participants over a two-week period. The FATF's detailed procedures for conducting evaluations are designed to ensure that they are fair, accurate, and consistent. The *Handbook for Countries and Assessors* lays out the necessary instructions and guidance for all countries and bodies that are conducting assessments.

---

[101] *Mutual Evaluations Programme*, FATF-GAFI, http://www.fatf-gafi.org/pages/0,3417,en_32250379-32236982_1_1_1_1,00.html (last visited Dec. 5, 2010).

The findings of the FATF assessment team are compiled in a *Mutual Evaluation Report*, which describes in detail that jurisdiction's system in place and which assesses and rates its effectiveness. A summary of each report is published on the FATF website, and FATF members have agreed in principle to make public the full evaluation reports (with the ultimate decision being left to each FATF member for its own report).

The FATF's relatively more aggressive approach to monitoring has become more popular as cross-border financial regulation has become a bigger global priority. Not only is the FSB adopting more intensive and ostensibly mandatory peer-review processes, but so is IOSCO, the quintessential universal standard-setting body. Specifically, as a precondition to joining IOSCO, prospective members must first become signatories of the MMOU. Regulators must formally indicate their commitment to mutual cooperation and assistance among IOSCO members, and demonstrate that they have the rights and powers under their own national laws to comply with the terms and conditions of the agreement.[102] The applicant regulator is required to fill out a questionnaire concerning the applicant's home state laws that relate to its ability to carry out the terms of the MMOU.[103] Based on a review of the questionnaire responses, coupled with additional information gained from coordinating, either by telephone or email, with officials from the applicant country, IOSCO verification teams make specific recommendations to a screening body as to the applicant's ability to comply with each MMOU provision mentioned in the questionnaire.[104] IOSCO officials then decide whether to accept the application. This process employs a range of different institutional actors: The screening group volunteers from both the Emerging Market and Technical Committees. Verification teams come from the screening group, though they include members with expertise in enforcing securities and derivatives laws. Countries that meet the criteria then qualify to be listed under Appendix A of the agreement as full signatories, and thus are referred to as "Appendix A" countries. Those that do not meet the criteria, but are working to do so, are listed as (and referred to) "Appendix B" countries. This hierarchy generates reputational pressures, incentivizing Appendix B countries to update or improve their local regulatory systems.

As is evident from the above discussion, formal peer-review processes can involve various degrees of intensity, depending on the approach to review and

---

[102] IOSCO, Multilateral Memorandum Of Understanding Concerning Consultation and Cooperation and the Exchange of Information 12 (2002), *available at* http://www.iosco.org/library/pubdocs/pdf/IOSCOPD126.pdf.

[103] *Id.* at 16–19.

[104] *Id.* at 12.

the particular issue area involved. Some approaches are formalistic, largely involving an academic examination of the laws on the books of a particular country. Other than queries concerning the interpretation of those laws and the views of domestic regulators on how to achieve optimal oversight, little contact may be made with national officials. At the other end of the spectrum, formal peer review processes can involve on-site inspections in which members of standard-setting bodies visit one another's countries in order to learn from, and observe regulators carrying out, their supervisory mandates.

Nongovernmental Monitoring

A third and final available option is nongovernmental expert monitoring – a form of monitoring that requires expertise beyond the level of government bureaucrats and even the state. In these cases, monitoring is undertaken by a diverse set of stakeholders and commentators from various institutions, ranging from universities to the private sector.

For example, some private actors have attempted to step into the breach to assist with ROSC data interpretation. The most significant of these actors has been the e-Standards Forum, a private initiative involving, among others, Oxford Analytica and the Wharton Financial Institutions Center, which assesses publicly available ROSC data and examines compliance. These efforts are not perfect: private examinations are at arm's length – "assessments of assessments" – and do not involve the actual monitors and the knowledge that they accumulate on the ground and through their interactions with private and public stakeholders. Private actors thus largely depend on publicly available information, unlike most existing regulatory regimes. Nonetheless, they can provide important relevant information to the market about a country's regulatory environment.

Expert monitoring also takes place through the daily activities of financial services professionals. For example, since transnational law firms routinely advise their clients as to international rules and regulations governing the conduct of business in foreign jurisdictions, these firms need to remain abreast of regulatory developments abroad and their practical consequences. Thus, when international regulatory authorities raise standards for ultimate implementation domestically, lawyers must learn about the new requirements and determine how they compare with local practices. Similarly, investment banking analysts, investment advisers, and other participants may, as part of the due diligence requirements for particular transactions, monitor bank capital levels and, in doing so, apply international standards in their assessment, or at a minimum, standards derived from them. And perhaps most importantly, auditors and credit-rating agencies routinely examine the health of banks and other financial institutions, often by assessing the capital adequacy and ongoing financial-reporting operations. All along, these professionals routinely pass on the information they gain from their work. Some times this is done voluntarily, such as when web pages of many of the leading law firms, for example, regularly produce reports on new regulatory requirements for cross-border firms, just as continuing education programs provide a platform for professionals to share their perspectives and their knowledge of peers' encounters with foreign regulatory bodies. At other times, information sharing may be statutorily promoted, such as where supervisors have the right to meet with external auditors to discuss their findings, or more commonly, where auditors are required to communicate directly with local supervisory agencies when they discover abusive practices by the management of audited companies.

Finally, civil society can play an important role in monitoring. Scholars and researchers in fields as diverse as law, business, and political science often report on important developments in foreign regulatory jurisdictions. In doing so, they both disseminate information on the substantive content of new laws and track compliance with best practices and international standards, helping estimate the degree of enforcement intensity observed in the jurisdictions in question. They also develop more detailed, longer-range studies and analytical insights than are available to other governmental monitors and researchers focused on more short-term solutions and challenges to the financial system.

Despite its virtues, nongovernmental monitoring is often an incomplete and haphazard source of compliance-related information. Since academic scholarship is, by its nature, typically rewarded more for theory than empiricism (especially in foreign or international law), the prospects of deep international studies on compliance, at least in the short term, are limited. Furthermore, academics generally develop narrow disciplinary and subdisciplinary specialties, further reducing the likelihood of broad, multisectoral studies and raising the likelihood of highly diverse analyses, methodologies, and conclusions.

As for market participants, their monitoring of compliance with international standards depends upon their market incentives. Even when compliance with international standards may decrease investment risks, if such compliance is too expensive, market participants and also financial services professionals will likely focus their efforts on tracking firm compliance with *national* standards. Insofar as compliance with international standards is important, they may choose to concentrate only on those developments that are estimated to have the largest or most obvious regulatory impact on the relevant firms. Both they and other third-party monitors may avoid or ignore smaller regulations and requirements that are viewed as minor or as having an inconsequential impact on a firm's activities – especially where such monitoring would be resource intensive.

MONITORING AND THE COMPLIANCE DECISION

The varying strength of monitoring indicates that the costs of sanctions must be discounted by the likelihood of detection. No matter how many rules that an international organization might have in place for regulating members, if the organization has little capacity to monitor the commitments, countries that do not want to comply will discount the sanctions by the likelihood of detection. Suppose, for example, that FATF countermeasures could cost a regulator's market participants $2 billion in lost transactions. If a regulator has a 50 percent chance of evading detection, the net costs of noncompliance would be calculated at $1 billion. On the other hand, if a regulator believed its noncompliance certain, it would calculate costs at the full $2 billion. These costs, along with reputational considerations and others, would then be measured against the potential competitive advantages, along with the increased ability to draw in transactions, that would result from noncompliance.

The quantification of the likelihood of detection is as much an art as a science, for it deals with an external assessment of institutional processes and procedures. But it is not impossible to make rough estimations. Other things equal, a mandatory, formalized process of verification will be more comprehensive than informal or voluntary means of oversight. Similarly, well-designed verification procedures such as on-site inspections, along with active input by civil society and market participants, can bolster the quality and accuracy of self-reported information, as well as help prevent countries from merely jumping through regulatory hoops – and doing the bare minimum to meet expectations of international monitors.

As we have already seen, the effectiveness of different international regulatory regimes varies substantially. FSAP monitoring has been undermined by low participation and, to a lesser extent, by publication challenges. The program is largely considered a weak global tool for compliance and discipline. In the only public study of compliance with the Basel *Core Principles*, conducted in 2002, World Bank and IMF staff found that of the sixty countries that had undertaken FSAP reports at the time, thirty-two were compliant with ten or fewer of the thirty standards involved, and only five were fully compliant with twenty-five or more.[105] A more recent assessment by the IMF suggests that full implementation of the IOSCO principles remains a challenge.[106] As of 2006, only four of the thirty principles have been implemented by 80 percent or

---

[105] IMF & WORLD BANK, IMPLEMENTATION OF THE BASEL CORE PRINCIPLES 8 (2002), *available at* http://www.imf.org/ external/np/mae/bcore/2002/092302.pdf [hereinafter Implementation Report].

[106] Ana Carvajal & Jennifer Elliott, *Strengths and Weaknesses in Securities Market Regulation: A Global Analysis* 11 (INT'L MONETARY FUND, Working Paper No. 07/259, 2007), *available at* http://www.imf.org/external/pubs/ft/wp/2007/wp07259.pdf.

more of IOSCO's members.[107] For four other principles, the levels of implementation fall below 50 percent.[108] The results would probably be even lower if one was to investigate the implementation of the more extensive, ever increasing body of international standards, rules, and reports issued by international organizations. Indeed, the core standards issued by standard-setting bodies and incorporated into FSAP reports represent a small fraction of the prescriptive analyses adopted and backed by the international regulatory community.

The degree of implementation revealed in FSAP reports contrasts sharply with the degree seen in regimes with robust monitoring and stiff sanctions – for example, as seen in the FATF, especially with regard to the reforms undertaken by blacklisted jurisdictions. When combined, robust monitoring and stiff sanctions tend to give international financial law something resembling considerable force and actually induce change – even when jurisdictions incur significant adjustment costs or erosion of their local market competitiveness. Despite being informal "recommendations," the FATF's main legislative products can take on a mandatory, prescriptive effect.

The effectiveness of the approach naturally raises the question as to why more regulators do not adopt stricter monitoring technologies in order to promote high standards. To be sure, monitoring requires less coordination than coordinated punishment, such as capital market sanctions. No agreement is necessary as to a specific sanction, and members are not required to impose forms of punishment that potentially hurt local firms and market participants. That said, monitoring does potentially raise the sovereignty costs for all players in the international regulatory system. When surveillance is strong, and information about defections from standards are shared with the market, firms from countries that are slow to adopt international rules may experience heightened costs of capital, and national regulatory agencies may suffer their own reputational costs. When, as is particularly the case with finance, the strategic advantages or costs of any one approach are unclear, national regulators may seek to avoid cooperative frameworks that cast light on the extent to which their firms abide by standards that are not directly propagated (and controlled) by them.

BEYOND THE HARD LAW/SOFT LAW DICHOTOMY

The complex operations of the international financial system challenge traditional academic frameworks that classify hard and soft law along different continua of legal obligation. Since international financial regulation imposes

[107] *Id.*
[108] *Id.*

no formal legal requirements on parties, it is consistently regarded by scholars as soft law. Nevertheless, international financial regulation, at its strongest, defies a number of common, and indeed foundational, assumptions regarding the operation and compliance pull of informal legal obligations.

First, international financial law weakens, and even dispels, the general criticism of soft international law as inherently less coercive – and by consequence, less credible – than hard international law. As we have seen, theorists generally presume that, although hard law may make coordination more difficult, it is ultimately more durable. Legalization (as hard law) is seen as capable of imposing deep reputational harm that is beyond the capacity of soft law. Defections from hard law agreements are violations of international law, which make cooperation in the future more difficult. Furthermore, legalization presumably legitimizes retaliation, which forces states to internalize the consequences of their decisions.

Casual observation shows that such dichotomies do not hold well. Plenty of hard law, treaty-backed regimes are not especially durable. UN resolutions concerning human rights and the environment are often ignored, just as commitments under trade regimes can be suspended, especially in times of economic stress. Moreover, as we have seen, soft law can have its own hard edges. Reputational costs arising from backtracking or ignoring international regulatory standards can be high, even when agreements are informal. When regulators fail to live up to their commitments, it may be more difficult for them to put forward their policy preferences in the future, and market participants may internalize higher costs of capital. Regulators have leverage and are capable of leveraging institutions and markets in ways that make defection from even informal law more costly.

International financial regulation also challenges traditional conceptions of hard law as a qualitatively different form of regulatory control exerted by national authorities. As Abbott and Snidal argued in their classic article, *Hard and Soft Law in International Governance*, hard law has long been considered more technocratic than its soft law counterpart:

> Legalization entails a specific form of discourse, requiring justification and persuasion in terms of applicable rules and pertinent facts.... [T]his discourse imposes some constraint on state action: governments will incur reputation costs within the legal community, and often beyond, if they act without a defensible position or without reasonable efforts to justify their conduct in legal terms.[109]

---

[109] Abbott & Snidal, *supra* note 17, at 429.

From this perspective, hard law can be viewed as possessing technocratic features that not only enable, but also require, elaboration and debate. These characteristics, it is suggested, make formal international law uniquely capable of mobilizing legally oriented interest groups and expanding the role of legal bureaucracies "within foreign offices and other government agencies."[110]

Under closer inspection, however, these ostensible comparative advantages are difficult, if not impossible, to generalize. Certainly, international financial legislation is often pitched at high levels of generality in order to gain consensus from parties. But so are many instances of hard law. Treaties are not necessarily prescriptive and detailed; indeed, many, especially in the realms of human rights and international criminal law, are vague. International financial law can itself be strongly prescriptive and can, like hard law, involve implementing methodologies, consultative reports, and clarifying instruments – processes that lend considerable "legality" to the substance of soft law by removing ambiguity and better defining regulatory commitments. International financial law often articulates best practices, commitments, and regulatory agreements with a detail far surpassing traditional treaty instruments. And precisely because of the broad implications of international financial law for market participants and their supervisors, it, too, involves considerable participation from bureaucracies, lobbyists, and, not infrequently, the private bar.

Ultimately, then, international financial regulation suggests that attempts to classify law as soft or hard on the basis of formal legal obligation is fraught with hazard and may actually be impossible. In some ways, employing the soft law label disguises the potential effects on regulatory activities and expectations. It overlooks that the true nature of "legality" may not be so much the formal status of a particular rule, but the range and activity of supplemental measures supporting the legal mandate. International financial law is at times "harder" than many conventional hard law instruments. Human rights treaties and UN conventions, for example, are regularly ignored by despots; and when they are, few disciplines can get them to change behavior. Similarly, a country that ignores its Kyoto commitments may face fewer reputational or economic sanctions than, for example, countries that end up on the FATF's blacklist.

Collectively, these observations seem to underscore Andrew Guzman's recent observations that in many ways hard law and soft law operate along a spectrum and are not dichotomous or qualitatively different forms of regulatory control. Treaties can certainly indicate solemnity, but not necessarily more seriousness than that associated with some of the commitments and expectations undergirding informal obligations. Indeed, the degree to which rules

---

[110] *Id.* at 428.

are "binding" should not be conflated with whether they imply a formal legal obligation. Whatever their qualitative character as hard or soft, commitments need to be analyzed and understood against their institutional backdrops and disciplining mechanisms.

This is not to say, of course, that international financial regulation is like all other forms of international law. Embedded in soft law instruments, international financial law is highly responsive to changing conditions and, as such, are easily distinguishable in this respect from the static legal instruments, such as treaties, common in more traditional areas.[111] And unlike traditional public international law, or even other areas of the law that address global challenges like human trafficking or the environment, international financial law inherently engages a wider tool set for regulatory discipline. As in many classic international law systems, reputational disciplines are available, along with institutional remedies, each of which can speak to commitments with various degrees of solemnity. International financial regulation can also apply to or engage market participants themselves in ways that differ from more traditional, state-centric approaches like trade embargoes and even tariff barriers. In doing so, international financial law not only draws on reputational and institutional disciplines, but it also leverages the interest of firms to maximize their profits when transacting with one another.

Because of the range of potential disciplinary devices, international financial law can speak to a far greater variety of (distributive) coordination problems than the traditional public international law literature anticipates. Soft law need not, in short, speak only to pure coordination problems. Rather, soft law also speaks to issues with deep distributive consequences by imposing costs for defection. And as traditional soft law theories have long suggested, soft law mechanisms like international financial law can avoid the expensive formalities and domestic political wrangling, not to mention delays, typically accompanying the creation of formal international law instruments. The benefits of such flexibility are not without costs, however. As I show in the following chapter, in demanding compliance while sidestepping what many consider to be core democratic processes, the system of international financial law raises questions about its own institutional claims to legitimacy – which some scholars believe to be a necessary element of any international legal regime.

[111] Lawrence Baxter, *The Internationalization of Law – The 'Complex' Case of Bank Regulation*, in THE INTERNATIONALISATION OF LAW: LEGISLATING, DECISION-MAKING, PRACTICE AND EDUCATION (Mary Hiscock & William van Caenegem eds., 2010).

4

How Legitimate Is International Financial Law?

For over half a century, ferocious academic and policy debates have addressed the legitimacy and accountability of the global economic system. Key international organizations, including the WTO, World Bank, and IMF, have long exhibited organizational characteristics that, in the eyes of many, are not consonant with democratic principles. Wealthier countries, for example, have dominated the policy and rule making of these institutions, and developing nations have had relatively little voting power. Commentators from around the world have called on radical organizational reform in order to bolster the acceptability of these key institutions in monetary affairs and international development.

As international financial law has become more prominent over the last two decades, it, too, has become subject to various criticisms regarding the legitimacy of its constituent processes. Soft institutions can be coercive – a point underscored in the previous chapter. As in the case of many international economic institutions such as the WTO, countries are not equal and do not have the same input into the formulation of international financial standards by new institutional actors such as the G-7, G-8, or G-20. Indeed, in some cases, countries (and their publics) may be excluded from any formal participation in the articulation of international financial rules, and even stakeholders in participating countries may have little opportunity to inform the rulemaking process. Thus, not all countries are treated in a fair and equitable manner, and their populations are effectively sidelined. In terms of established democratic theory, these structural inequities present a serious challenge to legitimacy.

The implications of such democratic deficits – though perhaps overlooked from the standpoint of systemic risk – have long been anticipated by international legal theorists. From Immanuel Kant to Thomas Franck, theorists have argued that, in one way or another, states obey, and should obey, only those rules perceived to have been born by legitimate processes. If international rules and standards are considered illegitimate and are unaccountable to national and international publics, they are unlikely to be persuasive, authoritative, and compelling, even when organizations exert coercive influence. According to this line of argument, illegitimate or unaccountable international financial law will inescapably fall short in any efforts to impose discipline on the global financial system and to address emerging financial and market risks.

Assessing the legitimacy of international financial law is tricky, however, and frameworks developed in traditional international law map poorly onto the relatively new financial institutional structures. The primary actors, as we have discussed at length, are generally not states but regulatory officials and agencies. As such, international financial law requires a more elaborate theory of democratic governance that incorporates some of the institutional features of administrative rule making into an analysis of legitimacy and that also takes into account the particular structure of the international financial system. The disaggregated nature of the international system, along with the heterogeneity of design features of standard-setting bodies, allows for combinations of inter-agency cooperation and for forms of cooperation between international and domestic actors that affect the legitimacy of the international regulatory system as a whole. In addition, bureaucratic processes common to administrative rule making – and central to the international financial system – depart from more traditional notions of treaty ratification yet still present compelling claims to legitimacy because of the participation by stakeholders and the varied ways of obtaining and integrating domestic-level input. We explore each of these dynamics below.

DEFINING "LEGITIMACY" AND "ACCOUNTABILITY"

International legal experts, as well as international relations gurus, perennially struggle with what legitimacy means (or should mean).[1] Part of the difficulty

---

[1] For examples of the range of definitions available given various issue areas and theoretical starting points, *see* MAX WEBER, ECONOMY AND SOCIETY: A CRITICAL COMPANION (1978) (distinguishing traditional charismatic and legal-rational legitimacy); Thomas M. Franck, *The Power of Legitimacy and the Legitimacy of Power: International Law in an Age of Power Disequilibrium*, 100 AM. J. INT'L L. 88–106 (2006); Robert O. Keohane et al., *Democracy-Enhancing Multilateralism*, 63 INT'L ORG. 1 (2009), *available at* http://www.princeton.edu/~amoravcs/library/multilateralism.pdf; Daniel Bodansky, *The Legitimacy of International Governance: A Coming Challenge for International Environmental Law?*, 93 AM. J. INT'L L. 596 (1999). Another good piece is Paul B. Stephan, *Accountability and International Lawmaking: Rules, Rents and Legitimacy*, 17 NW. J. INT'L L. & BUS. 681 (1996–1997); Ian Hurd, *Legitimacy and Authority in International Politics*, 53 INT'L ORG. 379 (1999), *available at* http://www.gesellschaftswissenschaften.uni-frankfurt.de/uploads/images/952/Hurd.pdf; T. Alexander Aleinikoff, *Transnational Spaces: Norms and Legitimacy*, 33 YALE J. INT'L L. 479

is that legitimacy is a political and often normative concept. My purpose here is not to get bogged down in the particularities of these debates, but to develop a framework for examining the legitimacy claims of actors in the international regulatory system. Suffice it to say, scholars largely reduce legitimacy to various categories. The most dominant approach splits legitimacy into two categories: the first, known as "input" legitimacy, involves a more explicit conception of consent by the governed, whereas the second, usually referred to as "output" legitimacy, involves a conception of implied consent based on the optimality of the rules that governors produce. Accountability, meanwhile, gauges the extent to which regulators are responsive to stakeholders and the public when wielding their power.

Legitimacy

Scholars of democratic theory have tended to stress input legitimacy when assessing domestic and international legal regimes. For them, authority to make societal decisions is legitimated to the extent to which it is given or transferred from individuals to elected or selected actors via democratic processes. When individuals can select decision makers, they enjoy full authority as *representatives* of their respective publics. As such, their rule making is justified and, regardless of discipline, will likely constitute a source of the authentic will of the people. It is therefore more likely that those who are governed will comply with the representatives' decisions, particularly if representatives serve for a specified term and can be replaced in subsequent elections.

By contrast, output legitimacy takes a post hoc view to rules promulgated by institutions to determine whether or not they have been effective. Two metrics have been traditionally used by political scientists – first, in our context, whether relevant countries comply with international laws and standards, and second, whether or not the rules themselves have been successful in achieving a desired outcome. Theories of output legitimacy thus justify authority not so

(2008); Niels Petersen, *Customary Law Without Custom? Rules, Principles, and the Role of State Practice in International Norm Creation*, 23 AM. U. INT'L L. REV. 275 (2008); John H. Jackson, *Sovereignty-Modern: A New Approach to an Outdated Concept*, 97 AM. J. INT'L L. 782 (2003); THOMAS M. FRANCK, THE POWER OF LEGITIMACY AMONG NATIONS (1990); Jens Steffek, *The Legitimation of International Governance: A Discourse Approach*, 9 EUR. J. INT'L REL. 249 (2010), *available at* http://ejt.sagepub.com/content/9/2/249.abstract; THOMAS RISSE, CTR. FOR TRANSATLANTIC FOREIGN AND SEC. POLICY, TRANSNATIONAL GOVERNANCE AND LEGIT-IMACY (2004), *available at* http://userpage.fu-berlin.de/~atasp/texte/tn_governance_benz.pdf; Ernst-Ulrich Petersmann, *Constitutionalism and International Organizations*, 17 NW. J. INT'L L. & BUS. 398 (1996–1997); Friedrich Kratochwil, *On Legitimacy*, 20 INT'L REL. 302 (2006), *available at* http://ire.sagepub.com/content/20/3/302.short.

much on the basis of processes and formal organizational qualities, but on the basis of an institution's accomplishments. In a world of complex decision making, authority can be legitimized by its success in producing the desired outcomes – for example, social welfare gains or global financial stability. Thus, an "institution derives legitimacy from its ability to solve problems that cannot be addressed by other means."[2] Public participation is not necessary for an institution to be legitimate, so long as organizations can lay claim to high-quality, welfare-enhancing, or otherwise effective actions.

As between the two approaches, input legitimacy has tended to be of secondary concern to the international regulatory community. As discussed below, technocratic decision making is commonly seen as necessarily an elite process, with the consequence that departures from democratic processes are inescapable. Moreover, the very goal of financial stability, along with the costs involved in financial market disruptions, has led many to emphasize the baseline importance of effective international coordination through structures that facilitate and maintain cross-border communication and action. That is not to say, however, that international financial law does not face challenges with regard to the effectiveness of its institutions and specifically with regard to output legitimacy as an evaluative metric of democratic authority. Owing to the at times considerable incentives to comply with international standards outlined in the preceding chapter, compliance is by itself of limited use in gauging whether a country's national practices reflect its deference to, and respect for, international rules and standards. Evaluating the "success" of regimes can be also be challenging inasmuch as such judgments inescapably depend upon the goals or policy objectives to be achieved, about which opinions may sharply differ.

Accountability

In contrast to legitimacy, which concerns the right of decision makers to wield power over their publics and stakeholders, accountability concerns the actual responsiveness of decision makers to constituents and stakeholders in the course of making policy. Key objectives of accountability are that individuals subject to regulation be protected from arbitrary governmental intrusions and that government officials act with due care and with proper attention to the issues that come under their jurisdiction.[3] Accountability as a normative goal

---

[2] Michael J. Warning, Transnational Public Governance: Networks, Law and Legitimacy 183 (2009).

[3] Lisa S. Bressman, *Beyond Accountability: Arbitrariness and Legitimacy in the Administrative State*, 78 N.Y.U L. Rev. 461, 499 (2003).

also aims to ensure that governmental authorities internalize the costs of their decision making such that they are rewarded (either politically or with more power or funding) when they are effective and are punished or overruled when their decisions undermine public welfare or unduly promote narrow, special interests.

There are several hallmarks of accountability in the regulatory context. The first is "transparency" – that is, the extent to which authorities divulge (specific) information on their upcoming policy goals, the rules and policies relied on to meet those policy goals, and the effectiveness of those strategies. This kind of information can be and is disclosed in a wide variety of ways. Announcements may be made in government-sponsored reports, websites, conferences, and a host of other popular media and professional forums. Minutes of meetings may be kept and made public, and some meetings may even be open to third-party observers. In some situations, private discussions with political authorities are used when the nature of the information may be sensitive to markets and market stability. Assessing the level of transparency is a qualitative, rather than empirical, matter that involves questions of degree, not absolute determinations of whether actors are accountable to their principles and for their actions. That said, transparency is a critical element of accountability and of well-governed organizations because it is needed in order to evaluate the performance of decision makers. As such, it is often a condition precedent for determining the (output) legitimacy of an actor. It also both helps to ensure that actors exercise care in fulfilling responsibilities and incentivizes responsiveness to the needs and concerns of stakeholders.

Another important feature of accountability can be broadly referred to as "review" – that is, the ability of stakeholders to evaluate, assess, and, if necessary, criticize or overturn suboptimal decisions made by their representatives. Accountability thus normally involves

> not just the provision of information about performance, but also the possibility of debate, of questions by the stakeholders and eventually of judgment of the actor by the stakeholders. Judgment also implies the imposition of formal or informal sanctions on the actor in case of malperformance, or, for that matter, of rewards in case of adequate performance.[4]

The belief is that transparency facilitates effective review – the public scrutiny and participation by elected officials and stakeholders – with the consequence that regulatory decision makers will have fewer opportunities to exploit their

[4] Mark Bovens, Analysing and Assessing Public Accountability: A Conceptual Framework 9 (European Governance Papers, No. C-06-01, 2006), *available at* http://www.connex-network.org/eurogov/pdf/egp-connex-C-06-01.pdf.

situation and act on the basis of private information. The public or their representatives will have better information about the actions of decision makers, and when decision makers fail to act in the pubic interest, they can be disciplined. Thus, with transparency and review, decision makers are most likely to internalize the costs of their decision making and, for that reason, to be more accountable to their principals.

LEGITIMACY AND ACCOUNTABILITY AS NATIONAL-LEVEL CHALLENGES

International financial law, as we have already seen, operates on two levels. At the local level national regulators promulgate standards – either local standards with international import or international standards produced by international organizations. Meanwhile, at the international level, international organizations promulgate international rules, best practices, and reports. Because of this dual structure, it is useful, and indeed necessary, to examine the parameters of legitimacy and accountability for *both* domestic and international regulatory processes. This section sketches out the parameters of national-level accountability and legitimacy. As will be seen below, financial regulation, even when practiced at the local level, is subject to various levels of criticisms. How important such criticisms are for any given domestic regulatory agency will depend largely on how much authority has been delegated to it from democratically elected legislatures and on the transparency and openness of local bureaucratic agencies.

Legitimacy

Financial regulation has always been the subject of considerable criticism from the standpoint of legitimacy, largely because of the foundation upon which authority and power stand. As we have already discussed, even at the local level, elected officials and politicians have very circumscribed roles in the day-to-day supervision and regulation of financial markets. Instead, unelected regulators – bank supervisors, finance officials in treasury departments, and so on – are the key individuals who make decisions on areas of national economic concern like disclosure for firms, deposit insurance, interest rates, and other issues. Although this type of regulatory decision making may help ensure expertise and technocratic know-how, it is not consent based and does not, in itself, reflect the values of (input) legitimacy.

The lack of input legitimacy has been a matter of popular concern, now and again, over the years. During the 1960s and 70s, when financial authorities worked in relatively narrow silos and regulation remained unconnected to larger macroeconomic (and political) issues, relatively few voices criticized

---

Text box 4.1. "Chain" of Domestic Regulatory (Input) Legitimacy

Election of representatives to legislatures → delegation of authority by legislatures to regulators → regulators implement statutes and fill gaps

---

the legitimacy of financial rule making – notwithstanding the broader, ideological jabs aimed at the capitalist system. However, as financial regulators came to make decisions that affect increasingly broad swaths of economic life worldwide, the legitimacy of their decision making has come under increased scrutiny. For some commentators, expertise serves as an insufficient proxy for political legitimacy; after all, technocrats make policy decisions that affect not only narrow regulated market participants but also the general public. Active involvement of political actors is consequently viewed as an important part of a regulatory regime.

Administrative law, in general, and delegation theory, in particular, offer what most observers agree is one of the most robust responses to such concerns. Simply put, although regulators are not elected, their power derives from the operation of political processes: voters elect representatives to participate in legislatures, who in turn delegate their authority to financial authorities under laws that are blessed by the executive. A chain of authority thus derives from democratic mechanisms that imbue regulatory authorities with input legitimacy, formalized by and under domestic statutes and accords. These controls can often be supplemented by other forms of oversight, such as appropriations powers exercised by legislatures over agency budgets.

Under this dominant interpretation of input legitimacy, regulatory power is legitimate because it has been authorized (and funded) by a higher political and democratic authority. See text box 4.1. Thus, securities regulators, for example, may craft rules that affect the cost of capital for a country's firms, and a bank regulator may supervise banks in a way that effectively limits a country's money supply – so long as they do not violate the explicit grants of authority provided to them by democratically elected legislatures in relevant statutes and accords. This standard is not always a clear one, however, particularly when legislatures' grants of powers to agencies are ambiguous. For example, the Federal Reserve's 2008 intervention in US capital markets sparked considerable debate about the institution operating as an unelected fourth branch of government and, indeed, as one that operated well beyond the scope of its national mandate by lending directly to financial firms like Bear Stearns, which were outside the Federal Reserve's regulatory net.[5] Yet even

---

[5] David Wessel, In FED We Trust: Ben Bernanke's War on the Great Panic 160 (2009).

in this example, in one of the most dramatic displays of regulatory authority in history, the issue of legitimacy has been circumscribed. Instead, concern focused on the proper scope of administrative action and not the legitimacy of the institution itself.

Arguments in favor of output legitimacy have largely rested on the perceived advantages of technocratic expertise discussed earlier in the book. Given the complexity of financial regulation, leadership wielded by technocrats and civil servants maximizes the likelihood of sound, accurate policymaking. Specialist training and experience in finance and financial market regulation give decision makers an expert understanding of the consequences of different policy approaches.[6] They also ensure that financial authorities possess a deeper skill set with which to harness market forces and direct them in ways that do not undermine financial stability. When this "expert" output legitimacy is coupled with delegation by generalist legislators, regulators are empowered to make decisions with the authority and blessing of the democratic electorate but without being directly subject to the pressures of reelection that can empower special interest groups. Indeed, administrative rule making can even help to undercut that sort of influence insofar as bureaucratic agencies wield their own rulemaking powers independent of the legislature and legislators.

Accountability

Accountability is a high-profile objective of many national financial regulatory systems, in part due to the stakes involved in financial regulation. Decisions pertaining to markets and the provision of capital affect many actors in a direct manner and even more actors indirectly. Moreover, the sums of money involved in financial transactions and the potential profits to be made from them are increasingly large, just as are the sizes of the institutions that participate in them. Efforts geared toward regulating capital and market participants consequently attract enormous attention from those with large, direct stakes in regulatory decision making.

Accountability is important, in part, because financial regulation, even when practiced by regulatory agencies, is potentially prone to a range of strategic and practical problems that undermine sound policymaking. Since the economic stakes involved in financial regulation are often greater than other, more socially oriented areas of regulation like education or welfare services, the temptation is always present for regulators to seek the favor of regulated

---

[6] Amichai Cohen, *Bureaucratic Internalization: Domestic Governmental Agencies and the Legitimization of International Law*, 36 GEO. J. INT'L L. 1110 (2005).

industries in the hope of securing future employment upon leaving the agency. Financial regulators in some countries (though certainly not all) are staffed or led by individuals with close ties to finance and the financial industry. On the one hand, such ties and professional experience provide financial authorities with considerable expertise and market-level experience. On the other hand, however, the interconnectedness can create conflicts and pressures to appease actors that may be employers for decision makers in the not so distant future.

Regulatory agencies may also be subject to a narrowing of outlook and a lack of creativity. Precisely because of the highly technical nature of policymaking and the professional training needed to become a financial regulator, the personnel in agencies charged with financial market regulation tend to share the same education, social background, and professional experience. These traits are also shared with the executives in the industries and markets they regulate. Administrative agencies are consequently often subject to group think, and ideas are often accepted and acted on without sufficiently critical attention.

In the absence of adequate accountability tools, financial authorities may find it relatively easy to hide their own policy failures. Suppose that an individual banking regulator has had long-standing responsibilities for ensuring the stability of a set of banks, one of which now has insufficient reserves due to the individual's own lackluster supervision. In that situation, the individual involved faces a tough situation. If the regulator recommends intervention – perhaps in the form of stiffer regulatory requirements or shutting the bank down altogether – he may draw attention to his own supervisory inadequacies and shortcomings. With that in mind, a regulator may ignore ominous signs of a bank's insolvency or grant it relief from compliance with minimum capital requirements or other regulations in hopes that its financial position improves. Forbearance is often costly, however, to society. To the extent that a regulator does not act in a timely manner to wind up or shut down a bad bank's activities, they risk exacerbating the likelihood and size of a bank's failure. And if the bank fails, it is the public's money that is likely to be used to bail out or guarantee the bank's deposits.

For these reasons, many legislatures have promulgated a range of rules and statutes requiring agencies to produce information that allows the legislatures to monitor and judge the actions, policies, and procedures of regulatory agencies. In some countries, regulatory agencies are required to publish reports that document the basis of its regulatory decision making. In others, bureaucratic agencies and policymakers are required, under "notice and comment" procedures, to inform the public of rules that they are considering or that they are planning to implement, and to solicit views from outsiders. In some instances,

---

Text box 4.2. Key Sources of Domestic Accountability

- Notice-and-comment procedures
- Due process
- Procedural transparency

---

third-party observers may even be permitted to attend meetings. See text box 4.2.

The objectives of such administrative innovations are all directed toward enhancing accountability. By requiring regulatory agencies and bureaucracies to publish information about their activities, principals – both legislatures and the people who elect them – are in a better position to monitor the actions of agencies and their effectiveness. The ability to evaluate the factual record used to make regulatory decisions also allows the public to scrutinize the wisdom and reasonableness of regulatory decisions and to help identify the circumstances that give rise to poor regulatory decisions. Notice-and-comment requirements – which put regulators in touch with the concerns and perceptions of outsiders, including the general public – help overcome tunnel vision, ideological blinders, and the potential impact of social and professional connections by broadening the scope of information that regulators receive.

Accountability to legislatures also enhances review, though the effectiveness may vary from country to country, depending largely on the particular context. Domestically, legislatures can intervene by enacting statutes that preempt the rule making of agencies. Courts can act to constrain agencies that overstep their mandates, misapply rules, or fail to comply with administrative requirements. Whether such review actually provides significant checks, however, is questionable. Although legislatures retain the right and ability to rein in the actions of financial authorities, intervention has at least historically been challenging due to difficulties involved in deciding upon a single approach and course of action, since the interests and perceptions of the legislators themselves are so varied. Likewise, although the executive branch may have considerable influence over the appointment of financial authorities, particularly regulatory agencies and supervisors, the branch's authority to remove them may be limited, especially in cases involving central bank governors and supervisors whose terms have not expired.

As a result, in democratic societies that have developed political systems with separation of powers, courts are commonly viewed as the best hope for ensuring regulatory accountability. But even with well-resourced judiciaries, the capacity of courts to intervene and discipline is likely to be weak. For one, the scope of administrative review is typically narrow and largely applies to issues of process established by legislatures. When judgments on substantive policy are required, courts are inclined to defer to agency expertise. Deference is especially likely when regulatory actions involve considerable discretion or involve judgments or guesses concerning the value of assets that may not have a market, such as bank loans in an environment of high risk aversion.[7] In such circumstances, courts and third parties more generally are in a poor position to second-guess or to evaluate the supervision of regulators or the judgments that they make.

LEGITIMACY AND ACCOUNTABILITY AS GLOBAL REGULATORY CHALLENGES

International law complicates national legitimacy and accountability. At the local level, national regulators act as agents of national legislatures (which have delegated authority to them) and of the national publics that have elected the national legislatures. At the international level, national regulators continue to serve legislatures and domestic audiences through agenda- and standard-setting organizations of various institutional designs, which promulgate global standards. Thus, at the international level, questions of legitimacy and accountability revolve around the degree to which regulators represent their local publics and whether international organizations like the Basel Committee, International Organization of Securities Commissions, and the Financial Stability Board are responsive to and represent particular special interests, national interests, or the global welfare.

Legitimacy

Legitimacy in global financial regulation is more problematic than in its domestic counterpart. The link to domestic political processes is more attenuated than at the domestic level. International standard-setting bodies originate global standards, and their constituents are not a "global public" per se but, instead, national regulatory organizations that represent their publics through appointment and political delegations. In international rule making, rules and standards are the product of "long and opaque chains of delegation":[8] people

---

[7] Daniel K. Tarullo, Administrative Accountability and International Regulatory Networks 33–34 (Nov. 4, 2008) (on file with author).

[8] Robert O. Keohane & Joseph S. Nye, Jr., *The Club Model of Multilateral Cooperation and Problems of Democratic Legitimacy, in* POWER AND GOVERNANCE IN A PARTIALLY GLOBALIZED WORLD 229 (2002).

elect legislatures that delegate power to regulators who then create (with their international counterparts) organizations responsible for promulgating global standards. Thus, with each additional link, claims to represent publics become progressively weaker, as it is not so much the principals as the agents themselves that transmit authority (either implicitly or explicitly) to other organizations. And some international financial organizations, like the Bank for International Settlements, have no clear responsibilities to any public.

The attenuated proximity to core democratic processes is problematic for some observers, especially because regulatory decision making at the international level is often more political than it is at the domestic level. In particular, coordination at the international level arguably involves more policy judgments that are not value neutral. In bargaining with international counterparts over various regulatory approaches, regulators make what are inherently political decisions that can determine winners and losers in particular industries. And when regulators bargain or interact over different sectors, they may be forced to prioritize different policy objectives (like financial stability, perhaps, over transparency) that arguably should not be resolved by technical experts alone.

Equally important, international financial law at times avoids the domestic political processes that accompany and legitimize more formal types of international law. As we have already discussed, there is no ratification procedure required. Thus, unlike "real" sources of international law, international financial law can avoid formal political legitimizing processes. To be sure, local administrative regulations may require various forms of public participation domestically through notice-and-comment obligations. However, no affirmative votes of legislatures are required for international financial rule- or policymaking or even, in most circumstances, authorization by heads of state. Instead, international administrative agencies are largely required only to acknowledge, and perhaps defend, their policy arguments. Thus, international financial law does not require the formal blessing of nationally elected officials. It is thus arguably illegitimate, even if it possesses lawlike qualities, such as compliance pull and even coercive force.

Perhaps the most damaging criticism of the legitimacy of international financial regulation concerns the "democratic deficit" in the standard-setting process. As we have already seen in the preceding chapter, most agenda- and standard-setting bodies have various degrees of exclusivity. Some organizations constitute clubs, whose members are mostly developed countries. Others, though universal in membership, are directed by exclusive policy cores. This exclusivity has important legitimacy implications. By definition, international financial regulation affects "global" finance and therefore all countries. If it is to be just, it should involve participation by all countries – at least those that are themselves democratic – in order to allow the full range of countries affected by the rules to have a voice in influencing their substantive content. Many scholars have, in this context, railed against G-groups and their concomitant standard-setting forums for their narrow, Euro-American "first world" dominance.

Excluded countries have strong arguments that "sovereign equality mandates their equal participation in forming the rules by which international finance is conducted."[9] Under international law, all states have equal status as legal persons, and in the absence of any formal agreement to the contrary, all states presumably have the right to equal input with regard to the crafting of international law. Theoretically, the same principles should apply to soft law standards when they have a coercive effect because of their implied "global" or universal application. Core notions of sovereignty are possibly ignored if governments do not have equal standing.

If universality is not reflected in an organization's institutional structure, it risks sacrificing its credibility. Take, for example, the following critique of the Basel Committee, dominated until recently by the G-10 central bankers. Critics have long argued that rich and poor countries may differ considerably on what kind of risk is acceptable to banks. More developed countries, for example, may be more risk averse with regard to loans extended to smaller and midsize companies and may require banks to hold more capital on their books for lending in that sector. Developing countries may need more credit to flow to middle-market firms and thus may want to place fewer limits on lending activities. Because poorer countries will be more likely to have more "high risk" borrowers than their richer counterparts, they may face larger costs with regard to their financing activities and thus prefer more flexible standards that promote development. In such circumstances, exclusion in itself can become the source of skepticism regarding virtually any international standard promulgated. When an organization like the Basel Committee excludes a government (or many governments), it risks being viewed as an undemocratic or unrepresentative regime imposing its will on nonparticipating (and often democratic) governments.[10] Richer countries can be seen as pushing rules that serve highly sophisticated global financial markets regardless of the developmental needs of smaller, poorer countries. The very credibility of its standards may consequently be undermined because of the regulatory environment in which it was created, whatever its technocratic merits.

[9] Robert P. Delonis, *International Financial Standards and Codes: Mandatory Regulation Without Representation*, 36 N.Y.U. J. Int'l L. & Pol. 563, 618 (2004).

[10] *Id.* at 619.

Accountability

The accountability of international financial law has also been subject to considerable criticism by commentators. Opprobrium has largely focused on the absence of any obligations by international standard-setting bodies to engage in processes that enhance transparency. In contrast to many domestic regimes, where legislatures periodically promulgate wide-ranging rules regarding administrative procedural requirements, no corresponding agreement, hard or soft, exists at the international level. Even the Vienna Convention on the Law of Treaties, which deals specifically with issues of treaty formation, only formalizes international law issues relating to consent and the capacity of states to enter treaties; no attention is given administrative law measures that might be incorporated into a treaty to help ensure transparency in law- or policymaking processes.

The charters and other foundational documents of international agenda- and standard-setting bodies have historically not specified a particular administrative process for promulgating international standards (though recently some headway has been made, as will be discussed below). Indeed, unlike traditional international organizations, which have more elaborate rules of order – the UN General Assembly, for example, has promulgated over 160 rules of procedure – international standard setters are open ended rather than restrictive.[11] In IOSCO, for example, the President's Committee is granted all the powers necessary to achieve the purposes of the organization, just as the International Association of Insurance Supervisors' bylaws permit its executive committee to undertake all decisions necessary to achieve those objectives.[12] The organizational documents rarely specify administrative processes that require or enhance accountability.

As a result, international financial law rarely evinces the transparency often available or desired in the domestic administrative processes of advanced developed countries. Outside observers are not permitted to participate in most meetings of international agenda- and standard-setting organizations. And historically, organizations have shied away from notice-and-comment mechanisms, which involve distributing minutes of meetings and even conducting public deliberations concerning the justifications for policies. This opacity of the international rulemaking process is characteristic of virtually all international agenda- and standard-setting bodies, though perhaps nowhere

---

[11]   David T. Zaring, *International Law by Other Means: The Twilight Existence of International Financial Regulatory Organizations*, 33 TEX. INT'L L.J. 281, 302 (1998).

[12]   *Id.*

as consistently and frequently as with the process associated with the Basel I Capital Accord in the late 1980s. In that instance, global rules were formulated, as noted by Miller and Barr, in closed meetings with little transparency and little to no input from the public or affected stakeholders.[13] As David Zaring explains, the final rule, when announced, was a "fait accompli."[14]

The problem of limited administrative transparency has been exacerbated in the past by the standard-setting process being – to use a phrase used by Keohane and Nye in a similar circumstance – largely "decomposable" from the rest of the system. That is, standard setters have generally operated independently of one another without deep and regular interactions horizontally.[15] For some commentators, this institutional discontinuity has allowed regulators to act in the privacy of the institutions and networks built around their mandates and issue areas.[16] By removing themselves from public scrutiny, many financial regulators have been able to develop "close working relationships with their colleagues from other countries, limiting the disruptive force of parochial concerns emanating from domestic politics."[17] And by keeping their internal deliberations confidential, decision makers have been able to strategically manipulate information and also to make compromises that would otherwise be impossible because they would undercut or disgruntle particular special interests.[18] Limited transparency makes it "difficult for outsiders to understand the actual positions taken in negotiations, how firmly they were held and the bargaining dynamics that produced compromises; therefore, it is hard to hold negotiators accountable for their actions."[19]

As with legitimacy, the absence of strong accountability mechanisms can undermine the credibility of international financial law. Rules imposed without the participation of those affected by the laws often translates into a lack of ownership and buy-in by stakeholders. There is skepticism and suspicion of the substantive quality of the rules adopted. While a closed process and little transparency may not necessarily lead to bad policy, the exclusion of input from affected stakeholders, outside observers, and third parties can lead to the misrecognition of problems uniquely encountered by those populations.[20]

---

[13] Michael S. Barr & Geoffrey P. Miller, *Global Administrative Law: The View from Basel*, 17 Eur. J. Int'l L. 15, 24 (2006).

[14] *Id.*

[15] Keohane & Nye, *supra* note 8, at 220.

[16] *Id.* at 221.

[17] *Id.*

[18] *Id.*

[19] *Id.*

[20] Delonis, *supra* note 9, at 617.

Policies can thus be less persuasive and less popular among stakeholders, as well as substantively incomplete and lackluster.

Weak accountability at the international level does not necessarily signify a loss of accountability in an absolute sense, but it does put considerable pressure on domestic accountability processes. In particular, even if international levels of policymaking are opaque, transparent domestic processes should be able to allow relevant political decision makers and stakeholders to pry into the bargaining process and understand the implications of international rules. However, as we have already seen above, domestic processes can themselves be weak and not quite up to this task. As they were in approaching accountability on the domestic level, courts and legislatures may not feel entirely competent or comfortable second-guessing regulators, given their greater expertise – especially since courts would thereby be moving into the deeper, unfamiliar waters of international affairs. Indeed, there may be little or no legal basis for interference at all. Jurisdiction on administrative law issues largely depends on whether administrative agencies are implementing or promulgating rules. Thus, for oversight to arise, the domestic agencies would have to be seeking the translation of international standards into domestic rules. Many standards, however, do not entail changes in existing legal regimes but affect only supervisory practices. Similarly, international standards may more modestly promulgate, though not actually impose, new norms, or they may help establish market expectations as to best practices for relevant firms. In such situations, financial authorities would likely not seek, or even need, new domestic rules; no domestic administrative law processes will be triggered.

THE INTERNATIONAL TREND TOWARD GREATER LEGITIMACY

The criticisms outlined above did little to provoke system-wide changes in the international regulatory architecture. To be sure, throughout the 1990s, new regional groupings and policymaking forums were developed (including the G-20) to broaden participation in a more conceptual sense, but the international architecture with regard to standard setting itself underwent relatively modest adaptations in institutional design.

The 2008 credit crisis ultimately had a dramatic impact on international institutional design and, with it, on the legitimacy and accountability of the global regulatory architecture. For the most part, as we have already seen, the changes were not due to a normative breakthrough but came about of necessity – and, in particular, because of the need to increase the buy-in of a larger group of economically relevant financial regulators by allowing them to take part in deliberations. Legitimacy did play a role, however, in the sense that exclusive clubs dominated by the G-8 were perceived not only as unfair, but also as unjustified in view of the central role that agenda setters played in causing the crisis. Ossified institutional structures could not, in short, rest easily on claims of input or output legitimacy.

The international regulatory system has responded to the perceived deficits in legitimacy in two ways. First, the standard-setting process has become increasingly politicized through the G-20 and FSB. Prior to 2008, most international standard-setting bodies, though coordinating through the then Financial Stability Forum, were relatively autonomous organizations that would set their own priorities with little guidance from G-groups in any formal sense. If G-groups did involve themselves, policy agendas – which rarely dealt with financial matters, though occasionally touched on economic issues – originated not only from the more politically inclined finance ministers of the G-7, but also from the G-10 central banks, which were more technocratic and separated from any political pressures or consequences due to their largely independent status.

The reforms introduced in 2008, along with the architecture outlined in chapter 2, have altered the political character of the financial system. The G-20, now considered the leading forum for economic policymaking, has been holding periodic leaders' summits that involve the heads of state from member countries. These meetings regularly address financial regulatory issues along with more traditional topics relating to monetary affairs. As a result, international standard-setting bodies, dominated by regulators and technocrats, now report at least indirectly to heads of state, enabling greater accountability to political actors, most of which are democracies. Meanwhile, the reform and elevation of the FSB offers a means of direct political involvement in the standard-setting process since finance ministries are involved in coordinating agendas and formulating standards across a wide variety of financial sectors. Although finance ministers in most countries are not responsible for representing heads of state per se but are instead tasked with pursuing the public interest, they are appointed by the executive and usually operate within executive agencies and departments, making them especially sensitive to domestic political issues and concerns. They may also, as mentioned above, be elected officials serving as members of their respective legislatures. Their leadership in the FSB, along with the FSB's increasingly central role in agenda setting, has thus led to greater structural opportunities for political influence.

One way to understand the greater vertical integration of the international regulatory system is from the perspective of organizational "linkage," meaning that more politically "legitimate" regimes can incorporate the rules of other,

TABLE 4.1. *Newly represented countries*

G-20	FSB	BCBS	IOSCO technical committee	CPSS
Argentina	Argentina	Argentina	Brazil	Australia
Australia	Brazil	Australia	China	Brazil
Brazil	China	Brazil	India	China
China	India	China		India
India	Indonesia	Hong Kong		Mexico
Indonesia	Mexico	India		Russia
Mexico	Russia	Indonesia		Saudi Arabia
Russia	Saudi Arabia	Mexico		South Africa
Saudi Arabia	South Africa	Russia		South Korea
South Africa	South Korea	Saudi Arabia		Turkey
South Korea	Spain	Singapore		
Turkey	Turkey	South Africa		
		South Korea		
		Turkey		

Source: GLOBAL FINANCE IN CRISIS: THE POLITICS OF INTERNATIONAL REGULATORY CHANGE 7 (Eric Helleiner et al. eds., 2010).

more technocratic ones. Simply put, by combining the technocratic expertise of standard setters with the largely (though not entirely, as in the case of China) democratic authority of political actors, institutions can bolster one another's various claims to legitimacy. The G-20, for its part, can operate as a kind of democratic-enhancing mechanism to technocratic standard setters, just as those standard setters can provide more technical substantive content for more political actors.

The second important response to perceived legitimacy deficits was the dramatic expansion of the number of countries participating in the agenda- and standard-setting process. See Table 4.1. Though discussed briefly in chapter 2, it is worth repeating here the kinds of expanded-membership reforms undertaken by the global financial system. At the outset, the G-7's displacement by the G-20 ushered in a systemic change in representation and membership across the global regulatory system. The FSB, Basel Committee, and Committee on Payment and Settlement Systems largely mirror the G-20's membership's expansion by bringing in new members like Brazil and South Africa. IOSCO made similar, though less expansive, changes by bringing in new, systemically important developing countries like Brazil, China, and India into its most important decision-making body, the Technical Committee. And the International Accounting Standards Board took the step of guaranteeing

TABLE 4.2. *Number of representatives on FSB by country*

Country	1	2	3
Argentina	X		
Australia		X	
Brazil			X
Canada			X
China			X
France			X
Germany			X
Hong Kong	X		
India			X
Indonesia	X		
Italy			X
Japan			X
Mexico		X	
Netherlands		X	
Russia			X
Saudi Arabia	X		
Singapore	X		
South Africa	X		
South Korea		X	
Spain		X	
Switzerland		X	
Turkey	X		
UK			X
US			X

Source: GLOBAL FINANCE IN CRISIS: THE POLITICS OF INTERNATIONAL REGULATORY CHANGE 7 (Eric Helleiner et al. eds., 2010).

"geographical diversity on its Board for the first time in a manner that guaranteed developing country representation."[21]

Representation nonetheless differs among parties, so that even among those that participate, the intensity of participation can vary dramatically. See Table 4.2. Most political scientists believe that the variations in representation serve as checks to some of the obvious developments in legitimacy, such as the expansion of membership ranks in many key standard-setting bodies. Owing to a growth in general membership, the international regulatory system has become more representative of not only the world economy, but the world itself. Nevertheless, just as with other, more traditional international organizations like the World Bank and IMF, where certain countries (for example,

[21] GLOBAL FINANCE IN CRISIS: THE POLITICS OF INTERNATIONAL REGULATORY CHANGE 6 (Eric Helleiner et al. eds., 2010).

Text box 4.3. Notice-and-Comment Procedures Among Agenda- and Sectoral Standard-Setting Bodies

G-20	FSB	BCBS	IAIS	IOSCO	IASB
None	De facto	De facto	De facto	Required, though according to broad standards and principles	Required by constitution

---

the United States) have greater representation than others, countries are not treated equally with regard to their representation at international financial standard-setting forums.

GROWTH IN INFORMAL AND FORMAL PROCEDURE

Various international standard-setting bodies have undergone organizational changes to mimic checks on administrative procedure that are common in the United States and EU. Notice-and-comment procedures are the most common, though regulators have committed to them to different extents and to varying degrees, with some organizations adopting no such procedures, others adopting them in practice (de facto), and others explicitly requiring such procedures according to internal mandates. See text box 4.3.

Basel I was prepared in largely closed meetings with limited transparency, and negotiations were conducted without public input.[22] By contrast, the Basel Committee adopted Basel II through a notice-and-comment rulemaking process that made public input possible.[23] During that process, through its website, the committee issued various papers for public consultation, collected comments about them, and gave reasons that made it easier for the public to assess whether the committee was being responsive to its expressed concerns. The committee also issued background papers to inform the public about its opinions on key issues. It held workshops and consultations with banking regulators from over one hundred countries, including developing ones, and allowed them to provide input.[24] Finally, as part of the notice-and-comment rule making, the committee engaged in explicit cost-benefit and economic analyses in support of its conclusions and judgments.

Similarly, the Basel III process has also involved considerable consultation with the public. In December 2009, the Basel Committee released a

---

[22] Barr & Miller, *supra* note 13, at 24.

[23] *Id.*

[24] Kern Alexander, *Global Financial Standard Setting, The G10 Committees, and International Economic Law*, 34 BROOK. J. INT'L L. 861, 872 (2009).

proposal for bank reform and petitioned any interested party for comments. Stakeholders from industry, finance, and banking lobbied both their domestic national regulatory agencies and international forums. Some of this lobbying was nationalistic, leading various countries to argue for exemptions that would benefit their local banks. Because of the public input, regulators recognized that some of the December 2009 proposals had unforeseen consequences for banks.[25] An analysis in the *Financial Times* reported:

> A plan to make banks stop counting as tier one capital flew in the face of the way emerging markets such as India and China worked with western banks. Another rule tossing out deferred tax assets – tax credits expected in future years – would have discouraged Japanese and Italian banks from setting aside money against future losses, exactly the opposite of what regulators were trying to achieve. A third proposal banning the fees banks receive for handling mortgages – despite American regulators' experiences that so-called mortgage servicing rights were saleable in a crisis – would have hit US banks particularly hard.[26]

Input such as this, along with additional studies by the Basel secretariat concerning the practicability of the initial proposals, provoked considerable changes in the follow-up proposal issued seven months later.

The Basel Committee is not the only major standard setter to have moved toward greater administrative openness. Both IOSCO and the IAIS have opted for more transparent decision-making processes. IOSCO has issued a document outlining a public consultative process geared toward soliciting views and comments from the international financial community. One of the objectives of such notice and comment is to benefit from the expertise of nonparticipants and to facilitate dialogue with the private sector, especially when the standards are likely to affect the business practices of regulated entities.[27] Meanwhile, IAIS lists all of its consultations on its websites, and it uses notice-and-comment procedures for almost all important policy decisions.

Perhaps the IASB has made the most notable changes. Since the early 2000s, in an effort to attain more credibility from national regulators, the private legislature has instituted a slew of formal "due process" changes in its constitution and implemented reforms in institutional design. The reforms include new rules for agenda setting, project planning, developing and publishing International Financial Reporting Standard, and reviewing such standards after

---

[25] Brooke Masters & Megan Murphy, *Banking Reform: Suspense Over*, Fin. Times, Aug. 19, 2010, http://www.ft.com/cms/s/o/ab02375c-aafb-11df-9e6b-00144feabdc0.html#axzz1KCsNAn3U.

[26] *Id.*

[27] Exec. Comm., Int'l Org. of Securities Comm'ns [IOSCO], IOSCO Consultation Policy and Procedure (2005), *available at* http://www.iosco.org/library/pubdocs/pdf/IOSCOPD197.pdf.

they are published. As part of this reform process, the IASB has a permanent Web portal open for notice-and-comment rule making; the IASB now invites public comments on all proposals that are published as discussion papers, exposure drafts, draft interpretations, and draft amendments to interpretations. The IASB also publishes final drafts of accounting standards so that companies and investors can learn the content, and a standing committee of the trustees, the Due Process Oversight Committee, has been established to monitor compliance with due process and examine complaints of alleged noncompliance. This committee is the only review mechanism in the field of international financial standard setting.

The G-20 and FSB have been relative laggards regarding accountability. Indeed, only the FSB has circulated consultative papers, and thus far has done so only rarely. Several reasons may account for this. First, as relatively new institutions, they have had insufficient time to develop such mechanisms. Second, the G-20 and the FSB, being more overtly political institutions, may feel that transparency is unhelpful when policies need to be negotiated and priorities set. Moreover, as semi-political institutions they may more directly internalize the costs of bad regulatory decisions by constituents, limiting in effect the need for transparency. Third, transparency may be both inefficient and of little value at the G-20 and FSB, given their function in the international regulatory system as agenda setters and not as more granular standard setters and rule makers.

OVERLOOKED SOURCES OF LEGITIMACY IN GLOBAL FINANCIAL GOVERNANCE

The structural reforms instituted in the wake of the crisis have failed to quell criticism from some commentators that international financial standard setting is illegitimate or unaccountable. Membership, for one, can serve as a weak indicator of organizational legitimacy. For example, some of the new members of the FSB have only one representative and, as such, do not enjoy the same level of representation as the original G-7 countries, of which each, along with the BRIC countries, has three representatives. Furthermore, as we see in organizations like IOSCO, some organizations have privileged positions in policymaking cores, whereas others are outsiders. And even after recent reforms, over three-fourths of the world's countries – 150 countries with one-third of the world's population and 20 percent of the world's GDP – have no representation at all on the G-20 and FSB.[28]

---

[28] Anthony Payne, *How Many Gs Are There in 'Global Governance' After the Crisis? The Perspectives of the 'Marginal Majority' of the World's States*, 86 INT'L AFF. 729 (2010).

The upshot is that many countries may be subject to what Michael Dorf describes in a similar context as a de facto "dynamic incorporation" of international financial laws; that is, standards adopted by foreign bodies and institutions may be incorporated domestically with little participation in international deliberations by domestic political leaders or regulatory agencies.[29] This "mini-lateralist" organizational dynamic arguably violates fundamental principles of international cooperation by arrogating to unrepresentative institutions important financial decisions that arguably should be shared by all countries.[30] It also erodes the sovereign rights of small countries by generating rules that countries are expected to follow despite having no voice or input in the decision-making process.[31]

Additional legitimacy concerns have centered on the practical implications of members' unequal representation on standard-setting bodies. Generally, a country's number of delegates affects its effectiveness and power. In consensus-based systems, problems of imbalance of power are less obvious since, in theory, strong disagreement voiced by any one member should be sufficient to stymie the proposal in question. Whether South Africa sends one representative or three, strong opposition by the country should be sufficient to block a policy proposal, though the peer pressure on the representative casting the lone vote, as opposed to three colleagues casting three votes, could more subtly disadvantage a country. Limited delegations also may have implications for the effectiveness of any one country in gathering information, coordinating with others, and promoting its views. At the FSB, for example, not all countries send three delegates, which affects the ability of smaller delegations to take part in key working groups and committees, and limits the number of votes that can be cast in plenary sessions of the body. A smaller country delegation may also have fewer opportunities to bargain with others and, as a result, may have less information about the needs and priorities of other members or about the negotiations in which they might be involved.

[29] Michael C. Dorf, *Dynamic Incorporation of Foreign Law*, 157 U. Pa. L. Rev. 103 (2008).

[30] This is an issue that is pervasive in the context of issues regarding the G-20. *See, e.g.*, Payne, *supra* note 28; Tony Porter, *The Democratic Deficit in the Institutional Arrangements for Regulating Global Finance*, 7 Global Governance 427 (2001). For some, however, mini-lateralism is considered to be the only way of achieving any international consensus. *See, e.g.*, Moises Naim, *Minilateralism: The Magic Number to Get Real International Action*, Foreign Pol'y, July-Aug. 2009, *available at* http://www.foreignpolicy.com/articles/2009/06/18/minilateralism.

[31] This has, perhaps not surprisingly, led to at times significant public criticism by outsiders. Indeed, at least one commentator has gone so far as to liken the evolving financial architecture as reminiscent of Prince Metternich's concert of great powers in Vienna which, among other things, was hostile democracy and set the stage for imperial conquests later that century. *See* Anders Aslund, Op-Ed., *The Group of 20 Must Be Stopped*, Fin. Times, Nov. 26, 2009, http://www.ft.com/cms/s/0/37deaeb4-dad0-11de-933d-00144feabdc0.html#axzz1K481fYoj.

Yet the consequences of the above shortcomings – which are real – are overstated by critics. It is worth reiterating that expectations must be reasonable, and the goal of achieving full democratic representation, participation, and legitimacy in these organizations is largely unrealistic, if not impossible. After all, the conditions for democracy cannot be met at the global level because not all countries are democratic; for those that are not, the country might be represented in an organization, but its people would not be. With the expansion of the G-7 to the G-20, which inaugurated the participation of nondemocratic (for example, China) and only marginally democratic (for example, Russia) countries in key regulatory processes, democratic legitimacy was arguably eroded instead of bolstered (or only symbolically bolstered). Even assuming that all countries were democratic, additional sources of potential illegitimacy arise when membership is determined. The relative size of a country's economy or its population comes into play here. For example, should countries be represented in organizations on a one country–one vote basis or on the basis of their relative populations?

Legitimacy can be understood as encompassing a variety of different values – consent, representation, expertise, responsiveness – which sometimes conflict with one another and also with the larger policy goals of international financial regulation. As we have already seen, coordination is more easily achieved when fewer individuals negotiate, fewer preferences need to be identified, and fewer players need to be appeased. As membership numbers increase, not only must more players be appeased or at least be satisfied with legislation, but opportunities multiply for players to exploit unanimity and to hold up the legislative process in order to secure their policy preferences. At the extreme, the standard-setting organization would become virtually incapable of producing new legislation.

Gains in input legitimacy can thus be outweighed by losses in output legitimacy, and vice versa. That is, when input legitimacy improves in terms of representativeness, beyond a certain threshold the output may suffer due to delays, conflicts, strategizing, and heterogeneous interests. If absolute representational legitimacy becomes a priority of institutional design, the institution's other priorities or objectives may be thwarted.

The challenge of international regulatory governance is thus to identify the countries that should get a seat at a table that has a likely finite number of chairs. Most organizations have undertaken pragmatic reforms geared toward increasing geographic diversity while also making sure to involve those players that oversee the largest financial markets. Thus, the G-20 and FSB have at least one representative from each of the world's regions but have tended to engage the largest economies. Similar choices have been made in IOSCO's expansion of its Technical Committee. Involving "big" countries makes sense. The regulatory community has assumed that wealthier countries will have the resources and expertise with complex issues to make better decisions when voting on various policy initiatives. Furthermore, regulators of large markets will have the largest stake in financial regulation in absolute terms and thus may pay closer attention to policy initiatives and the form that they eventually take.

Still, choices have costs, which include the legitimacy costs for excluded countries. One of the key challenges under the old G-7 and G-8 regimes was that the international regulatory architecture was led by a handful of countries that shared similar cultures, histories, and macroeconomic interests. Developing countries felt this difference keenly and viewed the pre-crisis order as providing the means by which former colonial or neocolonial powers could co-opt and dominate the southern hemisphere and Asia. Legitimacy costs grow as excluded (emerging) countries come to have more economic clout.

From this standpoint, the G-20 is noteworthy in that it both reflects shifts in the global economy and dilutes the concentrated power of traditionally dominant countries. Among other things, diversified membership has opened the door to greater input from wealthy, or soon to be wealthy, countries that have large domestic populations that are poor. The needs of these countries dovetail with the needs of developing countries. Thus, the G-20's diversification, though limited in the actual number of members, makes for greater de facto representation of interests. For example, although Botswana does not participate in G-20 (and other) international negotiations, South Africa does, and it is thus likely that shared economic interests of the region will be represented.

These observations do not discount the fact that even under more pragmatic models of legitimacy, some countries excluded from formal international regulatory processes may not have much in common with countries that do regularly participate. Even so, however, these countries will often find some sort of an opening in the international regulatory architecture. First, they may be able to participate in some of the regional consultative bodies that, as we have already seen, act as liaisons to international standard-setting bodies. The Fiji Islands, though not a member of the Financial Action Task Force, can communicate both informally and formally through the organization's regional partner organizations, of which it is a member. Likewise, the Democratic Republic of Georgia, though not a member of the Basel Committee, can articulate its concerns or demands regarding capital adequacy through the committee's regional group.

Second, and not to be overlooked, virtually any country can leverage either global or national accountability processes to access channels through which their voices can be heard. To the extent that an international standard-setting body uses notice and comment processes, outside stakeholders will be able to offer their views as to the effectiveness and implications of prescriptive policies and reports. Likewise, when members themselves require notice-and-comment processes, as is often the case, stakeholders can express their opinions on regulatory initiatives through domestic channels.

Third, in order to explore whether particular rules are optimal for their own populations, countries unrepresented at the global level can open up their own domestic administrative processes – a point highlighted in the growing international administrative law literature.[32] This kind of openness does not actually mitigate the lack of a participatory role globally, but it does enable a country's otherwise unrepresented stakeholders to wield voice and influence concerning internationally adopted rules. It also provides a route for stake-holders to reform or adjust policy proposals in ways that are suitable for local market participants. Thus local hard law, though informed by international soft law processes, will largely remain the product of domestic interests and preferences (which is not to say that domestic participants may not incur costs for deviating from the international standards involved).

A CLOSER INSPECTION OF ACCOUNTABILITY IN GLOBAL FINANCIAL GOVERNANCE

As with legitimacy reforms, accountability reforms at the global level of accountability have failed to impress many scholars. Although notice and comment is available in many standard-setting bodies, it is not often prac-ticed by those that set the international regulatory agenda. Moreover, when notice-and-comment procedures are in principle available or even espoused by regulators, they are used largely at the discretion of regulators. Indeed, such procedures are often perceived as a form of de facto *noblesse oblige*. (See text box 4.3.) In most cases, there is no formal obligation to explain or justify conduct. As a result, many measures geared toward establishing transparency are ad hoc and can be circumvented to the advantage of regulators. One note-worthy exception is the IASB, which displays a highly formalized commitment to transparency that informs its standard-setting processes.

These problems are real, but critics have overlooked a variety institutional processes that have the effect of at least mitigating some of the most damaging accountability deficits. Perhaps most important are domestic administrative processes. As we have already seen, international reforms of standard setting

---

[32] *See, e.g.*, Benedict Kingsbury et al. *The Emergence of Global Administrative Law*, 68 LAW & CONTEMP. PROBS., nos. 3 & 4, 2005, at 15, 31 (2004–2005) (noting how domestic institutions have taken the lead in trying to check absences in accountability in international regimes).

now increasingly trigger formal stakeholder involvement at the national level. The perceived problems of earlier, high-profile global compacts, like Basel I, generated a broad awareness of the importance of international regulatory rule making. Whereas the interest and participation in the Basel I process was low, by the time of the second phase, Basel II rule making, US agencies issued numerous Advanced Notices of Proposed Rulemaking about the potential reform of banks' capital requirements, and also made available the Basel Committee's draft accord.[33] The agencies involved also received and published 125 comments online.

Like the United States, the EU has launched its own consultation processes in connection with multilateral standard-setting processes, both to enhance international transparency and to expedite the EU's own rulemaking process. In particular, the European Commission drafted a consultative paper exploring the implications of new capital requirements in the EU context. Moreover, as Giulia Bertezzolo notes, whenever the Basel Committee decided to extend its timetable, the procedure agenda for the European Community was rescheduled accordingly in order to ensure consistency between European Community and the global rules.[34] The parallel rulemaking process allowed the commission to present a proposal on a directive concerning capital adequacy[35] immediately after the Basel Committee agreed to and published the final text of Basel II.[36]

The likelihood of backtracking on accountability at the international level is also extremely low. Whether formally embodied in charter documents, published on a website, or a matter of tradition, notice and comment as an administrative technique is now squarely a matter of expected international administrative practice, at least with regard to major standard-setting initiatives. Those bodies that have incorporated accountability would find it difficult to backtrack in the full public glare. The fallout from such action would be significant. Affected stakeholders in member countries could retaliate against political executives for failing to integrate them into the rulemaking process,

---

[33] Barr & Miller, *supra* note 13, at 29.

[34] Giulia Bertezzolo, *The European Union Facing the Global Arena: Standard-Setting Bodies and Financial Regulation*, 34 EUR. L. REV. 257 (2009). *See, e.g.,* Press Release, European Comm'n, Commission Welcomes Basel Committee's Review of the Impact of New Capital Accord (Dec. 19, 2001), *available at* http://ec.europa.eu/internal_market/bank/archives/index_en.htm.

[35] The final version of the *Basel II* was endorsed in June 2004 while the European directive proposal was presented July 14, 2004. *See Commission Proposal for a Directive of the European Parliament and of the Council . . . Relating to . . . Credit Institutions and . . . Capital Adequacy of Investment Firms and Credit Institutions*, COM (2004) 486 final (July 14, 2004).

[36] The directive was adopted on June 14, 2006 and the BCSB Basel II was adopted on June 2, 2006, *see Basel II: Revisited International Capital Framework*, BANK FOR INT'L SETTLEMENTS, http://www.bis.org/publ/bcbsca.htm (last visited Dec. 5, 2010).

and countries that have benefited from, and seen the value of, notice-and-comment procedures, whether at the national or international levels, could refrain from endorsing and accepting new international legislation. Rather, the greatest threat to accountability lies in those issue areas where there is no precedent.

Domestic accountability is not a fail-safe mechanism. It is, for one, not always available. Many lower-profile areas of regulation, particularly in the world of norm setting, are not accompanied by any kind of formal process. Reports may be issued with little public participation or notice, and MOUs signed without gauging public support. International best practices, reports stating records of fact, and general prefatory guidance and principles to upcoming regulatory initiatives are not subject to domestic accountability mechanisms since they do not consist of laws meant for direct implementation. Because these products are promulgated for largely normative, strategic purposes, domestic notice-and-comment procedures will not usually be activated, even when noncompliant international initiatives may have implications for firms by influencing the expectations of investors and other market participants. Thus, failures at the international level will have few checks domestically.

The timing of notice-and-comment processes can also be critical. As a general matter, these processes are most effective when they take place at the same time as the international rulemaking process. Otherwise, domestic accountability processes can be upended, and regulatory agencies may face unexpected opposition from domestic firms – which can undermine coordination processes. In 1999, for example, the SEC launched notice-and-comment procedures intended to conform the disclosure requirements in its Form 20-F concerning nonfinancial statements by foreign private issuers to the international disclosure standards endorsed by IOSCO. During the domestic notice-and-comment process relating to Form 20-F, however, the SEC encountered considerable opposition from the investment community on both substantive and procedural grounds. Specifically, the administrative processes employed by the SEC were perceived to be inadequate and belated since IOSCO had already endorsed final international standards drafted by the organization's Technical Committee, of which the SEC was the dominant member. As a result, by the time that the domestic notice-and-comment procedures were under way, the SEC was perceived as having little leeway for using domestic comments to shape international deliberations and was viewed as trapped into implementing most of the reforms anyway – regardless of domestic responses by stakeholders. As a result, at least one prominent law firm, Sullivan & Cromwell, lamented during the domestic notice-and-comment process that it should "have been possible for the SEC to have published, and invited comments on, a[n earlier] draft of the IOSCO standards."[37]

Perhaps the most effective organizational charters would include commitments by members to inform domestic legislatures of their global activities in real time or, at a minimum, to provide legislatures prospectively with the agency's international annual agenda. In this way, administrative processes could be synchronized in order to ensure more public participation. Legislators themselves might become more heavily involved in creating their own associations with which to police international agenda and standard setters. At a most fundamental level, legislatures could create hubs of information sharing with which to monitor the work of regulatory networks and prevent the development of overly complex and ultimately opaque chains of regulatory decision making.[38] Legislators could also, with the help of regulatory agencies, launch cross-border working groups with the sole responsibility of identifying problems in transnational regulatory networks (much like the role of an auditor-general in national politics). Over time, legislative networks and interactions, in the absence of regulatory networks, could work toward producing an international agreement (hard or soft) on guiding principles for the promulgation of standards. Specifically, best practices could be developed and endorsed that respond to the interests of legislative bodies in ensuring transparent activity by regulators in the development of transnational policies. Cost-benefit reports, regular updates to policymakers, and other initiatives could in this way become more formalized and standardized across borders.

OVERCOMING THE COORDINATION CONSTRAINT

How can legitimacy be bolstered, given that organizations often become less effective once the number of active participants increases beyond what is institutionally optimal? For some, the answer lies in the delegation of authority from the legislature directly to the international organizations themselves. Heads of state could sign treaties for approval by local legislatures – a process that would give full legal force to the prescriptive laws and rules emanating from existing international agenda and standard setters (or a new organization altogether). Through these formal acts of international delegation, the

---

[37] Memorandum from Sullivan & Cromwell to Jonathan G. Katz, Sec'y of the Sec. & Exch. Comm'n (Apr. 12, 1999), *available at* http://www.sec.gov/rules/proposed/s7399/sullivan.htm.

[38] Eric Helleiner & Tony Porter, *Making Transnational Networks More Accountable, in* RE-DEFINING THE GLOBAL ECONOMY 22 (Sara Burke ed.) (Friedrich-Ebert-Stiftung Dialogue on Globalization, Occasional Paper No. 42, 2009), *available at* library.fes.de/pdf-files/iez/global/06293.pdf.

organizations would possess the same international law-making legitimacy that domestic regulators possess legitimacy within their own legal systems. Indeed, the organizations would have a mandate – handed to them by domestic legislatures directly elected by the people (at least in the case of democratic country members) – and would act within the scope of that mandate.

The practical challenges of such delegations of power would be considerable since the process would involve heavy sovereignty costs, and the legislatures of most countries would not likely agree to such an infringement on their domestic powers of policymaking and governance. But aside from that issue, there is no clear indication that delegation would necessarily enhance the overall acceptance of an international organization or its policies or pronouncements. As proof, one need look no further than the protests surrounding the IMF, World Bank, and WTO over the last decade, with the most violent being the Seattle protests against the WTO Ministerial Conference in 1999 and the anti–IMF/World Bank protests in the early 2000s. Part of the impetus behind the protests involved the specific policies of the institutions, especially the IMF and WTO, which have left wealthier countries to their own devices but have pushed poorer countries toward market liberalization and the adoption of what have sometimes been disruptive social policies. Many argue that the hypocritical and occasionally cruel nature of IMF and World Bank decision making reflects the membership and representation of those organizations, which operate according to weighted voting structures. Decisions are directed from wealthy countries, not developing ones, and thus reflect the policy preferences of traditional economic powers.

The examples and arguments above again underscore input legitimacy as a multilayered concept in international regulatory affairs. Explicit delegation may help bolster domestic legitimacy for participant countries by partly removing one chain of principal-agent relationships, but it does little to address the global legitimacy and sovereignty challenges associated with organizations that are exclusive or that have unequal representation. Full legitimacy would require a global treaty or agreement by *all* countries (or at least all democratic ones) on issues concerning an organization's mandate, powers, and processes – an even steeper coordination challenge than that among bodies with limited numbers, such as the G-20. Mere reform efforts concerning issues of representation in the IMF and World Bank have consumed nearly two decades of negotiation and have yet to furnish clear reforms on voting powers and representation by emerging and developing economies. Indeed, informal organizational forms have, in some ways, stronger claims in terms of legitimacy; they allow more easily for reforms that take into account both changing economic realities and legitimacy implications – as seen in the G-8's quick transformation into the G-20 in 2008 – which would be impossible under hard law agreements. The degree of representation within an organization is likely more important in determining popular conceptions of legitimacy than whether or not they have been created by formal treaties or hard law processes.

Moving beyond the coordination/legitimacy constraint requires rethinking the modes of representation enabled by organizational membership. Perhaps the most obvious approach would involve the adoption of a universal model of membership by agenda setters and standard setters. A broader swath of countries could participate in the standard-setting process, aided by more effective, centralized management. To help alleviate coordination problems, a multi-chamber approach could be adopted as seen in organizations like IOSCO and the IAIS. Thus, both the G-20 and the FSB could create a larger general assembly consisting of all regulators and financial authorities, as well as a second, more exclusive executive council in which a small core of privileged members would participate.

One key issue for such an approach would be the nature of the relationship between the two chambers. Structurally, one could require that all executive decisions receive the blessing of both chambers. Thus, under this approach, the executive council could operate as the initiator of international legislation, with the larger general assembly required to approve it. In each particular case, different decision rules could be employed to reflect the various coordination dynamics. Thus, for example, consensus could be required in the executive committee, and majority rules required for the general assembly. Alternatively, each body could be empowered to independently promulgate its own legislation, thereby facilitating standard setting and the avoidance of strategic delays. However, reliance on both chambers as sources of standards would create the potential for inconsistent rules, and to the extent that rules lack the full backing of the institution, they could exhibit limited compliance pull and staying power.

Under either of the above alternatives, membership would remain, as always, a thorny issue. Who should be permitted to participate in the executive council? Ideally, one would like to restructure membership universally, according to explicit criteria, perhaps along key dimensions of size, location, and economic power – an approach suggested in the popular press by Robert Wade and Jakob Vestergaard.[39] The challenge in such approach, however, would lie in convincing existing privileged players, or at least some of them, to

---

[39] Robert Wade & Jakob Vestergaard, *Overhaul the G-20 for the Sake of the G-172*, FIN. TIMES, Oct. 22, 2010, http://www.ft.com/cms/s/0/a2ab4716-dd45-11df-9236-00144feabdc0 .html#axzz17MRmWCpZ.

relinquish their status and influence in international bodies and to participate only in the broader general assembly. In the past, such restructurings were possible, as we saw in IOSCO's growth from a regional organization. Whether or not such flexibility would be forthcoming from most countries in an age in which finance is increasingly important to national economies – and highly politicized in the wake of successive financial crises – is unlikely.

For this reason, perhaps the most pragmatic route to reform would be to build onto existing bodies while orienting new membership allocations around existing regional bodies or geography. Smaller, exclusive organizations like the Basel Committee, as well as policy cores like IOSCO's Technical Committee, could expand by adopting a rotating-membership model for new participants, with the space allocated on the basis of regional location (economy size and population are already largely taken into account). There could also, for example, be at-large African, South American, and Asian seats. Membership could be determined on the basis of a vote of regional regulators, or if a universal membership body complements a club, by a vote of the entire organization's membership. In this way, greater geographic and economic diversity could be achieved. Countries rotating through would furthermore be incentivized, due to regular organizational elections, to represent the group's long-term interests instead of individual short-term interests. Working groups and committees supporting an organization's standard-setting activities could additionally be staffed or chaired equally from developed and developing countries, and chairs could rotate periodically as seen in institutions like the G-20.[40]

Meanwhile, to help poorer countries carry out their responsibilities at the global level, organizational secretariats could be strategically expanded to bolster, and not reduce, the legitimacy of international standard setting. This suggestion is a controversial one, given that the core of international civil servants that help make possible international standard setting are generally viewed with suspicion by theorists. The FSB, IAIS, and Basel Committee, for example, have secretariats funded in large part by the BIS, supplemented by regulators seconded temporarily to Basel. As a result, the organizations' civil servants are in many ways autonomous actors that are unaccountable to political or national constituencies. This autonomy, however, need not erode the legitimacy of the organizations. Helleiner and Porter note that "powerful states can also manipulate informal settings where there are no clear

---

[40] Eric Helleiner, *The Financial Stability Board and International Standards* 7 (Ctr. for Int'l Governance Innovation, G-20 Papers No. 1, 2010), *available at* http://www.cigionline.org/sites/default/files/G20%20No%201_2.pdf.

rules or procedures to protect the weak. Without the same technical capacity, developing country representatives may lose out in an informal setting where expertise can become a form of influence."[41] From this perspective, secretariats can help to level the playing field in international organizations. Specifically, their mandate can be expanded to help poorer countries analyze and assess the impact of international regulatory standards and to offer tailored guidance in pursuing best policies for financial market stability and growth. Secretariats can thus bolster more informed and ultimately more legitimate policymaking at the international level.

CONCLUSIONS

The absence of legitimacy can be viewed as a potential source of systemic risk in the global financial system. To the extent that rules are not embedded in democratic processes and that rule making does not allow states and individuals to participate, the compliance pull of standards – particularly soft institutional norms and standards – can be limited. And when regulators and market participants ignore stability-enhancing rules, the global financial system is weakened.

Nevertheless, the legitimacy risks posed by the existing institutional architecture are not as acute as dominant voices seem to suggest. In most democratic societies, delegation by legislatures of administrative power to regulatory agencies provides the latter with sufficient authority to act on the international stage, at least insofar as doing so falls within their mandates. Domestic processes can furthermore act as a useful backstop when international accountability falls short. Key problems remain, however, especially given the exclusivity of different organizations and the at times limited participation by stakeholders. That said, international standard-setting bodies are evolving rapidly, incorporating novel processes to include both nonmembers' advice in the process of rule making and standard setting, and developing outreach mechanisms to generate increased buy-in of the standards adopted after consultations. However, additional innovations in membership are still needed – ones that acknowledge the pragmatic coordination difficulties of universal participation but that allow for broader and more diverse involvement in the global standard-setting processes.

[41] Helleiner & Porter, *supra* note 40, at 18.

5

Soft Law and the Global Financial Crisis

We turn now from theory to address what is (quite literally) the trillion dollar question: what role did international financial law play in the financial crisis? Given the prominence of regulatory failures in the United States, many commentators answer, "very little." After all, the financial crisis occurred in America's backyard, helped along by weak regulatory oversight by local officials. US financial authorities suppressed interest rates and, in the process, encouraged speculative real estate lending practices for subprime borrowers. Loans were pooled, sliced, and sold off to undercapitalized banks and financial institutions that relied on unregulated derivatives transactions like credit default swaps to hedge their risk. Credit-rating agencies, mired in significant conflicts of interest, barely scrutinized the underlying real estate risk posed by these complex derivatives. And in the absence of regulations concerning executive compensation, Wall Street bankers had perverse incentives to take outsized risks to maximize their pay. Bankers' short-term goal of earning high annual salaries outstripped any concern for the long-term stability of the institutions for which they worked, and exacerbated the impending financial crisis.

Even so, US rules and regulations were not solely responsible for the failure to anticipate or mitigate the financial crisis. Despite the plethora of widely publicized international codes and standards, the international regulatory community was unable to anticipate or avert the crisis. In fact, in some cases, it made the situation worse. And because of the limited effectiveness of international financial rules, the impact of the financial crisis, which originated in the United States, reverberated throughout the world. The international regulatory community was thus roused to brace itself against similar, future failures. An impressive array of global reforms was launched in the wake of the financial crisis to complement and support national efforts aimed at better regulation of cross-border systemic risks generated by increasingly interconnected financial markets. This chapter examines those responses in light of the preexisting gaps in the international regulatory architecture. It also draws on the crisis to tease out a fuller picture of some of the key limitations of international financial law as a mechanism of cross-border regulatory cooperation.

MARKET CAUSES OF THE 2008 FINANCIAL CRISIS

The causes of the global financial crisis have been well rehearsed in the literature, so I offer only a brief summary of them. It is generally accepted that the most immediate cause of the crisis was the bursting of the US housing bubble in mid-2006. Throughout the 1990s and 2000s, the US Federal Reserve Bank's aggressively low interest rates, along with large inflows of foreign capital seeking better yields in US capital markets, had increased speculation in US real estate in unprecedented ways. Most conspicuous was the increased lending to subprime borrowers – the riskiest category of borrowers since they did not qualify for traditional loans. Instruments like adjustable rate mortgages boomed in popularity. Borrowers were granted easy initial terms for loans that they used to purchase real estate, often in the belief that the long-standing trend of appreciating housing markets would continue and eventually allow refinancing at more attractive terms. Similar kinds of loans were used in other retail spaces, including credit card and auto loans, leading to unprecedented levels of consumer debt.

Fueling the lending spree was the popular technique of loan securitization. In essence, banks and other financial institutions that extended loans were not required to keep the loans on their books. The loans could be bundled, packaged, and sold off to investors. An important consequence of the "originate to distribute" model of banking was that lenders no longer had to concern themselves with the ultimate ability of borrowers to repay loans. Instead, the risks could be transferred from the originators of loans to the end purchasers of the securities. The process removed risk from balance sheets and freed up capital for a new round of origination and lending. Purchasers of the securities believed that securitization enabled greater portfolio diversification, moving away from concentrated risk exposures. If enough subprime mortgages could be packaged together from different parts of the country, and different tranches of securities generated from them, one could diversify holdings such that a substantial quantity of the subprime mortgages could enjoy AAA-rated prices, provided the correlation between mortgage defaults is low.[1]

---

[1] RAGHURAM G. RAJAN, FAULT LINES: HOW HIDDEN FRACTURES STILL THREATEN THE WORLD ECONOMY 134 (2010).

Eventually, investment banks, hedge funds, and other minimally regulated entities entered the financial real estate market as speculators. Demand for mortgage-backed securities increased, and the bonds became more complex and exotic. Pooled investments were sliced into different tranches based on perceived levels of risk in so-called *collateralized debt obligations* (CDOs). To minimize exposure on their investments, investors commonly entered into bilateral contracts, called *credit default swaps* (CDSs): one party (the protection buyer) would be entitled from the other party (the protection seller) the par value of the bond on which the contract was made should the third-party borrower default on its payments. Eventually, even "synthetic" CDOs were created, based on a portfolio of CDSs and other instruments, where two or more counterparties entered into payment obligations with respect to the underlying referenced securities. Because of the conflicts of interest at the credit-rating agencies charged with rating risk, the underlying risk posed by these complex derivatives received minimal scrutiny. Although designed to rate risk, credit-rating agencies were paid by the sponsors of the investments they rated and were incentivized to grant high ratings lest sponsors turn to competitors. Many financial services employees earned most of their compensation from large bonuses, which were tied to short-term performance. In other words, bankers were incentivized to make outsized risks, thereby maximizing their earnings.

During the housing boom, speculation involving such derivatives instruments and complex securities skyrocketed since they seemed to be relatively sure bets. Both the number and value of financial instruments and other agreements based on real estate consequently increased – just as the real estate market itself benefited from speculation. Additionally, more transactions were enabled due to financial innovation. With the advent of synthetic instruments, for example, traders no longer needed even to originate new mortgage loans in order to make bets on their performance. They could simply make an infinite number of bets on the bonds that already existed, assuming investors were available on the other side of the bet. Similarly, the securitization of credits expanded the number of potential securities transactions since banks, insurance companies, and financial institutions throughout the world used securitization and CDSs to pass risk to other investors and thereby remove liabilities from their balance sheets.

In 2006 and 2007, however, interest rates began to rise, and housing prices started to drop, making refinancing more difficult. As house values fell below outstanding balances on home mortgages, homeowners (usually those who had lost their jobs during the recession) were forced to default on their payments. When the housing bubble popped in 2008, global financial institutions reported major losses because of their borrowing against, and exposure to, subprime mortgage-backed securities investments. The firms that were first affected by the downturn were those directly involved in home construction finance and mortgage lending, like the US mortgage giant Countrywide Financial. Over one hundred mortgage lenders went bankrupt during 2007 and 2008 as the US real estate market crashed, and even the biggest financial institutions, with the value of their assets falling precipitously, could no longer obtain financing through the credit markets.

Ultimately, the crisis spread as it became apparent that major banking and financial institutions all over the world held large exposures of "toxic" assets tied to US real estate. General mistrust among banks about one another's solvency and the robustness of payment systems caused the quasi-disappearance of interbank lending. Huge swaths of the US financial system either failed, were bailed out through government-sponsored acquisitions, or were taken over by the government. The affected institutions included commercial banks like Washington Mutual and Wachovia, investment banks like Lehman Brothers, and brokerages like Bear Stearns and Merrill Lynch. Government-sponsored entities like Fannie Mae and Freddie Mac, as well as the insurance giant AIG, were crippled. Across the globe, similar financial market turmoil erupted due to bailouts required for Germany's Landesbanken, Belgium's Fortis and Dexia banks, the United Kingdom's Northern Rock, and many others exposed either directly or indirectly to the US mortgage finance industry.

GLOBAL SYSTEMIC RISK REGULATION, B.C. (BEFORE THE CRISIS)

The global regulation of systemic risk prior to the financial crisis was focused on four potential sources of instability: banks, payment systems, credit-rating agencies, and accounting practices. A variety of instruments had been devised to coordinate regulatory approaches and standards among financial authorities. The most important are listed below.

The Basel I Capital Accord

The most central way of regulating systemic risks – and in the process preventing, or at least mitigating, the impact of financial crises – has been through the regulation of "capital" held by financial institutions. "In its simplest form, capital represents the portion of a bank's assets which have no associated contractual commitment for repayment."[2] It thus represents the cushion between

---

[2] Douglas J. Elliott, Brookings Inst., Basel III, the Banks and the Economy 3 (2010), *available at* http://www.brookings.edu/~/media/Files/rc/papers/2010/0726_basel_elliott/0726_basel_elliott.pdf.

TABLE 5.1. *Basel I capital formulas*

Total tier 1 capital ≥ 4% of risk-weighted assets	Tier 1 + tier 2 capital ≥ 8% of risk-weighted assets

a bank's assets and liabilities that can be drawn upon if banks make investment decisions that turn out to be unprofitable. Capital both keeps banks solvent and provides a credible signal to creditors that they will be able to pay back their obligations.

Reaching consensus on international capital standards has not always been easy – a point reiterated by political scientists. In the wake of banking failures in the 1970s and 1980s, US and UK banking regulators proposed higher quality banking standards among the top banking markets. The ability to do so was constrained, however, by highly profitable Japanese banks, which had suffered few bank losses (due, in part, to interventions by the country's finance ministry). It was only in 1988, after considerable compromise – and the implicit threat of capital market sanctions against Japanese banks operating in the United Kingdom and United States – that an international agreement came into existence, now commonly referred to as the "Basel I Capital Accord" (or simply, "Basel I Accord").[3]

Under the Basel I Accord, all banks are required to meet one of two capital-adequacy requirements – two ratios that measure the capital on a bank's books in relation to the bank's risk-weighted assets. The first ratio, set at 4 percent, measures the amount of highest-quality, "tier 1" capital – for example, common stock, reserves, and equity as determined by the difference of assets and liability. The second ratio is based on a broader range of "tier 2" capital, including subordinate debt and preferred stock. It is set at 8 percent of the bank's risk-weighted assets. See Table 5.1.

The risk weighting of assets for the denominator, which includes assets both on and off the balance sheet, is set according to one of four risk categories – 0, 20, 50, and 100 percent. The least-risky assets, which are assigned 0 percent (and thus require no set asides by banks), include government securities issued by Organisation for Economic Co-operation and Development countries and purchased by banks. The riskiest assets, weighted at 100 percent (meaning the full amount is generally included in the denominator), include most of a bank's nonmortgage loans to corporations and individuals. Interbank lending is weighted at 20 percent, and mortgages secured on residential property

---

[3] *See generally* DAVID ANDREW SINGER, REGULATING CAPITAL: SETTING STANDARDS FOR THE INTERNATIONAL FINANCIAL SYSTEM (2007).

TABLE 5.2. *Key risk weights under Basel I*

No risk assigned	20%	50%	100%
Claims on OECD central government Claims on non-OECD central government in national currency	Cash in collection Claims on OECD banks and regulated securities firms Claims on non-OECD banks of <1 year maturity Claims on OECD public sector entities	Residential mortgage loans	Claims on the private sector (corporate debt, equity, and so on.) Claims on non-OECD banks of >1 year maturity Claims on non-OECD governments not in national currency

Source: Heidi Mandanis Schooner & Michael W. Taylor, Global Bank Regulation: Principles and Policies 150–51 (2009).

are subject to a risk weighting of 50 percent. These requirements, as Heidi Schooner and Michael Taylor have masterfully summarized elsewhere, can be presented as follows (Table 5.2).

The Basel II Capital Accord

Although the Basel I Accord was an improvement over having no global standard for capital regulation, it posed a variety of problems that became increasingly apparent as member countries implemented it. Most importantly, the risk-weighting system was somewhat arbitrary and failed to fully distinguish risks among creditors belonging to the same risk category – a topic that I address in more depth below. Because of this insensitivity to creditors, there was no guarantee that the risk weighting would fully capture the credit risk posed by any particular asset.

The Basel II Capital Accord, a second-generation initiative aimed at refining the 1988 agreement, had only been partially implemented in many countries (including the United States) by the time of the crisis. Over ten times the length of the Basel I, it articulates three different forms of supervision: minimum capital requirements ("Pillar One"), supervisory review ("Pillar Two"), and transparency and market discipline ("Pillar Three"). Of the three, Pillar One is widely regarded as the most important. It refines the risk-weighting approaches

TABLE 5.3. *Risk weightings under Basel II's standardized approach*

Rating	Risk weight for sovereign borrower	Risk weight for corporate borrower
AAA to AA −	0%	20%
A+ to A −	20%	50%
BBB+ to BBB −	50%	100%
BB+ to B −	100%	100%
below BB −	150%	150%
nonrated	100%	100%

Source: HEIDI MANDANIS SCHOONER & MICHAEL W. TAYLOR, GLOBAL BANK REGULATION: PRINCIPLES AND POLICIES 140 (2009).

for determining the adequacy of bank capital and provides two broad methodologies: "standardized" and internal, risk-based approaches. Under the first, asset risk is determined by the rating assigned to the borrower or issuer in question. That is, when a borrower has a credit rating from a recognized rating agency (for example, Moody's or Standard & Poor's), the lending bank can use that rating as a basis for calculating the risk associated with that borrower. In short, the higher the borrower's credit rating, the lower the capital requirement associated with that debt. It that way, banks can distinguish between governments and corporations that would have carried the same risk weighting under Basel I.

In an even more significant departure from Basel I, Basel II allows the largest international banks to use their own internal risk calculations as a basis for calculating capital charges under various iterations of the "Internal Ratings–Based Approach" (IRB). Specifically, banks are allowed to develop their own empirical models for calculating risk-weighted assets. These models, which are themselves subject to regulatory oversight and supervision, enable the banks to estimate the probability of default for individual clients or groups of clients and, in some cases, the banks' exposure to, and projected losses from, potential defaults. Providing banks with discretion regarding their methodologies and management systems aligns regulatory risk calculations with the more sophisticated risk models used by banks, thereby tying capital charges more directly to the actual risks posed by assets.

Bank ratings systems are generally based on quantitative credit risk models, which have been developed by outside vendors but are often customized for a particular bank by the vendor or the bank's own credit risk experts. Banks will use data specific to particular borrowers (and, as appropriate, different forms of borrowing by the same entity). These ratings are recalibrated regularly, presumptively once each quarter.[4]

Basel II addresses capital requirements not only in relation to credit risk, but also in relation to market and operational risks. Market risk relates to the assets held on a bank's trading books. In contrast to credit risks (lending), regulators determined that the primary risk level of assets was largely dependent on the extent to which they could lose value before an institution could shed those assets. Basel II therefore adopted a value-at-risk approach, which uses statistical techniques based on historical data to estimate how much value assets on trading books could lose under unfavorable market circumstances.[5] Operational risks are those associated with internal inadequacies or failure of various sorts, such as incompetence, fraud, inadequate controls, and management failures.[6] Basel II adopts a variety of approaches that range from using a simple formula relating to an institution's gross income, to using more complex internal systems, like the IRB approach, that rely on an institution's own risk-management assessments.

Basel II addresses other matters than capital requirements, as noted above. Pillar Two speaks to the need for supervisors to evaluate banks' internal capital-adequacy assessment. It also requires banks to hold capital in excess of the minimum threshold set by Pillar One to account for risks not captured under Pillar One, including risks generated by economic conditions. Pillar Three meanwhile imposes requirements for the public disclosure of, among other things, capital structure, capital adequacy, and interest-rate risk.

Basel Core Principles

Supplementing the Basel Capital Accords are additional pieces of international legislation to bolster bank supervision. Included in this category are the Basel *Core Principles*, a set of broad, prudential standards relevant to the deficiencies underlying the financial crisis:

- Principle 7 states that banks must have a well-developed process of monitoring credit relationships.[7] Supervision needs to ensure that the credit and investment function at individual banks is objective and grounded

---

[4] *Id.* at 152.
[5] ELLIOT, *supra* note 2.
[6] SCHOONER & TAYLOR, *supra* note 4, at 174.
[7] BASEL COMM. ON BANKING SUPERVISION [BASEL COMM.], CORE PRINCIPLES FOR EFFECTIVE BANKING SUPERVISION 3 (2006), *available at* http://www.bis.org/publ/bcbs129.htm [hereinafter BASEL COMM. Core Principles].

in sound principles. Lending and investment activities should be based on prudent underwriting standards that are approved by the bank's board of directors.

- Principle 8 states that when banks have problems, they need to enhance their financial strength. Banking supervisors must be satisfied that banks establish and adhere to effective policies, practices, and procedures for evaluating the quality of assets. Supervisors should assess a bank's policies and be satisfied that these policies are being reviewed regularly and implemented consistently.
- Principle 9 notes that banks should not have a concentrated exposure either to individual borrowers or groups of borrowers. Banking supervisors must be satisfied that banks have information systems that identify concentrations within their portfolios. Supervisors must set prudential limits to adequately restrict bank activities that result in a large exposure to single borrowers or groups of related borrowers.

Payment Systems

By 2007, payment systems had attracted considerable attention. Financial stability increasingly rested on parties' confidence that they would receive payments from each other when entering financial transactions; that is, the parties to any transaction needed to have sufficient capital to cover their obligations to each other. As early as 1998, International Organization of Securities Commissions had included in its *Objectives and Principles of Securities Regulation* that "there should be initial and ongoing capital and other prudential requirements for market intermediaries that reflect the risks that the intermediaries undertake."[8] By 2001, the concept had been extended to payment systems. The Committee on Payment and Settlement Systems promulgated its *Core Principles for Systemically Important Payment Systems (Core Principles)*, which described ten general principles that characterize the functioning of sound financial systems and also the role that central banks should play in supervising systemically important institutions. As with the IOSCO rules, a focal point of the *Core Principles* was that financial institutions participating in payment systems need to know, as funds flow between accounts, that they will receive payments from other participants. Building on this focus and other earlier reports, the CPSS and IOSCO jointly developed a set of recommendations for both securities-settlement systems and clearinghouses that could operate as counterparties (and thus insurance

[8] *Objectives and Principles of Securities Regulation*, INT'L FIN. RISK INST., http://riskinstitute.ch/ 145100.htm (last visited Dec. 5, 2010).

agents) for transactions, thereby improving the safety and efficiency of these systems.

Credit-Rating Agencies

As credit-rating agencies began to provide ratings for investors and financial authorities to use in evaluating risk for investment and regulatory purposes, they, too, came to attract more scrutiny from international standard-setting bodies. In 2003, IOSCO's Technical Committee formed a task force of its members' principal representatives to study the role of credit-rating agencies in the global capital market, with careful attention to any activities that could affect the quality of the ratings they published.[9] In addition, the Technical Committee published a set of principles that regulators, credit-rating agencies, and other market participants could follow to better guard the integrity of the rating process and to ensure that investors were provided with timely, high-quality ratings. In 2004, the Technical Committee released its *Code of Conduct Fundamentals for Credit Rating Agencies* (*Code of Conduct*), which was intended to provide all credit-rating agencies with a model for their own, internal codes of conduct. The *Code of Conduct* contained

> more than 50 different provisions that IOSCO's Technical Committee believes should govern the activities of [credit-rating agencies] to help them guard against conflicts of interest, ensure that their rating methodologies are used consistently by their employees, provide investors with sufficient information that they can judge the quality of a [credit-rating agency]'s ratings, and generally help ensure the integrity of the rating process.[10]

International Accounting Standards

Finally, alongside international efforts aimed at regulating the conduct of international market participants have been disclosure-related initiatives and approaches geared toward helping investors better understand the financial health and stability of financial firms. Specifically, regulators have long relied upon a system of financial statement preparation – generally referred to as "fair value" accounting – to shed light on the balance sheets of companies, including financial firms, thereby helping stakeholders to better understand the stability of the companies in question.. Under fair value accounting – which has been adopted under both the United States' Generally Accepted

---

9 Technical Comm., Int'l Org. of Securities Comm'ns [IOSCO], The Role of Credit Rating Agencies in Structured Finance Markets 1 (2008), *available at* http://www.iosco.org/library/pubdocs/pdf/IOSCOPD270.pdf [hereinafter The Role of Credit Rating Agencies].
10 *Id.*

Accounting Principles and International Financial Reporting Standards – all company assets, including financial assets, are generally accounted for, and priced in light of, their current market value. Fair value differed substantially from other approaches that focused on the historic cost of assets – which potentially enabled firms to create hidden reserves on their balance sheets. The capacity to generate reserves has the benefit of enabling management to smooth out acute crises by decreasing the probability of defaulting on loans, thereby lowering risk. But it also enables executives to "manage the books" and avoid pressure by shareholders – and may, in the process, lead to a slower response to emerging financial problems.[11]

Fair value accounting was presumed to reduce the risks of balance sheet manipulation while improving prospects of financial stability. Executives, for their part, are required to disclose the market value of their firms' assets to investors, and thus are incentivized to take immediate action to improve their firms' financial health should the value of their firms' assets erode, ultimately putting the executives' own jobs at risk over poor firm management. Fair value accounting counteracts regulatory forbearance – when, for example, embattled banks are allowed to delay recognizing their losses because regulators trust that, over time, the banks can raise enough capital to offset those losses. Regulatory forbearance, not to mention poor regulatory oversight, is also evident when regulators refrain from closing a bank in the hope that general upswings in the economy will ultimately improve the value of the bank's assets. Against a background of transparency and public scrutiny, when banks account for their assets and record losses promptly, regulators have little opportunity to provide banks with extra leeway. As a result, fair value accounting imposes discipline on firms and regulators alike.

GAPS IN THE INTERNATIONAL REGULATORY SYSTEM

Despite the presence of international rules and standards, the global financial system suffered from important gaps prior to the financial crisis. Indeed, deficiencies in the substantive content and scope of international agreements helped make the crisis possible and likely even exacerbated it.

Shadow Banking Institutions

In the 1990s and 2000s, a web of "nonbank" financial institutions – hedge funds, investment banks, money market funds and securities firms – had expanded

---

[11] GLOBAL FINANCE IN CRISIS: THE POLITICS OF INTERNATIONAL REGULATORY CHANGE 53 (Eric Helleiner et al. eds., 2010).

such that their collective assets, which peaked at $20 trillion in 2008, eclipsed the $13 trillion of assets in banking proper. Yet even though these institutions had become central sources of credit in many leading economies, international standards provided little guidance as how (or even whether) to regulate them. In 1989, for example, IOSCO had flagged the issue of systemic risk and the implications for securities firms. In a brief report, the organization summarized a range of methodologies for determining the minimum capital requirements for firms, though offered few specific judgments about them besides embracing value at risk as a central tool in mitigating risk.[12] And later in 2007, IOSCO revisited the issue as part of a consultative report on the valuation of financial instruments by hedge funds, though again no specific model or approach for doing so was adopted except to urge hedge funds to ensure the consistent application of policies and procedures in their internal valuation procedures.[13]

Meanwhile, the considerable headway made by the Basel Committee with regard to prudential and capital buffers had limited implications for the shadow banking industry because such institutions were not deposit-taking "banks," as traditionally understood and defined by existing regulations. Neither the Basel Capital Accords nor the Basel Committee's *Core Principles* originally laid out what it meant to be a "bank." Instead, the Basel Committee had merely proposed that the Accords be extended to include holding companies of banking groups, though these groups were themselves defined as activities that "may be" defined to include securities and other financial activities conducted "within a bank or banking group."[14] They did not explicitly define "banking" clearly or expansively, much less the capital requirements for firms that did not engage in banking activities. And notably, even where banking was concerned, the Accords' focus was on internationally active banks and not on banks that operate primarily at the national level.[15]

[12] TECHNICAL COMM., IOSCO, METHODOLOGIES FOR DETERMINING MINIMUM CAPITAL STANDARDS FOR INT. ACTIVE SECURITIES FIRMS WHICH PERMIT THE USE OF MODELS UNDER PRESCRIBED CONDITIONS (1998), *available at* http://www.iosco.org/library/pubdocs/pdf/IOSCOPD77.pdf.

[13] TECHNICAL COMM., IOSCO, PRINCIPLES FOR THE VALUATION OF HEDGE FUND PORT-FOLIOS (2007) (consultation report), *available at* http://www.iosco.org/library/pubdocs/pdf/IOSCOPD240.pdf.

[14] *See* BASEL COMM., A NEW CAPITAL ADEQUACY FRAMEWORK 21 (June 1999) (consultative paper), *available at* www.bis.org/publ/bcbs50.pdf. For more, *see* DAVID FLINT, CENTRAL BANK REFORM: THE RESERVE BANK OF NEW ZEALAND IN INTERNATIONAL MONETARY LAW 303 (2000).

[15] Internal Market Directorate General, *A Review of Regulatory Capital Requirements for EU Credit Institutions and Investment Firms*, at 9, European Comm'n Doc. MARKT/1123/99 (Nov. 22, 1999), *available at* http://ec.europa.eu/internal_market/bank/docs/regcapital/1999-consult/1999-consult_en.pdf.

The result, in practice, was that national authorities could choose the extent to which the Basel Capital Accords would apply to their local (nonbank) financial institutions. As a result, different countries have adopted varying approaches. In the EU, most banks were subject to both the Basel I and II requirements, whereas financial holding companies were subject to the requirements on a consolidated basis. EU officials later argued at international meetings held in Basel that capital requirements and appropriate regulatory supervision ought to be applied at all levels of financial companies and at every individual credit institution and investment firm. Even in the EU, however, some firms – notably, hedge funds – escaped rigorous supervision and prudential regulation.

By contrast, the United States was slow to implement Basel II and had little interest in imposing steep capital and supervisory requirements on securities firms. Moreover, "[w]hen Congress passed the Gramm-Leach-Bliley Act, it created a significant regulatory gap by failing to give to the SEC or any agency the authority to regulate large investment bank holding companies, like Goldman Sachs, Morgan Stanley, Merrill Lynch, Lehman Brothers, and Bear Stearns."[16] At the time that the act was passed, the political will to delegate such regulatory authority was lacking. Ultimately, however, due to pressure from the EU, a supervisory approach was adopted under the Consolidated Supervised Entities (CSE) program. As in Europe, the program did not apply to entities like hedge funds that fell outside of the traditional banking sector. Under the CSE program, companies could opt for a regulatory regime whereby investment bank holding companies would report their capital, maintain liquidity, and submit to leverage requirements. The SEC would then monitor and respond to financial operational weaknesses in CSE holding companies or their unregulated affiliates, including domestic and foreign registered banks and broker-dealers. However, the CSE program's effectiveness and institutionally mandated authority were weak because participation in the program was voluntary and investment bank holding companies could withdraw from the program at will. The program also suffered several highly public setbacks. For example, the failure of Bear Stearns drew attention to the high leverage of supervised firms and the program's inability to address concentrations of risk in mortgage securities.

---

[16] James Hamilton, *SEC's Consolidated Supervised Entities Program Ended*, JIM HAMILTON'S WORLD OF SECURITIES REGULATION BLOG (Sept. 28, 2008, 10:00 AM), http://jimhamiltonblog .blogspot.com/2008/09/secs-consolidated-supervised-entities.html; Financial Services Modernization (Gramm-Leach-Bliley) Act of 1999, Pub. L. No. 106-102 (codified in scattered sections of U.S.C.).

Derivatives

Not only had shadow banking largely escaped the attention of the international regulatory community, but so had the activities in which they were often dominant participants. Of special note here are CDSs, which contributed significantly to the downfall of institutions like AIG and Lehman Brothers. CDSs obligated their writers to compensate holders for defaults on the loans that they purchased. Prior to the crisis, however, no international best practices or standards were developed to address such instruments or the infrastructure supporting derivatives trading. CDSs, as well as other derivatives, were commonly traded off exchanges in most countries and escaped registration and disclosure obligations that would ordinarily apply in the case of most securities transactions. Moreover, because no record-keeping and reporting requirements were in place, most transactions escaped public oversight, and limited information was available as to the underwriting activities of systemically important financial institutions. US regulators – and, indeed, the entire international regulatory community – had little knowledge of the particularities of private derivatives transactions, much less of the trillions of dollars of aggregate speculative derivatives exposure building up in financial markets and threatening the global economy.[17]

Payment Systems

Despite the considerable headway made in the last decade to generate best practices for payment and settlement systems at the international level, existing rules had a limited prescriptive effect, especially with regard to the issues spurring the 2008 crisis. The CPSS *Core Principles* were expressly designed to ensure that they would be broadly applicable in all countries, and financial authorities stressed that the principles do not represent a blueprint for the design or operation of any individual system. To that end, and in contrast to certain other international financial standards such as the *Basel Core Principles for Effective Banking Supervision*, the CPSS *Core Principles* do not provide a methodology for assessors. Moreover, the recommendations, which are geared toward reducing risks in the infrastructure for settlement, focus on simpler, standardized products meant to be traded on exchanges. Reflecting the dominant regulatory approach in the United States, little attention was paid to clearing and settlement in the over-the-counter derivatives market. Although standards touched on areas like margin requirements for some vanilla

[17] Id.

transactions, no rules were promulgated covering more complex situations where markets are thinner and where more stringent prudential regulations may be necessary.

Too Big to Fail

Critically, no global rules were in place to limit the size of banks or the degree to which they interacted with one another, or for that matter non-banks that also served as sources of credit in financial markets. As a result, institutions could become very large and interdependent, with the consequence that the failure of one could upend the broader system. In such situations regulators face a difficult choice: let the institution fail, and accept the resultant financial and economic turmoil; or inject taxpayer money to keep it afloat. Politically, the first option is often untenable because the failure of financial institutions can undermine markets and the real economy with long-lasting (even decades-long) effects. The second option sets an unhealthy precedent of implicit support. Institutions that have reached sufficient size and importance may engage in high-risk, speculative activities because they can presume that the government will bail them out in times of trouble. Furthermore, large institutions may acquire competitive advantages over smaller, less systemically important institutions simply because lenders and counterparties may also presuppose government support for them. Thus, the "too big to fail" institution becomes a more attractive borrower or market participant.

The absence of global rules targeted at the too-big-to-fail problem meant that financial institutions were able to transact at a scale few regulators would have imagined just a decade earlier. In the absence of coordinated national and international regulation of bank size, institutions like AIG and Citigroup reached such scope that they became too big and interconnected to fail, and would ultimately benefit from bailouts when faced with the prospect of insolvency. Even today, the thirty largest institutions around the world are deeply international. They have, on average, 53 percent of their assets abroad, and of their one thousand subsidiaries, 68 percent operate abroad, including 12 percent in offshore financial centers.[18]

Cross-border Resolution Cooperation

Exacerbating the too-big-to-fail problem was the lack of an efficient, international program or process for closing down large international financial

---

[18] Stijn Claessens et al., Ctr. for Econ. Policy Research, A Safer World Financial System: Improving the Resolution of Systemic Institutions (2010), *available at* http://www.voxeu.com/index.php?q=node/5280.

institutions that had failed. Although the Basel Committee had provided extensive guidance on prudential regulation, particularly capital-adequacy and risk-management procedures, no cooperative mechanism was developed for large, failed banks, either commercial or investment.[19] The Basel Committee's *Core Principles for Effective Banking Supervision* acknowledge that a necessary part of an efficient financial system is the prompt and orderly exit of banks that are no longer able to meet supervisory requirements, and that supervisors should be responsible for, or assist in, such an orderly exit. Yet these principles, as well as their accompanying methodology, do not identify the particular processes that should be followed as part of an effective exit policy.[20] A Basel report entitled *Supervisory Guidance of the Basel Committee* describes, in contrast, possible responses by bank supervisors when banks fail, but offers no specifics regarding an appropriate or even default approach for cooperation.[21] Prior to the financial crisis, the International Association of Insurance Supervisors had also published numerous papers on insurer solvency, but had never articulated a robust global methodology for assessing it or winding down failing multinational insurance companies. As a result, the international insurance supervisory community lacked basic tools for determining the risk and solvency positions of immense insurers like AIG or international reinsurers.

In most cases, the failure of multinational financial institutions, rather than setting off united international reinforcement efforts, leads to independent attempts at stabilization by multiple national legal frameworks. The disparate patchwork of responses was evident during the failure of Fortis, a Belgian financial conglomerate listed on both Euronext Amsterdam and Brussels. Fortis had a large presence in Belgium, Luxembourg, and the Netherlands and was an important clearing member on several exchanges. When the bank failed in the wake of both an unwise acquisition and high exposure to US mortgage-backed securities, cooperation among authorities, even within Europe, was minimal: governments were willing to engage in recapitalization schemes for the parts of the company within their respective countries, but not for the rest of the holding company. As a result, the separate national governmental efforts to respond to the situation failed to calm international markets, exacerbating the effects and ultimate costs of the bailout.[22]

Likewise, when Lehman Brothers failed, efforts to shore up the troubled bank were borne primarily by the United States – even though the firm had over two hundred subsidiaries and was a participant in over one hundred

[19] BASEL COMM. Core Principles, *supra* note 9.
[20] Eva Hupkes, *Insolvency–Why a Special Regime for Banks?*, *in* 3 CURRENT DEVELOPMENTS IN MONETARY AND FINANCIAL LAW 474 (Int'l Monetary Fund Legal Dep't ed., 2005).
[21] *Id.*
[22] CLAESSENS ET AL., *supra* note 20, at 49.

payment and settlement systems around the world.[23] US officials provided financing for an orderly resolution of the broker/dealer arm of Lehman Brothers based in the United States, and helped facilitate a merger with Barclays Capital. However, there was no cooperative effort to help overseas Lehman subsidiaries – not even the subsidiary in the United Kingdom, which hosted major banking and financial operations.[24] Most international authorities agree that the United States' domestic focus, coupled with poor international cooperation, impeded the return of client money and the efficient unwinding of the firm's operations.[25]

Executive Compensation

Even fewer tools and agreements had been developed to deal with executive compensation. This is in part because executive compensation was not really considered a matter of systemic risk. Markets, it was assumed, along with firms (by virtue of their self-interest), would pay bankers appropriately according to the profits that they earned for the banks' shareholders. However, this laissez-faire attitude, both at the national and international level, was misguided. It overlooked the nature of many pay contracts for bank employees, which incentivized employees to take outsized risks that would generate large year-end bonuses. The structuring of bonuses also discouraged employees from considering the long-term benefits of particular trades and positions; they were paid on a yearly basis and could leave their firms long before the investments that they made turned out bad. A banker could, in short, purchase risky, mortgage-backed securities in the red-hot 2007 market, with little concern for their viability as good investments, and be paid long before the wisdom of his investment was proven. The incentive structure in many banks undermined the institutions' long-term viability and stability.

Credit-Rating Agencies

Although IOSCO's 2004 *Code of Conduct* for credit-rating agencies listed recommendations for better managing conflicts of interest, it failed to fully address some of the key challenges that helped fuel the US real estate bubble in the last decade. For example, the code did not identify the impropriety of

---

[23] John Lipsky, First Deputy Managing Dir., Int'l Monetary Fund, Towards an International Framework for Cross Border Resolution, Remarks at the ECB and its Watchers Conference XII (July 9, 2010), *available at* http://www.imf.org/external/np/speeches/2010/070910.htm [hereinafter Lipsky Speech].

[24] CLAESSENS ET AL., *supra* note 20, at 46.

[25] Lipsky Speech, *supra* note 25.

analysts working as unsolicited consultants for clients to improve products that had been given poor ratings. It required neither reviews of the methodologies used in rating different products nor disclosure as to how they were applied. Finally, the code did not require credit-rating agencies to ensure that their employees had the appropriate knowledge and experience to develop sound opinions on rating different types of credit. These shortcomings, compounded by the absence of national-level regulation in the area and the failure of the US subprime market, led investors to question the accuracy of ratings as well as their usefulness as risk-detection devices.

THE PROBLEM OF ARBITRAGE

The existence of regulatory gaps at the international level enabled market participants to arbitrage differences in regulatory approaches across national boundaries. That is, in the absence of clear global standards and international convergence, a financial services holding company could exploit the gaps in the international regulatory architecture to minimize its compliance obligations. For example, AIG was able to exploit the absence of derivatives regulation in the United States by executing trades in the United Kingdom. The UK subsidiary, though it was regulated neither as a bank nor an insurance company, was treated as a bank by counterparties for their risk-weighting purposes and for its own CDS credit exposures.

In addition to the differences in national regulatory regimes, the broad nature of existing international commitments enabled considerable regulatory arbitrage within the parameters of the international regulations themselves. The use of just four categories of risk (under Basel I) generated imprecise risk assessments. Specifically, the determination of risk based solely on the character of the borrower (for example, corporation, commercial bank, sovereign) did not necessarily reflect the actual credit risk posed by individual borrowers in any particular category. As a result, considerable capital arbitrage was possible under the regime. Because all commercial loans were weighted at one hundred percent, a bank could charge higher rates to a riskier borrower but be subject to the same capital charge. That is, a bank could earn greater returns by lending to a less than creditworthy corporation than to an established company with a better credit history.[26] Similarly, the distinction between Zone A and Zone B countries was arbitrary; among other things, assigning zero risk weighting to all OECD countries was unjustified. A bank could seek to lend

[26] Daniel K. Tarullo, Administrative Accountability and International Regulatory Networks 23 (Nov. 4, 2008) (on file with author).

to the riskiest institutions in a particular risk bucket (for example, lending to Greece instead of Germany) in order to increase its returns – assuming, of course, that the bank believed that the borrower country would not default.

Basel I encouraged, as Schooner and Taylor note, securitization over other loan structures:

> Under Basel I, if a legal opinion supported the view that the originating bank no longer had a claim on the securitized assets, these assets could be treated as off-balance-sheet for regulatory purposes, and banks did not have to hold capital against them. Thus, a bank could securitize residential mortgages, provide the credit enhancement and take the first loss piece of the securitization, and still find that its capital requirements were lower than if it had held the original assets on its own balance sheet. Nonetheless, the bank [could] still retai[n] most of the risk of default, just as it would have done had it not securitized the assets.[27]

Thus, Basel I could fail to capture a bank's exposure and consequently understate the bank's risk exposure.

Basel II addresses some of the loopholes created by Basel I. With respect to banks' capital charges, Basel II incorporates credit ratings into risk-weighting determinations. Borrowers within a particular category (and among categories) can be better differentiated according to their credit risk. Basel II rules also address capitalization risks posed by securitization and off-balance-sheet arrangements – though not those risks associated with originate-to-distribute models of fee generation. For banks under the standardization approach, all positions retained by a bank securitizing its assets are subject to capital reserve requirements. Under the IRB approach, mathematical formulas determine the capital required to be retained by banks. In both cases, the Basel rules are designed to address "situations in which a bank provides "implicit support" – that is, when "an institution provides support to a securitization in excess of its pre-determined contractual obligation" – though even here banks could partially evade the requirements by selling assets to special-purpose vehicles that they had to support when market conditions deteriorated.[28]

Despite the more sophisticated approach of Basel II, banks have discovered new opportunities for capital arbitrage. For example, IRB approaches, which allow banks to develop and apply their own risk assessments, can be used to yield lower costs for large banks. Similarly, certain securitization products are now more attractive than others from a capital standpoint. According to Fitch, the international ratings agency, an IRB bank seeking exposure to the

---

[27] Schooner & Taylor, *supra* note 4, at 161.
[28] *Id.* at 162.

credit card and commercial markets is better off, from a regulatory capital perspective, if it chooses to invest in a rated securitization structure rather than holding or purchasing an equivalent pool of unsecuritized assets.[29] Thus, in the case of securities backed by credit cards, commercial mortgages, or residential mortgages – many of the same instruments that faltered in the wake of the 2008 financial crisis – banks are incentivized to invest in securitization structures rather than to hold a comparable pool of unsecuritized assets.[30]

Finally, it is worth emphasizing that both Basel I and II were designed to allow regulatory arbitrage in ways that encouraged lending in desired areas of the economy. Consider, for example, the risk-weighting approaches to sovereign debt. Under Basel I, sovereign debt enjoys a zero risk weighting for OECD lending. Even under Basel II, governments have lower capital charges than companies enjoying the same or, in some instances, better credit. The disparity with some countries – for example, the United States and, to a lesser extent, EU members – is partially explained by the reserve status of their currencies, which ensures the ability of the borrower to repay. Nevertheless, the extension of the policy to all OECD members reflects fundamental political considerations. Of special note is that lowering the risk weighting of government debt incentivized banks to enter the sovereign debt and also, indirectly, lowered the interest charges that governments faced when borrowing capital. Similar rationales informed the risk weighting of mortgage lending. Under Basel I, for example, lending for housing purposes (including purchases of mortgage-backed securities) was weighted at 50 percent, whereas corporate lending was weighted at 100 percent, even though some corporate borrowers were more creditworthy than home buyers. The reason underlying this particular policy is that some countries, especially the United States, had longstanding policies of promoting home ownership and sought to encourage lending in that sector.

The policy choices discussed above did not always have the desired outcome. In the case of sovereign lending, arbitrage led to loans for less-than-creditworthy governments, thereby facilitating irresponsible fiscal activities of spendthrift national governments. Low capital charges for residential mortgages activated not only speculative lending, but also real estate bubbles, which in 2008 crippled the global economy once asset prices quickly eroded following widespread mortgage delinquencies.

---

[29] Martin Hansen, Fitch Ratings, Basel II: Bottom-Line Impact on Securitization Markets (2005), *available at* http://www.securitization.net/pdf/Publications/Fitch_BaselII_Sept05.pdf.

[30] *Basel II: The 'Bottom-line' Impact on Securitization Markets*, Risk Ctr., Sept. 14, 2005, http://www.riskcenter.com/story.php?id=11459.

THE PROBLEM OF PROCYCLICALITY

International regulatory approaches were not always designed in a way that prevented risks. Indeed, sometimes they exacerbated them. Measuring risk for the purpose of regulating capital has proven to be a particular challenge. Basel II has been roundly criticized for promoting practices among banks that aggravate risks associated with procyclicality – that is, movement in the same direction as the overall economy. Under IRB approaches, measures of risk and the assumptions underlying them tended to be highly procyclical. Banks developed templates involving a series of risk factors to help determine the riskiness of assets. These templates, however, were collected from recent borrowers and were expected to serve as good predictors of a borrowers' ability to repay.[31] Additionally, they relied in part on near-horizon estimates of quantitative inputs that included short-term volatility, asset and default correlations, and probabilities of default and loss. But they failed to take into consideration far-horizon models, along with the risks and vulnerabilities that could accumulate during good times.[32]

One major target of criticism was the Basel Committee's adoption, in 1996, of the value-at-risk (VaR) method of risk assessment used by banks to calculate their required capital reserves for trading book assets. VaR is an estimate of the maximum loss that a given portfolio of financial assets could potentially incur over a specified period of time.[33] It is attractive to many practitioners because it effectively sums up the risk presented by a portfolio in a single number.[34] Like many other methods of measuring financial risk, VaR relies on principles of probability and randomness, and also on the assumption that decisions made by portfolio managers operate independently of one another and thus do not affect market prices. To calculate VaR, a risk manager typically considers the conditions and kinds of risks that affect value in a particular portfolio, including historical changes in prices and market rates. From that information the manager generates estimates of value.[35]

VaR has a variety of important advantages but has also had two unintended consequences. First, VaR's ability to distill risk into a single number requires a manager to identify a historical baseline against which risk is modeled. In

---

[31] SCHOONER & TAYLOR, *supra* note 4, at 154.

[32] FIN. STABILITY FORUM [FSF], ADDRESSING PROCYCLICALITY IN THE FINANCIAL SYSTEM 9 (2009), *available at* http://www.financialstabilityboard.org/publications/r_0904a.pdf [hereinafter FSF Report on Procyclicality].

[33] SCHOONER & TAYLOR, *supra* note 4, at 172.

[34] Charles K. Whitehead, *Destructive Coordination*, 96 CORNELL L. REV. 323, 341 (2011).

[35] Id.

practice, however, trading portfolios are measured over short holding periods using data that do not capture full credit cycles. As a result, risk measurements exacerbate procyclicality by encouraging market participants to extrapolate from current conditions and to ignore or downplay long-term averages.[36] Second, VaR presumes that portfolio managers act independently and that market prices are unaffected by a manager's trading decisions. Yet, if VaR is incorporated into regulation and is used as a market standard, it can promote greater price uniformity. Managers continue to work separately, but a decision to buy or sell assets is more likely to be replicated by others using the same risk measure. The resulting sales can cause price declines, prompting further trading as managers adjust and readjust their portfolios.[37]

Standard accounting practices were subject to similar complaints. The International Accounting Standards Board, under IAS 39, had adopted (along with the Financial Accounting Standards Board, the US accounting authority) fair value accounting methods for financial assets and liabilities, and for derivatives. Although promoting transparency, in strong markets fair value accounting allows institutions to record excessively high values for assets such as derivatives contracts and mortgage-backed securities. High asset valuations, in turn, feed high recorded profits on investments, inflate bonuses for financial services executives, and lead de facto to more irrational exuberance in a self-enforcing cycle.[38] By the same token, when market cycles turn and markets crash, procyclicality may fuel irrational despair. Marking the value of assets to a market in which no investor wants to risk capital potentially undervalues assets. Market prices are not always an accurate reflection of an instrument's underlying cash flow or of the price at which the instrument might eventually be sold. Additionally, falling prices can activate margin calls and contribute to a downward spiral in market prices.[39]

A core aspect of fair value accounting was the impairment model of recognizing losses. The idea behind impairment is that an asset is not carried, for financial-reporting purposes, at an amount that exceeds its recoverable amount. To do so would have the effect of overstating a reporting company's financial health and performance.[40] As a result, prior to the crisis, most banks recognized losses only when they occurred. The consequence was that even

---

[36] FSF Report on Procyclicality, *supra* note 34.

[37] Whitehead, *supra* note 36, at 347.

[38] Fin. Serv. Auth., The Turner Review: A Regulatory Response to the Global Banking Crisis 65 (2009).

[39] Global Finance in Crisis: The Politics of International Regulatory Change, *supra* note 13, at 43.

[40] European Fin. Reporting Advisory Grp., Impairment of Financial Assets – The Expected Loss Model 3 (2009), *available at* http://www.efrag.org/news/detail.asp?id=485.

as troubles were arising in the financial system in 2005 and 2006, reporting companies were not allowed to consider the effects of expected losses on their balance sheets. The logic of this approach is that it is less subjective than other methods that potentially rely on interpretations and on estimates of future cash flow prepared by the reporting firm. The trade-off, however, is that this incurred-loss model is characterized, like fair value, by higher revenues in the period immediately after initial recognition, followed by a lower net income if credit losses are incurred.[41] As such, it is viewed as contributing to procyclicality and as potentially destabilizing the financial system when markets are under severe stress.

Collectively, poorly conceived risk-measurement techniques failed to identify risks in financial activities that were building up during good economic times. In fact, many banks did not adequately assess their risk burden so as to set aside necessary reserves for trading and credit activities. Yet, in an economic downturn, as credit quality and market asset values fell, the risk weightings of assets rose. Financial institutions confronted rising capital requirements and were compelled to seek financing in risk-adverse markets.

THE PROBLEM OF IMF/WORLD BANK MONITORING

In addition to gaps in the international regulatory architecture, weaknesses and flaws in the legislation of the time helped contribute to financial instability. First, compliance monitoring was poor, especially with regard to participation in global surveillance systems. As I have already argued in chapter 3, monitoring and surveillance in the international system has generally been weak. Although the program initiating *Reports on the Observance of Standards and Codes* was launched in 1999, few countries were under direct pressure to undertake the assessments. Germany's first and last ROSC appeared in September 2003. The United States, the epicenter of the 2008 financial crisis, had not undertaken *any* complete assessment under the IMF's Financial Sector Assessment Program prior to the financial crisis. Its first FSAP review was initiated in 2010. This is not surprising, of course, in light of the voluntary nature of surveillance under the FSAP. Additionally, wealthy countries like the United States have never relied on IMF financing – an important source of institutional discipline in the form of conditionality. Reputational and market discipline has been less than robust due to institutional shortcomings.

Surveys of national regulators over the last ten years suggest, perhaps not surprisingly, that standards memorialized in the *Core Principles* have been

---

[41] *Id.* at 5.

implemented only haphazardly across jurisdictions, despite their broad-based character and general applicability. Although most developed countries that were assessed by the IMF and World Bank are fully compliant with the *Core Principles*, a recent, 2008 study indicated that countries with low or low-middle incomes were compliant just over half the time.[42] Furthermore, some types of regulation have low compliance regardless of wealth and geographic location. For example, nearly half of the jurisdictions assessed in the 2008 study did not meet the standards set for supervising banks' risk-management practices for country markets, as well as for supervising other risks, such as those associated with liquidity, foreign exchange, and operations. Although most jurisdictions now use a risk-weighting framework along the lines of Basel I for credit (demonstrating its pervasiveness as an international standard), the requirements were not applied consistently across firms, and key risks (including market risk) have not always been incorporated into the capital calculation.

Weak compliance with the *Core Principles* is in many ways predictable. Adjustment costs accompanying the adoption of some principles are often significant, especially when local banks have to forgo attractive, but higher-risk investment opportunities that, due to stiffer prudential regulation and supervision, would necessitate an increase in the banks' capital reserves. Furthermore, countries can adopt the standards in name and under-implement them in practice – an easy tactic when monitoring is low or nonintrusive and when market or official sector discipline is virtually nonexistent. Even when market discipline is tougher, as with capital adequacy, evasion of implementation is possible and, in some cases, common. Thus, the value of the *Core Principles* has traditionally been in articulating desirable norms. Their function has been as such directed toward articulating best practices and not necessarily proscribing specific conduct. Even so, the *Core Principles*, like their counterparts in other fields, were highly negotiated, probably as much for their long-term agenda-setting significance as for any prospective, short-term demands for compliance.

THE GLOBAL REGULATORY SYSTEM, 2008–2011 "A.D."
(AFTER THE DEBACLE)

In the wake of the financial crisis, many countries, including the United States, were motivated to reform their domestic regulatory systems as well as the

---

[42] Martin Cihak & Alexander Tieman, *Quality of Financial Sector Regulation and Supervision Around the World* 10 (Int'l Monetary Fund, Working Paper No. WP/08/190, 2008).

international regulatory system. Taking the lead in coordinating at the global level was the G-20, which took over the G-7's previous role as the leading agenda setter for international finance. In the organization's first "Leaders' Summit" in 2008, heads of state tasked finance ministers with, among other things, enhancing global financial regulation and promoting the integrity and stability of international financial markets. Working groups were established to make recommendations in diverse areas – such as accounting and disclosure, and prudential oversight – including ones to dampen cyclical forces in the financial system. The Washington Summit's *Declaration* additionally contained a detailed action plan based in part on the principle that all financial markets, products, and participants – including shadow banking institutions – must be subject to sufficient prudential regulation.[43] In 2009 in London, the G-20 published a *Leaders' Statement* that took a step forward by committing to whatever was necessary to strengthen global financial supervision and regulation.[44] Participating countries laid out a framework for improving prudential regulation, tackling a range of specific issues inadequately addressed in the previous regulatory order, such as hedge funds, credit derivatives, and executive compensation. The work of these two summits continued in Pittsburgh (2009) and in Seoul (2010), and covered not only financial regulatory matters, but also trade, currency, and monetary affairs. Below is a general overview of some key financial market initiatives following the crisis of 2008.

Broad-Based Capital Reforms Under Basel II and III

The centerpiece of initial international regulatory efforts was the introduction of broader wholesale reforms of capital ratios for banking regulatory purposes. First, the methodology for determining risk weighting of trading assets was made more comprehensive – and stringent.[45] Additional stress testing was required, as well as back testing and value-at-risk testing, in order to increase the robustness of banks' internal credit models. Most banks experienced trading book losses in excess of the minimum capital requirements under Basel II's capital-adequacy rules. Thus, the Basel Committee, in a first stage of reforms, required banks to calculate a "stressed" value at risk that takes into account a potential one-year period of significant losses. This stressed value at risk must be calculated in addition to the standard value at risk, which is based on the

---

[43] Group of Twenty Summit on Financial Markets and the World Economy, Wash., D.C., Nov. 14–15, 2008, *Declaration: Summit on Financial Markets and the World Economy* (Nov. 15, 2008).

[44] Group of Twenty Summit on Financial Markets and the World Economy, London, U.K., Apr. 2, 2009, *The Global Plan for Recovery and Reform*.

[45] ELLIOTT, *supra* note 2.

most recent one-year observation period. This additional requirement reduces the procyclicality of the minimum capital requirements for market risk.

Under the formal Basel III process completed in 2010, regulators moved from the issue of risk weighting (the denominator in capital-adequacy ratios) and took aim at capital requirements themselves (the numerator in the ratio). Specifically, under Basel III, banks are required to hold three times as much capital on reserve – an effort to move banks toward more conservative positions and to force them to fashion a larger cushion against potential losses. The central feature of the agreement is a measure that requires banks to raise the amount of common equity they hold – considered the least risky form of capital – to 7 percent of assets from 2 percent by 2015. In addition, banks will be subject to an additional "conservation buffer" of 2.5 percent in times of strong economic growth, which means, in effect, that banks will need 7 percent common equity, 8.5 percent tier 1 capital, and 10.5 percent tier 2 capital to meet their capital requirements. If a bank cannot meet this conservation requirement, it should not be permitted to pay dividends. Finally, when the provision of credit in a country appears to be expanding faster its gross domestic product, a country can unilaterally require banks within its borders to hold extra capital against potential losses, up to of 2.5 percent.[46] Regulators in other countries would then have to reciprocate by imposing capital taxes on their own financial institutions, based on the extent to which they have exposure to the country imposing the buffer.

The Basel Committee also introduced several new capital ratios, alongside risk-weighted prudential requirements, in order to enhance the stability of the global financial system. Banks must now satisfy a leverage ratio measuring the bank's degree of debt. Risk-weighted asset calculations – whether based directly on historical experience, as with the internal ratings used by the large banks, or indirectly, as with the risk weightings set by the Basel Committee – failed to fully anticipate the steep decline in assets possible with market fluctuations. The Basel III rules therefore include a leverage ratio of tier 1 assets at 3 percent – which limits lending to thirty-three times their capital – as an additional test of capital adequacy and serves as a "safety net" against undue exposures of financial institutions to market risk. Because leverage ratios are absolute limits on financial institution indebtedness and are not risk weighted, they are blunt instruments, and a financial institution has to reserve as much capital to back a US government bond as to back a risky loan. But the approach does address the risks that can arise from inappropriately low risk weightings.[47]

---

[46] Felix Salmon, *Basel III Arrives*, REUTERS: FELIX SALMON BLOG (Sept. 12, 2010, 2:37 PM), http://blogs.reuters.com/felix-salmon/2010/09/12/basel-iii-arrives/.

[47] ELLIOTT, *supra* note 2.

Two additional liquidity ratios have been introduced in order to prevent a repeat of the liquidity crunch following the fall of Lehman Brothers in 2008. The first ratio, the Liquidity Coverage Ratio, requires financial institutions to maintain an "adequate level of assets that can be converted into cash to meet [their] liquidity needs for a thirty calendar day time horizon under a significantly severe liquidity stress scenario specified by national banking supervisors."[48] As unencumbered assets that present low credit and market risk, have ease and certainty of valuation, and are listed on a developed and recognized exchange market, they can be readily converted to cash to meet a bank's liquidity needs for a thirty-day time horizon under the severe-liquidity-stress scenario specified by national banking supervisors. The ratio, which has been fixed at 100 percent, includes a denominator comprising the projected cash outflows less capital inflows in a severe-stress scenario, while the numerator comprises a stock of unencumbered assets (that is, securities that present low credit and market risk, have minimal correlation to risky assets, and are traded on exchanges) to cover any shortfall. A second ratio, the Net Stable Funding Ratio, is designed to promote resilience over a longer, one-year period. The ratio requires that the sum total of a bank's funding expected to stay with the bank in the case of an extended stress be at least equal to the value of each asset adjusted for its liquidity, on a scale of 0 percent to 100 percent, with cash receiving a factor of 0 percent.

Shadow Banking

Significantly, the international regulatory community moved to better supervise institutions that have traditionally fallen below the radar of banking regulation. At the November 2010 Summit, the G-20 leaders requested that the FSB, in collaboration with international standard-setting bodies, develop recommendations to strengthen the regulation of the shadow banking sector. In response, the FSB formed a task force to develop initial recommendations that would define "shadow banking," set out potential approaches for monitoring it, and explore regulatory measures to address systemic risk and regulatory arbitrage concerns.[49] These recommendations are to be submitted to the G-20 by the fall of 2011 for their consideration and possible endorsement.

---

[48] Daniel Pruzin, *Basel Panel Issues Final Basel III Package; Version Contains New Liquidity Rule Details*, Int'l Bus. & Fin. Daily Online (BNA) (Dec. 17, 2010).

[49] Fin. Stability Bd. [FSB], Progress in the Implementation of the G20 Recommendations for Strengthening Financial Stability 4 (2011), *available at* http://www.financialstabilityboard.org/publications/r_110219.pdf [hereinafter 2011 Financial Stability Report].

Additionally, in October 2010, the FSB issued its report on the *Intensity and Effectiveness of SIFI Supervision*, which recommends that all global systemically important financial institutions, whatever their legal status, should have higher capital charges than those enumerated even under the improved Basel III Accord. This framework was then endorsed by G-20 leaders and their finance ministers and central banks several months later, and the FSB, along with the Basel Committee and the IAIS, has been working since to assess the systemic importance of financial institutions at a global level, regardless of their bank or nonbank status. The FSB also announced that by the end of 2011, likely at the G-20's Leadership Summit, it would present "criteria for assessing which institutions pose global systemic risk,"[50] in order to help ensure consistent implementation throughout its members' jurisdictions.

Regulators also redoubled efforts at promulgating international standards for hedge funds in view of their increasing role in financial transactions. Specifically, the G-20 called for mandatory national registration of hedge funds and their advisers, just as IOSCO amended its *Objectives and Principles of Regulation* to include the statement that regulators should ensure that "hedge funds and/or hedge funds managers/advisers are subject to appropriate oversight." The IOSCO Technical Committee published a report with six high-level recommendations for risk-based regulatory oversight of hedge funds, focused particularly on systemically important and higher-risk hedge fund managers.[51] According to its recommendations, hedge fund managers should provide information to help regulators protect investors and to monitor systemic risk and risks to hedge fund counterparties. Ideally, the information supplied through the registration process would provide adequate transparency of the hedge fund manager's business and should also be made available to all prospective clients prior to the execution of the investment management agreement. The disclosure should include assets under management, fees charged, investment strategies, risk tools employed, and conflicts of interest. IOSCO also declared that regulations require hedge fund managers to have comprehensive and

---

[50] FSB, Progress Since the Washington Summit in the Implementation of the G20 Recommendations for Strengthening Financial Stability 8 (2010), *available at* http://www.financialstabilityboard.org/publications/r_101111b.pdf [hereinafter 2010 Financial Stability Report].

[51] James Hamilton, *IOSCO Recommends Hedge Fund Regulation as Part of Systemic Risk Oversight*, Jim Hamilton's World of Securities Regulation Blog (Apr. 16, 2009, 1:00 PM), http://jimhamiltonblog.blogspot.com/2009/04/iosco-recommends-hedge-fund-regulation.html; Technical Comm., IOSCO, Hedge Funds Oversight (2009), *available at* http://www.hedgefundlawblog.com/wp-content/uploads/2009/06/iosco-hedge-fund-regulation-report.pdf.

independent risk management functions that measure risks across the whole of the business, including market, liquidity, credit, and operational risks.

Derivatives

Shadow banking "activities" attracted more attention following the crisis, especially derivatives transactions. The Basel Committee developed new capital weightings to better account for the risk exposures generated by complex financial instruments. For example, it was recognized that financial intermediaries tend to suffer highly correlated losses when they act as counterparties, especially in the derivatives space. The Basel III Accord therefore increased credit-risk weights when counterparties to derivative transactions are financial intermediaries with over $100 billion in assets, and these increases apply automatically when a counterparty is an unregulated financial intermediary, like a hedge fund. A smaller weight is applied, however, whenever a party transacts with a recognized central counterparty, thereby incentivizing actors not to transact bilaterally, but through a third-party clearinghouse, thereby mitigating credit risk. Under Basel III, banks will also need to create models predicting the impact of credit downgrades on their liquidity and quality of collateral used and on their collateral for derivatives transactions. Meanwhile, models used by banks to determine risks posed by counterparties are subject to various back-testing procedures and other metrics.

Payment Systems

Along with risk weights, the international regulatory community has acted to directly address derivatives trading and transparency, as well as their impact on trading systems. A key element of these efforts has been to increase the use of central counterparties to reduce risk. Central counterparties act as middlemen between buyers and sellers of securities and derivatives, meaning that if one party defaults it absorbs the loss. In October 2010, the FSB issued twenty-one recommendations in a report *Implementing OTC Derivatives Market Reforms*, which itself addressed practical issues that national authorities could encounter in implementing earlier G-20 commitments to shore up over-the-counter derivatives market by the end of 2012. Among other things, financial authorities are instructed to ensure that "appropriate incentives" are put into place for market participants to use standardized derivatives products, and the industry is urged to commit itself to increasing both standardization and the volume of centrally cleared transactions.[52] Additionally, in May 2010, the CPSS

---

[52] FSB, IMPLEMENTING OTC DERIVATIVES MARKET REFORMS (2010), *available at* http://www .financialstabilityboard.org/publications/r_101025.pdf.

and IOSCO published a consultative report, *Guidance on the Application of the 2004 CPSS-IOSCO Recommendations for Central Counterparties to OTC Derivatives CCPs*, to promote consistent application of existing central counterparty standards to better address risks associated with clearing OTC derivatives and to bolster the effectiveness of central counterparties as risk-mitigating devices.[53] Similarly, the CPSS and IOSCO published a consultative report, *Considerations for Trade Repositories in OTC Derivatives Markets*, which lays out factors that trade repositories should consider in designing and operating their services and that relevant authorities should consider in regulating and overseeing trade repositories.[54] Finally, the two organizations have planned to launch notice-and-comment procedures regarding twenty-four principles to be adopted by 2012 and observed by the repositories of important payment and settlement systems and by central counterparties.

Complementing these broader initiatives to articulate better prudential frameworks, and in an effort both to encourage the use of central counterparties and to anticipate risks associated with them, the Basel Committee put forth new capital rules in Basel III, whereby trade exposures to a qualifying central counterparty receive a 2 percent risk weight. In doing so, Basel III raises the risk weighting from what, under the prior Basel II framework, permitted all bank exposures to central counterparties to be free of risk capital. These risk weights would be significantly lower, however, than the risk weights applicable to bilateral transactions with more risky or low-rated corporations and financial institutions – and would thus incur a smaller capital charge.

Resolution Authority and Crisis Management

Regulators have sought to improve the cross-border resolution of large financial institutions, whatever their legal or regulatory identity, in a variety of forums. In March 2010, the Basel Committee issued its final *Report and Recommendations of the Cross-border Bank Resolution Group*, which "set out recommendations concerning strengthening national resolution powers, firm-specific contingency planning and reducing contagion."[55] Additionally, the committee and International Association of Deposit Insurers developed *Core Principles for Effective Deposit Insurance Systems*, which will be included in a revised *FSB Compendium of Standards* and, in 2011, will be accompanied

---

[53] COMM. ON PAYMENT AND SETTLEMENT SYS. & TECHNICAL COMM. OF IOSCO, GUIDANCE ON THE APPLICATION OF THE 2004 CPSS-IOSCO RECOMMENDATIONS FOR CENTRAL COUNTERPARTIES TO OTC DERIVATIVES CCPs (2010), *available at* http://www.bis.org/publ/cpss89.htm.

[54] 2010 Financial Stability Report, *supra* note 52, at 13.

[55] *Id.* at 8.

by a methodology to presumably be used for future FSAP reviews. The IAIS has also started to develop a white paper on crisis management and cross-border resolution of insurance companies.[56] Even the IMF, as part of its role as lender of last resort, has published its own proposals for improving coordination of cross-border banking. Finally, and perhaps most importantly, the FSB announced that, as part of its efforts regarding SIFIs, it would begin work on identifying the key attributes of effective resolution regimes, including the minimum level of legal harmonization and legal preconditions required to make cross-border resolutions effective."[57] These criteria are meant to draw on the work by the Basel Committee, IMF, and IAIS, and to eventually help establish a peer review process to assess whether the measures developed are applied consistently across countries.

Accounting

Accounting reforms have focused on simultaneously harmonizing and converging US GAAP and IFRS accounting standards. In September 2009, the G-20 called on the IASB and US accounting authorities to redouble their efforts at converging on a universal, global set of standards by the end of 2011. Part of this process has included enhancing the ability of investors and other users of financial information to understand the accounting of financial assets – a task that focuses on replacing IAS 39 in three main phases (to be completed by 2020). Toward that end, in 2009, the IASB promulgated a new standard, IFRS 9, as the first phase of accounting reforms. That standard addresses the classification and measurement of financial assets, whereas the second and third phases will address impairment and hedge accounting, respectively. The major advantage of IFRS 9 is its simplicity and effectiveness at measuring financial instruments. IAS 39, the older accounting regime, categorized all assets according to four different asset categories. By contrast, "IFRS 9 requires all financial assets to be measured subsequently at either amortized cost or fair value after considering (a) the business model of the entity for managing the financial asset and (b) the contractual cash flow characteristics of the financial asset."[58]

This approach is important insofar as amortized cost is less sensitive to market conditions than fair value. Under the evolving rules, the amortized cost

---

[56] *Id.* at 9.

[57] *Id.* at 8.

[58] *Significant Changes to the Classification and Measurement of Financial Assets: IFRS 9 Financial Instrument*, PRICEWATERHOUSECOOPERS (Feb. 23, 2010), http://www.pwc.com/us/en/alternative-investment/alerts/IFRS-9-financial-instruments.jhtml.

model will apply when the objective of the business model is to hold assets, specifically debt instruments, in order to collect contractual cash flows, and when the contractual terms of an asset give rise, on specified dates, to cash flows that are themselves solely payments of principal and interest on the principal outstanding under the terms of the loan.[59] Other financial assets are to be measured at fair value. Thus, through these reforms, nonfinancial institutions that tend to hold their assets and not trade on them, as well as institutions that exercise traditional commercial (deposit-taking) banking activities, would likely apply fair value assessments less frequently than under the previous IAS 39, and thus be less severely exposed to dramatic procyclical shifts. Notably, fair value measurements will also have to disclose when measurements are based on models with unobservable data.

Executive Compensation

The promulgation of rules and standards for executive compensation was rapid after the onset of the crisis, despite the relative novelty of compensation as an object of international regulation. Just before reestablishing itself as the Financial Stability Board in 2008, the Financial Stability Forum developed the *Principles for Sound Compensation Practices* aimed at mitigating incentives by bankers to engage in short-term speculation that could mortally wound their firms.[60] The principles are intended to apply to all securities firms and banks but are especially critical for large, systemically important financial institutions. In sum, they obligate firms in the financial industry to change their compensation practices such that employees' incentives are better aligned with the long-term profitability of the firm. The principles require compensation practices to reflect risk outcomes and to be more sensitive to the time horizon posed by investment risks. Supervisory examinations of firms are required at the national level. To this end, the Basel Committee has developed a set of *Compensation Principles and Standards Assessment Methodology* for national authorities to use with local financial institutions.[61] The *Methodology* seeks to foster supervisory approaches that are effective in promoting sound compensation practices at banks and that help to maintain a level playing field. The

---

[59] KPMG, IFRS Briefing Sheet: IFRS 9 Financial Instruments (2009), *available at* http://www.kpmg.com/Global/en/IssuesAndInsights/ArticlesPublications/IFRS-briefing-sheets/Documents/IFRS-briefing-sheet-160.pdf.

[60] Fin. Stability Forum, Principles for Sound Compensation Practices (2009), *available at* http://www.financialstabilityboard.org/publications/r_0904b.pdf.

[61] Basel Comm., Compensation Principles and Standards Assessment Methodology (2010), *available at* http://www.bis.org/publ/bcbs166.htm.

Basel Committee has also sought to strengthen banks' corporate governance more generally. As early as 2006, the Basel Committee issued eight corporate governance principles for banking organizations and their parent companies, though to little fanfare or attention. In 2010, in the wake of the crisis, the committee issued a new paper, *Principles for Enhancing Corporate Governance*,[62] which built upon OECD reports on corporate governance and the financial crisis, and attracted comparably more attention. It covers issues relating to best practices for banks' boards of directors and risk officers, and requires greater involvement of the board and senior management in overseeing their institutions' compensation systems.[63]

Credit-Rating Agencies

Credit-rating agencies have also not escaped new regulatory reforms at the international level. IOSCO's *Objectives and Principles* were revised to include a principle stating that credit-rating agencies "should be subject to adequate levels of oversight."[64] Additionally, the FSB released principles to reduce reliance on private credit-rating agencies in relation to market standards, laws, and financial regulations. Among the goals are to gradually eliminate references to credit-rating agencies in standards, laws, and regulations, to replace old standards with "suitable alternative standards of creditworthiness," and to force market participants to "make their own credit assessments." A mechanistic reliance on credit-rating agency ratings had meant that rating downgrades had large procyclical effects.

IOSCO's *Code of Conduct for Credit Rating Agencies* was revised in 2008 by the organization's Technical Committee to address the risks posed by structured financial products.[65] Included in the revisions are provisions that prohibit credit-rating agency analysts from making proposals or recommendations on the design of structured finance products that the relevant credit-rating agency rates. Additionally, the code requires that credit-rating agencies establish and

---

[62] Basel Comm., Principles for Enhancing Corporate Governance (March 2009) (consultative document), *available at* http://www.bis.org/publ/bcbs168.pdf.

[63] *See* Org. Econ. Co-operation & Dev., Corporate Governance and the Financial Crisis: Key Findings & Main Messages (2010), *available at* http://www.oecd.org/dataoecd/3/10/43056196.pdf; *see also* Gregory P. Wilson, Managing the New Regulatory Reality: Doing Business under the Dodd-Frank Act 234 (2011) (explaining how the Basel Committee leveraged the OECD's work).

[64] IOSCO, Objectives and Principles of Securities Regulation (2010), *available at* http://www.compliance-exchange.com/governance/library/ioscoprinciples2010.pdf.

[65] Tech. Comm., IOSCO, Code of Conduct Fundamentals for Credit Rating Agencies (2008), *available at* http://www.iosco.org/library/pubdocs/pdf/IOSCOPD271.pdf.

implement a rigorous oversight mechanism whereby methodologies and models, as well as any significant changes, are reviewed. A range of disclosures are required during the rating process, including those on rating financial products with limited historical data, which are more likely to be inaccurate. As part of the initiative, IOSCO developed an examination module to identify and promulgate best practices among regulators and converted what was an ad hoc credit-rating agency task force to a permanent Standing Committee on Credit Rating Agencies.[66] A central component of the IOSCO initiative for promoting compliance with its credit-rating agency code has been its February 2007 report on thirty-two credit-rating agencies and its March 2009 report on twenty-one credit-rating agencies from six jurisdictions (Brazil, Canada, Germany, Japan, Switzerland, and the United States) in March 2009. Both reports compared the wording of the IOSCO code with the wording of credit-rating agency codes as published on their websites.[67] In 2010, the FSB issued broad principles exhorting both market participants and regulators not to depend on credit ratings for their assessment of firm risk.

Enhanced Monitoring and Regulatory Surveillance

The IMF has approved financial stability assessments as a mandatory part of the fund's surveillance for members in systemically important financial sectors. Previously, participation in the FSAP process was voluntary for all fund members. Now, however, participation will be mandatory for all countries determined to have systemically important financial sectors. According to the IMF, mandatory financial stability assessments will comprise three elements:

- an evaluation of the source, probability, and potential impact of the main risks to macrofinancial stability in the near term;
- an assessment of each country's financial-stability policy framework, involving an evaluation of the effectiveness of financial sector supervision against international standards; and
- an assessment of the authorities' capacity to manage and resolve a financial crisis should the risks materialize, looking at the country's liquidity-management framework, financial safety nets, and crisis-preparedness and crisis-resolution frameworks.[68]

---

[66] GLOBAL FINANCE IN CRISIS: THE POLITICS OF INTERNATIONAL REGULATORY CHANGE, *supra* note 13, at 70.

[67] *Id.*

[68] Press Release, Int'l Monetary Fund, IMF Expanding Surveillance to Require Mandatory Financial Stability Assessments of Countries with Systemically Important Financial Sectors (Sept. 27, 2010), *available at* http://www.imf.org/external/np/sec/pr/2010/pr10357.htm.

In 2010, the IMF identified twenty-five jurisdictions as having systemically important financial sectors. For this purpose, the fund used a methodology that evaluated both the size and interconnectedness of each country's financial sector. The jurisdictions were as follows: Australia, Austria, Belgium, Brazil, Canada, China, France, Germany, Hong Kong SAR, Italy, Japan, India, Ireland, Luxembourg, Mexico, the Netherlands, Russia, Singapore, South Korea, Spain, Sweden, Switzerland, Turkey, the United Kingdom, and the United States.[69] Nearly 90 percent of the global financial system is represented by this group, as well as 80 percent of global economic activity.[70] It includes fifteen of the G-20 members, and over half of the membership of the FSB. Each country will have to undertake an FSAP assessment every five years, and all can volunteer for more frequent surveillance. The methodology is itself set to be reviewed periodically to ensure that it continues to capture countries that are systemically important to the global financial system.

Additionally, the FSB itself launched two general peer review processes – activities that had not been part of the FSF's activities. Included in these activities are "thematic" peer reviews that gauge countries' compliance with international financial standards and with policies that the FSB itself prioritizes, or that take stock of existing practices in particular policy areas. The FSB has declared that the objectives of the reviews are to encourage consistent implementation of standards across sectors and countries, to evaluate the extent to which standards and policies have had their intended results, and, when relevant, to help set agendas or make recommendations for potential follow-up by regulators, supervisors, and standard setters.[71] As such, the thematic peer reviews are envisioned to complement additional FSB "country" peer reviews, which will focus on the progress made by individual FSB members' jurisdictions in implementing FSAP regulatory and supervisory recommendations.[72]

CRITICISMS OF POST-CRISIS REFORMS

The initiatives enumerated above represent a significant improvement in the international regulatory architecture from both a substantive and architectural standpoint. Not only do they represent a step forward in stabilizing the international financial system, but they also create structures for cooperation and information sharing across a range of critical issue areas. Nevertheless, some

---

[69] *Id.*

[70] *Id.*

[71] *Thematic Review on Risk Disclosure Practices: Peer Review Report* (Fin. Stability Bd. Framework for Strengthening Adherence to Int'l Standards, Thematic Review No. 2, 2011), *available at* http://www.financialstabilityboard.org/publications/r_110318.pdf.

[72] *Id.*

writers consider the post-crisis period to be bad for global governance because reformers avoid tough decisions, with the consequence that the reforms are incomplete, ambiguous, or too broad. A full examination of each piece of legislation is beyond the scope of this book, but let us consider some of the more common criticisms.

Basel III

Although hailed by many commentators as strengthening the financial resilience of banks, Basel III has attracted three main criticisms. First, many experts have asserted that the core, tier 1 ratio is not high enough to cope with a downturn of a magnitude similar to the one experienced in 2008. It would not take much of a disaster to bring leveraged financial institutions close to insolvency and to panic uninsured creditors. Bailouts by national governments would be required again to stabilize the financial system. Consequently, some regulators have argued that the capital ratios that best serve the economy should be as high as 50 percent of risk-weighted assets. Meanwhile, other observers have criticized the ratios as largely discredited and risk weighting itself as a largely ineffective approach to regulation.[73]

Second, when the new standards were announced, their formal implementation was not required until 2019; it is widely held that the date was chosen to appease German banks that would have difficulties meeting the new capital requirements. In the interim period, regulators are free to continue complying with Basel II's lower capital requirements, thus giving time for distressed financial institutions to improve their balance sheets. A potential problem with this approach is that by 2019 the world will likely have lived through one or more new financial crises and will then have to respond by enacting new measures without knowing how effective the old ones were.

Third, although the G-20, along with the FSB, has gradually started to utilize broader references to "financial institutions," especially with regard to agenda-setting goals and policy planning concerning arbitrage, executive compensation, and procyclicality, Basel III's scope remains flexible. The calculation of risk weights remains at times ambiguous, especially with regards to complex issue areas like pension fund liabilities. And even Tier 1 capital is being interpreted in some jurisdictions, including Europe, as not limited to ordinary shares and potentially including insurance capital deductions. The potential for regulatory arbitrage through shadow-banking institutions also remains considerable. Risk activities taking place in commercial banks can,

---

[73] Martin Wolf, *Basel: The Mouse That Did Not Roar*, Fin. Times, Sept. 14, 2010, http://www.ft .com/cms/s/0/966b5e88-c034-11df-b77d-00144feab49a.html#axzz17NXexnsP.

quite simply, move to a new home – "within the sprawling mass of hedge funds, private equity firms, trading houses, even energy companies," all of which remain largely free of direct international (and national) capital requirements and regimes.[74] Additionally, some commentators fear that high capital requirements perversely incentivize banks to take more risks to compensate for decreased returns on capital, in order to satisfy potential investors.

Accounting

Both the IASB and the US Financial Accounting Standards Board reported continued progress toward convergence of their key financial instruments standards, and the US SEC is scheduled to make a determination by the end of 2011 whether to adopt or allow the use of IFRS for US issuers. Nevertheless, it is unlikely that the two organizations will finalize all key standards by the target date of June 2011. Although the IASB and FASB expect to complete deliberations with regard to the impairment of financial assets, balance sheet netting of derivatives, leasing, and revenue recognition, other standards will not likely be published until the second half of 2011.[75]

Meanwhile, to the consternation of some commentators, and despite the progress made by IFRS 9, which replaces the previous IAS 39, most financial assets continue to be reported at fair value. The only assets that can be held at amortized value are debt instruments. Under IFRS 9, financial assets are scheduled to be classified at "fair value through profit and loss," meaning that they are reported at fair value with corresponding changes in value affecting profit and loss each period. However, until at least 2013 (and possibility later), some financial managers will be allowed to continue classifying assets as "available for sale," meaning that changes in fair value are reported as direct adjustments to shareholders' equity on the balance sheet – and thus bypass the income statement altogether. The choice of reporting changes in fair value as a component either of earnings or of shareholder equity is an important one since that choice will affect the reported volatility of earnings. Readers of financial statements tend to react more, and pay more attention, to items that flow through the income statement. As a result, even with the introduction of IFRS 9, considerable procyclicality will remain embedded in the system. Furthermore, once the transition period ends and asset evaluations via a current profit-and-loss model will likely cause significant swings in the market valuations of affected firms.

---

[74] Patrick Jenkins & Brooke Masters, *Financial Regulation: The Money Moves On*, FIN. TIMES, Sept. 14, 2010, http://www.ft.com/cms/s/0/abf1599e-c02d-11df-b77d-00144feab49a.html.

[75] 2011 Financial Stability Report, *supra* note 51, at 7.

Shadow Banking

Although G-20 declarations and IOSCO's revised principles state that hedge funds should be subject to some form of prudential regulation and "appropriate oversight," just what that means remains largely ambiguous even two years following the summit. Neither the G-20 nor IOSCO adopted any particular national model for hedge fund regulation, and they also did not establish a multilateral framework under which hedge funds would have to register. And although IOSCO's hedge fund report outlines generally advisable disclosure elements, no capital or leverage requirements are promoted, and no efforts have been made to address disclosure issues like trading positions and trading strategies, valuation policies, and credit party exposure. Additionally, no agreement was reached as to whether or not such disclosures should extend beyond advisers to the actual funds under management.

Meanwhile, efforts at the G-20 and FSB to identify SIFIs have moved apace. For its part, the Basel Committee announced in July 2011 additional capital requirements for 28 globally systematically important banks ("G-SIBs") to be phased in beginning in 2016 and fully effective in 2019. However, the FSB has yet to identify any non-bank globally systemic financial institutions ("G-SIFIs") whose failure could undermine the global financial system. Indeed, global regulatory bodies are largely expected to avoid singling out any hedge funds, private equity funds, and other nontraditional market participants. Instead, the existing initiatives represent agreement as to *procedural*, as opposed to *substantive*, approaches for hedge fund regulation. Few funds, if any, are currently subject to the capital-adequacy requirements imposed in commercial banking. Partially in response to these challenges, IOSCO launched efforts in 2010 to create a methodology for assessing the implementation of hedge fund principles and published a template for the global collection of hedge fund information, with the initial data-gathering exercises to be carried out on a "best efforts" basis.

Consequently, international efforts have been unable to quash a persisting concern that the activities of high-risk businesses are not being adequately addressed through international financial law. Instead, many regulators believe that activities like highly speculative hedging, short selling, and derivative transactions will, even if subject to regulation in the banking sector, merely migrate beyond traditional banking institutions to new homes, most likely the vast complex of private equity funds, hedge funds, and trading houses that remain, for the most part, free of the capital requirements imposed on traditional banks. Indeed, although smaller than the $20 trillion high point reached in 2008, shadow banking is still larger than the assets in banking proper, with \$2 trillion in the highly leveraged and ultra-speculative hedge fund industry alone. Most experts consequently believe that nonbanks are essential sources of credit and that, as money flows to these institutions, their systemic importance will remain significant.

Derivatives Registration and Trading

With the exception of the enhanced Basel risk weights discussed in the previous section, few prescriptive standards have been articulated for derivatives. As of mid-2011, no internationally recognized best practices have been promulgated concerning disclosure requirements for derivatives instruments, the conditions under which they should be registered, or the institutions that should be permitted to deal in them. Instead, regulation has been urged, but only "where appropriate," giving authorities considerable leeway in determining the degree of transparency. Most standards promulgated since 2008 consequently concern derivatives trading itself. They provide general balancing tests to be administered by national supervisors for determining key issues – for example, whether an OTC derivatives product is actually "standardized" and thus can (or must) be traded on an exchange. Yet even here, limited instruction has been provided with regards to issues like the ownership of clearinghouses and the capital requirements for clearinghouse members, how (much) collateral should be posted for derivatives transactions. As a result, as with disclosure and registration, significant discretion has been left to national authorities in implementing the global standards.

National-level discretion presents at least the theoretical problem of regulatory arbitrage. In principle, given the prerogative of national regulatory authorities, a derivative transaction consummated in one part of the world could generate a lower charge in another. In practice, however, this decentralized approach has allowed the United States and the EU, the two parties enjoying the largest derivatives markets, to work on a largely bilateral basis on international derivatives policy through a series of letters between high-level finance ministries and supervisors. Still, even bilateralism has been difficult. Not only are key, growing derivatives markets in Asia likely to continue along a less regulated path (no matter what agreements are ultimately reached between the EU and the United States), but even the United States and EU have diverged from with one another along key points of policy implementation, particularly in the wake of sovereign debt crises in Europe. As the costs of Greek borrowing skyrocketed in the summer of 2010, French, German, and Greek leaders called on EU supervisors to ban so-called naked credit default swaps, where investors were purchasing insurance for bonds they never owned, reinforcing perceptions of possible EU bank and sovereign debt default. US regulatory

authorities, however, balked at outright bans because of the difficulty of policing such transactions and the substantial participation in such speculation by
US institutional investors. Similarly, although both the EU and the United
States have sought increased use of data repositories for recording over-the-
counter trades, the EU has sought more aggressive stances on information
sharing of repository information, and some authorities have even considered
requiring a treaty to memorialize commitments between EU members and
third-party countries to obligate deeper cooperation to that end. US authorities, by contrast, have resisted sharing potentially sensitive information about
trading positions of local market participants with foreign regulators. The EU
and the United States have even diverged concerning the institutional basis of
derivatives trading, with EU regulators adopting a more relaxed stance toward
banking and deposit-taking institutions participating in derivatives trading, and
US authorities adopting a stricter approach, partly due in part to the too-big-
to-fail considerations described below. The EU has consequently postponed
voting on European Markets Infrastructure Regulation, just as US and EU
regulators have pushed back the deadlines implementing derivatives reforms.

Because of these and other issues, the FSB has expressed its concern that
many jurisdictions may not meet the 2012 deadline of transitioning to more
robust derivatives infrastructure, and believes that differences in approaches
could weaken reforms in these markets, create possible opportunities for regulatory arbitrage, and subject market participants to conflicting regulatory
requirements.[76] Cross-border efforts aimed at data sharing or aggregating data
on a global basis may also be compromised insofar as national authorities adopt
divergent approaches to the reporting of transaction data. Finally, the FSB has
warned of possible future inconsistencies among countries in the following
areas: clearing requirements; margining and collateralization practices for
asset classes, products, and market participants; and regulatory requirements
for multi-dealer and single-dealer trading platforms.[77] In response to this challenge, IOSCO and CPSS issued in August 2011 a *Report on OTC Derivatives
Data Reporting and Aggregation Requirements*, which included draft guidelines relating to trade repository reporting that have yet to be scrutinized by
industry and market participants.

Too Big to Fail

Although considerable work has aimed at identifying SIFIs that are themselves
often "too big to fail," regulators have had difficulty in agreeing on *ex ante*

---

[76] Id.
[77] Id.

criteria for judging either how big financial institutions should be allowed to become or what kinds of activities any given institution should be permitted to participate in. As a result, each national regulator has its own approach, which can differ widely from that of other countries. Under the "Volcker rule," promulgated under Dodd-Frank, the US Congress instructed regulators to, among other things, ban deposit-taking institutions from trading securities on their own account and from investing more than 3 percent of their tier 1 capital in hedge funds and private equity firms, institutions that themselves engaged in high levels of speculation in securities and derivatives markets.[78] In the process, banks would to some extent have to reduce their "size" and riskiness. The idea was that speculative investments should not be funded by deposit-taking institutions. Meanwhile, proprietary trading not only presented conflicts of interest when banks traded against their customers' positions, but also could exacerbate volatility in bank earnings since banks could win (or lose) disproportionately from one quarter to the next. By contrast, continental Europe followed a different approach, one that reflects its long-standing traditions of universal banking, in which securities and deposit-taking activities have regularly taken place under one institutional umbrella.

Importantly, neither the G-20 nor the FSB addressed the too-big-to-fail issue head on, in part due to a preoccupation with more pressing negotiations regarding capital adequacy and reserve requirements. In the absence of detailed, prescriptive global standards, national regulators enjoy considerable discretion with regard to their local approaches. In practice, such flexibility means any one country's efforts to deal with the problem can potentially be undercut by another country's inaction. Here again, the Volcker rule provides an example. In theory, it works on a global basis and operates via direct extraterritoriality; for example, even the foreign branches of US institutions are banned from participation in hedge funds and private equity funds. Non-US entities can, however, relocate their trading activities from the United States to other locations, as long as they do not service US customers. These institutions can thus continue to grow larger – despite US regulatory attempts to address size – and can maintain diverse financial practices under one institutional roof. If large enough, the failure of such an institution, even if it is not US-based, could upend the international financial system, forcing both its home country and perhaps other foreign private and sovereign agents (potentially including the US government) to fund its bailout.

---

[78] Dodd-Frank Wall Street Reform & Consumer Protection Act, Pub. L. No. 111-203, 124 Stat. 1376-2223 (codified in scattered sections of U.S.C.).

Resolution Authority

Most commentators agree that, despite the work of the international regulatory community, the architecture for cross-border regulatory cooperation remains inadequate to deal with another financial crisis. No international plan has been developed whereby multinational banks and financial institutions can be liquidated in an orderly manner that imposes losses on creditors. Instead, coordination initiatives have been tentative. For its part, the FSB established a Steering Group to identify the essential features that national resolution regimes should have, and set up a Cross-border Crisis Management Group to help develop recovery and resolution plans for SIFIs and a framework for assessing and resolving multinational financial institutions. It has also published a consultative document, *Effective Resolution of Systemically Important Financial Institutions*, which proposes several additions to and improvements in domestic and cross-border resolutions regimes including living wills. The Basel Committee has similarly identified the need for greater coordination in light of the failures of the crisis and called on authorities to develop a framework for greater cooperation.

A key challenge in this context is to develop a coherent framework for the multitude structures and activities within global financial institutions – and a framework that effectively takes into account the diversity of risks that these structures and activities pose for the global financial system. An exacerbating factor is that many regulators do not have even the basic mandate or independence required to cooperate internationally, with the consequence that collaboration will likely develop slowly, over a period of years or even decades.[79] Much authority instead resides de facto with judges, who, unlike regulators, are less accustomed to international cooperation while carrying out their deliberations. As a result, the bankruptcy of a major financial institution today would cause the same chaos as failing institutions in prior crises and again require again major bailouts by governments.

Credit-Rating Agencies

Although the IOSCO *Code of Conduct* requires credit-rating agencies to change some of their internal procedures and created stricter divisions between the business development and actual ratings activities, it does not ban conflicts outright, so long as the consulting services are unsolicited. Furthermore, the *Code of Conduct* does not change or call for change in the business model of

---

[79] 2010 Financial Stability Report, *supra* note 52.

credit-rating agencies, with the consequence that they continue to earn fees from the institutions that pay them to rate their products. Besides such prescriptive limitations, the *Code of Conduct* remains technically voluntary. It has garnered its most high-profile criticism from the former EU Commissioner McCreevy, who notably described the initiative as a "toothless wonder" even though many credit-rating agencies were working to incorporate its guidelines. The FSB's more basic attempts to minimize reliance on credit-rating agencies have also met with only limited success. After much debate, Basel III continues to rely on credit ratings, though, as we have seen, it supplements risk weightings with stress testing, which itself remains suspect. National securities regulators, as well as various financial institutions, similarly use ratings as the basis for making determinations concerning the suitability of certain investments, the riskiness of institutions and provision of credit, and the access that some firms have to various investor classes. Only with regard to specific market segments – in particular, securitization – has robust coordination been secured at the global level to reduce reliance on credit-rating agencies. As a result, some regulators, especially in Europe, are considering a number of unilateral responses, including the creation of a European credit-rating agency, exposing credit-rating agencies to civil liability, and increasing opportunities for smaller credit-rating agencies to compete with the largest ones, which tend to dominate the ratings industry. Additionally, some EU policymakers have advocated restricting the extent to which ratings compiled outside the EU (and beyond the scope of EU territorial regulation) can be used for calculating regulatory capital.

Monitoring

Monitoring also remains weak along several dimensions. G-20 and FSB surveillance initiatives are not backed by overt sanctions or penalties for countries that do not fully participate in the programs or share information. And even when, as with the IMF, membership sanctions are potentially tied to surveillance like FSAP reviews, an absence of robust participation is, by itself, unlikely to affect a country's access to IMF credit facilities or World Bank loans. Thus, market disciplines may remain the primary disciplines, though the basis of information on which they would expected to operate may be limited. Indeed, it is worth emphasizing that most international reports and standards are not subject to the multilateral surveillance of any sort but are, instead, at most subject to informal peer review.

Finally, and arguably most important, even the FSAP as a whole is subject to "supervisory" shortcomings. FSAP evaluations generally remain obscure instruments and attract limited attention from market participants. Moreover, supervision is primarily carried out locally by regulators, and thus no direct supervision of financial institutions is carried out by international bodies. This nested mode of regulatory supervision is, in some ways, highly inefficient. As Eric Pan notes:

> The financial crisis stemmed from a series of governance and operational failures at various financial institutions: a breakdown in underwriting standards for subprime mortgages; erosion of market discipline by parties involved in the mortgage securitization process; flaws in credit rating agency assessments of subprime mortgages; risk management weaknesses at large financial institutions; and failure by financial institutions to mitigate these risk management weaknesses.[80]

As a result, Pan and others have argued that more intrusive supervision is needed at the international level. Financial innovation, in short, requires periodic examinations not only of legal structures, but of the financial institutions themselves. In the wake of the crisis, increasing attention was paid to the fact that national supervision of financial institutions can be weak, even when international standards were being used. EU assessments of bank stability through so-called stress tests gave Irish banks a passing grade even when utilizing some Basel-related standards – only to require a bailout several months later. Given the interest some regulators may have in undersupervising failed institutions, more effort (and power) should arguably be vested at the international level in order to evaluate the quality of banks' and other financial institutions' assets and to assess their risk-management practices.[81]

BACK TO THE BASICS: OBSTACLES TO POST-CRISIS REFORM

None of the issues addressed above is necessarily intractable, and two and a half years of regulatory coordination are hardly sufficient to declare the failure of international cooperation. And indeed, with some of the most immediate challenges (for example, capital adequacy) largely addressed, more resources may be available to focus in the near future on issues such as global SIFIs and cross-border resolution. Still, difficult, complex problems with few obvious solutions take time to resolve. National positions must be developed, a process that can involve everything from legislatively mandated studies – to examine the costs and benefits of prospective rules – to coordinating with local stakeholders and businesses. It is only after such domestic processes are complete that significant cross-border negotiation can even begin, and an agreement

---

[80] Eric J. Pan, *Challenge of International Cooperation and Institutional Design in Financial Supervision: Beyond Transgovernmental Networks*, 11 CHI. J. INT'L L. 243, 265 (2010).
[81] *Id.* at 266.

between national authorities be hammered out. Moreover, the complexities of this process often have significant roots in the dynamics and obstacles discussed earlier in the book. It is thus worthwhile to review these challenges now and to see how they apply to the financial crisis, enabling us, in turn, to better evaluate the prospects and limitations of international financial law as a coordinating mechanism.

Regulatory Philosophy

The initial responses to the 2008 crisis have highlighted that differences in regulatory philosophy have consistently stymied full agreement in many regulatory arenas. At the most basic level were differences in opinion concerning the role of the state and propriety of state intervention. Consider the example of executive compensation. As mentioned previously, in 2009, just prior to the G-20 meeting in Pittsburgh, calls were made by some countries – France's President Nicholas Sarkozy was especially vehement – to institute straightforward, international limits on the pay a banker could earn. Such an approach was in line with France's social democracy, which had long set pay scales for executives in various fields. The notion of government-dictated compensation clashed violently, however, with US notions of free-market capitalism, and the US government fiercely resisted any blunt constraints on regulating banker pay. Because of this deep difference in regulatory philosophy and the competitive considerations described below, the international community opted for a compromise, focusing not so much on the determination of pay but on the alignment of incentives between executives and their firms.

Similar clashes arose more generally with regard to prudential regulation and transparency initiatives. Even after the crisis and its taxpayer bailouts, many officials, especially in the United States, believed in the self-corrective power of the market – above all, in matters where sophisticated participants dominated specialized trading and financial markets. Calls to regulate well-heeled investors and institutions thus sat poorly with long-standing jurisprudential and legal traditions in the United States, which either expected or allowed sophisticated investors to fend for themselves in their dealings with one another rather than rely on government protections. US authorities thus often sought market-oriented approaches based on transparency and not on prudential oversight and supervision. In contrast, in the EU, as well as in parts of South America and Asia, regulators were more inclined to interfere in capital markets, even those that were dominated by sophisticated investors and institutions.

Different countries have also had genuine disagreements regarding the effectiveness of various approaches. Cross-border resolution provides an excellent example. In the United States, resolution has often focused on the notion of "fresh starts": Individuals and investors cut their losses such that debtors can either liquidate or restructure to carry on activities in the most productive way possible. The United States has emphasized the need for liquidated or restructured insolvent banks to emerge from the bankruptcy process unencumbered so that they are not "saddled with [the] shareholders debt, senior executives, or bad assets" of the old bank.[82] Banks can therefore exit bankruptcy with a fresh start and participate fully in financial markets and contribute to the real economy. Equally important, bankruptcy is an antidote to the too-big-to-fail syndrome and the moral hazards that it generates for bank managers: if necessary, insolvent banks can be liquidated and their executives dismissed.

European regulators, by contrast, have emphasized financial stability in their approach to bank insolvency. Liquidation dampens executive greed and allows purchasers of bank assets a fresh start with unencumbered assets, but it can also generate enough chaos to bring down the wider financial system. As a result, many European authorities have sought reforms where banks in financial distress issue "bail-in" debt, which converts into common equity when the crisis is past, thus enabling the bank can be quickly recapitalized. The EU has also sought authority to write down debt held by creditors of a failing firm at the point of resolution. The advantage of this approach is that the market instability that is often generated by insolvency can, at least in theory, be avoided if such plans can be executed swiftly in times of economic distress. On the downside, however, the approach potentially enables regulators to selectively choose how and when to impose regulatory requirements and allows bad banks to continue. In light of these drawbacks, US authorities have generally viewed such approaches with skepticism, though notably have not vetoed or blocked such initiatives in regulatory forums like the Basel Committee.

Similar cracks in the international regulatory consensus are apparent in deciding what kinds of activities banks should be permitted to participate in. European regulators support the universal banking model, with bank participation in securities markets and other complex areas of finance, enabling banks can diversify their sources of revenue and lower the exposure to any one set of risks. This approach has not been historically accepted by the United States, though liberalization efforts under the Gramm-Leach-Bliley Act of 1999 ultimately permitted affiliations between investment and commercial banks. Following the 2008 crisis, however, US regulatory policy veered away from

[82] John Gapper, *The Best Bet to Curb Too Big to Fail*, FIN. TIMES, Oct. 14, 2010, http://www.ft .com/cms/s/0/709a1486-d6fc-11df-aaab-00144feabdc0.html#axzz17NZbK0Yb.

Gramm-Leach-Bliley and readopted the country's historical approach framed under the Glass-Steagall Act of 1933, which sought to disconnect commercial banking from securities activities.[83] US regulators and policymakers did not want to direct the activities of banks on an individual level, but they increasingly believed that when deposit-taking institutions participated in riskier ventures like derivatives underwriting and took on less predictable assets, their stability was undermined and could pose a threat to national and international financial systems. European regulators, by contrast, have generally not backtracked from their universal banking model. These differences have made consensus on cross-border regulatory initiatives difficult to achieve, especially in relation to the permitted activities of financial institutions.

National Interest

Competitive considerations have informed virtually every element of regulatory decision making, even after the financial crisis. Consider, again, the Volcker rule. The legislation bars banks from dealing in derivatives and (mortgage-backed) securities, and from investing more than 3 percent of their capital in hedge funds and private equity. The Volcker rule was introduced as part of more extensive efforts in the United States to address the too-big-to-fail problem as well as conflicts of interest that often pitted banks against their clients. The rule gained little traction, however, among EU countries. Instead, by the mid-2011 only the United Kingdom had adopted anything remotely similar to the rule, though even in this instance, authorities have sought only to "ring fence" deposit-taking banks with higher capital charges.

The reason for such divergent practices reflects more disparate regulatory philosophies: if adopted in Europe, the Volcker rule would have forced many highly profitable European universal banks, themselves "national champions" heavily supported by or associated with the state, to fundamentally change their business models and potentially lose some of the competitive advantages of size, scale, and scope. For the United States, the adjustment costs would in some ways be less onerous. First, the US commercial banking market, in particular, is more fragmented and often animated by smaller banks that have less proprietary trading and fewer investments in private funds, and thus would be required to make few adjustments. Furthermore, even under the Volcker rule, some of the largest investment banks affected by it may still be able to trade on their own accounts to the extent to which they do so through "principal investments" that are subject to higher capital charges and held for

---

[83] Banking (Glass-Steagall) Act of 1933, Pub. L. No. 73-66, 48 Stat. 162 (repealed 1999).

TABLE 5.4. *Capital costs estimated under Basel III*

	Tier 1 capital	Short-term liquidity	Long-term funding
European Union	€1.1 trillion	€1.3 trillion	€2.3 trillion
United States	€600 billion	€570 billion	€2.2 trillion

Source: PHILIPP HARLE ET AL., MCKINSEY & CO., BASEL III AND EUROPEAN BANKING: ITS IMPACT, HOW BANKS MIGHT RESPOND, AND THE CHALLENGES OF IMPLEMENTATION (2010), *available at* http://bit.ly/kk9GWA.

a longer term. That said, it remains to be seen whether the United States will be able to maintain its course with the reforms; the general absence of any traction and reform among EU countries has sparked considerable concern among US congressmen that the Volcker rule, if robustly implemented, could still disadvantage US banks internationally.

A similar disparity was evident in capital-adequacy proposals. Compared to their US counterparts, major EU banks were slow to write down bad assets on their books in the wake of the financial crisis. Banking occupied a larger segment of their capital market, so higher capital requirements would be more costly for Europe; since banks there were comparatively more undercapitalized than those in the United States, they would be required to raise more capital (to be more precise, more equity) in order to meet the new, substantive obligations under Basel III. See Table 5.4.

Adjustments to regulatory regimes also meant that EU banks would face higher competitive disadvantages. Some financial institutions, especially German Landesbanken, would no longer be permitted to rely on a particular form of nonvoting capital, known as "silent participations," as the highest form of capital for capital-adequacy considerations; this type of capital does not absorb losses as long as a bank is still in operation. Additionally, according to a McKinsey & Company study published just prior to the crisis, Basel III would reduce banks' return on equity by an average of 4 percent in Europe versus only 3 percent in the United States.[84] Because of these and other challenges, some European financial authorities, especially German bank regulators, pushed strongly and successfully for a delayed implementation of the rules – which, as noted in the previous section, do not go into effect until 2019. Indeed, the only European country to institute robust standards beyond Basel has been Switzerland, where the government has acknowledged its inability, as a small country of less than ten million people, to rescue its two largest banks, UBS and Credit Suisse, if either was to fail.

[84] *Id.* at 1.

Regulators may also have diverging preferences with regard to attracting certain market participants. Consider the issue of executive compensation. In the wake of the damaging risk taking that helped undermine financial institutions in the first decade of the twenty-first century, France called for straightforward, international limits on the pay that bankers could earn. This policy proposal was met with strong resistance, however, by the United States and the United Kingdom. Both countries hosted among the highest-paid bankers in the world, whose presence generated considerable income tax revenue for the governments. International rules could, by contrast, have serious implications for the competitiveness of their labor markets. The standardization of compensation would level the playing field with regard to attracting financial market participants from other countries, at least in the sense that firms would have fewer incentives to set up outposts there. Instead, operations could simply move to other jurisdictions that enjoyed other kinds of competitive advantages. As a result, neither the United Kingdom nor the United States sought global standards in this area prior to the crisis, and afterward they were largely content to issue broad principles relating to the means, and not the amount, of compensation paid to executives. Similar stances were taken by Hong Kong and Singapore, known to attract top talent through high salaries. Neither center wanted to risk losing top performers to other countries. In the face of such resistance, Sarkozy never debated the proposal at the G-20.

National interests and concern about the mobility of mobile market participants have also stifled coordination of hedge fund and private equity regulation. The biggest push to regulate these forms of investment started in Germany. Although few funds are based in Germany (which continues to be dominated by banks), what has unsettled political leaders is that the country and some of its key institutions have been especially lucrative targets for such fund activities. In 2005, for example, British and American hedge funds forced top executives of the Deutsche Börse, Germany's top stock exchange, to resign after the exchange's unsuccessful bid for the London Stock Exchange. This foreign interference in the heart of German capitalism sparked widespread concern about the short-term interests of funds operating in the country, and prompted a party chairman of the then leading coalition to famously compared hedge funds to locusts stripping German firms of valuable assets. In the wake of the Deutsche Börse affair, the German government began to explore possibilities for regulating behavior of hedge funds and private equity firms. After several working groups were launched, however, officials concluded that national regulation was unlikely to be effective since most of these firms were based abroad. They recommended that international forums, such as the FSF, tighten surveillance.[85]

Tighter surveillance, however, required US and UK cooperation, and neither country was eager to lend it, especially prior to the crisis. Besides disagreeing as to the basic utility of hedge funds, leaders in both countries feared that tough global standards could diminish the attractiveness of their local financial centers as destinations for capital. Regulators in both countries believed that domestic financial services professionals had benefited greatly from the comparative institutional and regulatory advantages of a financial system that placed few disclosure and prudential barriers on hedge funds.[86] Thus, in 2000, when an array of countries sought to rein in and regulate what had been growing pools of unregulated capital, the two countries resisted, and the then FSF conceded that its members were unable to "reach a firm conclusion" regarding the risks posed by hedge funds and that it could "not recommend a further range of potential policy options."[87] By 2007, and just prior to the crisis, the G-7 had adopted only an "indirect supervision approach" in which the hedge fund industry itself was to be responsible for monitoring and enforcing a code of best practices.[88] Even after the crisis, fear of capital flight has caused national financial authorities to diverge considerably from one another with regard to their domestic regulatory approaches.

Sovereignty Costs

Finally, the perceived sovereignty costs accompanying stricter standards and institutional mechanisms can stymie extensive international coordination in many areas. International rules, in short, can potentially prevent governments from acting in the best interests of their local economies or in their preferred fashion. For example, many countries have shied away from cross-border resolution and bankruptcy cooperation since new rules could make it more difficult for local institutions, including local regulators, to determine when financial institutions are insolvent, as well as how the institutions are restructured or liquidated. The financial consequences could be very substantial, too, if a distressed bank is a systemically important institution that serves as the

---

[85] GLOBAL FINANCE IN CRISIS: THE POLITICS OF INTERNATIONAL REGULATORY CHANGE, *supra* note 13, at 127.

[86] K. Orfeo Fioretos, *Capitalist Diversity and the International Regulation of Hedge Funds*, 17 REV. INT'L POL. ECON. 696, 710 (2010).

[87] *Id.* at 708

[88] *Id.* at 713.

primary source of capital in a country. International rules could prevent courts from tailoring the disposition of assets to protect local creditors and achieve the most benefit for local economic interests. Instead, international program, though efficient, would likely treat foreign and local creditors equally, thereby limiting the government's control over the disposition of an institution's assets. Many national authorities are consequently reluctant to engage in far-reaching cooperation and prefer to retain flexibility and control over their own local industries, even in times of severe economic dislocations.

As yet another example, consider international accounting standards. Convergence has been difficult because national governments and regulatory agencies do not want to give up their sovereign prerogatives relating to how local companies are valued. The United States, for its part, has long enjoyed, via the SEC, FASB, and local stock exchanges, influence both at home and abroad with regard to the international adoption of its accounting standards. Companies wishing to sell securities in US capital markets or even borrow from large banks have traditionally been forced by regulations or the market to make disclosures according to US GAAP. Similarly, India and China have felt little pressure to cede to international accounting trends due to their impressive growth outlook; investors have been more flexible with local companies in order to escape the comparatively dismal economic prospects in developed countries.[89] The only major power to push vigorously for international standards has been the EU – which, notably, does *not* enjoy a pan-European accounting regulator. Embracing the IFRS and IASB has elevated, as opposed to eroded, its own ability to inform international accounting trends and standards.

International surveillance and monitoring of countries' compliance with best practices likewise generate considerable sovereignty costs. International standards exhibit their strongest compliance pull when they are acknowledged by the market as important and when both regulators and markets can evaluate a jurisdiction's compliance with them. When surveillance is strong, and information about defections from standards is shared with the market, firms in noncompliant countries may experience heightened costs of capital, and governmental authorities may suffer reputational costs in the international community. In 1999, many regulators – from both developed and developing countries – resisted efforts to make the FSAP (while it was still a pilot program) a formal requirement of membership in the IMF, or to impose obligations on

[89] Adam Jones, *Quest for Consistency Still Faces Hurdles*, FIN. TIMES, Jan. 27, 2011, http://www.ft.com/cms/s/0/e99f025c-2976-11e0-bb9b-00144feab49a.html#axzz1IQMVutOq.

all countries to adhere with its standards. Countries did not want to bind their hands with a particular regulatory policy, especially in the quickly evolving area of financial innovation, especially when regulators were unsure how the policy would affect the competitiveness of domestic market participants. The ultimate economic costs of poor financial supervision became increasingly evident in the years leading up to the 2008 crisis, however, and the crisis itself served to change the cost-benefit analyses of many countries. That said, although the G-20 has committed to participation, not every IMF member has done so. It remains apparent that the IMF has yet to take sufficient steps to heighten market discipline and transparency in relation to international standards – a topic we will return to in the final chapter.

THE LIMITS OF INTERNATIONAL FINANCIAL LAW – LESSONS FROM THE CRISIS

Our analysis of recent challenges, successes, and pitfalls experienced by the international regulatory community presents several practical and theoretical lessons. First, soft law does not necessarily ensure that parties "agree" on policy measures. As in other more traditional areas of international law, standard setting in international financial regulation is often fraught with misaligned and even antagonistic interests. When policies could result in steep distributive consequences that could potentially hamper local market participants, or when agreements could reduce the flexibility of governments to tailor solutions according to their policy preferences, gaps may persist throughout the regulatory architecture.

However, even when countries differ in regulatory philosophy and when distributive implications may be steep, attempts at coordination may actually prove to be successful. Germany, for example, ultimately acceded to higher capital standards – albeit with a delayed implementation timeline – demonstrating both regulatory and political will in the interest of financial stability. But acceptable compromises often require time and dialogue.

Take, for example, efforts to achieve consistent accounting standards under IFRS 9. Early in the negotiations, Germany, France, and Italy stridently disagreed with the United States and the United Kingdom with regard to the degree to which accounting standards should be reformed in light of procyclicality risks.[90] The United States and the United Kingdom, along with other

---

[90] *See generally* Paul J. Davies & James Wilson, *Insurers Worried by Fair Value Proposals*, FIN. TIMES, July 16, 2009, http://www.ft.com/cms/s/0/609e0e24-7169-11de-a821-00144feabdc0.html#

regulators, embraced fair value accounting as helping promote transparency – in their view, the paramount objective of financial disclosure. As a result, in 2009, they exerted significant pressure on the IASB to promote US-styled fair value rules.[91] By contrast, continental Europeans favored approaches to asset and liability valuation based on historic cost and amortization, rather than present market value.[92] These countries perceived fair value as having "exacerbat[ed] the credit crisis by providing [only] a snapshot of prices in a falling market" thus promoting financial instability.[93] Moreover, aggressive implementation of fair value could favor banks and insurance companies in jurisdictions that already mandated fair value over those that have not – and as such would have asymmetric costs.[94] These concerns led the EU to announce in November 2009 that it would delay introducing new global accounting rules for fear that they would require more widespread use of fair value accounting among global financial institutions.[95]

After several tedious rounds of negotiations that generated questions concerning the viability of the IASB as a standard-setting institution, the divergent philosophical and national interests found a compromise solution. The IASB's fair value standard creates under the IFRS 9 rule something in between the US and European approaches.[96] As we saw above, IFRS 9 uses a mixed-measurement model, requiring institutions to value some assets and liabilities at fair value and others, albeit fewer, at amortized cost, depending on the institution's business model, the cash-flow characteristics of the assets and liabilities, and whether they are held to maturity. According to the IASB's chairman, Sir David Tweedie, this middle road was ultimately well received: "The overwhelming reaction to IFRS 9 was, 'well you got the cut about

axzz1HSLtYdPh; Rachel Sanderson, *Tokyo Offers Support for 'Fair Value' Accounting Standard*, FIN. TIMES, Mar. 8, 2010, http://www.ft.com/cms/s/o/ffab4a04-2a50-11df-b940-00144 feabdco.html; Rachel Sanderson, *Japan Warns on Trend to US-style Fair Value*, FIN. TIMES, Dec. 31, 2009, http://www.ft.com/cms/s/o/d746cf6a-f563-11de-90ab-00144feab49a.html#axzz1 HSLtYdPh; Rachel Sanderson, *Europe's Schism Threatens Global Accounting Rules*, FIN. TIMES, Nov. 16, 2009, http://www.ft.com/cms/s/o/od14f81c-d217-11de-aof0-00144feabdco.html# axzz1HSLtYdPh.

[91] *See* Mario Christodoulou, *Tweedie: U.S. Fair Value Not Proving Popular*, ACCOUNTANCY AGE, Aug. 25, 2010, http://www.accountancyage.com/accountancyage/news/2268684/ tweedie-fair-value-proving; Sanderson, *Japan Warns on Trend to US-Style Fair Value*, *supra* note 93; Rachel Sanderson, *Chance for Change as Decade-Old Double Act Exits*, FIN. TIMES, Aug. 25, 2010, http://cachef.ft.com/cms/s/o/8c84585a-b073-11df-8c04-00144feabdco .html#axzz1HSMq3kTo.

[92] *See* Christodoulou, *supra* note 94.

[93] *See* Sanderson, *Tokyo Offers Support for 'Fair Value' Accounting Standard*, *supra* note 93.

[94] Davies & Wilson, *supra* note 93.

[95] Sanderson, *Europe's Schism Threatens Global Accounting Rules*, *supra* note 93.

[96] *See* Christodoulou, *supra* note 94.

right.'"[97] That said, some observers speculate that discord over the issue may still result in three separate sets of standards: a US set of standards, which requires widespread use of fair value; a European set of standards, which favors amortized cost; and a set of standards for the rest of the world that lies somewhere in the middle.[98] Thus, although the informal nature of the IASB enabled formal agreement, more negotiation likely lies ahead, and some industry players are pushing for delayed implementation of the rules.

The early challenges of international financial law demonstrate that, even when regulators agree on prescriptive best practices and principles, they may converge on the wrong rules and approaches – as seen most spectacularly in the Basel process. That process, viewed until recently as the apogee of international financial cooperation, has consistently failed to prevent bank failures and global economic crises, even with its ostensibly more stringent rules. Basel I arguably ended up encouraging risky short-term borrowing; recent experience has shown the inadequacy of Basel II's reliance on credit ratings and banks' own models to generate accurate risk weights for capital requirements; and as seen above, Basel III is already viewed by many commentators as far too weak in its capital requirements and as lax in its deadlines for global implementation.

Regulatory errors arise for various reasons. Again, the complexity of international finance cannot be underestimated. Rules often operate in contexts that few – including market participants – understand fully. Because regulators are not active participants in markets, they may not always have the on-the-ground understanding of deal dynamics required to appreciate the implications of any one regulatory approach. They may nevertheless have superior macro-level information when compared to private firms, as well as some insider information not accessible to those firms. More generally, approaches distilled from regulatory practices in one country and then standardized globally may well lead to unintended consequences locally – that is, as it is implemented in the context of each country's unique combination of politics, markets, and financial institutions.

Regulators, like business executives, are also human – and can be biased. In the course of their supervision and oversight, regulators may approach data with preconceived notions or expectations that can undermine their analyses and determine their degree of acceptance or rejection by governments and other financial actors. Excessive weight can be given to an unimportant, but salient feature, of a regulatory problem. Issues can be framed in ways that divert attention from more efficient solutions. Regulators may even be less

[97] *Id.*
[98] Sanderson, *Europe's Schism Threatens Global Accounting Rules, supra* note 93.

incentivized to search for and identify risks than their better-compensated counterparts in the private market. And they may also be swayed to work in ways that gain favor with regulated entities or political elites (who themselves may be captured by special interests in the financial industry) in the hope of gaining future (and very well compensated) employment.

Cross-border rules may additionally fail to hit their mark because they are, fundamentally, the product of cross-border negotiation rather than of robust, comprehensive regulatory oversight. To be sure, flexibility is a fundamental necessity in cross-border regulation: authorities in one jurisdiction must be prepared for give-and-take over shared or common regulatory alternatives and arrangements. Compromises between national financial authorities may not, however, always be driven by a search for optimal outcomes. Instead, the dynamics of negotiations may be driven in one or both jurisdictions by the interests of politically connected industries. Or similarly, overwhelming disparities in influence or bargaining power between negotiating parties may prevent balanced agreements between stakeholders to reached.. International rules and standards are thus not always, or even often, "optimal" in a strict regulatory sense and may not fully address the risks that enhanced or coordinated regulatory oversight presumably aims to prevent.[99]

The costs of regulatory error can be considerable, and regulation is, in itself, expensive. Governments must muster resources to devise and enforce new rules for powerful economic players like banks, insurance companies, and securities firms, and these regulated entities must then undertake appropriate steps to change their conduct and avoid falling foul of the new rules. This process often involves the hiring of third-party actors like lawyers, consultants, and accountants, and each of these costs is magnified when market participants make mistakes. And despite these costs, the regulations may be poorly designed or ineffective. Regulators may lack the capability to identify and address risky activities or emerging systemic risks. Regulators can impose insufficient capital buffers or adopt standards that either exacerbate bubbles and crises or enable regulatory and capital arbitrage. And without a tangible understanding of on-the-ground financial activities, regulators can force regulated entities to misdirect their efforts, spending unnecessary time and money on regulatory compliance with ill-designed regulations.

In any of these situations, international financial law can amplify errors throughout the global financial system. More often than not, regulations harmonize, at least in the sense of establishing common approaches to supervision.

---

[99] Katharina Pistor, The Standardization of Law and Its Effect on Developing Economies, Presentation at the G-24 Technical Group Meeting 2 (Mar. 2000).

As such, they not only prohibit, but also potentially prescribe, with the consequence that market participants across national boundaries are required to undertake the same actions. Financial market regulations thus commonly have world economy–wide implications. For example, raising common equity requirements is generally perceived to negatively affect GDP growth in countries that adopt them, at least in the short term.[100] Or when, in the case of banking regulation, capital reserve obligations are imposed, this situation can incentivize actors to adopt the same investment and risk-management strategies. International rules can thus take on "systemic" qualities with regard to their implications for financial markets. In short, in the absence of international financial law, the failure of one regulator to get its rules right may be buffered by other regulators instituting proper regulatory initiatives in their home jurisdictions (assuming regulatory competition has not bid down regulations globally). By contrast, when international regulators are wrong, and they fail to anticipate costs or risks, all actors, across boundaries, are likely to suffer if they have adopted the global standard.

Indeed, even when regulators reach an agreement and "get it right," the rules that are promulgated will not necessarily be implemented comprehensively at the global level. Although monitoring has been strengthened since 2010 in many important ways, especially with regard to key codes and best practices, most international financial law enjoys little, if any, formal surveillance. Discipline at times of defection can be weak. Furthermore, agreements can be drafted to dramatically narrow their scope or to drain them of meaning by avoiding key, defining terms, such as "registration," "prudential regulation," and "bank." Ultimately, international financial law, though embodied in soft instruments, not only resembles formal international law in its coordination and commitment-making functions, but also involves, for better or worse, many of the same legislative strategies employed in treaty making to smooth over disagreements between parties and to reach consensus.

[100] Wolf, *supra* note 75.

6

The Future of International Financial Law

The 2008 financial crisis serves as a reminder for both policymakers and the public of the fragility of the global financial system. It also unveiled with tragic clarity that the national and international regulations in place prior to the crisis to ensure global financial stability were far from adequate. In this book, we have examined the new institutional arrangements, standards, codes, and reports created to meet the challenges of global finance. We have also seen, however, the persistence of important gaps, sluggish and nationally oriented problem solving, and the high costs of regulatory error when international rules are flawed.

For some commentators, these limitations reveal defects in the very institutional foundations on which international financial law is built, and indicate that more radical changes and reforms are required beyond the revamped Financial Stability Board and G-20. Specifically, some experts have called for a more formal "World Financial Organization," akin to the WTO, that would act as the primary international standard setter for finance, free from the distortional effects of power politics. Under such a centralized, treaty-based international organization, more official "hard law" models of global governance could be leveraged to more effectively supervise mobile market participants.

This final chapter provides an overview of that position and then examines the likely future strategies and development of international financial regulation. The chapter casts considerable skepticism on the likelihood of greater supranational financial regulation. It shows that the call for more formal governance, whatever its merits, is simply impractical the same reasons that have historically inhibited the full coordination and implementation of international financial law. The chapter thus predicts that national regulatory authorities will continue to play important roles in a constantly evolving regulatory architecture, just as the accumulating body of international codes and institutions will set (and reset) the rules of engagement for cross-border market supervision. The chapter concludes by identifying the strategies of the most successful regulatory actors in this increasingly important, albeit far from perfect, world of international financial governance.

THE LOGIC OF A GREATER LEGAL FORMALITY — AND ORGANIZATION

Despite its technically nonbinding status, international financial law boasts many features of "legality": by triggering a range of market, institutional, and reputational responses, international financial law holds potentially enormous consequences for both regulators and firms, whether they make an effort to follow its dictates or simply ignore them. As such, international financial law exhibits *efficacy* or — what Hume described in speaking of the relationship of cause and effect — the "power of production."[1] Its more coercive guises show that even nonbinding rules "matter," and reveal a variety of enforcement mechanisms that counter legal positivist claims that have generally been skeptical of international law, formal and informal. Increased political participation at the head-of-state level, along with lower-level input mechanisms, also provide claims to *legitimacy* and *accountability*. Though not possessing the "moral" obligation associated with public international law, the codes, reports, and best practices of international financial law effectively communicate what "ought" to be done, even when compliance is technically not required. International financial law thus carries with it a general sense of *obligation*, and investors, markets, national regulators, and international organizations routinely impose penalties on noncompliant financial authorities, companies, and firms for derogating from established best practices.

Nevertheless, persistent gaps in the scope and substantive content of international regimes, coupled with the limited supervision of multinational firms, have encouraged commentators to radically question and rethink the global architecture. Some academics have called for greater legal formality and the establishment of a global financial authority, with its regulatory activities centralized under one institutional umbrella. The most extreme version of this type of proposal is, as noted above, the establishment of a new World Financial Organization that would function in much the same way as the WTO. Countries seeking access to foreign markets would have to become members and meet the organization's obligations for supervision and regulation.[2] An

---

[1] Joshua Kleinfeld, *Skeptical Internationalism: A Study of Whether International Law Is Law*, 78 Fordham L. Rev. 2451, 2505 (2010).

[2] *See* Kern Alexander et al., Global Governance of Financial Systems: The International Regulation of Systemic Risk 162 (2006) (arguing for the establishment of a Global

independent body of experts would then decide whether countries have met their obligations. Indirect dispute-resolution mechanisms could be added that would target members who backtrack on their international obligations – for example, through regulatory forbearance or other forms of under-enforcement, or by promoting new rules or exemptions for financial institutions and products that are destabilizing the global financial system.

Under an alternative version of this approach, an existing international organization, such as the FSB or the IMF (or even a new organization altogether), would be empowered not only to survey and monitor regulators, but also, when necessary, to issue rules regarding the behavior and conduct of market participants.[3] Ideally, these rules would include consequences for states that fail to comply, and the regulatory bodies would even possess direct powers of enforcement against financial institutions of all stripes for breaching the rules. Some academics have gone so far as to suggest formal treaties under-girding the international financial system in ways that mirror other contexts, like trade. It is argued that such an approach would address both the gaps in systemic risk regulation and the coordination problems that stifle regulatory cooperation.

The idea of a single regulator with a global mandate is appealing in several respects. At the most basic level, a global financial authority promises fewer gaps between national regimes, each with its own level of prudential regulation, since it could promulgate international standards across borders and would not depend on the national supervisors for their implementation. Additionally, by delegating power to one supranational entity, the opportunity for national regulatory competition would be restricted since individual authorities would not be able to undercut one another by offering weaker regulatory stances. Finally, a global financial authority could allow greater transparency and

Financial Governance Council based on treaty commitments by countries to abide by the highest regulatory standards); Raghuram Rajan, *Reforming Global Economic and Financial Governance, in* WHAT G-20 LEADERS MUST DO TO STABILISE OUR ECONOMY AND FIX THE FINANCIAL SYSTEM 24 (Barry Eichengreen & Richard Baldwin eds., 2008) (Ctr. for Econ. Policy Research, D.C.), *available at* http://www.voxeu.org/reports/G-20_Summit.pdf; *see also* Douglas W. Arner & Michael Taylor, *The Global Financial Crisis and the Financial Stability Board: Hardening the Soft Law of International Financial Regulation?* 54–57 (Asian Inst. of Int'l Fin. Law, Working Paper No. 6, 2009), *available at* http://papers.ssrn.com/sol3/papers .cfm?abstract_id=1427084 (discussing possible "hard law" approaches to international finance based on the WTO, IMF and the EU).

[3] Timothy Adams & Arrigo Sadun, Op-Ed., *Global Economic Council Should Oversee All,* FIN. TIMES, Aug. 17, 2009, at 9; *see also* Peter Mandelson, Op-Ed., *We Need Greater Global Governance,* WALL ST. J., June 19, 2009, at A13, *available at* http://online.wsj.com/article/ SB124536757998629319.html; GROUP OF THIRTY, FINANCIAL REFORM: A FRAMEWORK FOR FINANCIAL STABILITY 8 (2009) (arguing for stronger existing international mechanisms).

consistent regulatory intensity.[4] Multinational institutions would be subject, in particular, to the consistent application of international rules and disclosure, and to constant oversight and supervision by a single, unitary supervisor – one that, given its status, could successfully bargain with and oversee powerful mobile firms.

THE IMPRACTICALITY OF A WORLD FINANCIAL ORGANIZATION

Despite the potential attractions of a global regulator, the likelihood of the sort of supranational authority described above is small to nonexistent. First, and perhaps most obvious, it would be almost impossible to generate sufficient international support for the creation of a single, global regulator that would carry with it, for individual states, the relinquishment of national sovereignty and autonomy. Establishing a global authority would require countries to delegate authority to a supranational authority, an act involving a "dynamic" delegation of authority such that any decision made by that authority would create de facto changes in the domestic laws of member regulators.[5] It is unlikely that national legislatures would agree to compromise their domestic powers of policymaking and governance in that way, especially in relation to large domestic financial institutions and firms.[6] Financial regulation is also, as some scholars have recognized, increasingly linked to monetary and macroeconomic policy, owing to the central banks' role as lenders of last resort.[7] Nation-states are unlikely to cede power to a global financial regulator as long as they retain the responsibility for guaranteeing liquidity, serving as the capital providers of last resort, and protecting the public treasury.[8] Indeed, even when states have succeeded in centralizing vast swaths of financial authority in a regional body – as with the EU – power remains in many ways shared between local and supranational authorities.[9]

---

[4] Vanessa Blackmore & Esther Jeapes, *The Global Financial Crisis: One Global Regulator or Multiple Regulators?*, 4 CAPITAL MARKETS L.J. (Supp. 1) S112, S113 (2009).

[5] Michael C. Dorf, *Dynamic Incorporation of Foreign Law*, 157 U. PA. L. REV. 103, 103 (2008).

[6] Kenneth W. Abbott & Duncan Snidal, *Hard and Soft Law in International Governance*, 54 INT'L ORG. 421, 437 (2000) (noting that while sovereignty costs are relatively low when states make international legal commits limiting their behavior in particular circumstances, but that these costs rise where states accept external authority over significant decisions and where international arrangements impinge on the relations between a state and its citizens or territory).

[7] Blackmore & Jeapes, *supra* note 4, at S116.

[8] *Id.* at S116–17.

[9] Eilís Ferran & Kern Alexander, Soft Institutions and Hard-Edged Power: What Role for the European Systemic Risk Board? 27–29 (2010) (on file with author).

Differences in regulatory philosophy and national interest will, as we have seen throughout this book, continue to make cooperation difficult and would make delegation to an international regulatory authority a Herculean task. Desirable forms of financial regulation differ across countries, depending on their preferences and levels of development; nations sit at different points on their "efficient frontiers."[10] Some countries would want to purchase more financial stability than others – and have tighter regulations – at the price of giving up financial innovation. Others would seek to develop capital markets more quickly through looser standards, even at the price of stability. Because of such differences, countries would vie to assume strategic positions in organizations that endow them with particular influence or power over the provision of global law.[11] And as one sees today, powerful and rich countries are more likely to assume dominant positions. Although an international organization may have a secretariat and independent bureaucrats, the organization and its staff may still be beholden to those countries that provide the most funding and political support for the organization's operations.

Finally, even assuming delegation was possible, the benefit of a single decision maker is still uncertain. Delegation to a centralized rulemaking authority would further homogenize international approaches, amplifying the costs of regulatory error. Weak or poorly designed standards could affect and compromise financial systems across the globe would be susceptible to that weakness. Similarly, in the case of overly stringent standards or ones not entirely suitable to particular domestic regulatory regimes, firms would have no choice but to internalize the costs of potentially wasteful compliance measures. In the place of a system where regulatory agencies can effectively implement standards on their own, a global financial body would have authority to regularly punish regulators for any deviations from the laws promulgated by that body at the international level. This kind of regime differs considerably from the existing architecture, where compliance, though at times coercive, generally relies on regulatory reputational effects and assessments by market participants.

Because of the philosophical, sovereignty, and distributive issues involved in financial regulation, the time needed to negotiate the terms of a treaty would take years, if not decades.[12] In that time, one or two more financial crises would likely occur, revealing new thinking or better institutional practices. As with the EU's efforts to create a new federal resolution mechanism – which prompted a redrafting of the Lisbon Treaty and ratification efforts among

---

[10] Dani Rodrik, *A Plan B for Global Finance*, Economist, Mar. 14, 2009, at 80.

[11] *Id.*

[12] Lawrence G. Baxter, Exploring the WFO Option for Global Banking Regulation 4 (2010) (on file with author).

member states – new coordination efforts would require the participation not only of regulators, but of legislatures and heads of state, in order to nail down the details of a new regime.

Collectively, these observations suggest that developing an international regulatory order is likely to evolve along two paths. As we have seen with the creation of the Financial Stability Forum, FSB, the G-20, and many other organizations, times of economic crisis open up opportunities for deeper international regulatory cooperation. Political leaders and financial authorities come to appreciate the risks of loopholes in financial oversight, as well as the benefits of multilateral responses. In such moments, considerable institutional reforms are possible, to the creation of new forums and organizations, to the publishing of new standards like Basel III. More often, however, international legislative products evolve incrementally, from the broad to the narrow: the articulation of broad core principles is frequently the first step, followed by methodologies for interpreting the principles and one-off, timely reports and guidance on particular issues of special importance. At most, perhaps, in times of relative financial stability, one might be able to envision the ultimate creation of a process treaty outlining the terms by which organizations create standards. Yet even here, such an organization would likely face considerable challenges due to disparate allocations of power between members and the diverse experiences of countries with international cooperation.

THE PARADOX OF POST-CRISIS SUPERVISION

The impracticality of a world financial organization, combined with the decidedly decentralized nature of international financial standard setting, highlights the lasting importance of national regulatory supervision in global regulatory affairs, even in an age of transnational markets and market participants.

National regulators will almost always be the first responders in times of economic crisis; international responses, even when the global economy is at risk, may not be swift enough to address the challenges posed by constantly evolving financial markets and cross-border capital movements. Proposals formulated by international organizations reflect the result of heterogeneous, and at times complex, institutional processes, often need to the vetted by local administrative and political actors, and, for implementation, require coordination among many stakeholders – all of which have the effect of delaying the actual response. In the resulting legislative vacuum, national regulators are usually the first line of defense against financial instability. In the 2008 financial crisis, for example, national regulators adopted a variety of important initial responses – including bailing out financial institutions, imposing controls on executive compensation for firms aided by the government, enacting bans on short selling, and relaxing fair value accounting obligations.

Even when global rules are promulgated by robust and recognized international institutions, national regulators may still operate as gap fillers insofar as the international rules are vague or incomplete. Many international regulatory principles are too broad, reflecting political impracticalities, failures in design, or the lack of consensus the matter in question. International standards can be thus be vague about the interpretation or application of key provisions. In such instances, national regulators will be required to provide meaning and direction for unclear terms, principles, or approaches. In particular, when international regulatory standards fail to sufficiently control systemically risky actors and behavior, national regulators will have to step into the breach and provide prudential oversight. The ability of any particular regulator to serve as a gap filler, however – either by itself or in coordination with other like-minded regulators – will depend on many factors, perhaps most importantly on market size. As we saw in chapter 1, all else being equal, the larger the market a regulator oversees, the greater the reach of that regulator beyond its borders, even when it regulates international actors on a territorial basis.

Finally, national regulators, even in today's world of increasingly important cross-border regulatory activities, are the ones ultimately responsible for implementing rules. Implementation involves, of course, putting the laws down on one's books, as well as potentially supervising and enforcing the rules (and the objectives of the rules) in one's market. Supervision, at best, is by proxy because international financial law has political limits, meaning that regulators continue to have the ultimate say in how norms are implemented on the ground.

These national-level activities cause friction with the basic norms and objectives of international coordination that are discussed in the first chapters of the book. Intrinsic to international financial cooperation is an interest in, and commitment to, working with other countries in order to solve common problems. Resorting to unilateral (or even bilateral or regional) arrangements generates tension with other, broader efforts to regulate the global financial system. Unilateralism has its drawbacks, of course, for it can generate considerable reputational costs for regulators, especially when actions are viewed as violations of established norms of comity, and can expose regulators to possible retaliation. National regulation, when practiced against the backdrop of international financial law, can thus be a paradox of sorts: it may be necessary, considering the limits of international financial law, but it may also be seen as a breach of international decorum.

That said, there are plausible reasons to believe that the presence of international financial law can change the outcome and practical implications of unilateral conduct in surprising ways. International financial law can, for example, create cover for unilateral regulatory action, particularly with regard to reputation. Consider, for example, a situation where a country or a group of countries decides to exclude from their capital markets any foreign bank that fails to meet Basel capital standards. This particular form of exclusion and supervision may not necessarily be articulated under the accord, though it can certainly be viewed as operating in accordance with its spirit – and it even helps promote Basel capital standards, as other banks will have greater incentive to meet them. Or consider again the situation discussed in chapter 1, when the EU decided on new registration requirements for hedge funds. In theory, the decision to exclude certain banks could be viewed as unilateral, but the relevant national regulations also dovetail with earlier international agendas, reports, and proclamations in support of tougher regulation of the shadow-banking industry. Thus, when a regulator can credibly act in accordance with the objectives of international best practices, claims of unilateralism can be defused, even when its implementation is novel or divergent from dominant international practices. Context is, to be sure, of critical importance. How gap filling or back stopping is executed can have important consequences for how regulatory activities are perceived. If a country generates its own standards in ways that ignore international precedent or ongoing international activities, it can suffer significant reputational damages. Furthermore, if a country acts in ways that are perceived to preempt or complicate international processes, it exposes itself to claims of irresponsible unilateralism. Thus, in 2008, when Germany imposed a short-selling ban domestically – and just the EU was planning a collective regulatory response among its members – Germany's actions were met not only with skepticism, but with continent-wide repudiation.

SUCCEEDING IN A WORLD OF SOFT FINANCIAL LAW

All of these issues point to the increasing importance of strategy in international regulatory affairs. As increasing numbers of countries come to enjoy large or significant capital markets, the comparative advantages of any one regulator with regard to the promotion of its regulatory preferences derive not only from the size of the markets it regulates, but also from the practice of sound financial statecraft. Several tactics and approaches will be key to succeeding in the world of soft financial law.

"First in Time" Cooperation

As a matter of first-order principles, international power "works best against problems before, rather than after, they mature."[13] That said, international regulatory financial cooperation is most likely to arise when, as David Singer has noted, financial shocks generate such financial instability that regulators (and political elites) are incentivized, if not forced, to intervene in market activity and to do so collectively.[14] Yet as financial globalization moves apace, the increasingly dispersed power and interests of countries create negotiation costs, and the likelihood of cooperation is further complicated by each country's perception of the effect that any prospective or proposed interventions will have on its own domestic firms or economy. Moreover, because unilateral interventions by national regulators almost invariably create new compliance costs for firms, those regulators have long refrained from regulating firms prospectively. The upshot is that action on both international and national levels typically lags significantly behind need.

That said, significant tactical advantages will benefit national regulators most inclined and able to cooperate with other countries and with international bodies in financial regulatory affairs. As highlighted in chapter 1, rules are equalizers that promote efficiency not only in a regulatory sense, but also between actors. Rules and standards exhibit potential network externalities. As more and more firms and market participants adopt a particular standard, the more attractive that standard may become since economies of scale reinforce its desirability. Thus, once sufficient numbers of countries adopt a particular disclosure format or financial reporting approach, leading that approach to becomes dominant among market participants, other approaches are at a competitive disadvantage – in terms not only of cost, but also of ease of use. Put more concretely, once a critical mass of investors adopts a particular method for recognizing losses on a balance sheet or measuring tier 1 capital and becomes more familiar with it, users of other standards will be inclined to do the same and switch. Notably, this dynamic may occur even when various standards may solve a particular problem with equal effectiveness.

---

[13] Leslie H. Gelb, *Necessity, Choice and Common Sense*, FOREIGN AFF., May-June 2009, at 71.
[14] DAVID ANDREW SINGER, REGULATING CAPITAL: SETTING STANDARDS FOR THE INTERNATIONAL FINANCIAL SYSTEM 22 (2007).

Additionally, rules generated by organizations tend to exhibit staying power even when organizational membership changes. When a regulator joins an established international organization, that regulator will not usually be in a position to change the substantive content of the legislation that the organization has already passed unless external events or circumstances alter the preferences of incumbent members. Supermajoritarian decision rules and consensus can inhibit regulatory change by even powerful newcomers. Thus once international standard-setting bodies are established, they exhibit a staying power of their own as coordinating mechanisms.

Regulators should consequently be prepared to cooperate and to engage relevant regulatory partners *quickly*. For regulators of both small and large capital markets, such conduct is in some ways counterintuitive. As we have discussed, some regulators of large markets have been able to export their policy preferences through domestic rule making. Meanwhile, smaller countries, especially those that participate in international standard-setting organizations, have at times been incentivized to hold out on agreement, especially when high levels of agreement are required in order to obtain regulatory concessions and international standards more in line with its own policy preferences. Yet as we have seen, disengagement, too, can be risky. Regulators that first enter into cooperative alliances may be able to develop loose terms of membership, but, as such alliances grow, or as members themselves achieve larger market share, the alliances may transform into clubs and impose membership standards in ways that raise the cost of entry for future parties seeking to join. Moreover, early participants in coordination efforts and clubs can affect the process by which rules are considered, as well as the choice and membership of national regulators, bureaucracies, or institutions to address particular issues. Accordingly, as new issues and challenges arise, financial authorities seeking to promote resilient global standards in line with their own national interests should claim the initiative and seek out opportunities to strategically develop and leverage common standards throughout the international regulatory community.

Mastering the Art of Persuasion

In order to exert influence and achieve their strategic objectives in peer-to-peer regulatory environments, participants need to rely on the art of persuasion. Brash exertions of national interest are insufficient modes of rule making in a world of more diffuse threats and power. Instead, as Joshua Cohen and Charles Sabel have illustrated in some of their work on transnational experimentalism, rule making and cross-border coordination are likely to be most successful when regulators provide compelling rationales for their positions that are understood by foreign counterparts and the market participants to whom the rules would apply.[15]

That said, because national interest always undergirds international cooperation to some extent, regulators generally have to be convinced that their local market participants stand to benefit from a particular legislative initiative or that they will at least not lose disproportionately when compared to others. International agencies consequently need increasingly to identify overlapping regulatory interests upon which to base rule making. Senior regulatory officials from developed and developing countries alike should be sent abroad to learn about foreign regulatory traditions and market conditions. Where standards are roughly crafted (or opposed) to protect any one country's market participants, those standards will encounter both greater skepticism and a smaller chance of global adoption. Although previous unilateral models of financial sovereignty emphasized the separateness of regulatory – and specifically, territorial – authority, globalization creates new needs. Collective interests must be affirmed in the service of a now global public good: financial stability.

In exerting the soft power of persuasion, any divergence from established, sound policies needs to be justified or minimized. Indeed, proposed regulatory initiatives propagated by any regulator should be linked to widely accepted principles, reports, or standards promulgated by standard setters in the relevant sector or in functionally similar contexts. Since the "probability that an institutional change will succeed depends in part on its consistency with the wider order," it is important, in support of such a change, to "persuade others of the reform's strong links to well-established precedents."[16] Advocates of serious reform would also be wise to make sure that their policies do not contradict their own long-standing pronouncements regarding best practices, unless they have rethought their positions.

For purposes of persuasion, it is also important for national policies to be consonant with one another and for a country's different regularly bodies to speak with a unified voice – which is not always the case. For example, although the United States eventually adopted a unified stance on IFRS reforms, in the initial stages of the 2008 financial crisis, the Federal Reserve and SEC differed in important ways with regard to fair value accounting. Underlying the difference was the difference in their respective mandates. As a central bank the Federal Reserve was largely concerned about financial stability, which could

---

[15] Joshua Cohen & Charles F. Sabel, *Global Democracy?*, 37 NYU J. INT'L L. & POL., 763, 779 (2005).

[16] Stephen G. Brooks & William C. Wohlforth, *Reshaping the World Order: How Washington Should Reform International Institutions*, FOREIGN AFF., Mar.-Apr. 2009, at 60.

be undermined by mark-to-market accounting since it could expose a bank's weaknesses or undermine its balance sheet, whereas the SEC was focused on investor protection and thus especially concerned about transparency. And just as a middle course was eventually mediated internationally, so was a series of discussions and negotiations launched domestically between officials in the Treasury Department and bank and securities regulators.

Unified positions can be difficult for countries to develop because regulatory agencies both regulate and represent different market actors that often have divergent interests with regard to rules with implications that cut across financial sectors. For example, the US Federal Deposit Insurance Corporation, which is usually responsible for winding down large institutions and even insuring deposits, may be more interested in a larger, global list of systemically important financial institutions than that of the US Federal Reserve. Unlike the Fed, the FDIC is an insurer of deposits and ultimately pays out when institutions fail. It is thus more incentivized to seek out arrangements that cast the widest net possible in covering risky institutions. In the absence of a consolidated financial regulatory authority, even domestic agencies may place varying degrees of emphasis on certain issues or prioritize differing objectives or tools. Interagency coordination may, as a result, be necessary on a local (national) level as a predicate to international, cross-border cooperation. And it is here, in particular, that elected officials can facilitate international effectiveness by choosing and prioritizing policies for diverse constituents and economic stakeholders.

Leveraging Transparency

My colleague Dan Tarullo once noted that the more time that passes from the crisis, the higher the incentives of some countries to acknowledge international standards while implementing their own potentially divergent policies at home. Indeed, such risks will be especially high in the face of deteriorating economic and financial conditions that make limits on the ability of banks to provide credit – whatever their merits – less appealing. Transparency will, as a result, be an increasingly important instrument for improving and sustaining the efficacy of international financial law. Traditionally, transparency has been associated with governmental reputation and the costs that backtracking has on a government's ability to secure cooperation with counterparts in the future. But as we saw in chapter 3, transparency can also make possible other kinds of disciplines can be equally effective and, indeed, more significant when embedded in particular institutional or market contexts. The prospect of higher costs of capital for domestic firms, or of exclusion from standard setting forums, can incentivize financial authorities to raise standards. Likewise, when there is transparency and public information regarding the rules under which market participants operate, they may themselves adopt better disclosure practices, risk-management procedures, and capital-retention programs, even when their home regulators may not formally require them.

This is not to say that it is always preferable for international standard-setting organizations to produce ever greater volumes of information regarding compliance. There may be limits as to just how effective such approaches are if they become too commonplace or pervasive. If, for example, each standard setter not only begins to produce increasingly large volumes of standards, but also monitors compliance with each new standard with greater levels of intensity, market participants and regulatory authorities may become overwhelmed and incapable of processing (or unwilling to process, given the time and costs associated) the information received from proliferating monitors. In such instances, otherwise solicitous users of regulatory surveillance information may fall back on other potentially less credible sources of information concerning the legal and regulatory environment in which actors transact. As a result, international standard setters would be wise to be judicious as to just how many standards the international regulatory community as a whole produces, and for whom.

That said, this book has shown that under the right circumstances, *soft* law can be wielded in ways that evoke *hard* power, and efforts to make it more effective need not involve formal treaties, supranational regulators, or international organizations. Reforms of international surveillance and monitoring in the wake of the crisis help illustrate the point. In improving the effectiveness of the World Bank and IMF, no formal changes to the IMF Articles of Agreement were made, and no new global treaty was enacted. Instead, less dramatic changes have been introduced in the international system to increase the compliance pull of international rules and standards. Members of the FSB have committed to the Financial Stability Assessment Program, and the IMF has made Financial Sector Assessment Program reports mandatory for G-20 and other strategically important countries, and has done so without enacting new international rules. Individual standard-setting bodies – from the Financial Action Task Force to the International Organization of Securities Commissions and the FSB – are also increasingly involved in peer reviews, and the results of surveillance are increasingly published. Membership sanctions are at least implied, if not overtly applied, in many organizations – and all without resorting to the tedious and likely unachievable process of formal supranational legislation.

My point is not, however, to give a full-throated endorsement to the current international architecture, which, as we have already seen, still suffers considerable gaps. And to be sure, further innovation is still possible without supranational legislation. FSAP reports, in particular, could be better organized and be presented in ways more user-friendly for market participants. For the most part, information is disseminated in either very broad terms in financial sector assessments or in detailed, verbose observance reports. For market participants, a better approach would be to model assessments on investment prospectuses. In every annual assessment, an executive summary, for example, could be included, along with a general rating or scale of country compliance with especially important standards. Then, in addition to the executive summary, an in-depth explanation could be provided to explain the process of data gathering and the regulatory measures taken by the government in question. Finally, toward the end of the report, national regulators should be given the opportunity to contest the score that they earned or the merits of the international standard at issue, or to explain their reasons for not fully implementing that particular standard.

Transparency can, of course, be used as a means by which official pressures can be legitimized alongside other institutional and organizational sanctions, assuming sufficient political will and consensus is available to do so. More important, however, is that market participants can themselves enjoy the best material information possible concerning the products and institutions in which they are investing and transacting. Transparency does not by itself have to act as a means of vulgar governmental coercion, at least not in the way as commonly understood by international relations theorists. Even when operating on principles of voluntariness, transparency can still be effective in making actors internalize the costs of their decision making. Investors can evaluate the strengths and weaknesses of regimes, and reward market participants on the basis of the rules according to which they operate and to which they are subject. In that way, regulatory expectations and practices can reflect and inform behavior (even where there is a diversity of preferences), and can open a space for learning, information sharing among stakeholders, and possibly multiple regulatory solutions for common problems.

Leading by Example

In a world of soft law, leading by example is critical. Like globalization, this phenomenon is a relatively new one. Immediately following the Asian financial crisis, financial market risk and poor regulatory supervision were largely seen as problems of unsophisticated, developing countries, and not of wealthier ones. Major countries did not feel compelled to comply with all of the rules that they promulgated, much less to participate in international monitoring processes. Instead, rules were produced for the consumption of countries transitioning to, or striving for, a more vigorous level of development.

In the wake of both financial globalization and the 2008 financial crisis, such "do what I say, not what I do" policy contradictions complicate and undermine a country's financial statecraft. Pushing for reform at the global level is uphill work if a national regulator itself is unwilling to fully implement the standards in its home market. Unilateralism may be excused when a country acts independently to demonstrate the benefits of its regulatory strategy. But if a national regulator consistently engages in regulatory forbearance and ignores underperforming, or systemically risky firms that do not meet international standards, its actions could lose credibility and effectiveness.

This particular issue returns us to the concept of reputation – and the underlying question of whether a national regulator follows through with its commitments. If a regulator commits to international standards and then ignores them, it can gain a reputation for untrustworthiness and empty promises. By contrast, abiding by international standards – and under the right circumstances, switching to even higher standards than the international norm – can enhance a regulator's reputation for sound supervision. Regulators again gain in credibility when they urge others to follow their example and switch to higher standards, or when they impose domestic measures with extraterritorial reach. Furthermore, leading by example can reduce the risks for other jurisdictions and increase the likelihood of that standard gaining international prominence. Many countries will not follow a regulatory policy unless they can determine that it works or is not overly burdensome. They look to other jurisdictions that have the proposed rule in place to identify the associated costs and the benefits. Leadership by example can provide useful information for straggler agencies seeking to better understand the ramifications of adopting a particular regulatory approach.

Taking Legitimacy Seriously

Finally, legitimacy is important. It is often impossible to bring together every stakeholder for every decision of global import, and outsiders to decision-making processes will generally (and rightly) criticize the shortcomings of the international regulatory system as it exists. Thus, in order to maximize the compliance pull of standards, it remains critical that agenda and standard setters enjoy widespread recognition as the most legitimate representatives of the regulatory community. This practical objective suggests a rethinking of membership models and participatory structures in key international institutions.

Meanwhile, for countries vying for leadership, it is important for them, too, to realize regulatory and policy successes that inspire other countries to adopt their approaches. For nearly two generations, the United States had an unparalleled reputation for sound regulatory oversight and supervision, and thus its legislation enjoyed unprecedented "output" legitimacy. To be sure, it had its failures – the S&L crisis of the 1980s, the Enron & WorldCom frauds, and the hedge fund Long-Term Capital Management case (perhaps the most notable prior to the 2008 crisis) – but the overall strength, growth, and stability of US financial markets largely overshadowed these episodic shortcomings. The global financial crisis has largely undermined this reputational capital, however – and not only because the crisis occurred, but also because it was an enormous failure of oversight on many dimensions. Both globally and domestically, the United States failed to regulate or to help regulate a slew of important financial institutions and financial instruments, and ceded it ceded its supervisory responsibilities to market participants that were themselves critical of the need for supervision.

In the wake of the 2008 crisis, the Anglo-American model of financial regulation has been discredited in various respects. As Ian Bremmer succinctly notes, "American-style free-market capitalism and the idea of globalization have taken plenty of blame for the meltdown."[17] The crisis started in the United States and was enabled, perhaps above all else, by poor regulatory oversight. Meanwhile, countries that adopted US-style regulations and that had "opened themselves to trade and foreign investment took an especially tough hit, while . . . those less dependent on cross-border financial flows weathered the storm with fewer lasting problems."[18]

To be sure, other countries and jurisdictions face similar reputational challenges. Europe's own banks were bailed out alongside those in the United States, showing deep lapses in EU oversight regarding their exposure to US mortgage-related securities. And although Asia as a whole generally fared well in the crisis, East Asia's reputation for financial regulation remains in many ways suspect due to the supervisory failures that made possible the East Asian crisis in the 1990s. Similarly, various countries ranging from Mexico south through Central and South America have had their own series of crises that have undermined their reputations for strong regulatory management and supervision.

With the international system so unsettled and long-standing reputations in disarray, no particular regulatory model holds clear sway in the immediate

---

[17] Ian Bremmer, The End of the Free Market: Who Wins the War Between States and Corporations? 178 (2010).

[18] *Id.*

post-crisis environment. The situation is unlikely to change anytime soon; reputations for competence will be built incrementally over time. This will particularly be the case over the next decade as national regulators, like market participants, give more careful attention to issues not only of market and credit risk, but also of regulatory risk. Reputations for governance and stability will be strengthened or comprised based on the successes and failures of regulatory models at both the national and international levels. It is thus important for national regulators to adopt strategies that are advantageous to domestic market participants but that that also achieve the larger goal of overall regulatory effectiveness. Regulatory failures at home erode national reputations for policy competence.

THE NOT-SO-QUESTIONABLE FUTURE OF INTERNATIONAL FINANCIAL LAW

When the G-20 was established in 2008 as the world's premier economic organization, it was viewed in two ways: as a step just short of a global government, or as doomed to ineffectuality because of (among other things) its soft institutional structure and the nonbinding nature of its rules. This book has shown that neither view to be correct. A stream of international rule making emerged from the international financial system between 2008 and 2011 that bolstered cross-border cooperation and consensus on wide-ranging regulatory matters. To be sure, these efforts have not always been successful, and key gaps persist in the international regulatory architecture. Moreover, as concern for the state of the global economy grows, bridging the gaps may become even more difficult as slow-growth industrialized countries seek to bolster lending by financial institutions that could be hampered by additional financial regulation. But it is disingenuous to assert that significant improvements have not been achieved in the wake of the crisis, even in the absence of formal lawmaking and the emergence of an international financial organization parallel to the WTO. Many of these achievements have been hard won and even demonstrated considerable courage by regulatory agencies and national heads of state in resisting the pressure of well-heeled, influential domestic special interests.

Recent reforms reflect a growing awareness of the interconnectedness of markets and a gradual ideological shift away from the low-level regulatory intervention in markets that has characterized the last half-century. These changes have set in motion regulatory dynamics that will likely have their own self-sustaining qualities. Many of the most critical international financial rules have been refined in recent years by a process of ongoing prescriptive rule making – a process that is set in motion once standards have been promulgated. Core principles, for example, may have methodologies that add greater precision to their content; reports may be published by international bodies and endorsed by national regulators who, with counterparts, then publish additional interpretations and refinements of existing international legislation; and even surveillance tools like the FSAP reports may be developed to examine the implementation of international standards – in the process, giving greater clarity to their content.

As theorists of formal international institutions have long acknowledged, international organizations, once established, make cooperation easier. And soft institutions are no different from their formal counterparts. Like formal international organizations, international financial organizations can help condition participant members to cooperate, establish procedures for assessing problems, build trust, and pool resources for tackling common challenges. And all of these qualities can create a basis not only for creating international financial law, but for also elaborating rules and standards already promulgated by the international community. Equally important, these same dynamics can generate greater discipline. Surveillance may be enhanced as national regulators enjoy greater institutional and member feedback on policy proposals and become more familiar with one another's regulatory systems through informal peer review. As institutions become more important, shaming and exclusion will have greater consequences.

These qualities of the international regulatory system do not, in themselves, determine outcomes or guarantee results. Even with the significant utility that international financial organizations provide, governments remain highly sensitive to their national sovereignty and national interests, and can make consensus difficult to reach in agenda- and standard-setting processes. Conflicts between national regulators need not, however, be destructive. As other scholars have long recognized, where regimes successfully manage conflicts, faith in regimes generally rises. Moreover, the patterns of engagement and the substantive principles developed through frequent interactions among national regulatory authorities can, over time, enjoy "procedural weight, both through learning processes and the pragmatic necessity of building on experience."[19]

A common assumption among theorists is that as principles and procedures become more refined, hard law will emerge. On the domestic level, this assumption is certainly correct insofar as national authorities work (albeit to varying degrees) to comply with soft law by implementing local regulatory standards and reforms, and then enforcing those laws at home. At the

---

[19] Anne-Marie Slaughter, A New World Order 212 (2004).

international level, however, trust and experience are more likely to incrementally lead to greater innovation in soft law and its supporting institutions. One particular practice that may be prove to be especially susceptible to change is the consensus-based nature of many decision rules and, indeed, many organizations – which as we have seen, can generate a range of strategic hold-ups by parties. In a world of increasingly interdependent actors, consensus constitutes a potentially major barrier to cross-border coordination. The challenge, of course, is what kind of decision rule should replace it. Either majority- or even supermajority-based decision making would constitute a type of delegation to international bodies, in the sense that regulators would be required to implement decisions made by standard setters even when in disagreement with those decisions. Probably more likely is a subtle and less overt change, through organizational practice, in the very meaning of the term "consensus." Disagreements among members may simply be elided as chairpersons of working groups or committees find a "general" consensus where supermajorities exist. Whatever the ultimate form of consensus, as long as regulators' trust in the global regulatory system – and in their international homologues – increases, that system will ineluctably continue to evolve and to adapt to changing circumstances, including the maturation of its constituent players into comfortable actors on the global stage.

In sum, just as awareness of the interconnectivity and interdependence of financial markets and financial market regulation increases, so, too, will the global financial system adapt and continue to evolve. And although new institutions and new regulations and regulatory frameworks of various kinds will continue to emerge, many existing trends and strategies will likely continue to dominate cross-border decision making for a good time to come – including the key role of soft law as a coordinating mechanism. Against such a backdrop, competitive advantages will come to those regulators that enjoy or develop large and active financial markets and to those that best navigate and leverage the evolving international regulatory architecture. Successful financial statecraft will require a robust participation in international standard setting, as well as the smart deployment of transparency, persuasion, and leadership in order to realize national regulatory objectives – and achieve stability in the global financial system.

Index